HOLDER!

KEN AKAMATSU

vol.12

CHARACTERS

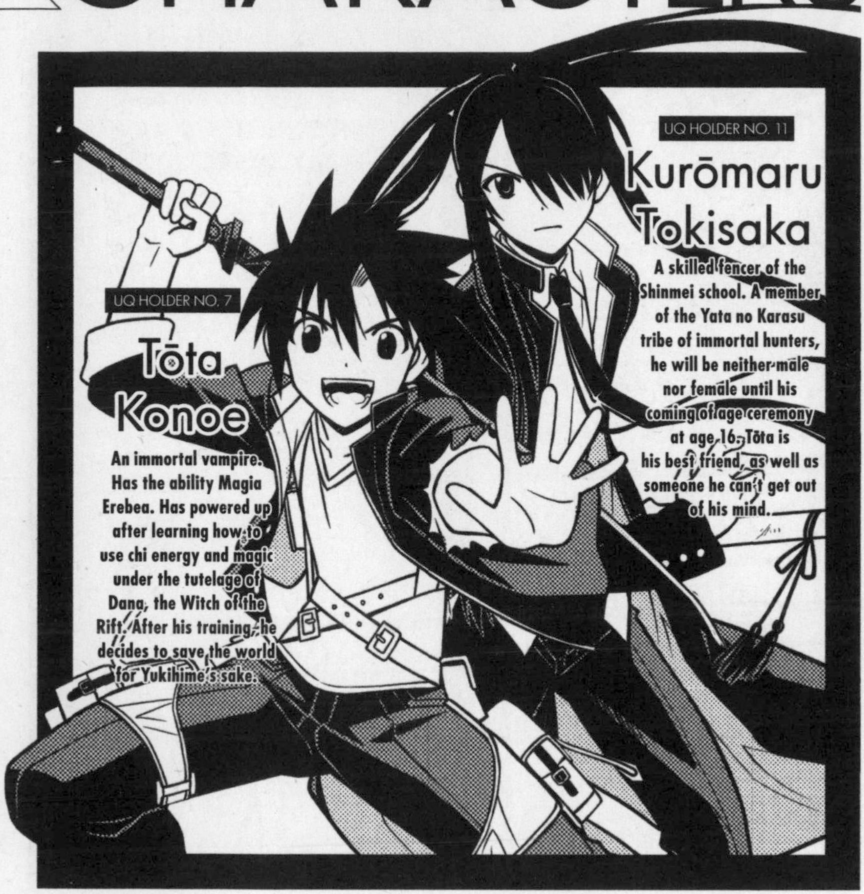
UQ HOLDER NO. 11
Kurōmaru Tokisaka
A skilled fencer of the Shinmei school. A member of the Yata no Karasu tribe of immortal hunters, he will be neither male nor female until his coming of age ceremony at age 16. Tōta is his best friend, as well as someone he can't get out of his mind.
UQ HOLDER NO. 7
Tōta Konoe
An immortal vampire. Has the ability Magia Erebea. Has powered up after learning how to use chi energy and magic under the tutelage of Dana, the Witch of the Rift. After his training, he decides to save the world for Yukihime's sake.

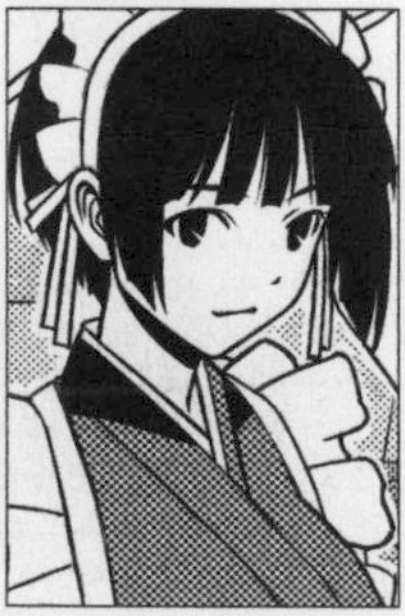

UQ HOLDER NO. 4

KARIN

Cool-headed and ruthless. Her immortality is S-class. Also known as the Saintess of Steel. Loves Eva.

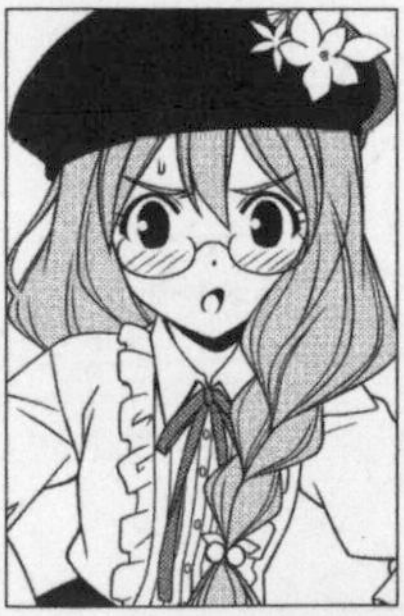

UQ HOLDER NO. 9

KIRIË SAKURAME

The greatest financial contributor to UQ Holder, who constantly calls Tōta incompetent. She can stop time by kissing Tōta.

UQ HOLDER! Ken Akamatsu Presents

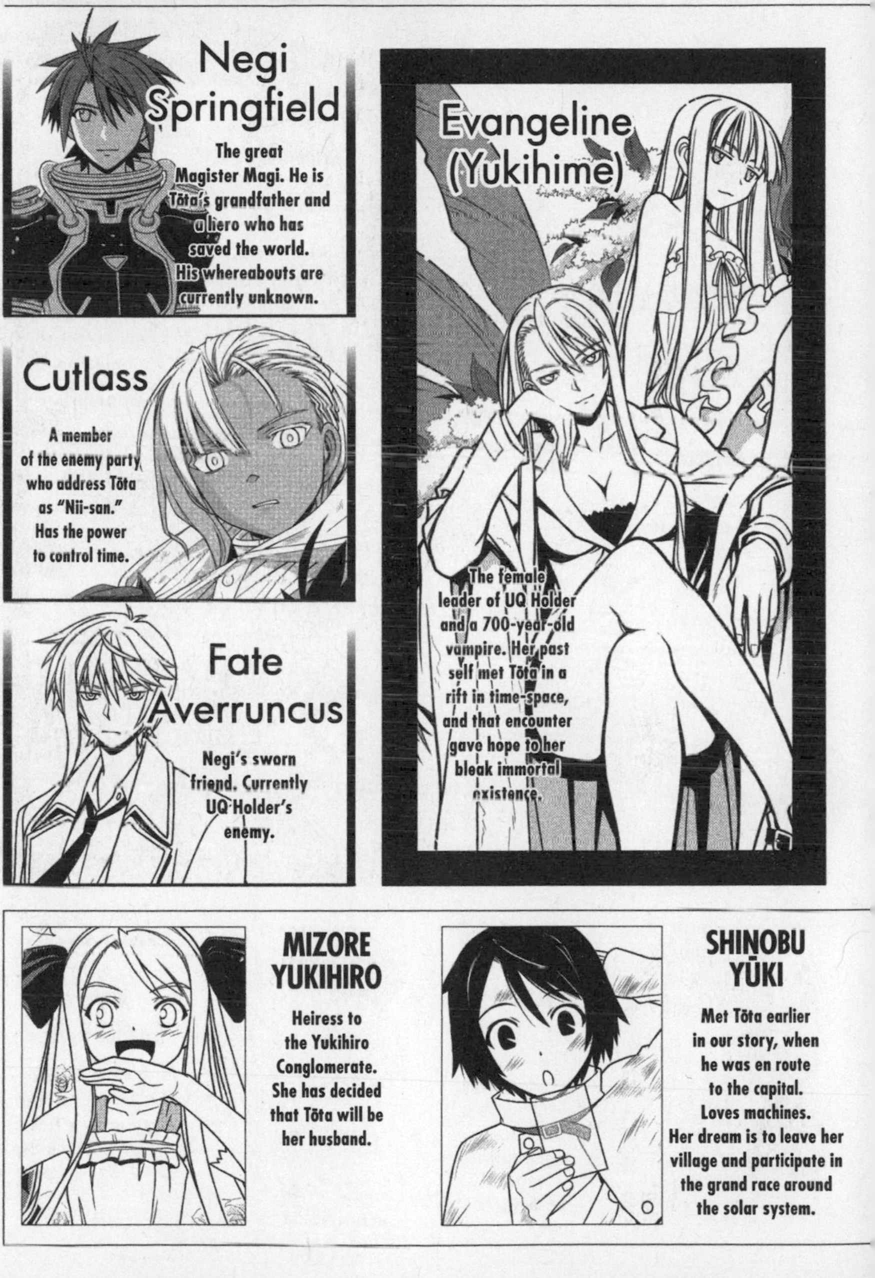
Evangeline (Yukihime)
The female leader of UQ Holder and a 700-year-old vampire. Her past self met Tōta in a rift in time-space, and that encounter gave hope to her bleak immortal existence.
Negi Springfield
The great Magister Magi. He is Tōta's grandfather and a hero who has saved the world. His whereabouts are currently unknown.
Cutlass
A member of the enemy party who address Tōta as "Nii-san." Has the power to control time.
Fate Averruncus
Negi's sworn friend. Currently UQ Holder's enemy.
SHINOBU YŪKI
Met Tōta earlier in our story, when he was en route to the capital. Loves machines. Her dream is to leave her village and participate in the grand race around the solar system.
MIZORE YUKIHIRO
Heiress to the Yukihiro Conglomerate. She has decided that Tōta will be her husband.

THE STORY SO FAR

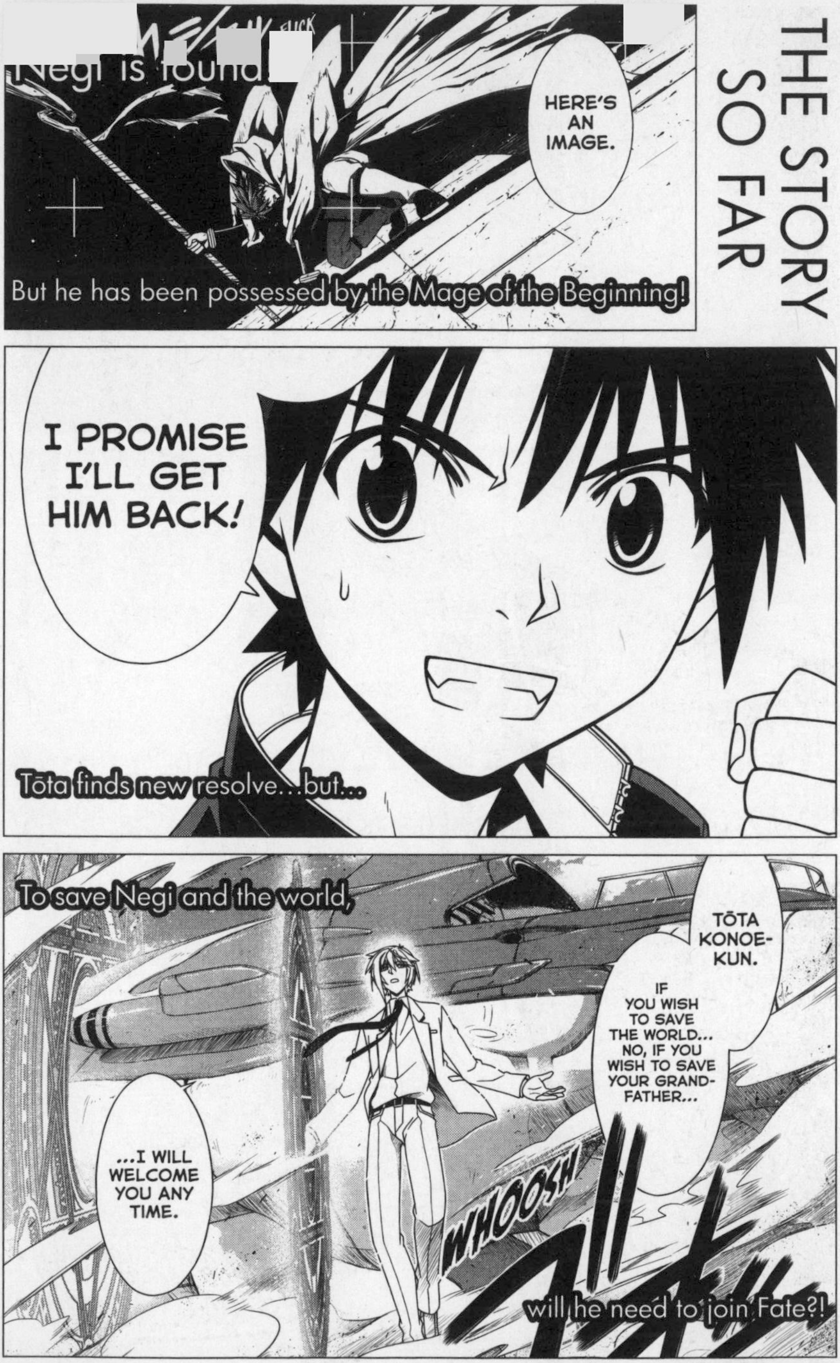

FLICK
Negi is found
HERE'S AN IMAGE.
But he has been possessed by the Mage of the Beginning!
I PROMISE I'LL GET HIM BACK!
Tōta finds new resolve…but…
To save Negi and the world,
TŌTA KONOE-KUN.
IF YOU WISH TO SAVE THE WORLD… NO, IF YOU WISH TO SAVE YOUR GRANDFATHER…
…I WILL WELCOME YOU ANY TIME.
WHOOSH
will he need to join Fate?!

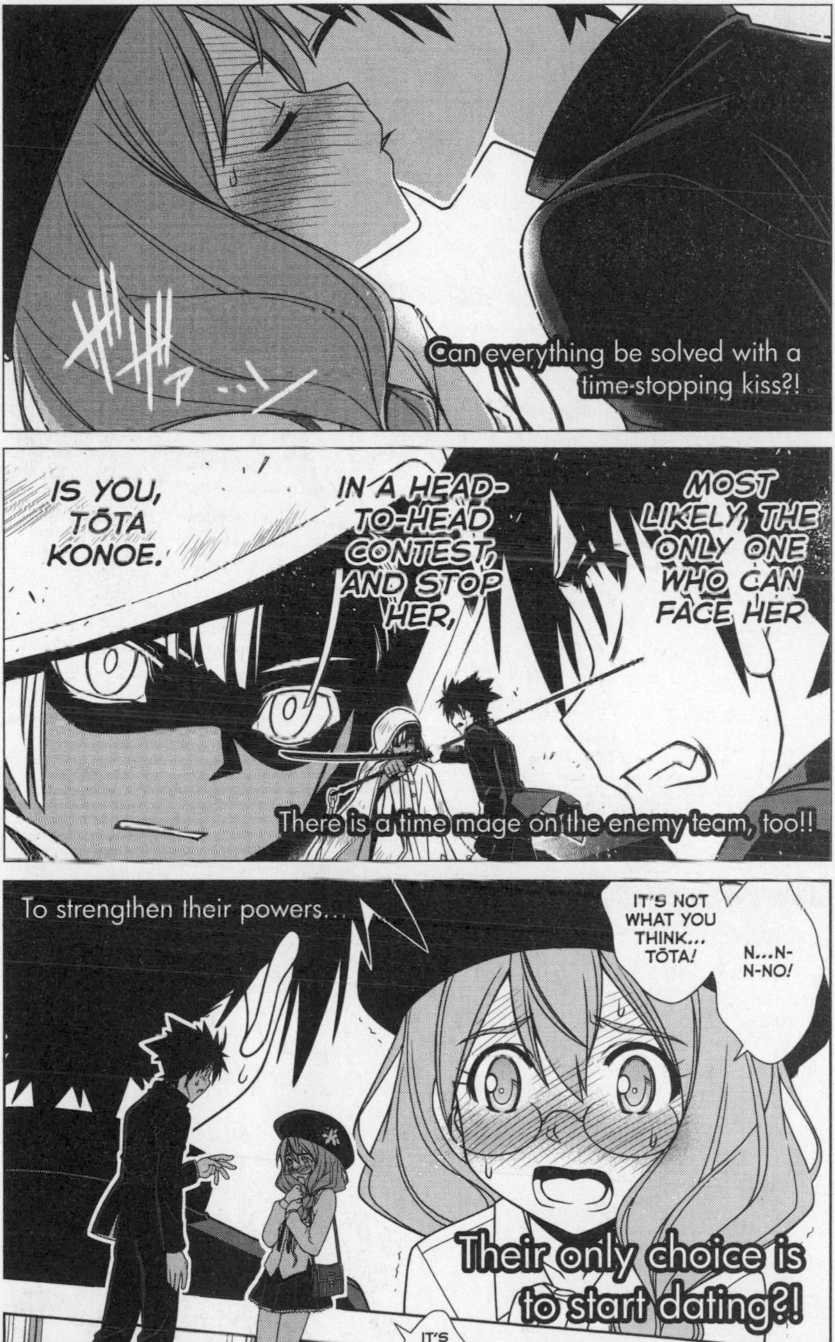
Can everything be solved with a time-stopping kiss?!
MOST LIKELY, THE ONLY ONE WHO CAN FACE HER
IN A HEAD-TO-HEAD CONTEST, AND STOP HER,
IS YOU, TŌTA KONOE.
There is a time mage on the enemy team, too!!
N...N-N-NO!
IT'S NOT WHAT YOU THINK... TŌTA!
To strengthen their powers...
Their only choice is to start dating?!
IT'S NOT...

CONTENTS

Stage.119 TŌTA AND KIRIË: WILL THEY OR WON'T THEY? 7

Stage.120 SPEEDER THREE-WAY................................ 25

Stage.121 RACING WITHOUT A STITCH 43

Stage.122 BECAUSE YOU ARE MIZORE'S BELOVED! 61

Stage.123 THE THREE TŌTAS' WISHES! 79

Stage.124 THAT'S HOW IT'S DONE!! 97

Stage.125 TIME MANIPULATOR CUTLASS...................117

Stage.126 IT ALL BEGINS 135

Stage.127 IT'S GOOD TO SEE YOU AGAIN 153

Stage.128 WE ARE UQ HOLDER!................................. 171

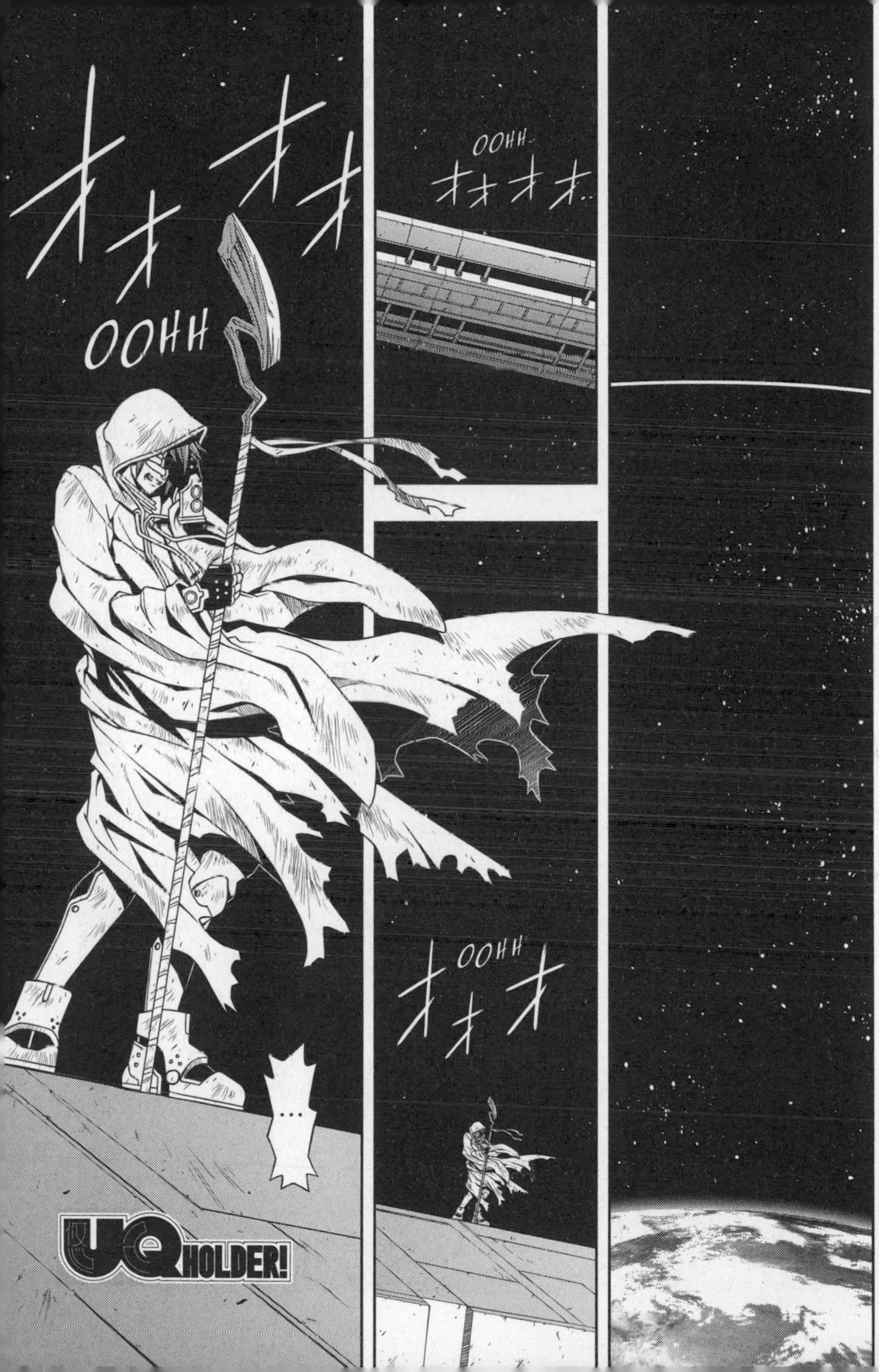
OOHH..
オォオォ..
OOHH
オォオ
オォオォ
OOHH
...
UQ HOLDER!

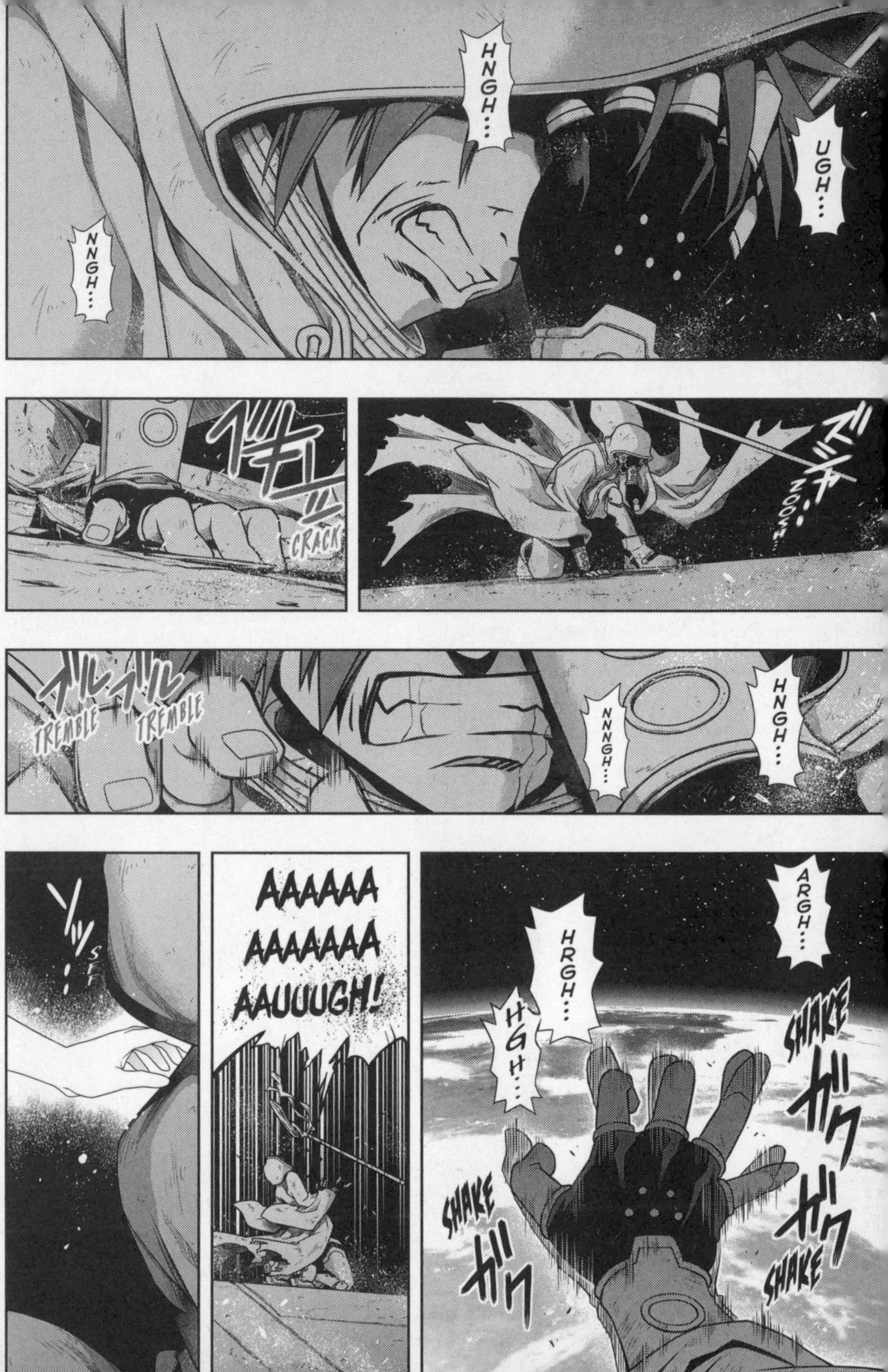
UGH...
HNGH...
NNGH...
ZOOSH...
CRACK
HNGH...
NNNGH...
TREMBLE
TREMBLE
ARGH...
HRGH...
HGH...
SHAKE
SHAKE
SHAKE
AAAAAA AAAAAAA AAUUUGH!
SFF

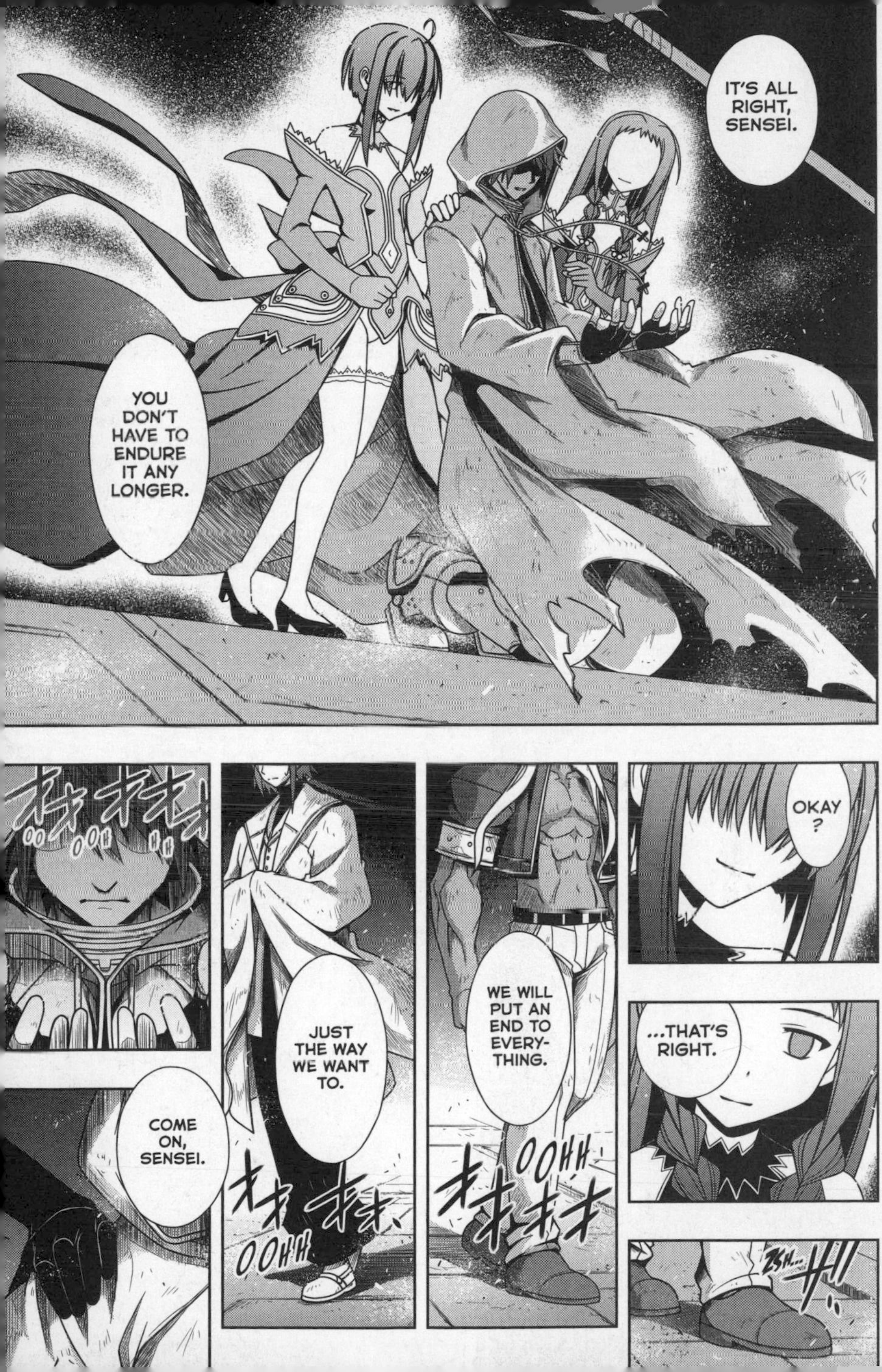
IT'S ALL RIGHT, SENSEI.
YOU DON'T HAVE TO ENDURE IT ANY LONGER.
OKAY?
...THAT'S RIGHT.
ZSH...!!
WE WILL PUT AN END TO EVERY-THING.
OOHH
JUST THE WAY WE WANT TO.
OOHH
OOHHH
COME ON, SENSEI.

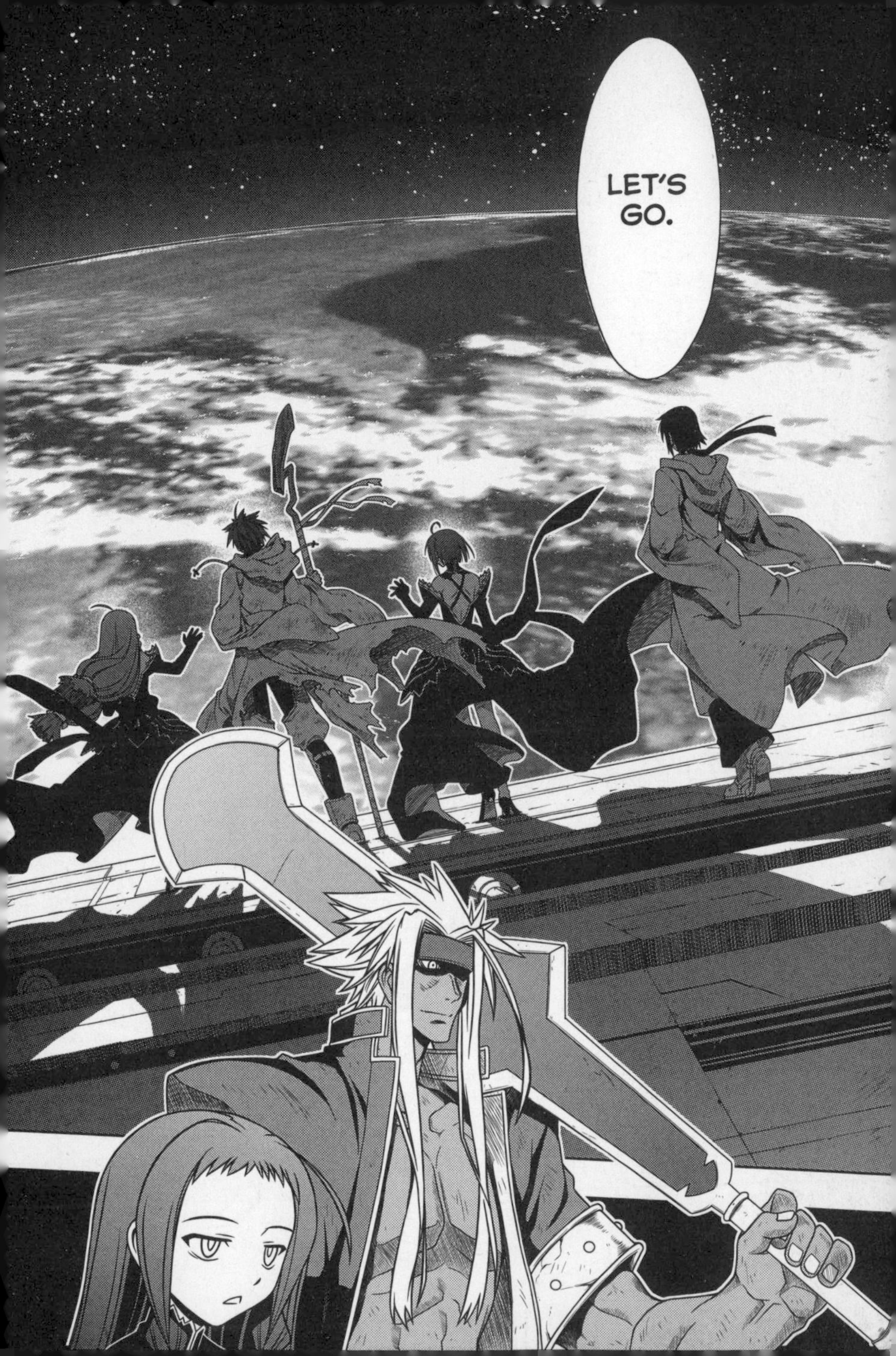
LET'S GO.

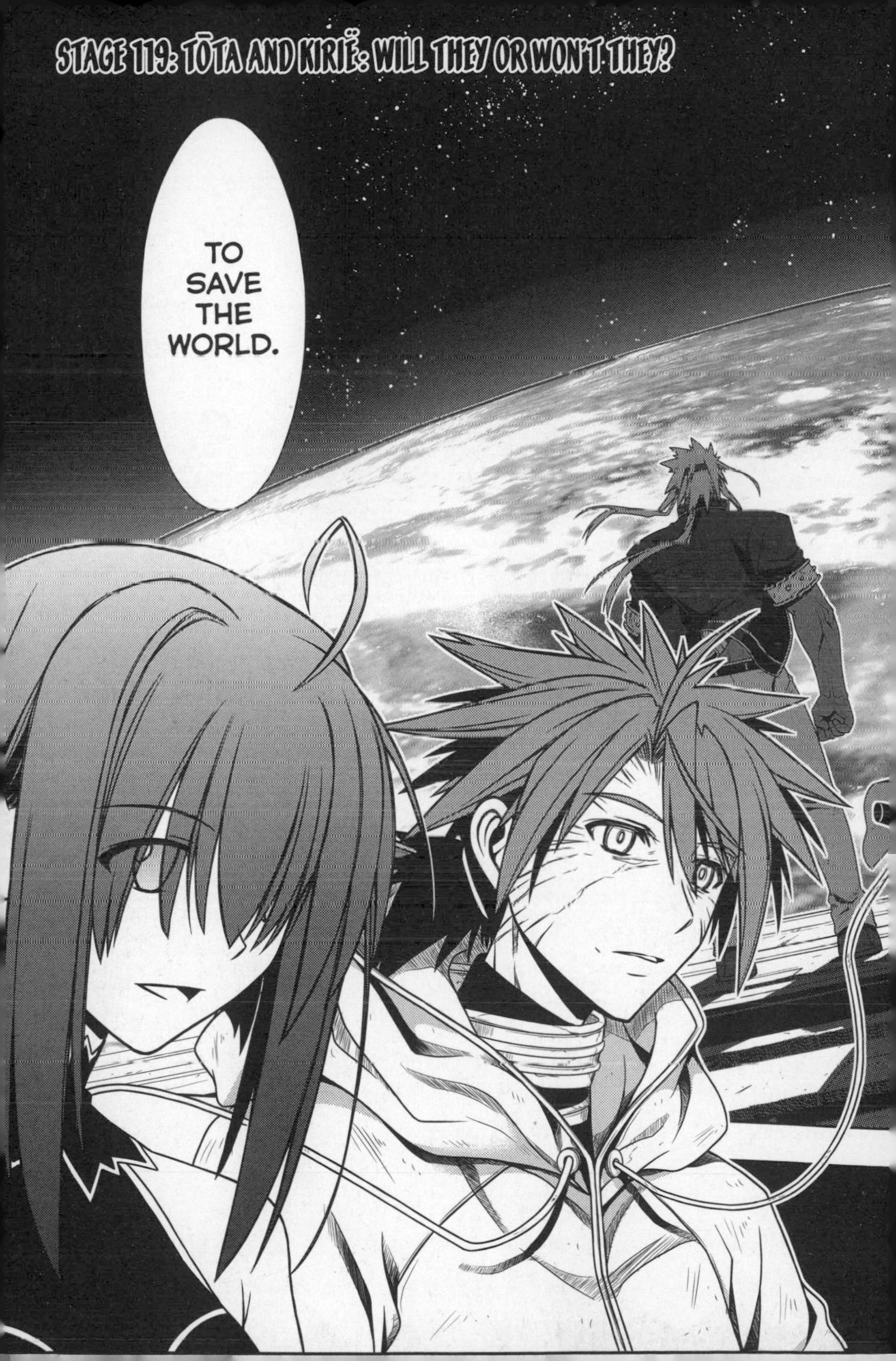
STAGE 119: TŌTA AND KIRIĒ: WILL THEY OR WON'T THEY?
TO SAVE THE WORLD.

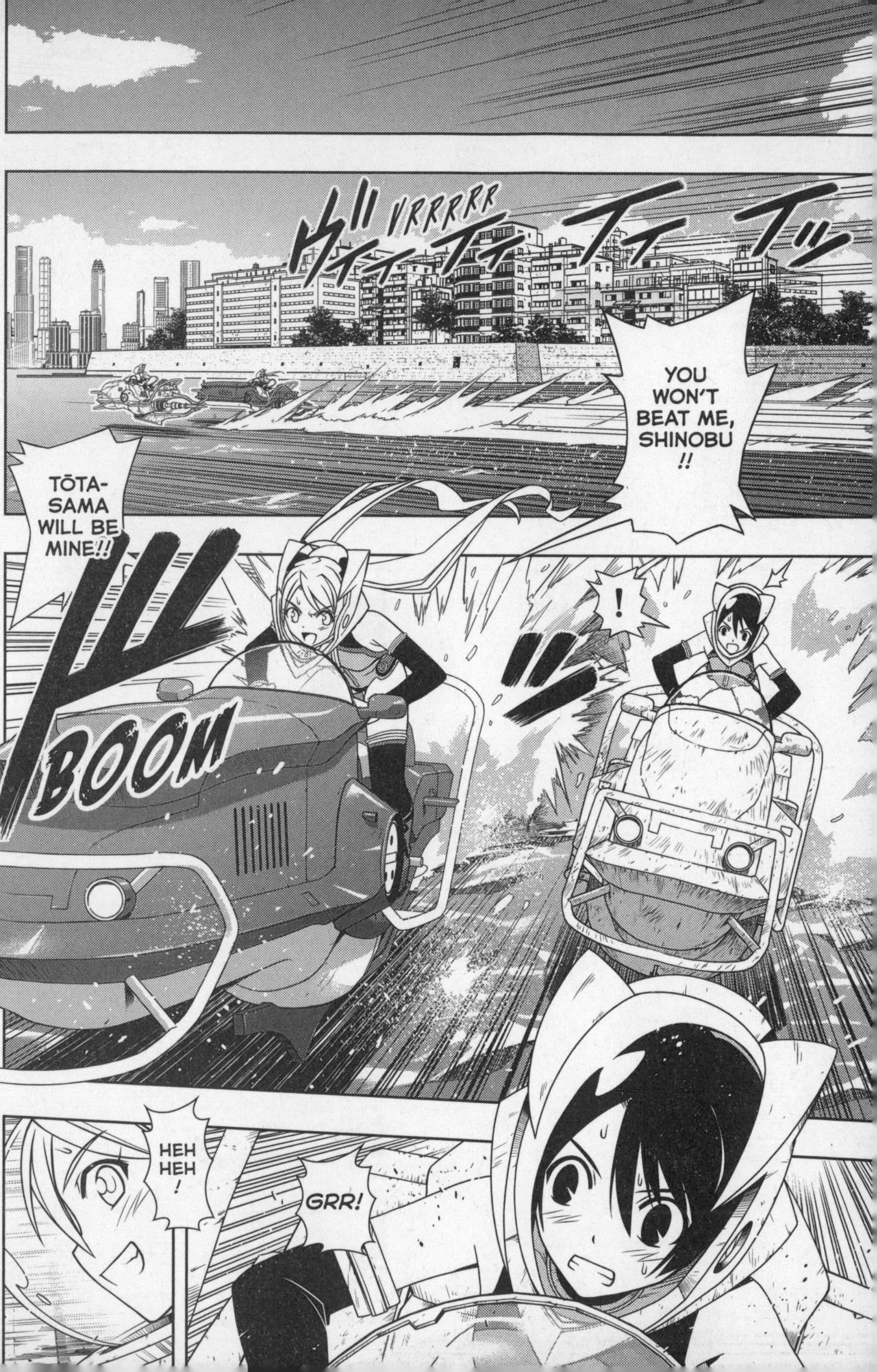
VRRRRR
YOU WON'T BEAT ME, SHINOBU!!
TŌTA-SAMA WILL BE MINE!!
!
BOOM
GRR!
HEH HEH!

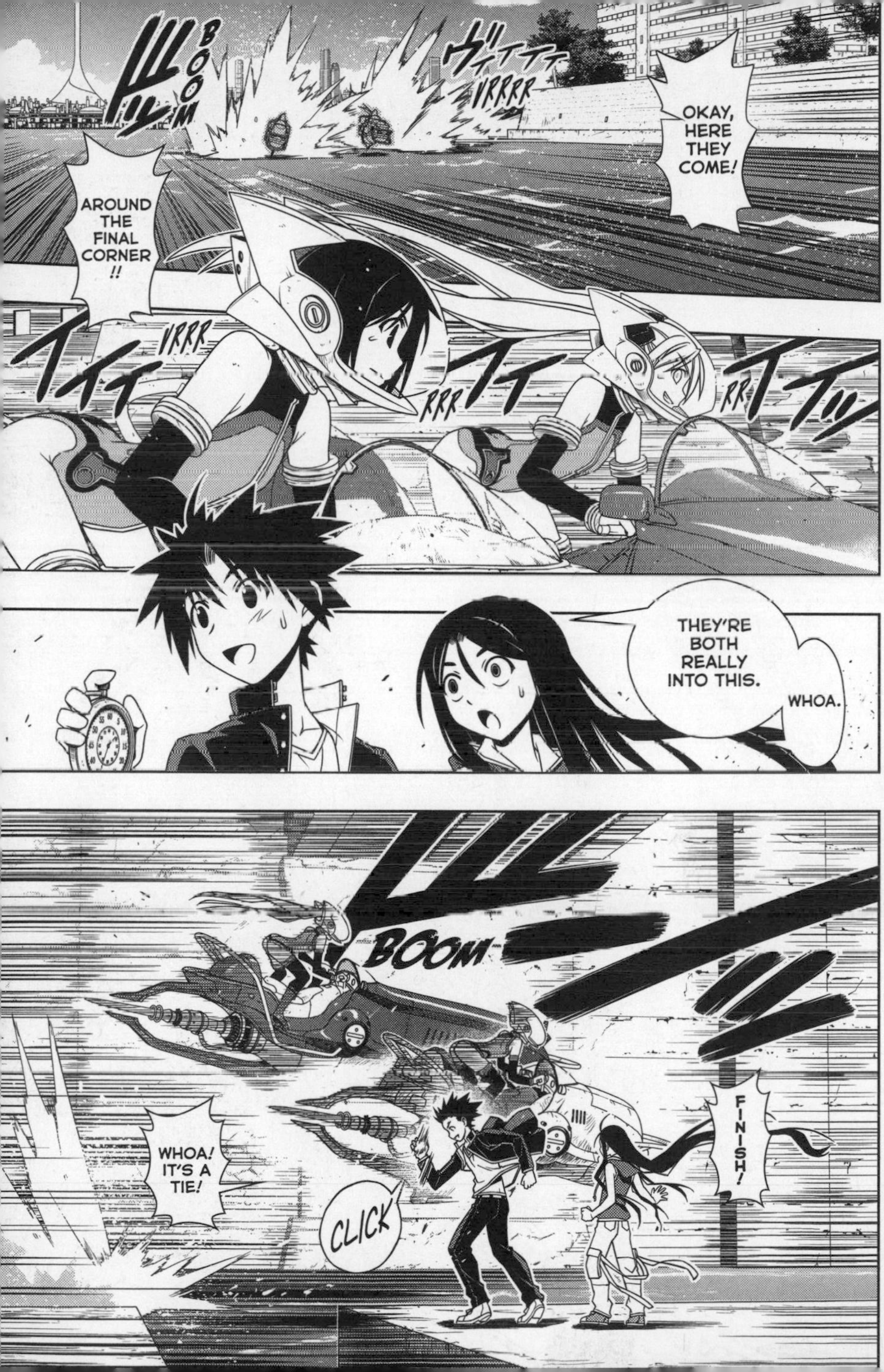

OKAY, HERE THEY COME!
ヴィイイイイ
VRRRR
BOOM
AROUND THE FINAL CORNER!!
RR
RRR
VRRR
WHOA.
THEY'RE BOTH REALLY INTO THIS.
FINISH!
BOOM
CLICK
WHOA! IT'S A TIE!

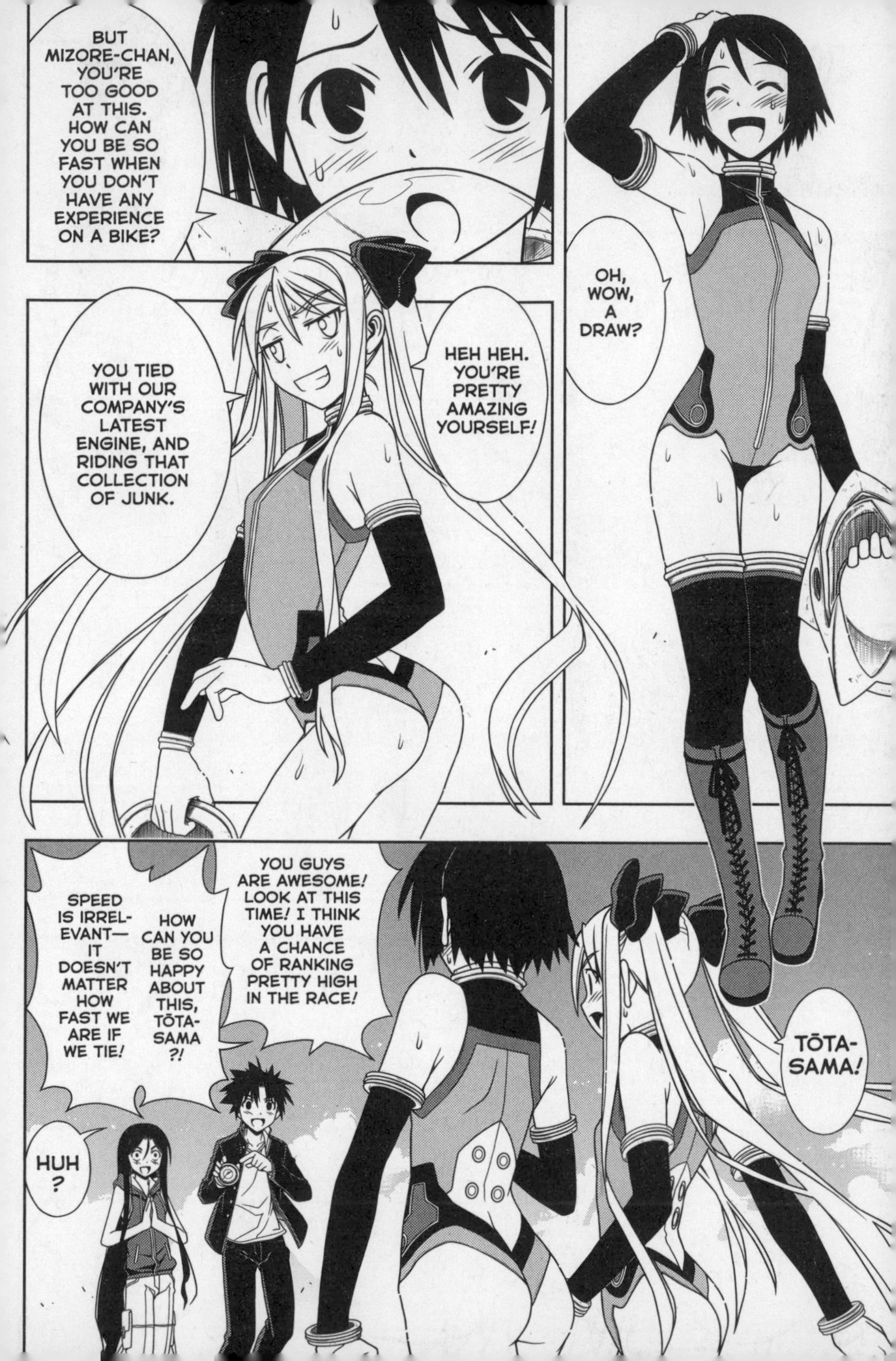
OH, WOW, A DRAW?
BUT MIZORE-CHAN, YOU'RE TOO GOOD AT THIS. HOW CAN YOU BE SO FAST WHEN YOU DON'T HAVE ANY EXPERIENCE ON A BIKE?
HEH HEH. YOU'RE PRETTY AMAZING YOURSELF!
YOU TIED WITH OUR COMPANY'S LATEST ENGINE, AND RIDING THAT COLLECTION OF JUNK.
TŌTA-SAMA!
YOU GUYS ARE AWESOME! LOOK AT THIS TIME! I THINK YOU HAVE A CHANCE OF RANKING PRETTY HIGH IN THE RACE!
HOW CAN YOU BE SO HAPPY ABOUT THIS, TŌTA-SAMA?!
SPEED IS IRREL-EVANT—IT DOESN'T MATTER HOW FAST WE ARE IF WE TIE!
HUH?

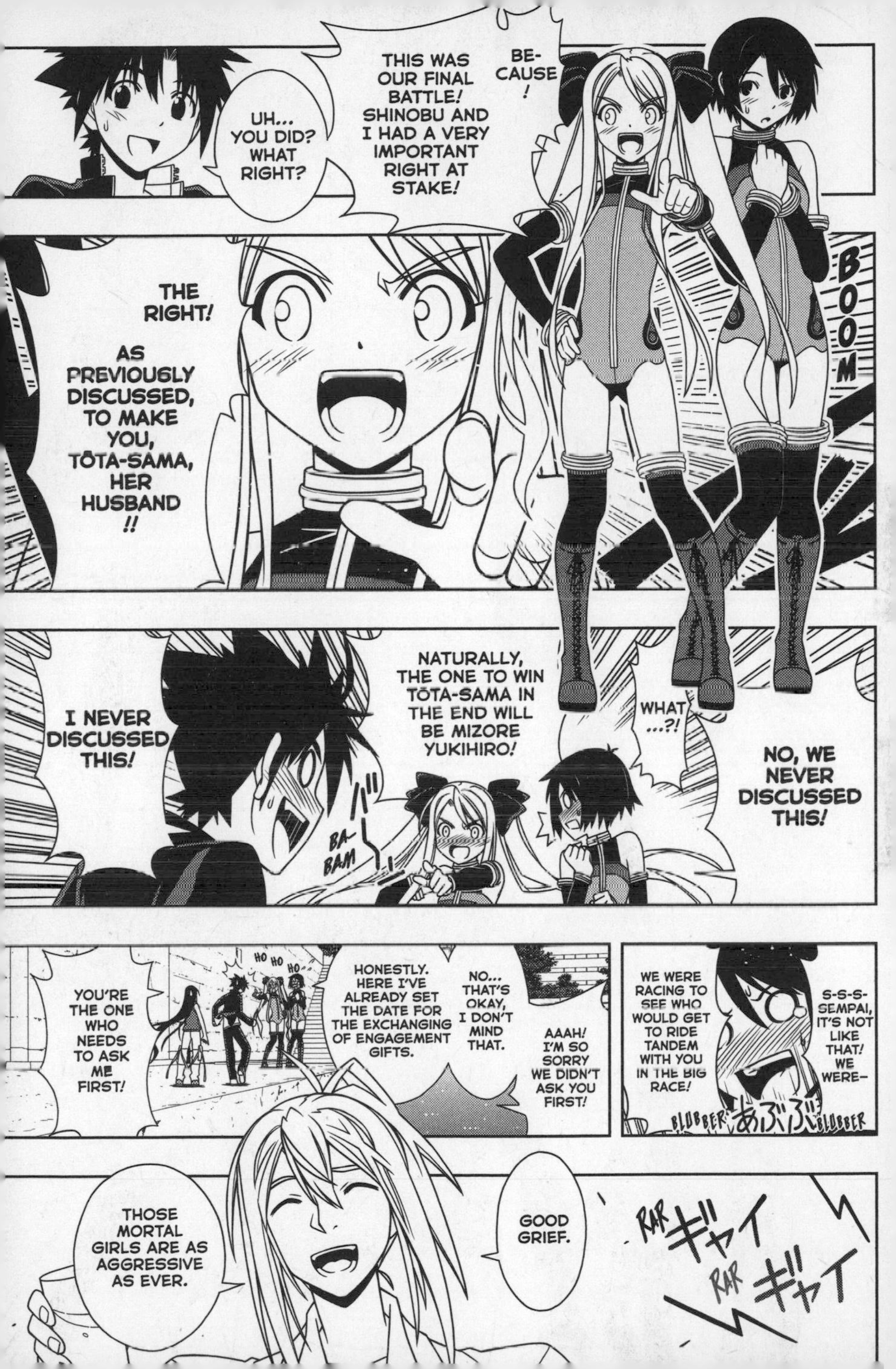
BE-CAUSE!
THIS WAS OUR FINAL BATTLE! SHINOBU AND I HAD A VERY IMPORTANT RIGHT AT STAKE!
UH... YOU DID? WHAT RIGHT?
BOOM
THE RIGHT!
AS PREVIOUSLY DISCUSSED, TO MAKE YOU, TŌTA-SAMA, HER HUSBAND!!
NO, WE NEVER DISCUSSED THIS!
WHAT...?!
NATURALLY, THE ONE TO WIN TŌTA-SAMA IN THE END WILL BE MIZORE YUKIHIRO!
BA-BAM
I NEVER DISCUSSED THIS!
S-S-S-SEMPAI, IT'S NOT LIKE THAT! WE WERE—
WE WERE RACING TO SEE WHO WOULD GET TO RIDE TANDEM WITH YOU IN THE BIG RACE!
BLUBBER あぶぶ BLUBBER
AAAH! I'M SO SORRY WE DIDN'T ASK YOU FIRST!
NO... THAT'S OKAY, I DON'T MIND THAT.
HONESTLY. HERE I'VE ALREADY SET THE DATE FOR THE EXCHANGING OF ENGAGEMENT GIFTS.
HO HO HO
YOU'RE THE ONE WHO NEEDS TO ASK ME FIRST!
RAR ギャイ
RAR ギャイ
GOOD GRIEF.
THOSE MORTAL GIRLS ARE AS AGGRESSIVE AS EVER.

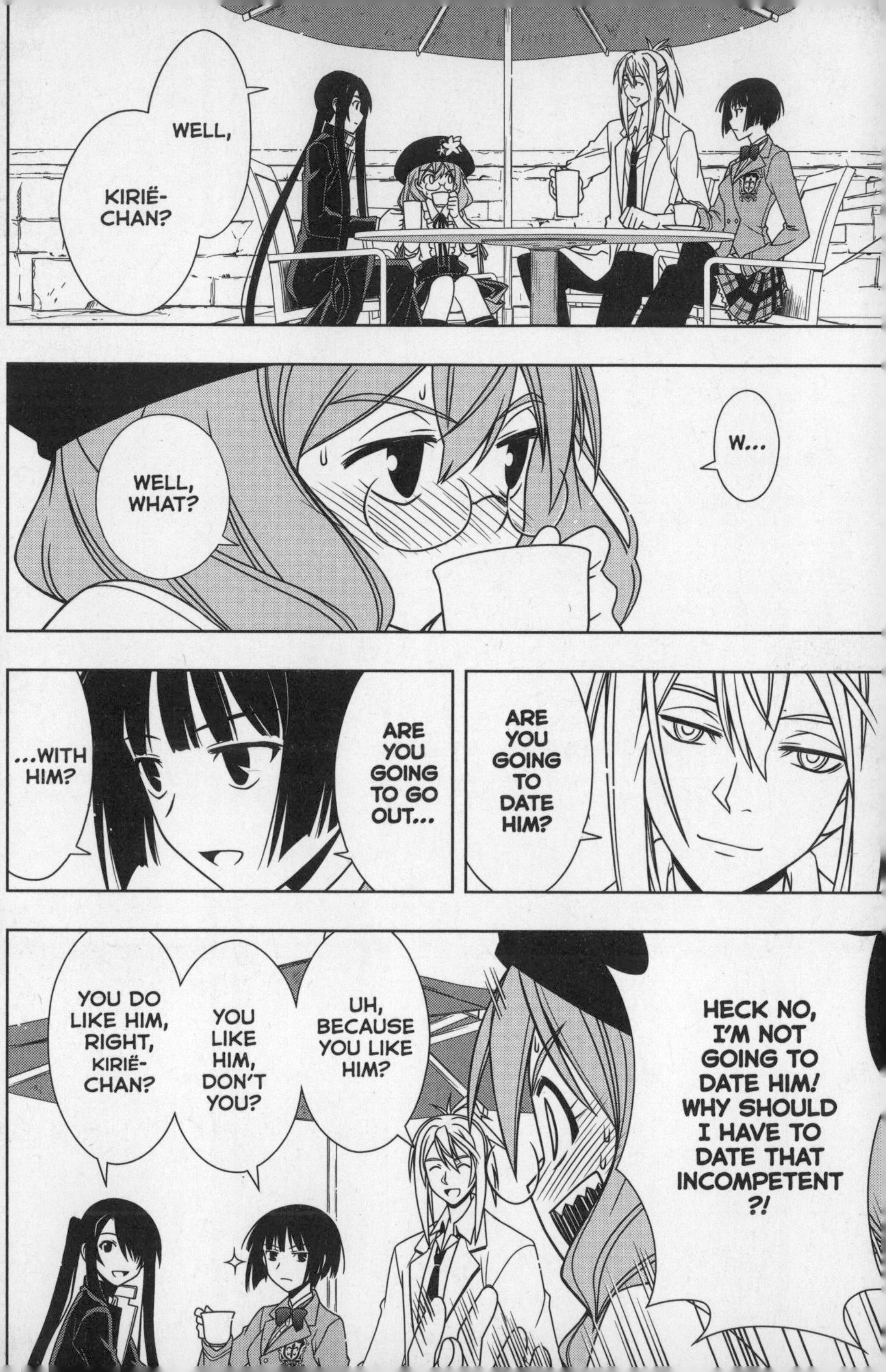
WELL, KIRIË-CHAN?
W...
WELL, WHAT?
ARE YOU GOING TO DATE HIM?
ARE YOU GOING TO GO OUT...
...WITH HIM?
HECK NO, I'M NOT GOING TO DATE HIM! WHY SHOULD I HAVE TO DATE THAT INCOMPETENT ?!
UH, BECAUSE YOU LIKE HIM?
YOU LIKE HIM, DON'T YOU?
YOU DO LIKE HIM, RIGHT, KIRIË-CHAN?

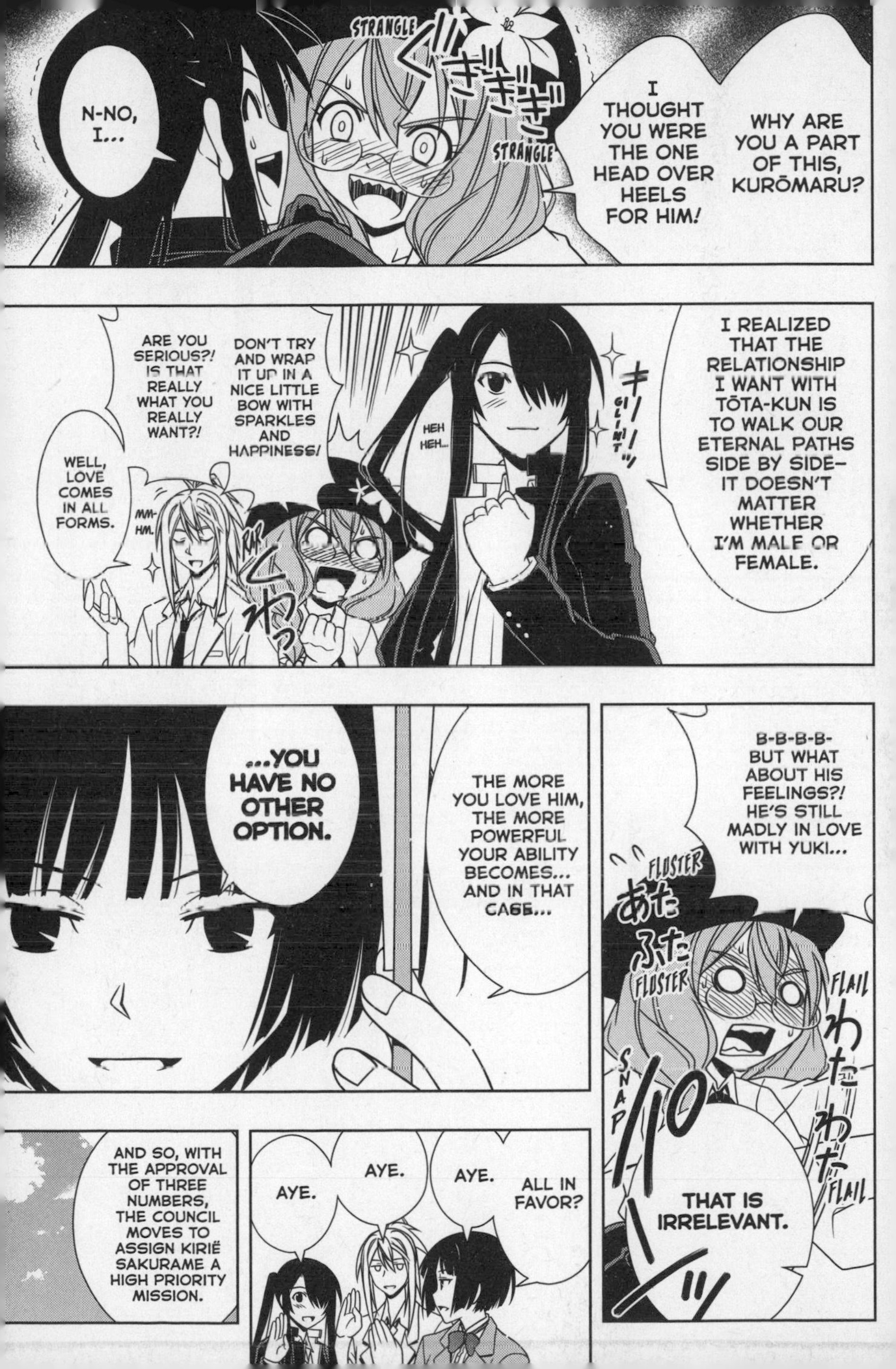
WHY ARE YOU A PART OF THIS, KURŌMARU?
I THOUGHT YOU WERE THE ONE HEAD OVER HEELS FOR HIM!
STRANGLE
STRANGLE
N-NO, I...
I REALIZED THAT THE RELATIONSHIP I WANT WITH TŌTA-KUN IS TO WALK OUR ETERNAL PATHS SIDE BY SIDE– IT DOESN'T MATTER WHETHER I'M MALE OR FEMALE.
GLINT
HEH HEH...
DON'T TRY AND WRAP IT UP IN A NICE LITTLE BOW WITH SPARKLES AND HAPPINESS!
ARE YOU SERIOUS?! IS THAT REALLY WHAT YOU REALLY WANT?!
RAP
MM-HM.
WELL, LOVE COMES IN ALL FORMS.
B-B-B-B-BUT WHAT ABOUT HIS FEELINGS?! HE'S STILL MADLY IN LOVE WITH YUKI...
FLUSTER
FLUSTER
FLAIL
FLAIL
SNAP
THAT IS IRRELEVANT.
THE MORE YOU LOVE HIM, THE MORE POWERFUL YOUR ABILITY BECOMES... AND IN THAT CASE...
...YOU HAVE NO OTHER OPTION.
ALL IN FAVOR?
AYE.
AYE.
AYE.
AND SO, WITH THE APPROVAL OF THREE NUMBERS, THE COUNCIL MOVES TO ASSIGN KIRIË SAKURAME A HIGH PRIORITY MISSION.

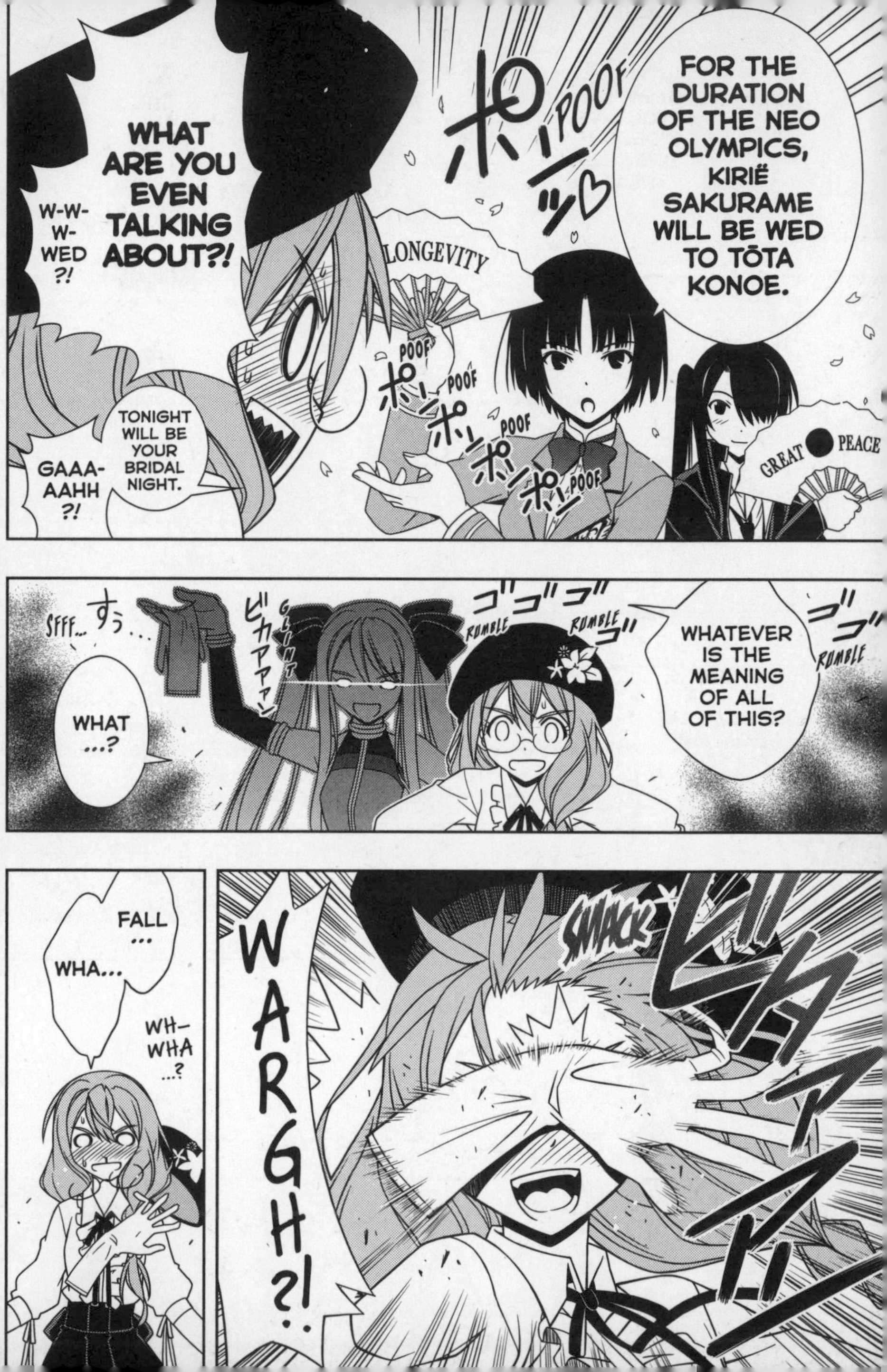
FOR THE DURATION OF THE NEO OLYMPICS, KIRIË SAKURAME WILL BE WED TO TŌTA KONOE.
POOF
GREAT ● PEACE
LONGEVITY
POOF POOF POOF POOF
WHAT ARE YOU EVEN TALKING ABOUT?!
W-W-W-WED ?!
TONIGHT WILL BE YOUR BRIDAL NIGHT.
GAAA-AAHH ?!
RUMBLE
WHATEVER IS THE MEANING OF ALL OF THIS?
RUMBLE RUMBLE
GLINT
SFFF...
WHAT ...?
SMACK
WARGH ?!
FALL ...
WHA...
WH-WHA ...?

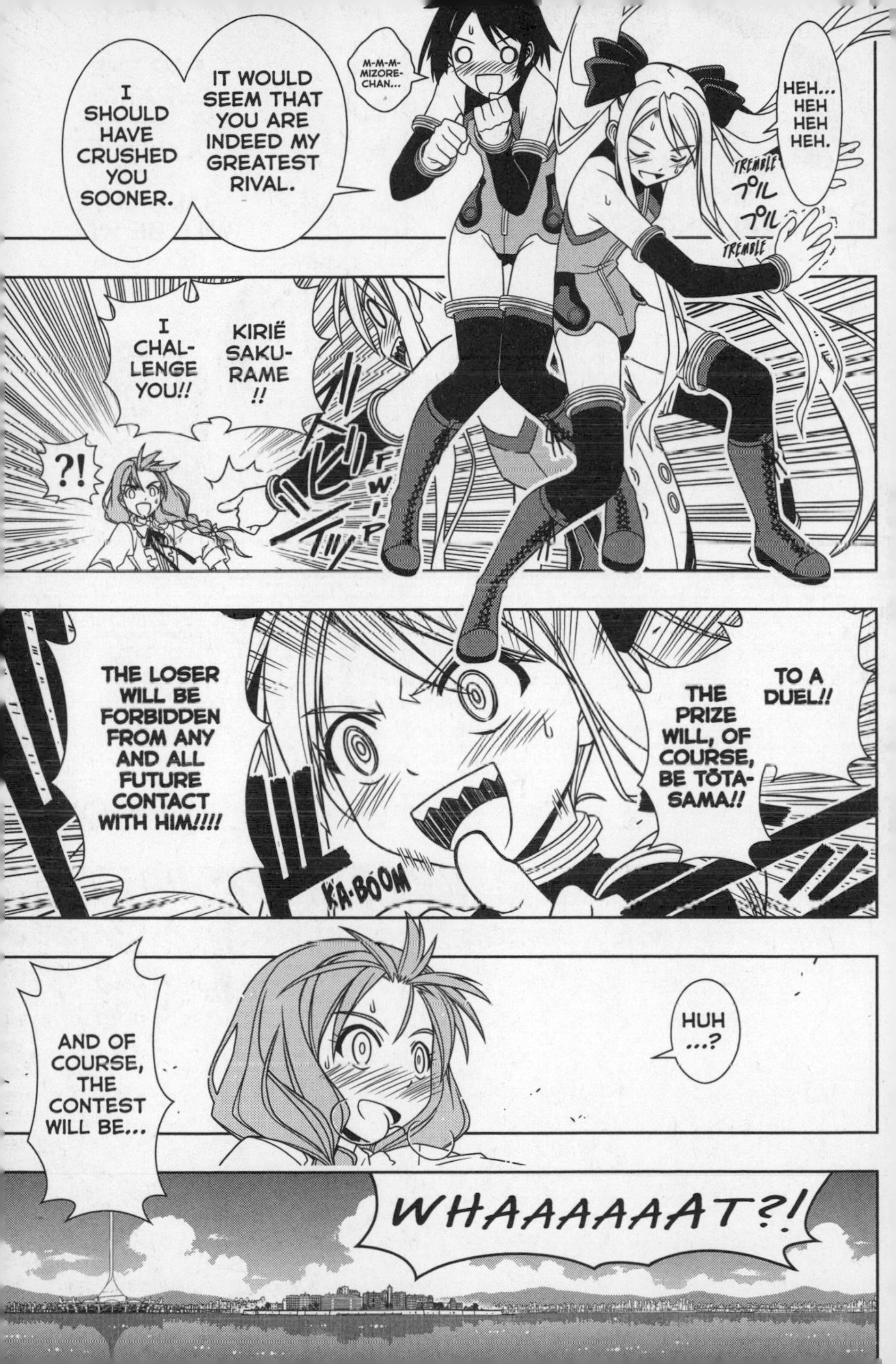
HEH... HEH HEH HEH.
TREMBLE
プル
プル
TREMBLE
M-M-M-MIZORE-CHAN...
IT WOULD SEEM THAT YOU ARE INDEED MY GREATEST RIVAL.
I SHOULD HAVE CRUSHED YOU SOONER.
KIRIË SAKURAME!!
I CHALLENGE YOU!!
FWIP
?!
TO A DUEL!!
THE PRIZE WILL, OF COURSE, BE TŌTA-SAMA!!
KA-BOOM
THE LOSER WILL BE FORBIDDEN FROM ANY AND ALL FUTURE CONTACT WITH HIM!!!!
HUH...?
AND OF COURSE, THE CONTEST WILL BE...
WHAAAAAAT?!

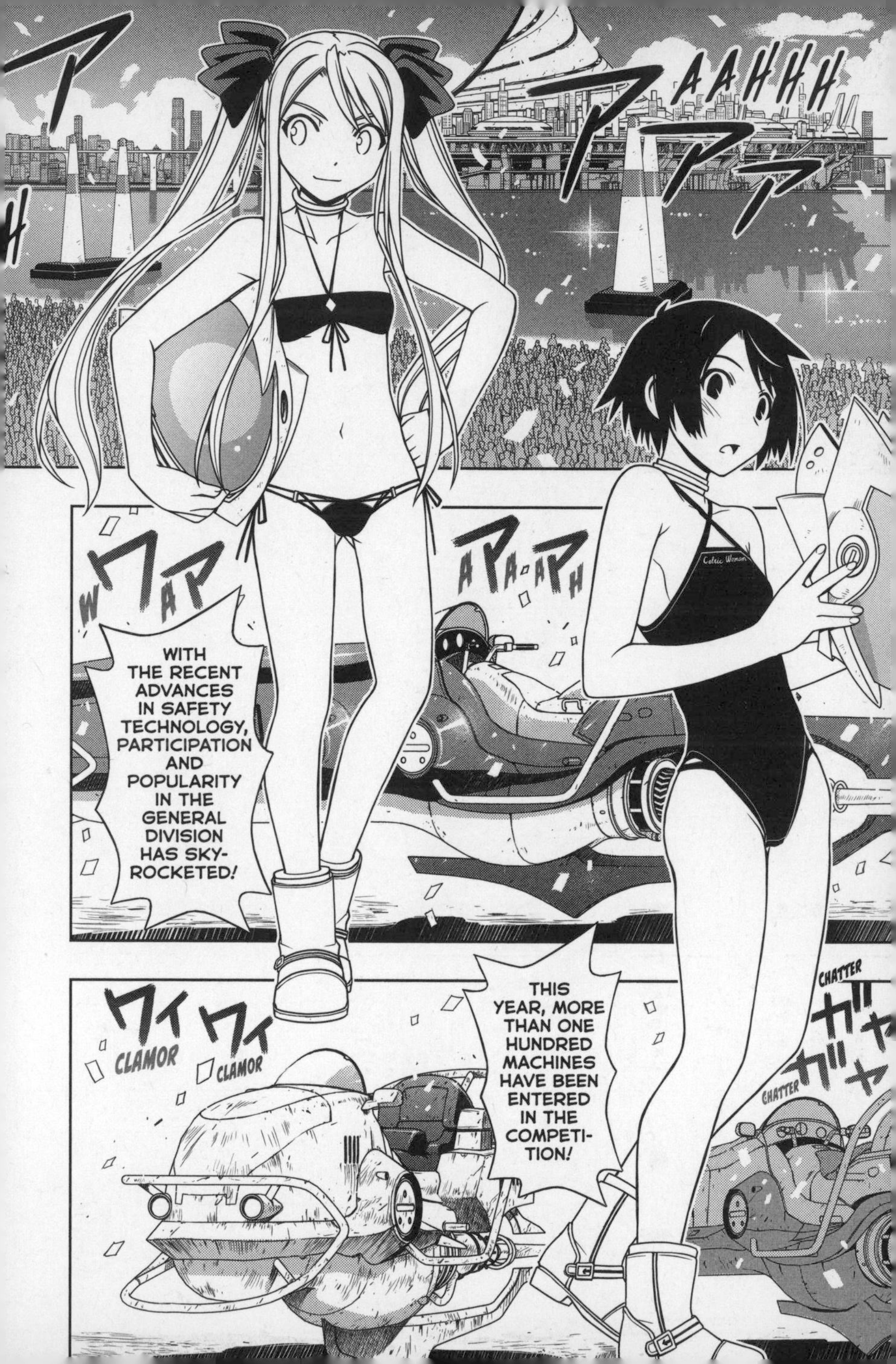
AAHHHH
H
APA-APH
Celtic Woman
WAP
WITH THE RECENT ADVANCES IN SAFETY TECHNOLOGY, PARTICIPATION AND POPULARITY IN THE GENERAL DIVISION HAS SKY-ROCKETED!
CHATTER
CHATTER
THIS YEAR, MORE THAN ONE HUNDRED MACHINES HAVE BEEN ENTERED IN THE COMPETI-TION!
CLAMOR
CLAMOR

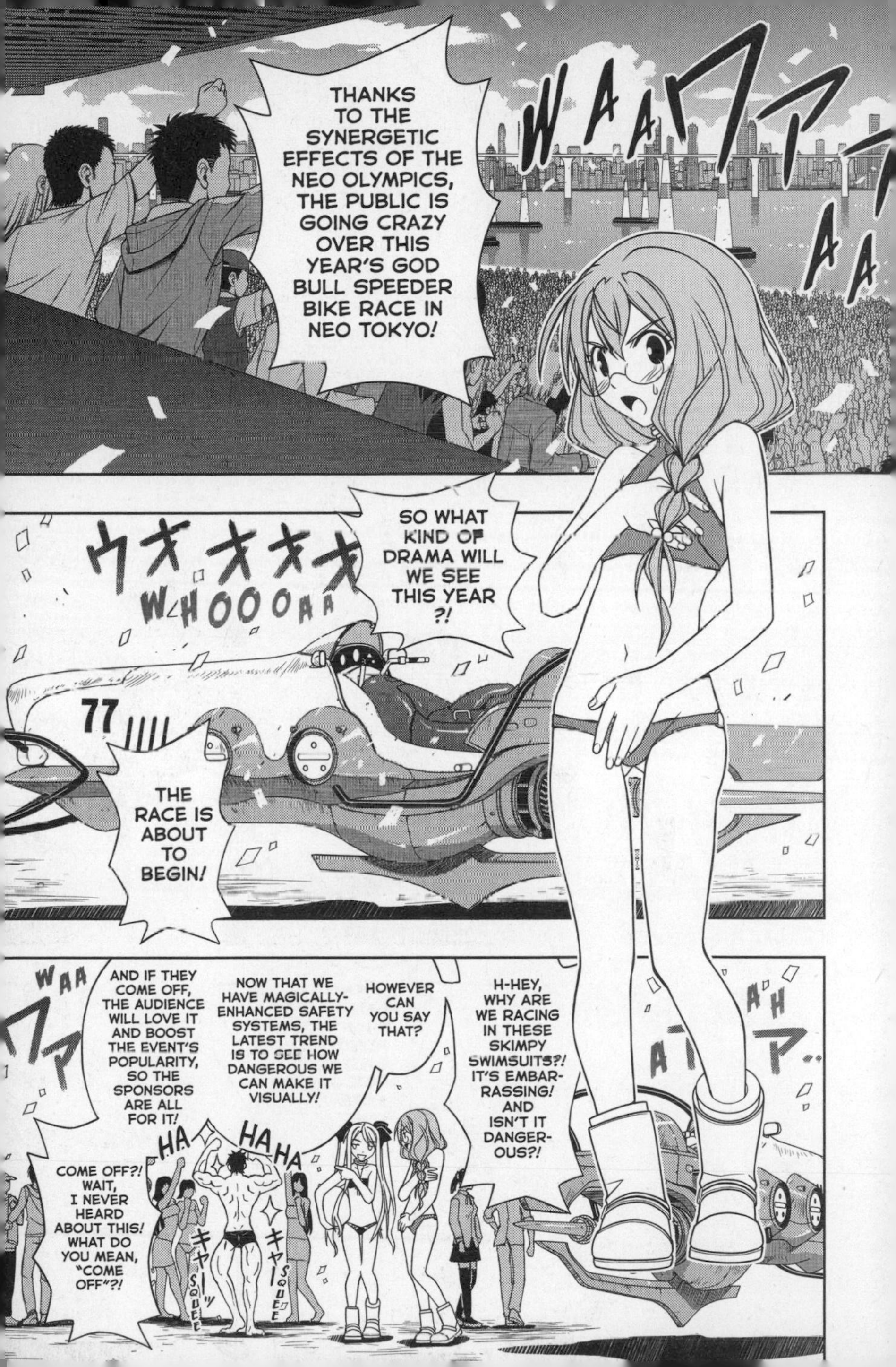
WAAAAA
THANKS TO THE SYNERGETIC EFFECTS OF THE NEO OLYMPICS, THE PUBLIC IS GOING CRAZY OVER THIS YEAR'S GOD BULL SPEEDER BIKE RACE IN NEO TOKYO!
SO WHAT KIND OF DRAMA WILL WE SEE THIS YEAR ?!
WHOOOAA
77
THE RACE IS ABOUT TO BEGIN!
AAH
H-HEY, WHY ARE WE RACING IN THESE SKIMPY SWIMSUITS?! IT'S EMBARRASSING! AND ISN'T IT DANGEROUS?!
HOWEVER CAN YOU SAY THAT?
NOW THAT WE HAVE MAGICALLY-ENHANCED SAFETY SYSTEMS, THE LATEST TREND IS TO SEE HOW DANGEROUS WE CAN MAKE IT VISUALLY!
AND IF THEY COME OFF, THE AUDIENCE WILL LOVE IT AND BOOST THE EVENT'S POPULARITY, SO THE SPONSORS ARE ALL FOR IT!
WAA
HA HAHA
SQUEE
SQUEE
COME OFF?! WAIT, I NEVER HEARD ABOUT THIS! WHAT DO YOU MEAN, "COME OFF"?!

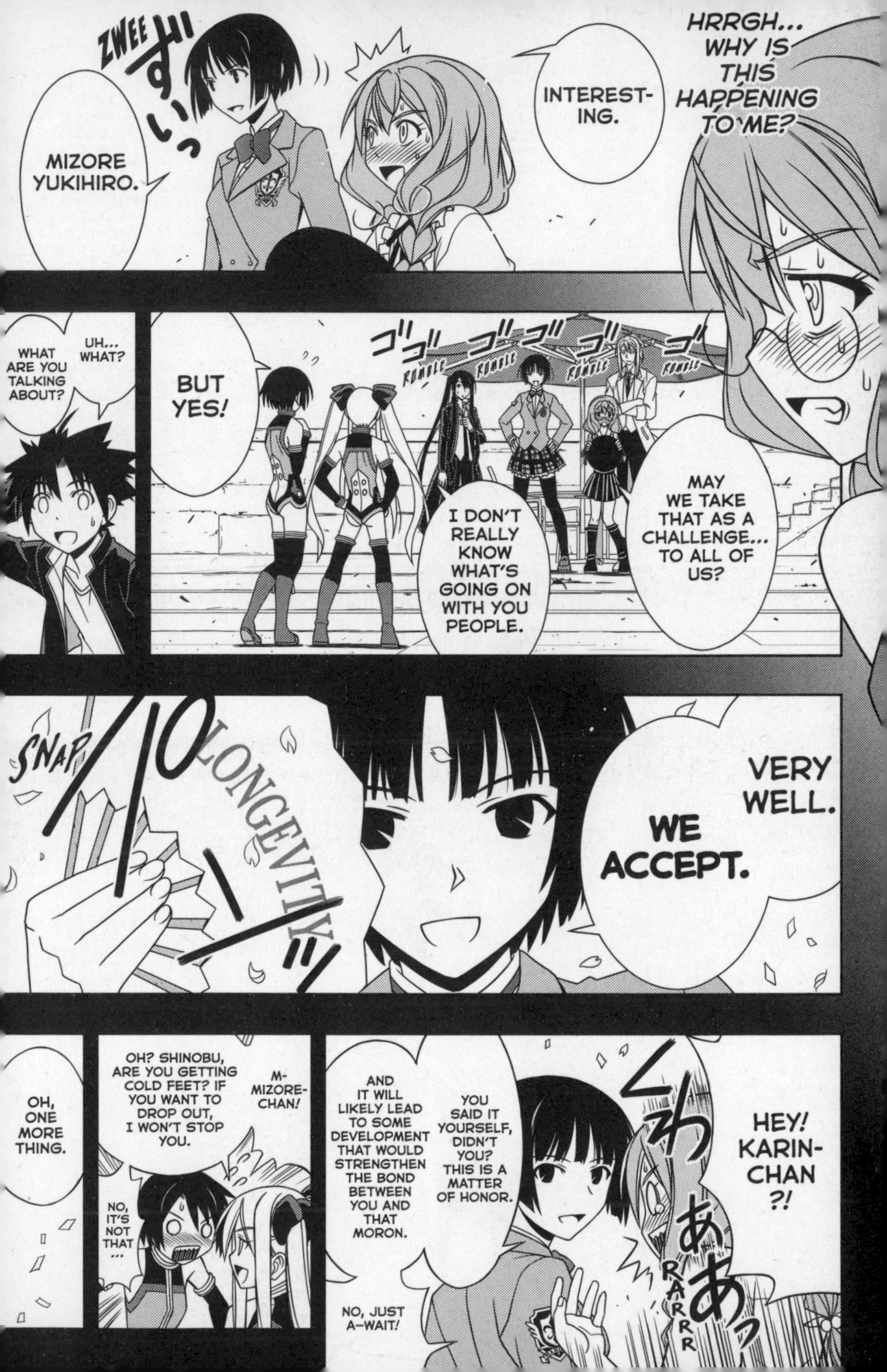
HRRGH... WHY IS THIS HAPPENING TO ME?
INTERESTING.
ZWEE
MIZORE YUKIHIRO.
MAY WE TAKE THAT AS A CHALLENGE... TO ALL OF US?
RUMBLE RUMBLE RUMBLE RUMBLE
I DON'T REALLY KNOW WHAT'S GOING ON WITH YOU PEOPLE.
BUT YES!
UH... WHAT?
WHAT ARE YOU TALKING ABOUT?
VERY WELL.
WE ACCEPT.
LONGEVITY
SNAP
HEY! KARIN-CHAN?!
RARRR
YOU SAID IT YOURSELF, DIDN'T YOU? THIS IS A MATTER OF HONOR.
AND IT WILL LIKELY LEAD TO SOME DEVELOPMENT THAT WOULD STRENGTHEN THE BOND BETWEEN YOU AND THAT MORON.
NO, JUST A-WAIT!
M-MIZORE-CHAN!
OH? SHINOBU, ARE YOU GETTING COLD FEET? IF YOU WANT TO DROP OUT, I WON'T STOP YOU.
NO, IT'S NOT THAT...
OH, ONE MORE THING.

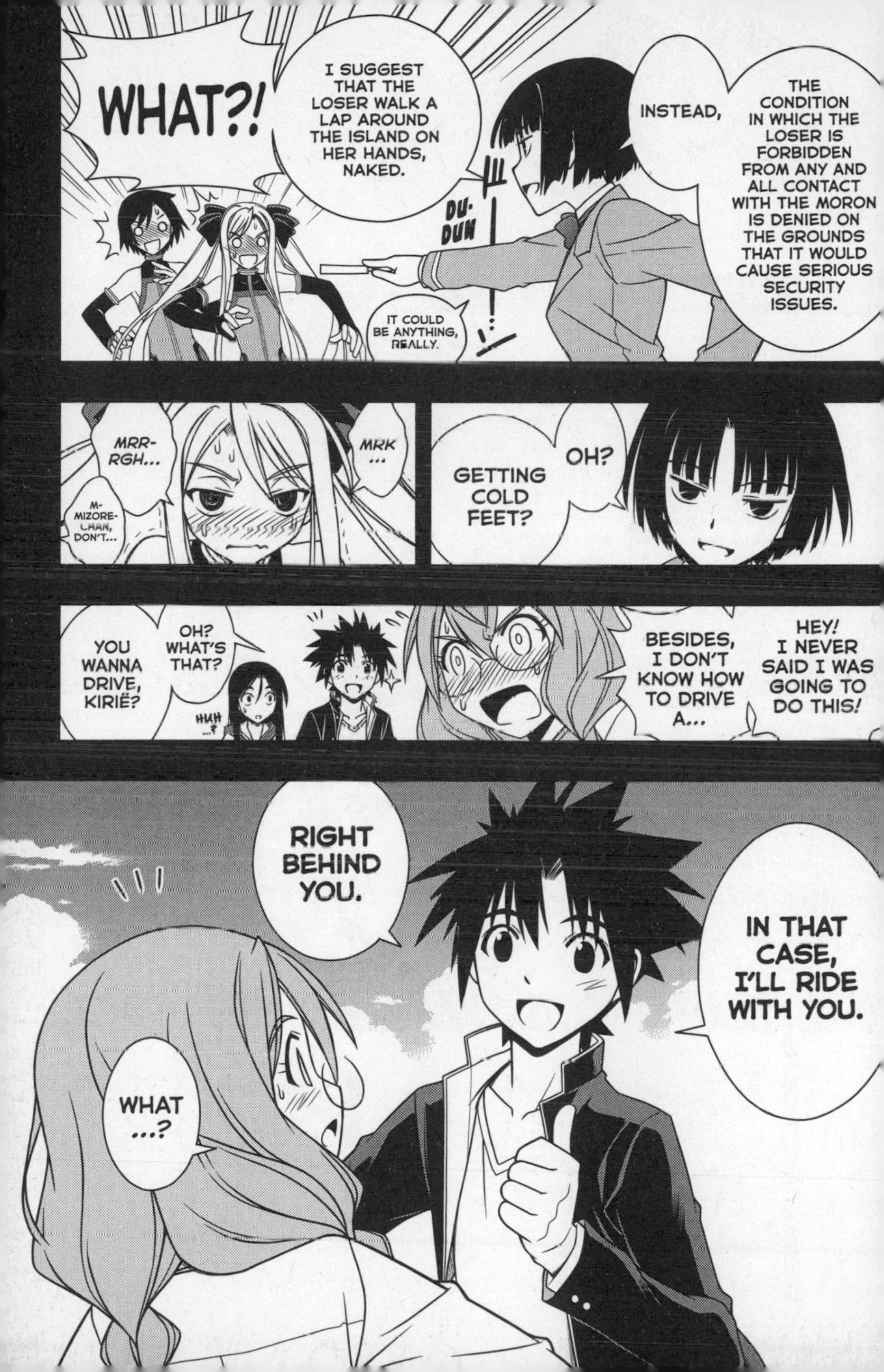
THE CONDITION IN WHICH THE LOSER IS FORBIDDEN FROM ANY AND ALL CONTACT WITH THE MORON IS DENIED ON THE GROUNDS THAT IT WOULD CAUSE SERIOUS SECURITY ISSUES.
INSTEAD,
I SUGGEST THAT THE LOSER WALK A LAP AROUND THE ISLAND ON HER HANDS, NAKED.
DU-DUN
WHAT?!
IT COULD BE ANYTHING, REALLY.
OH?
GETTING COLD FEET?
MRK...
MRR-RGH...
M-MIZORE-CHAN, DON'T...
HEY! I NEVER SAID I WAS GOING TO DO THIS!
BESIDES, I DON'T KNOW HOW TO DRIVE A...
OH? WHAT'S THAT?
YOU WANNA DRIVE, KIRIË?
HUH...?
IN THAT CASE, I'LL RIDE WITH YOU.
RIGHT BEHIND YOU.
WHAT...?

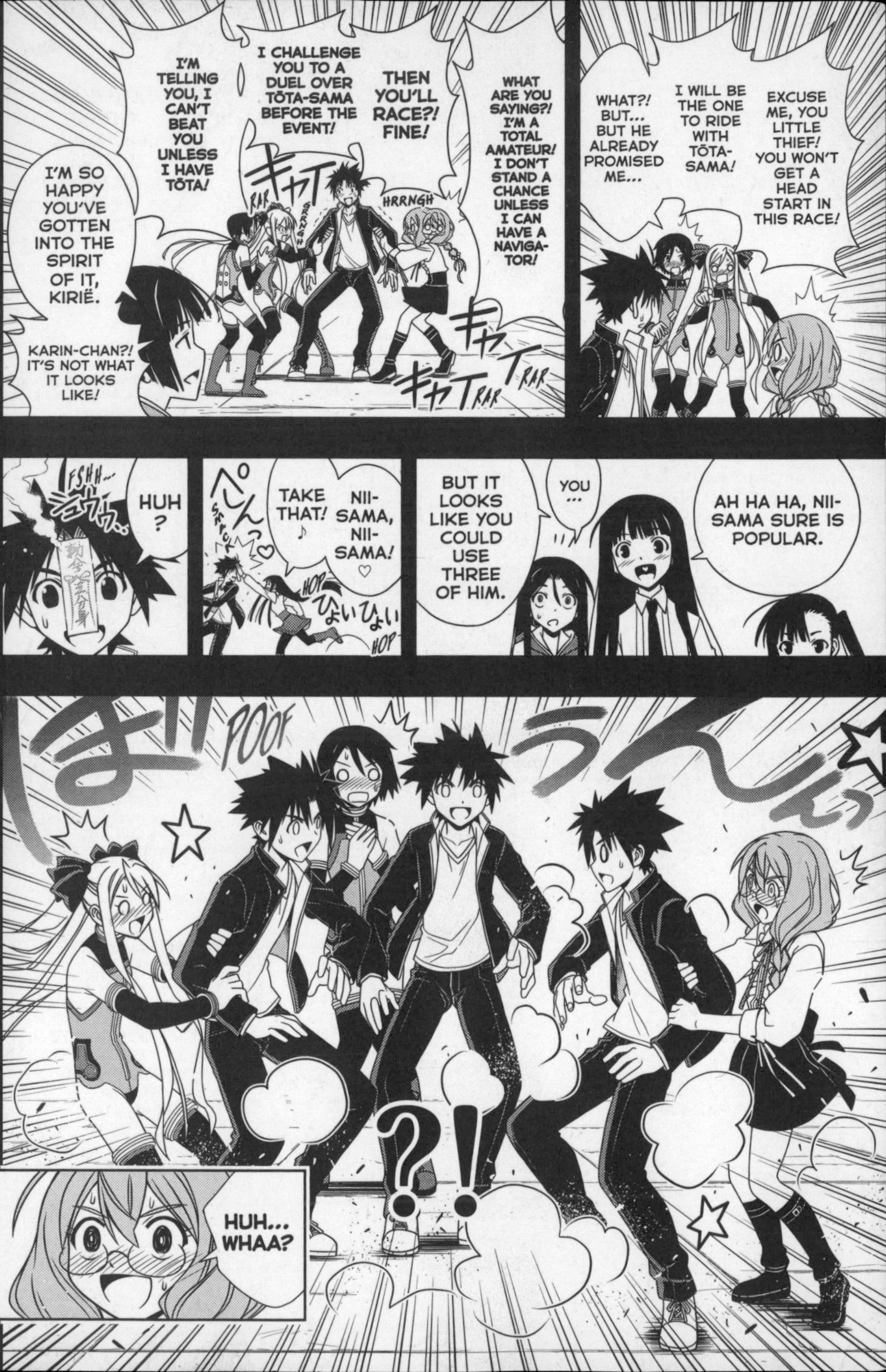
EXCUSE ME, YOU LITTLE THIEF! YOU WON'T GET A HEAD START IN THIS RACE!
I WILL BE THE ONE TO RIDE WITH TŌTA-SAMA!
WHAT?! BUT... BUT HE ALREADY PROMISED ME...
WHAT ARE YOU SAYING?! I'M A TOTAL AMATEUR! I DON'T STAND A CHANCE UNLESS I CAN HAVE A NAVIGATOR!
THEN YOU'LL RACE?! FINE!
I CHALLENGE YOU TO A DUEL OVER TŌTA-SAMA BEFORE THE EVENT!
I'M TELLING YOU, I CAN'T BEAT YOU UNLESS I HAVE TŌTA!
HRRNGH
SRRNGH
RAR
I'M SO HAPPY YOU'VE GOTTEN INTO THE SPIRIT OF IT, KIRIË.
RAR
RAR
KARIN-CHAN?! IT'S NOT WHAT IT LOOKS LIKE!
AH HA HA, NII-SAMA SURE IS POPULAR.
YOU...
BUT IT LOOKS LIKE YOU COULD USE THREE OF HIM.
NII-SAMA, NII-SAMA! ♡
TAKE THAT! ♪
HOP
HOP
HUH?
FSHH...
POOF
?!!
HUH... WHAA?

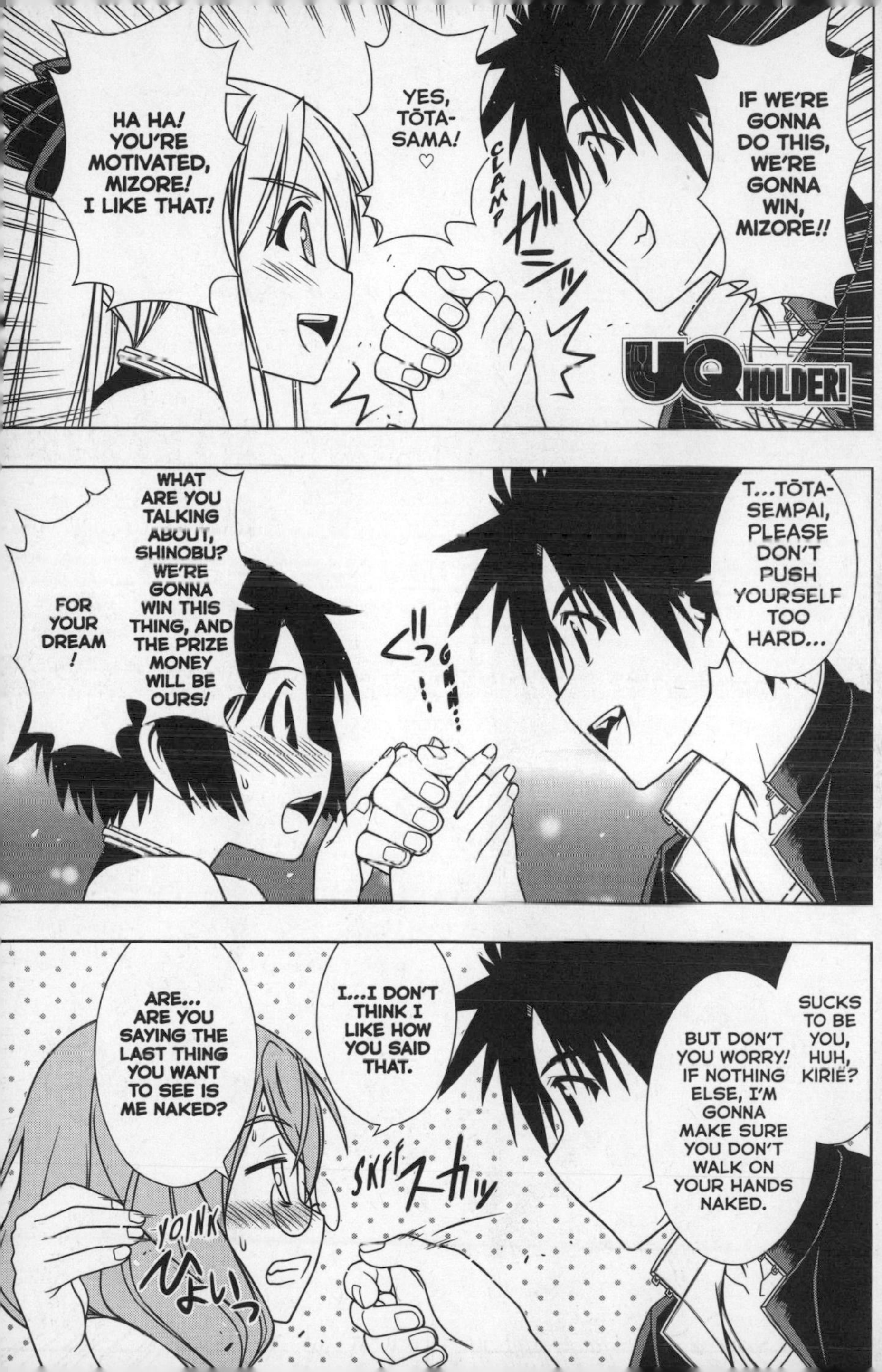
IF WE'RE GONNA DO THIS, WE'RE GONNA WIN, MIZORE!!
CLAMP
YES, TŌTA-SAMA! ♡
HA HA! YOU'RE MOTIVATED, MIZORE! I LIKE THAT!
UQ HOLDER!
T...TŌTA-SEMPAI, PLEASE DON'T PUSH YOURSELF TOO HARD...
GNN...
WHAT ARE YOU TALKING ABOUT, SHINOBU? WE'RE GONNA WIN THIS THING, AND THE PRIZE MONEY WILL BE OURS!
FOR YOUR DREAM!
SUCKS TO BE YOU, HUH, KIRIE?
BUT DON'T YOU WORRY! IF NOTHING ELSE, I'M GONNA MAKE SURE YOU DON'T WALK ON YOUR HANDS NAKED.
SKFF
I...I DON'T THINK I LIKE HOW YOU SAID THAT.
ARE... ARE YOU SAYING THE LAST THING YOU WANT TO SEE IS ME NAKED?
YOINK

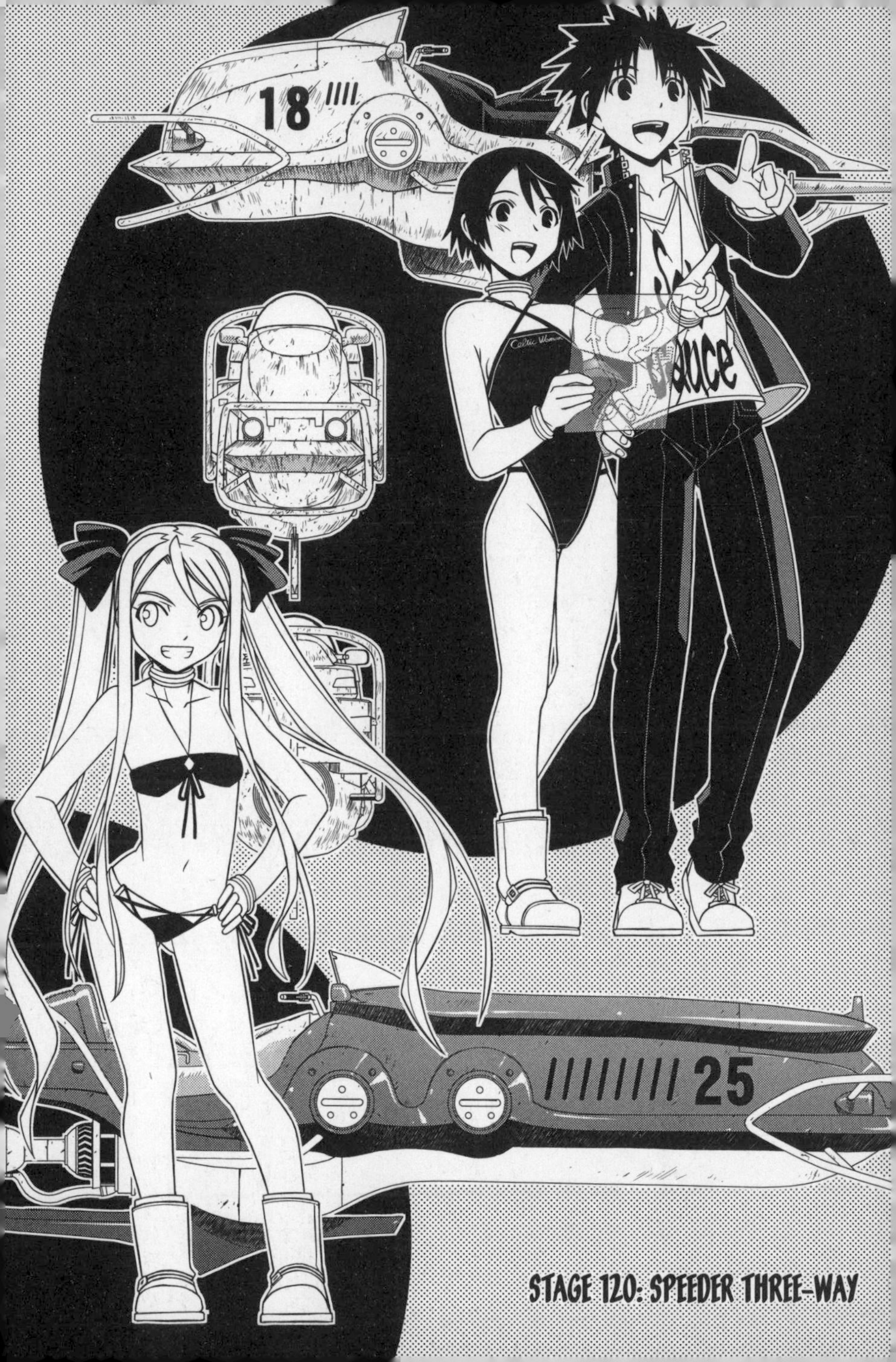
18
25

STAGE 120: SPEEDER THREE-WAY

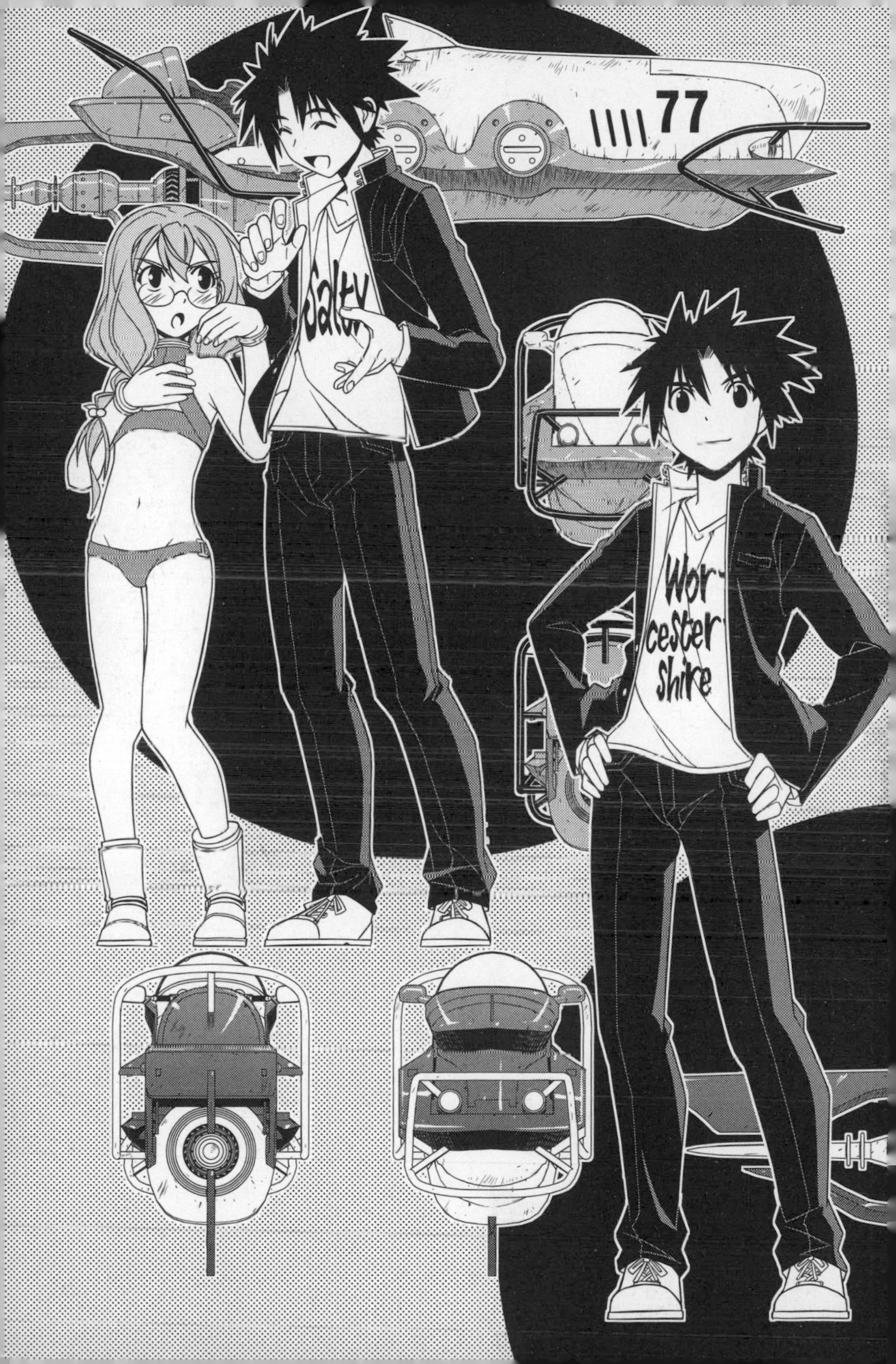
77
Salty
Wor
cester
shire

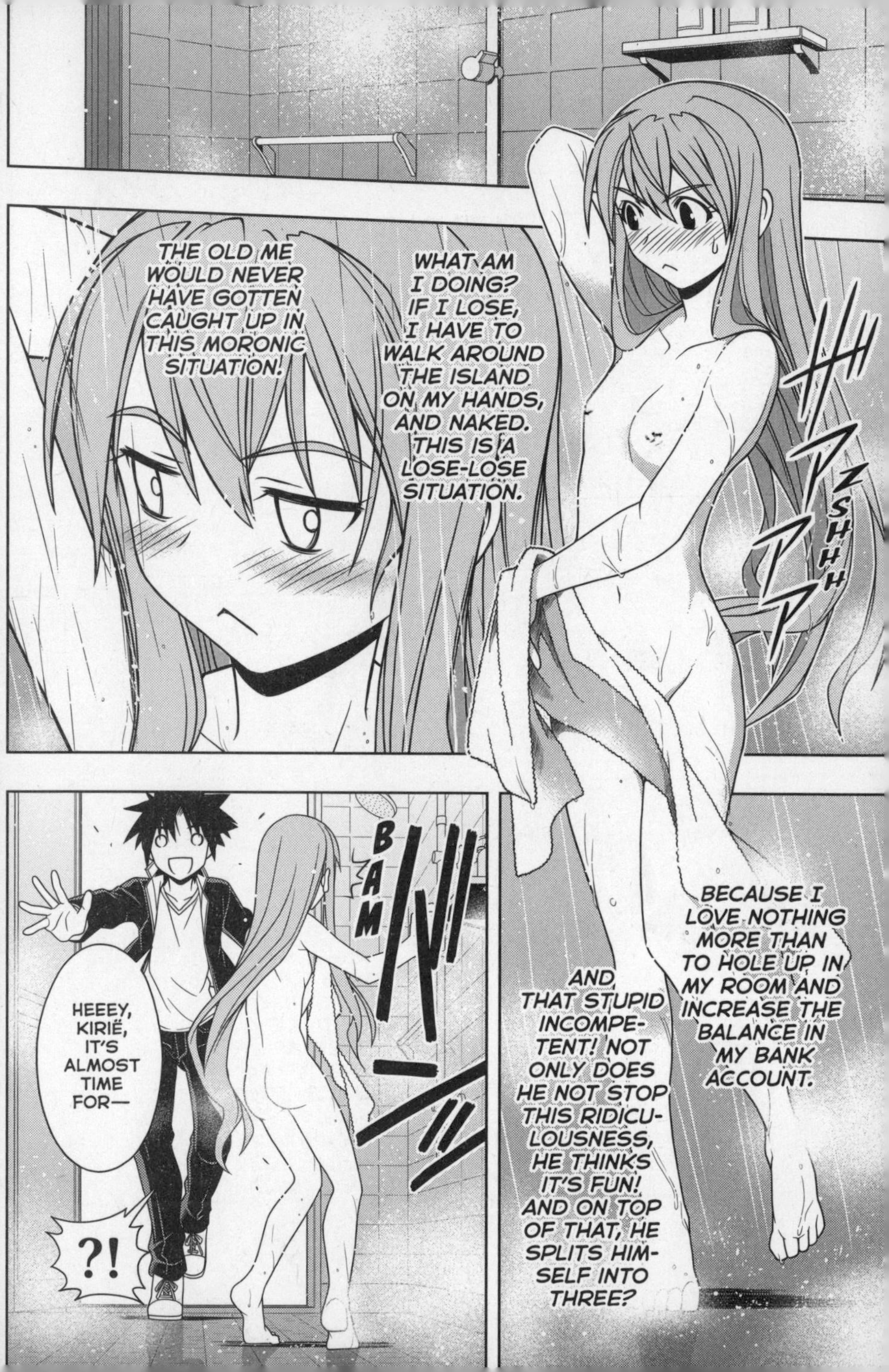
ZSHHH
WHAT AM I DOING? IF I LOSE, I HAVE TO WALK AROUND THE ISLAND ON MY HANDS, AND NAKED. THIS IS A LOSE-LOSE SITUATION.
THE OLD ME WOULD NEVER HAVE GOTTEN CAUGHT UP IN THIS MORONIC SITUATION!
BECAUSE I LOVE NOTHING MORE THAN TO HOLE UP IN MY ROOM AND INCREASE THE BALANCE IN MY BANK ACCOUNT.
AND THAT STUPID INCOMPE-TENT! NOT ONLY DOES HE NOT STOP THIS RIDICU-LOUSNESS, HE THINKS IT'S FUN! AND ON TOP OF THAT, HE SPLITS HIM-SELF INTO THREE?
BAM
HEEEY, KIRIË, IT'S ALMOST TIME FOR—
?!

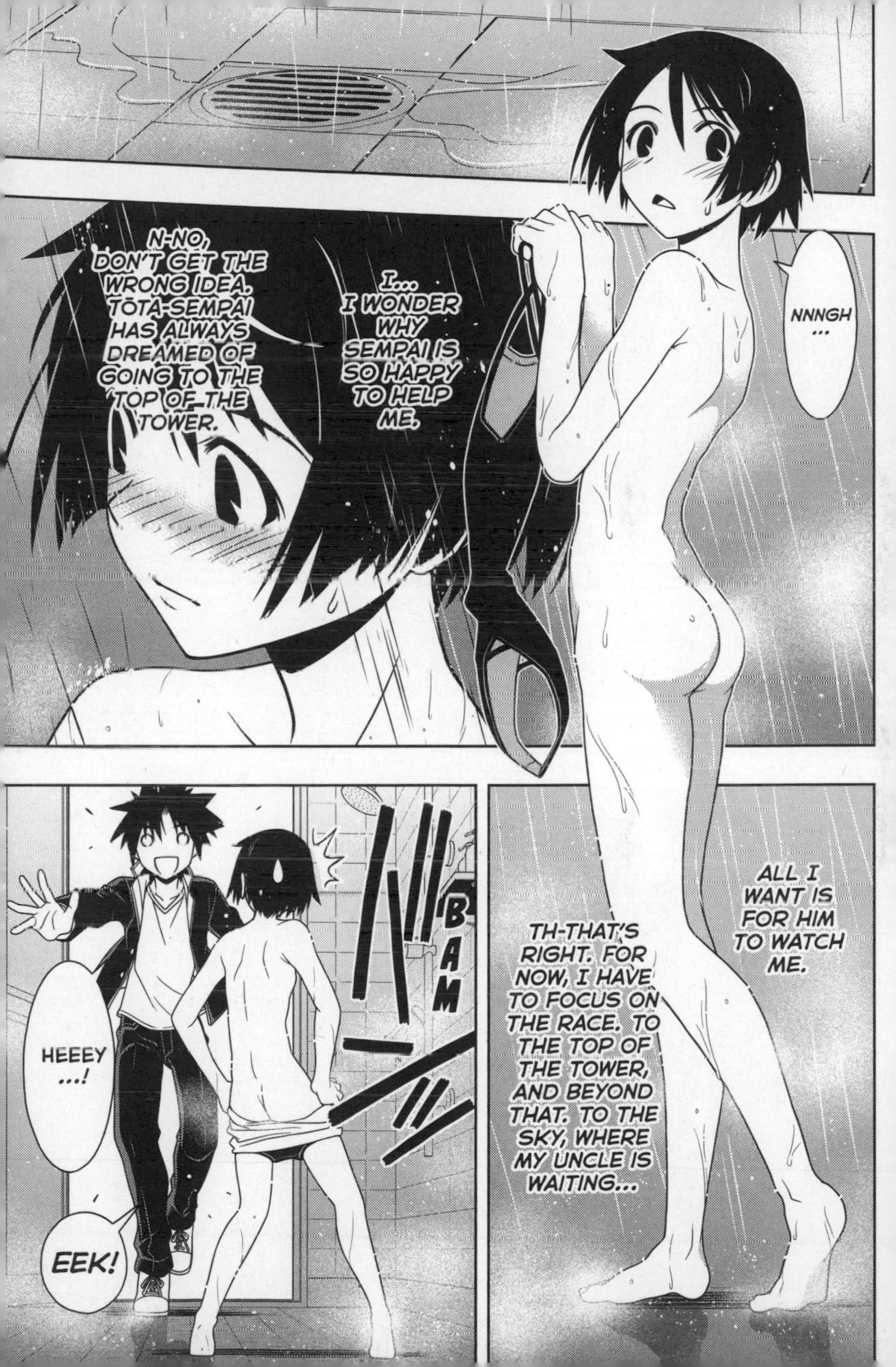
NNNGH...
I... I WONDER WHY SEMPAI IS SO HAPPY TO HELP ME.
N-NO, DON'T GET THE WRONG IDEA. TŌTA-SEMPAI HAS ALWAYS DREAMED OF GOING TO THE TOP OF THE TOWER.
ALL I WANT IS FOR HIM TO WATCH ME.
TH-THAT'S RIGHT. FOR NOW, I HAVE TO FOCUS ON THE RACE. TO THE TOP OF THE TOWER, AND BEYOND THAT. TO THE SKY, WHERE MY UNCLE IS WAITING...
BAM
HEEEY...!
EEK!

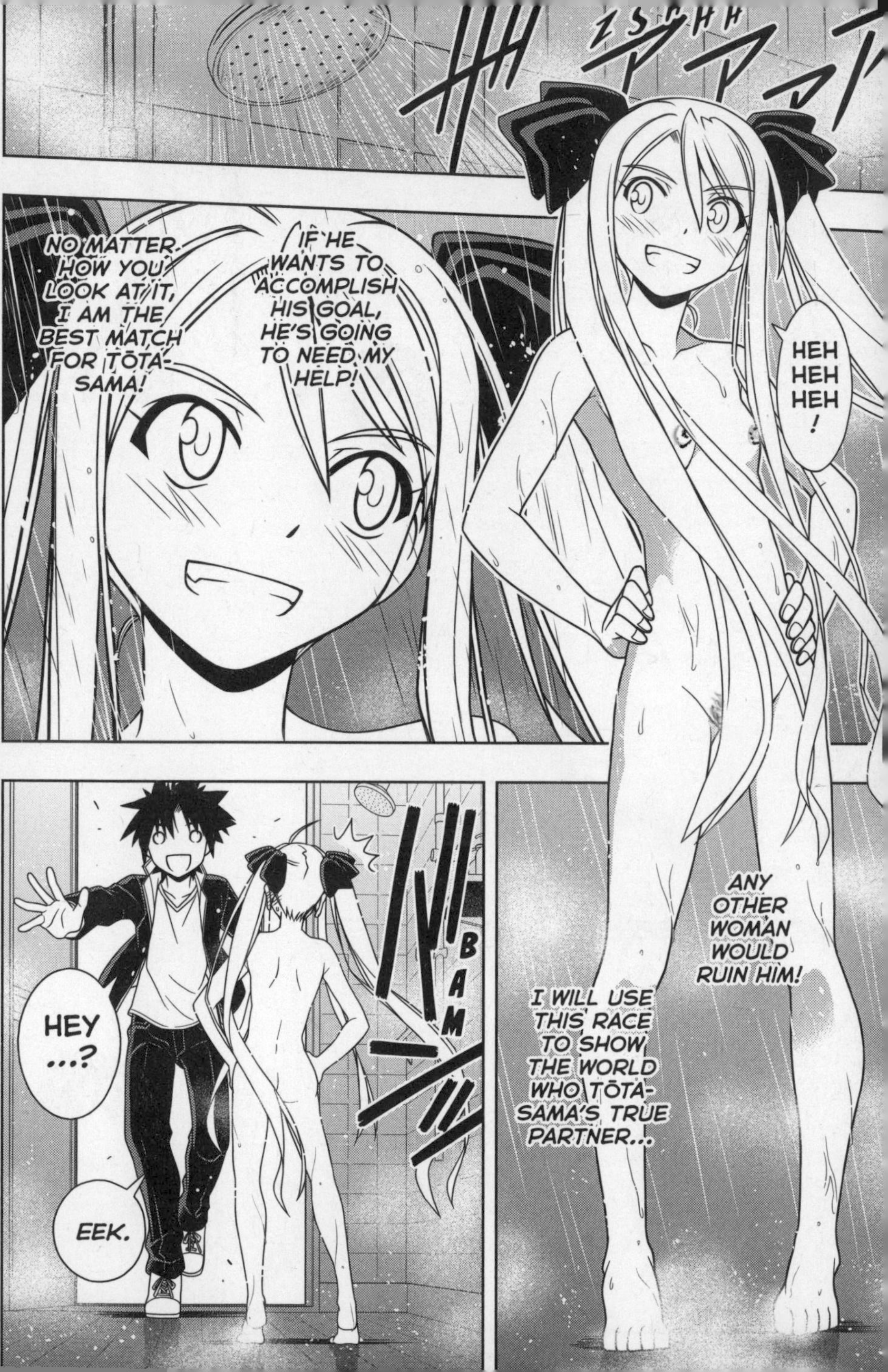
ZSHHH
HEH HEH HEH!
ANY OTHER WOMAN WOULD RUIN HIM!
I WILL USE THIS RACE TO SHOW THE WORLD WHO TŌTA-SAMA'S TRUE PARTNER...
IF HE WANTS TO ACCOMPLISH HIS GOAL, HE'S GOING TO NEED MY HELP!
NO MATTER HOW YOU LOOK AT IT, I AM THE BEST MATCH FOR TŌTA-SAMA!
BAM
HEY ...?
EEK.

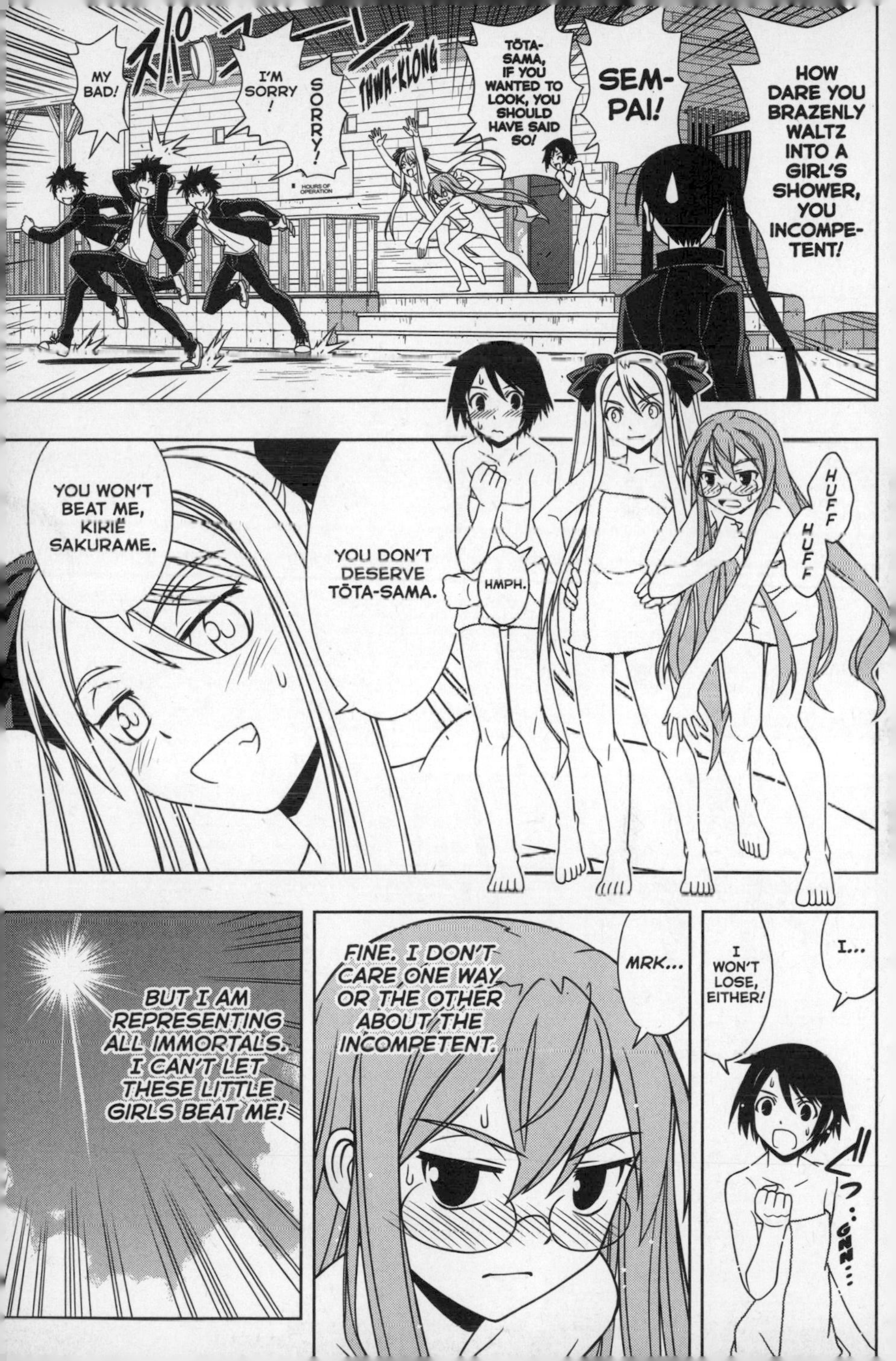
HOW DARE YOU BRAZENLY WALTZ INTO A GIRL'S SHOWER, YOU INCOMPETENT!
SEM-PAI!
TŌTA-SAMA, IF YOU WANTED TO LOOK, YOU SHOULD HAVE SAID SO!
THWA-KLONG
SORRY!
I'M SORRY!
MY BAD!
HOURS OF OPERATION
HUFF HUFF
HMPH.
YOU DON'T DESERVE TŌTA-SAMA.
YOU WON'T BEAT ME, KIRIE SAKURAME.
I...
I WON'T LOSE, EITHER!
GNN...
MRK...
FINE. I DON'T CARE ONE WAY OR THE OTHER ABOUT THE INCOMPETENT.
BUT I AM REPRESENTING ALL IMMORTALS. I CAN'T LET THESE LITTLE GIRLS BEAT ME!

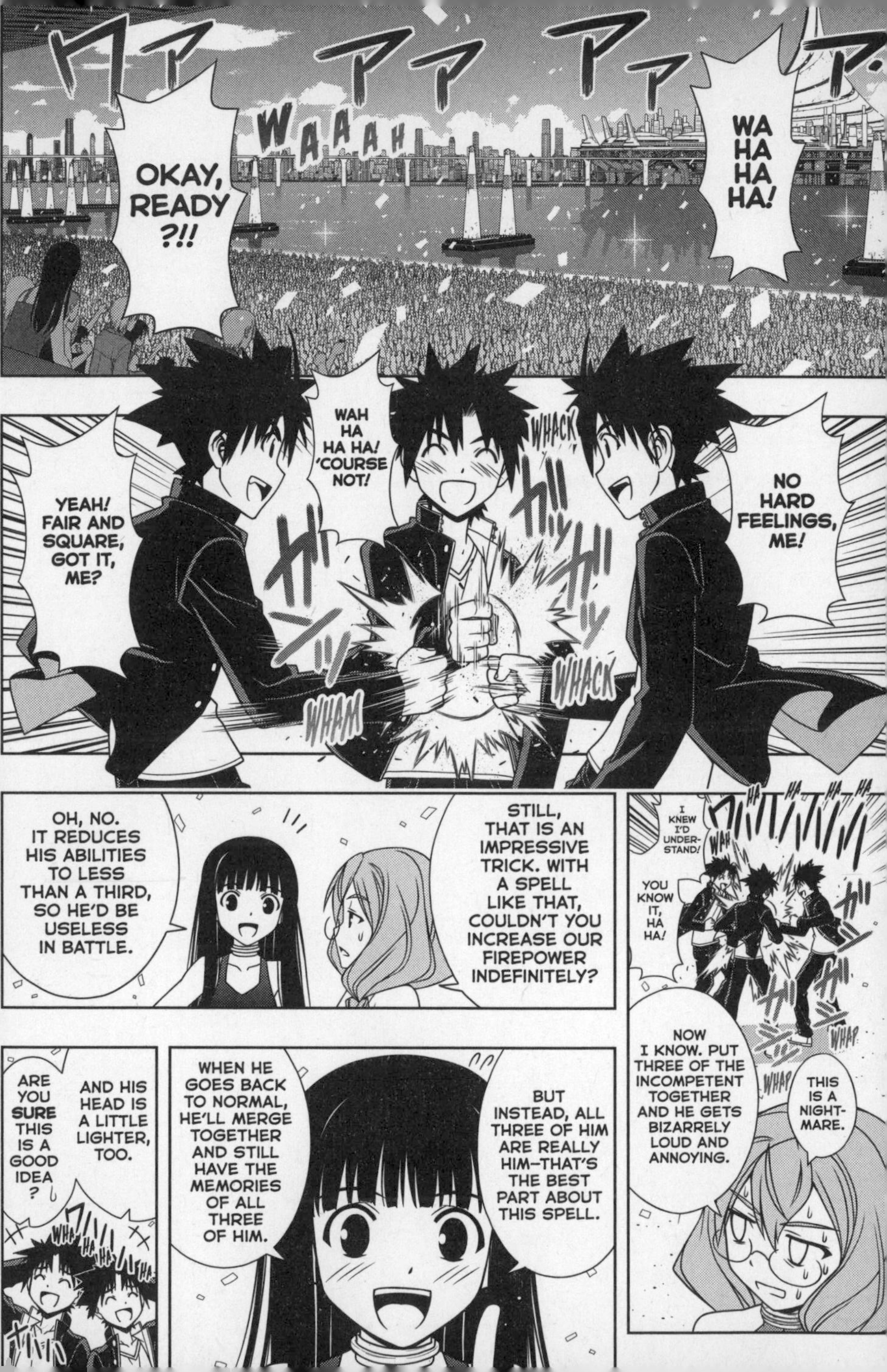
WA HA HA HA!
WAAAH
OKAY, READY ?!!
NO HARD FEELINGS, ME!
WHACK
WAH HA HA HA! 'COURSE NOT!
YEAH! FAIR AND SQUARE, GOT IT, ME?
WHACK
WHAM
HA HA HA HA
I KNEW I'D UNDER-STAND!
WAH
YOU KNOW IT, HA HA!
WHAP
WHAP
THIS IS A NIGHT-MARE.
NOW I KNOW. PUT THREE OF THE INCOMPETENT TOGETHER AND HE GETS BIZARRELY LOUD AND ANNOYING.
STILL, THAT IS AN IMPRESSIVE TRICK. WITH A SPELL LIKE THAT, COULDN'T YOU INCREASE OUR FIREPOWER INDEFINITELY?
OH, NO. IT REDUCES HIS ABILITIES TO LESS THAN A THIRD, SO HE'D BE USELESS IN BATTLE.
WHEN HE GOES BACK TO NORMAL, HE'LL MERGE TOGETHER AND STILL HAVE THE MEMORIES OF ALL THREE OF HIM.
BUT INSTEAD, ALL THREE OF HIM ARE REALLY HIM—THAT'S THE BEST PART ABOUT THIS SPELL.
AND HIS HEAD IS A LITTLE LIGHTER, TOO.
ARE YOU SURE THIS IS A GOOD IDEA?
WAH HA HA HA

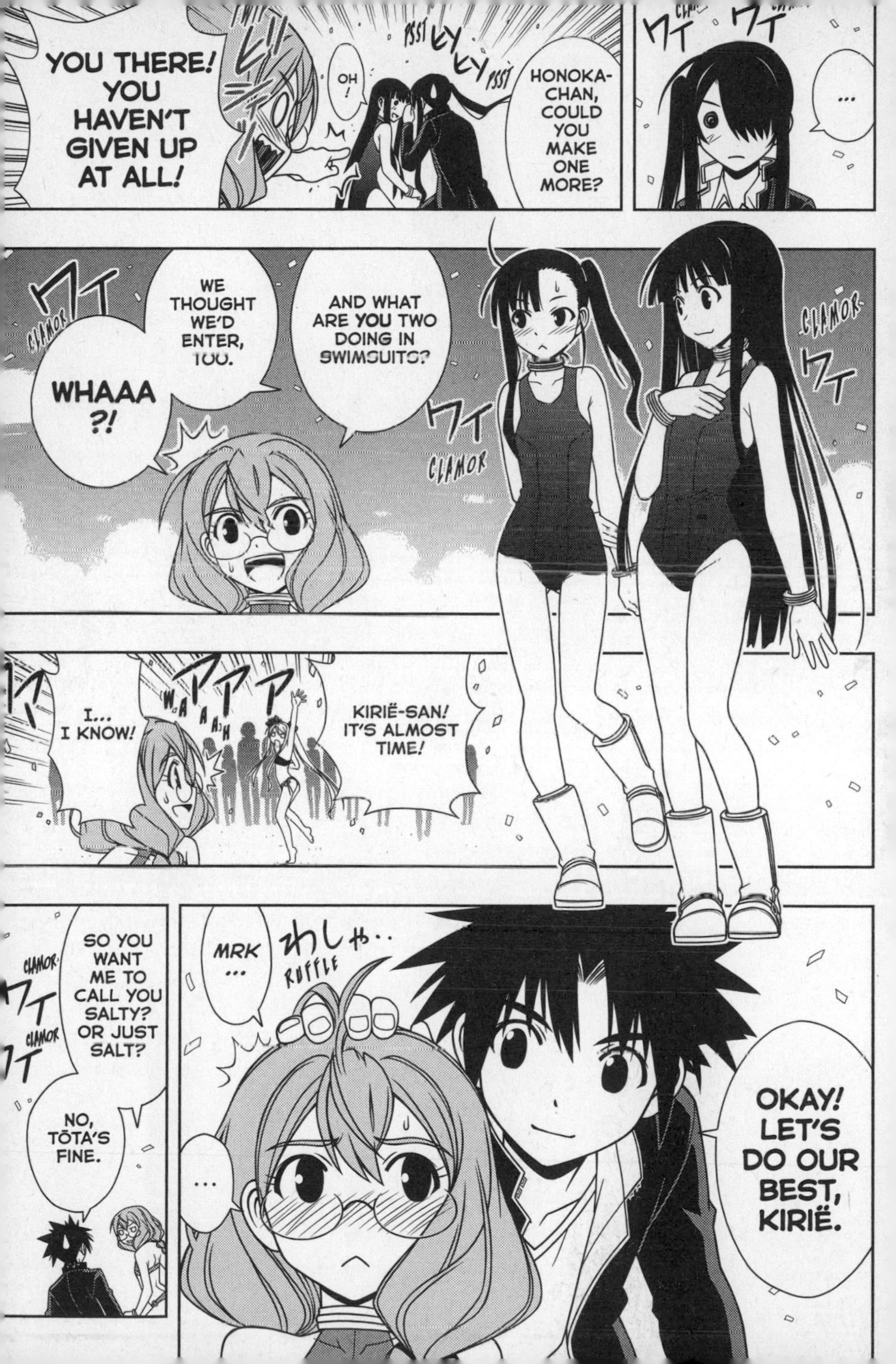
...
HONOKA-CHAN, COULD YOU MAKE ONE MORE?
PSST
PSST
OH!
YOU THERE! YOU HAVEN'T GIVEN UP AT ALL!
CLAMOR
CLAMOR
AND WHAT ARE YOU TWO DOING IN SWIMSUITS?
WE THOUGHT WE'D ENTER, TOO.
WHAAA?!
CLAMOR
KIRIË-SAN! IT'S ALMOST TIME!
WAAAAH
I... I KNOW!
OKAY! LET'S DO OUR BEST, KIRIË.
MRK...
RUFFLE
...
SO YOU WANT ME TO CALL YOU SALTY? OR JUST SALT?
CLAMOR
CLAMOR
NO, TŌTA'S FINE.

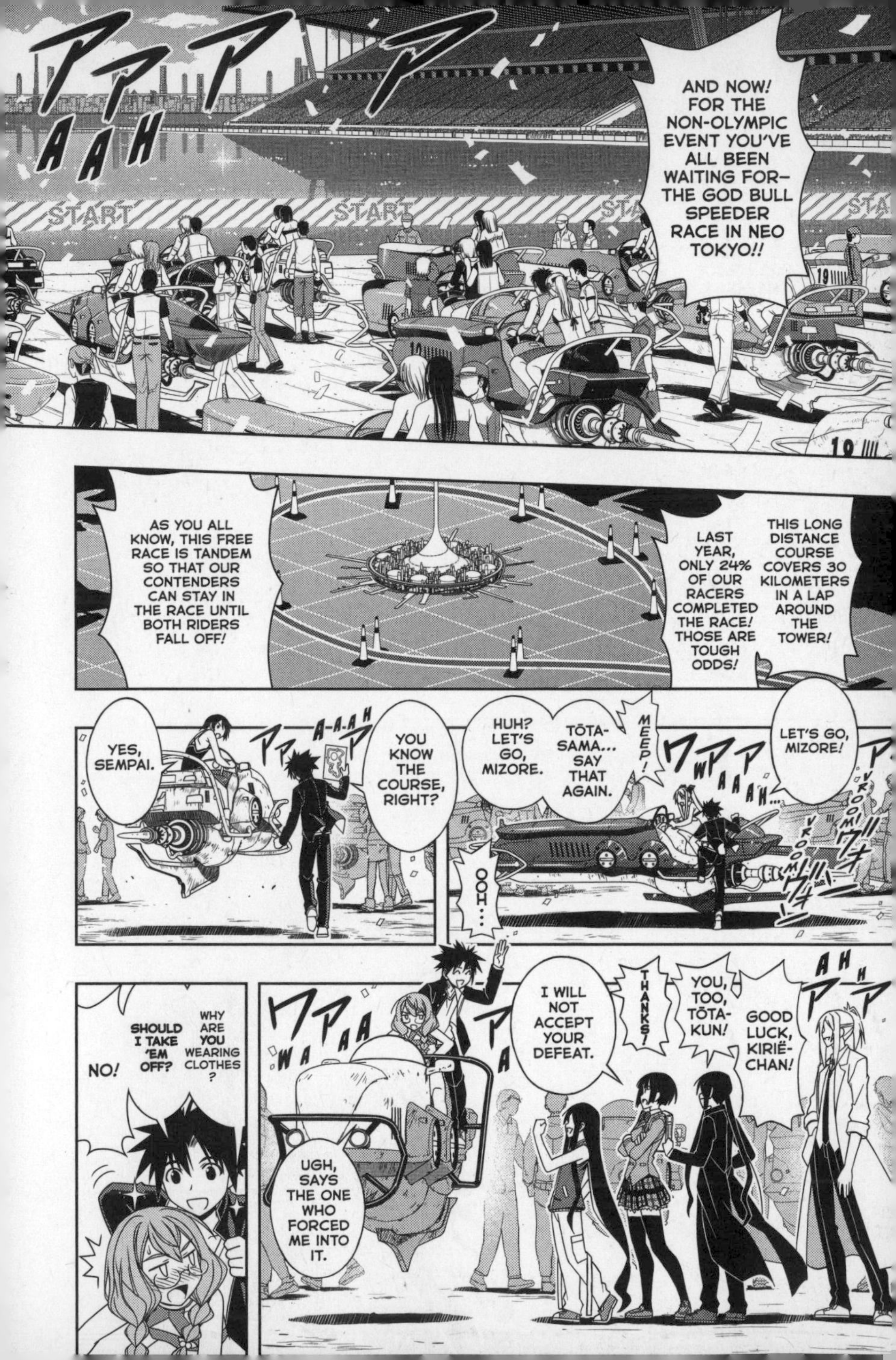
AAH
AND NOW! FOR THE NON-OLYMPIC EVENT YOU'VE ALL BEEN WAITING FOR—THE GOD BULL SPEEDER RACE IN NEO TOKYO!!
START
THIS LONG DISTANCE COURSE COVERS 30 KILOMETERS IN A LAP AROUND THE TOWER!
LAST YEAR, ONLY 24% OF OUR RACERS COMPLETED THE RACE! THOSE ARE TOUGH ODDS!
AS YOU ALL KNOW, THIS FREE RACE IS TANDEM SO THAT OUR CONTENDERS CAN STAY IN THE RACE UNTIL BOTH RIDERS FALL OFF!
LET'S GO, MIZORE!
WAAAH...
MEEP!
TŌTA-SAMA... SAY THAT AGAIN.
HUH? LET'S GO, MIZORE.
VROOM
VROOM
OOH...
YOU KNOW THE COURSE, RIGHT?
A-A-AH
YES, SEMPAI.
AHH
GOOD LUCK, KIRIË-CHAN!
YOU, TOO, TŌTA-KUN!
THANKS!
I WILL NOT ACCEPT YOUR DEFEAT.
WAAA
UGH, SAYS THE ONE WHO FORCED ME INTO IT.
WHY ARE YOU WEARING CLOTHES?
SHOULD I TAKE 'EM OFF?
NO!

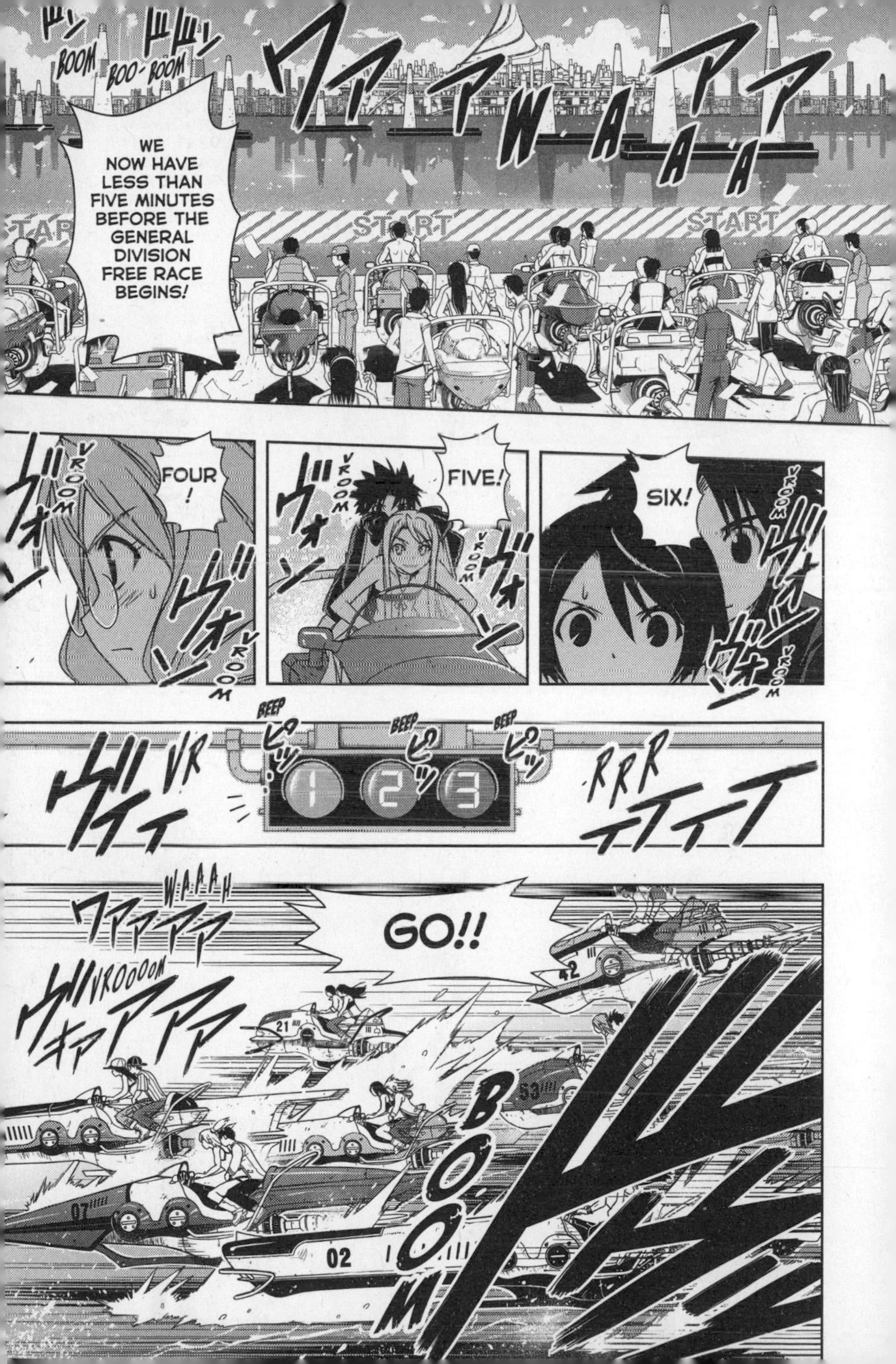

WAAA
BOO-BOOM
BOOM
WE NOW HAVE LESS THAN FIVE MINUTES BEFORE THE GENERAL DIVISION FREE RACE BEGINS!
START
START
VROOM
SIX!
VROOM
VROOM
FIVE!
VROOM
VROOM
VROOM
FOUR!
BEEP
BEEP
BEEP
1 2 3
RRR
VR
GO!!
BOOOM
WAAAH
VROOOOM

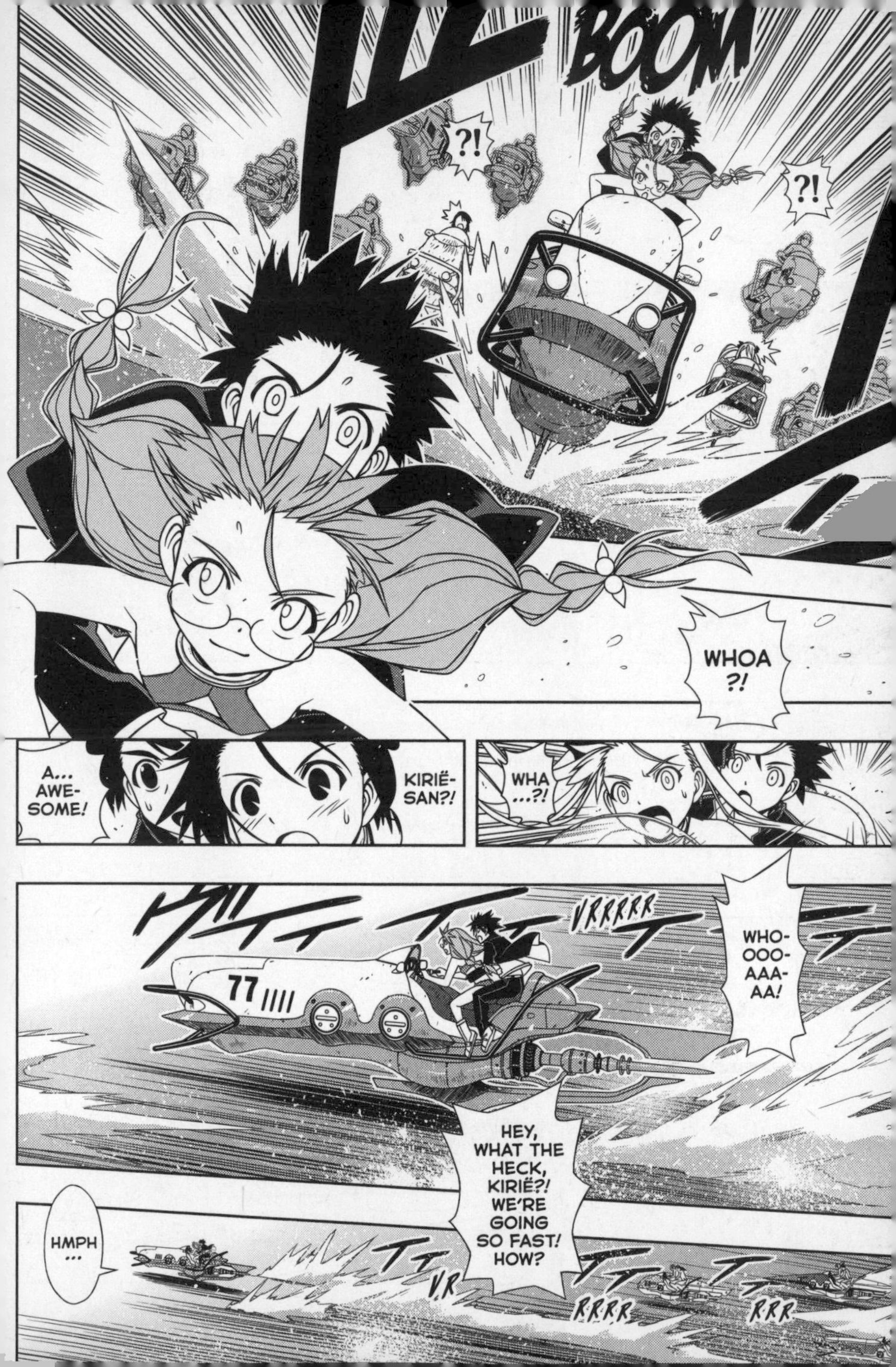

BOOM
?!
?!
WHOA ?!
WHA ...?!
KIRIË-SAN?!
A... AWE-SOME!
WHO-OOO-AAA-AA!
VRRRRR
77
HEY, WHAT THE HECK, KIRIË?! WE'RE GOING SO FAST! HOW?
RRR
RRRR
VR
HMPH ...

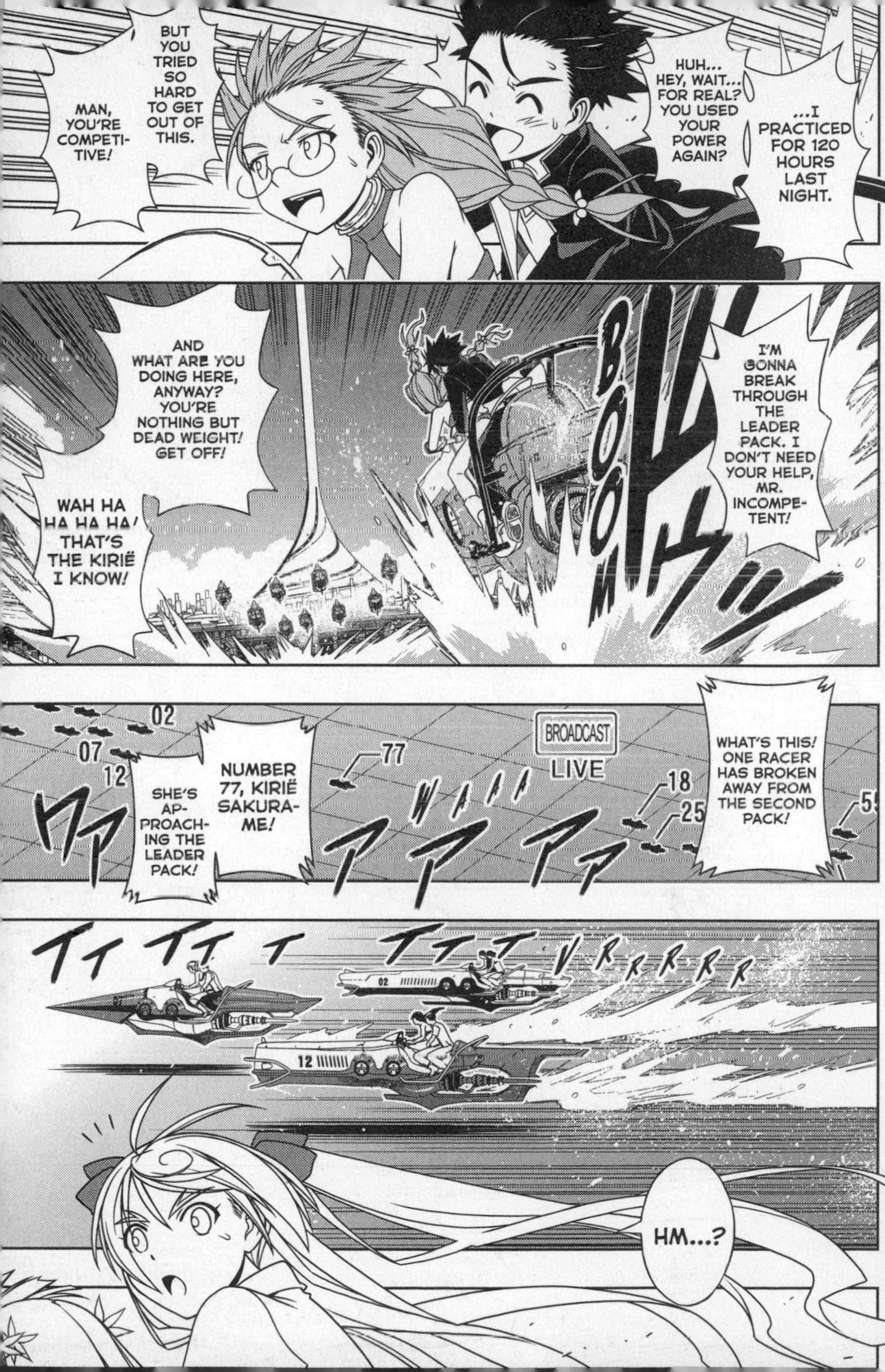
...I PRACTICED FOR 120 HOURS LAST NIGHT.
HUH... HEY, WAIT... FOR REAL? YOU USED YOUR POWER AGAIN?
BUT YOU TRIED SO HARD TO GET OUT OF THIS.
MAN, YOU'RE COMPETITIVE!
I'M GONNA BREAK THROUGH THE LEADER PACK. I DON'T NEED YOUR HELP, MR. INCOMPETENT!
AND WHAT ARE YOU DOING HERE, ANYWAY? YOU'RE NOTHING BUT DEAD WEIGHT! GET OFF!
WAH HA HA HA HA! THAT'S THE KIRIË I KNOW!
WHAT'S THIS! ONE RACER HAS BROKEN AWAY FROM THE SECOND PACK!
BROADCAST
LIVE
55
25
18
77
WAAAA
NUMBER 77, KIRIË SAKURAME!
SHE'S APPROACHING THE LEADER PACK!
02
07
12
VRRRRRR
02
12
HM...?

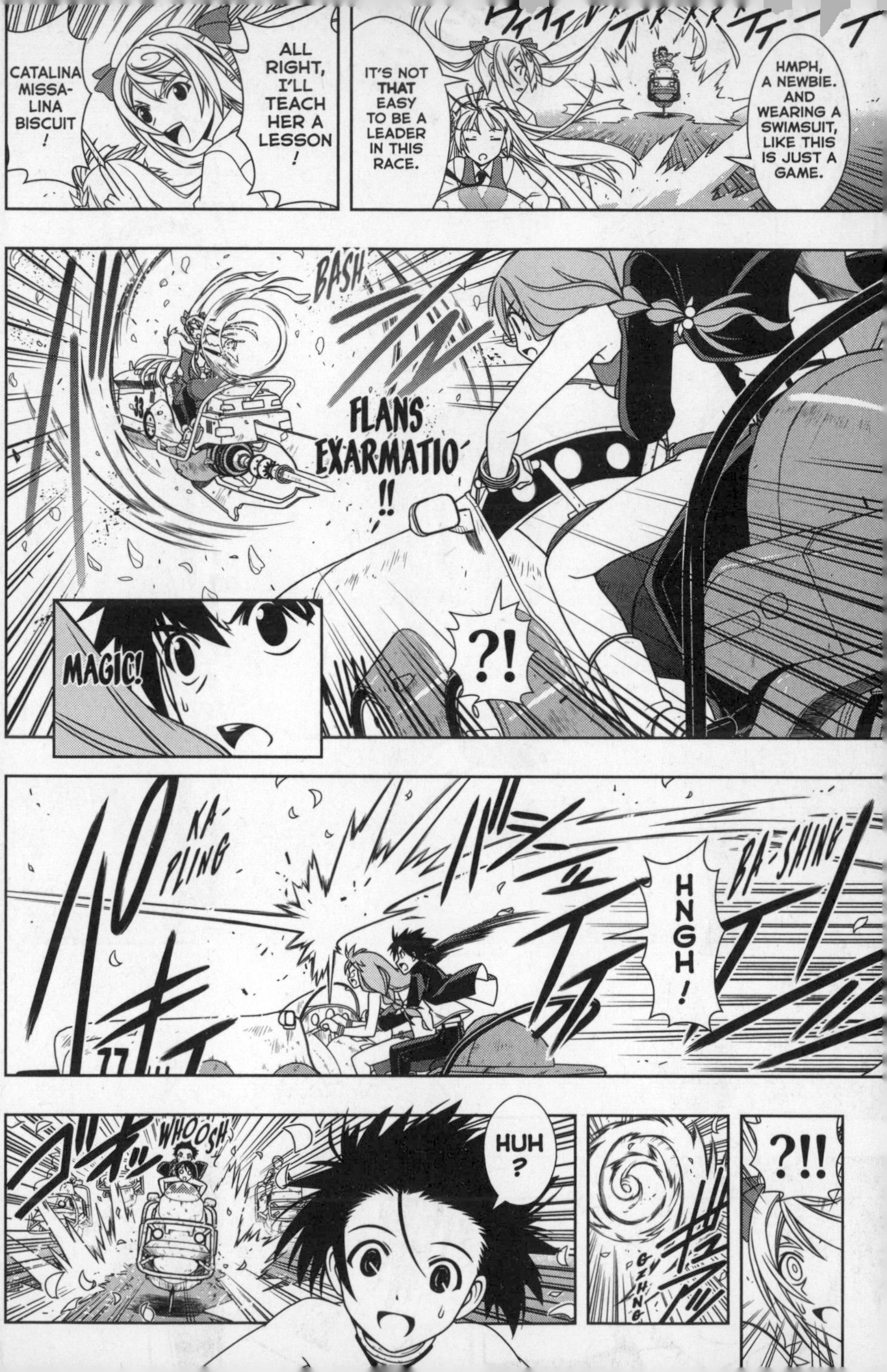
HMPH, A NEWBIE. AND WEARING A SWIMSUIT, LIKE THIS IS JUST A GAME.
IT'S NOT THAT EASY TO BE A LEADER IN THIS RACE.
ALL RIGHT, I'LL TEACH HER A LESSON!
CATALINA MISSALINA BISCUIT!
BASH
FLANS EXARMATIO!!
?!
MAGIC!
BA-SHING
HNGH!
KA-PLING
?!!
GZHNG
HUH?
WHOOSH

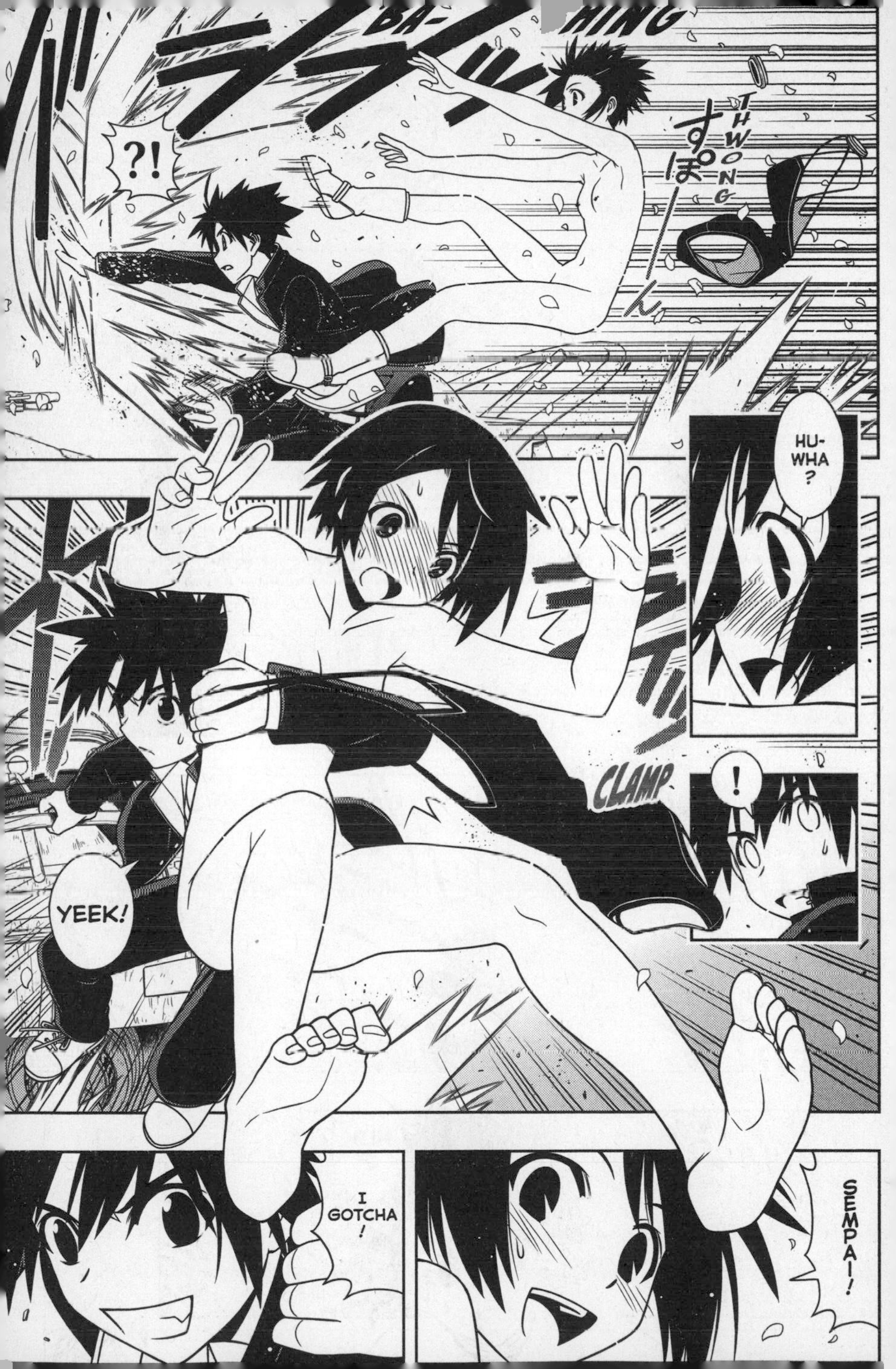

BA-
HING
THWONG
すぽーん
?!
HU-WHA?
!
CLAMP
YEEK!
SEMPAI!
I GOTCHA!

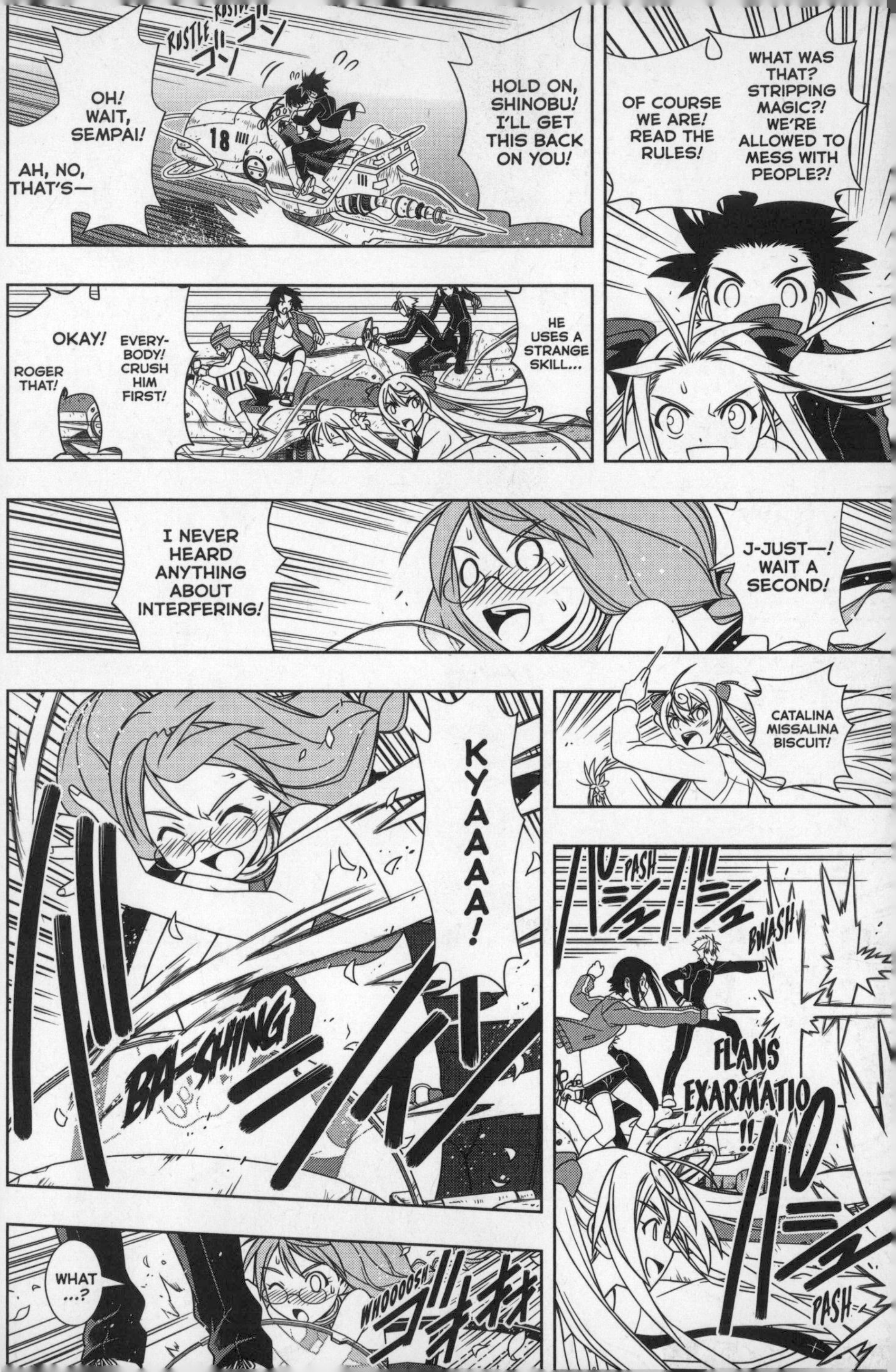
WHAT WAS THAT? STRIPPING MAGIC?! WE'RE ALLOWED TO MESS WITH PEOPLE?!
OF COURSE WE ARE! READ THE RULES!
RUSTLE
RUSTLE
HOLD ON, SHINOBU! I'LL GET THIS BACK ON YOU!
OH! WAIT, SEMPAI!
AH, NO, THAT'S—
HE USES A STRANGE SKILL...
EVERY-BODY! CRUSH HIM FIRST!
OKAY!
ROGER THAT!
J-JUST—! WAIT A SECOND!
I NEVER HEARD ANYTHING ABOUT INTERFERING!
CATALINA MISSALINA BISCUIT!
PASH
BWASH
FLANS EXARMATIO!!
PASH
KYAAAA!
BA-SHING
WHOOOOSH
WHAT ...?

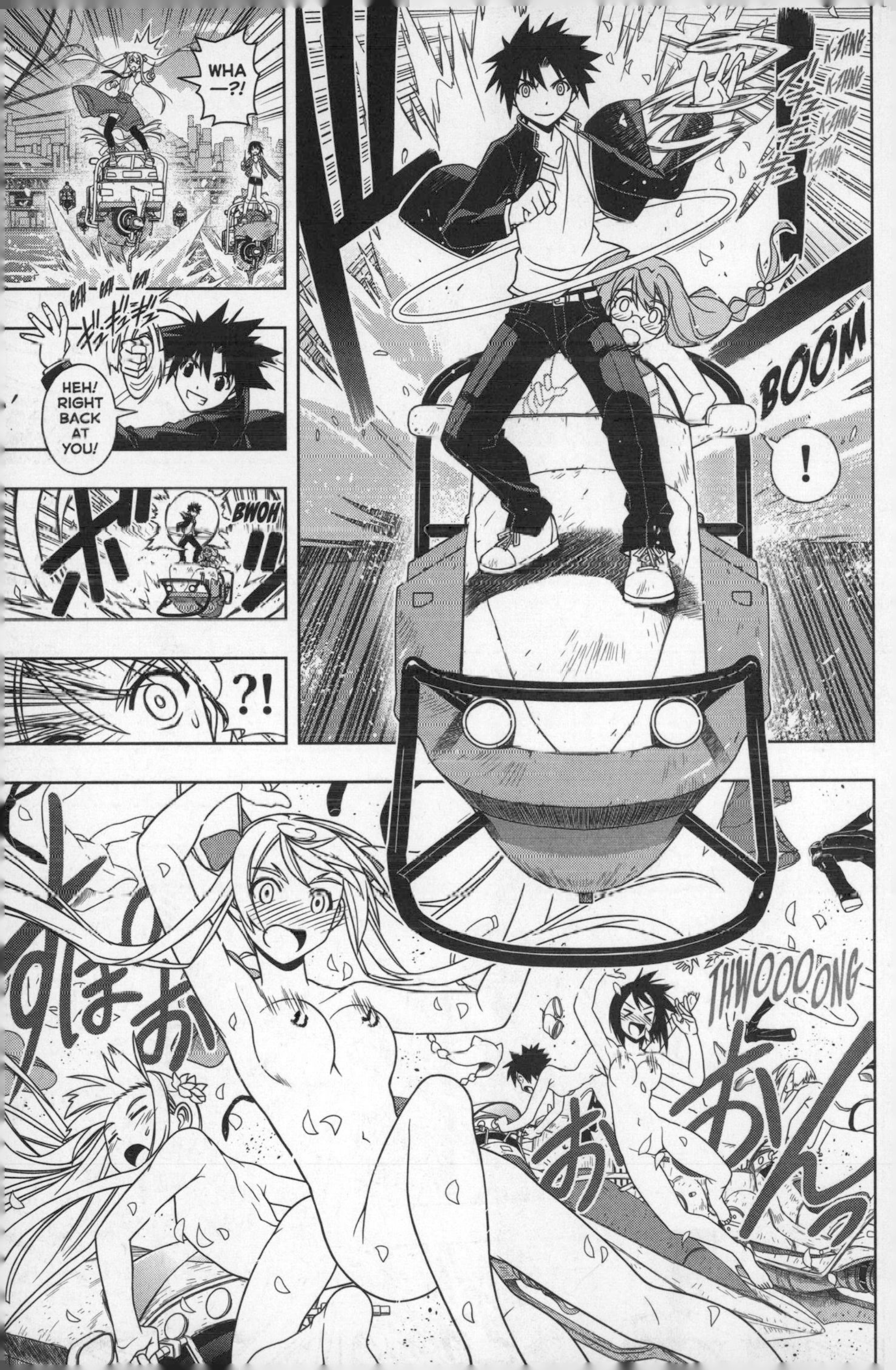
K-ZHING
K-ZHING
K-ZHING
K-ZHING
BOOM
!
WHA —?!
HEH! RIGHT BACK AT YOU!
BWOH
?!
THWOOOONG

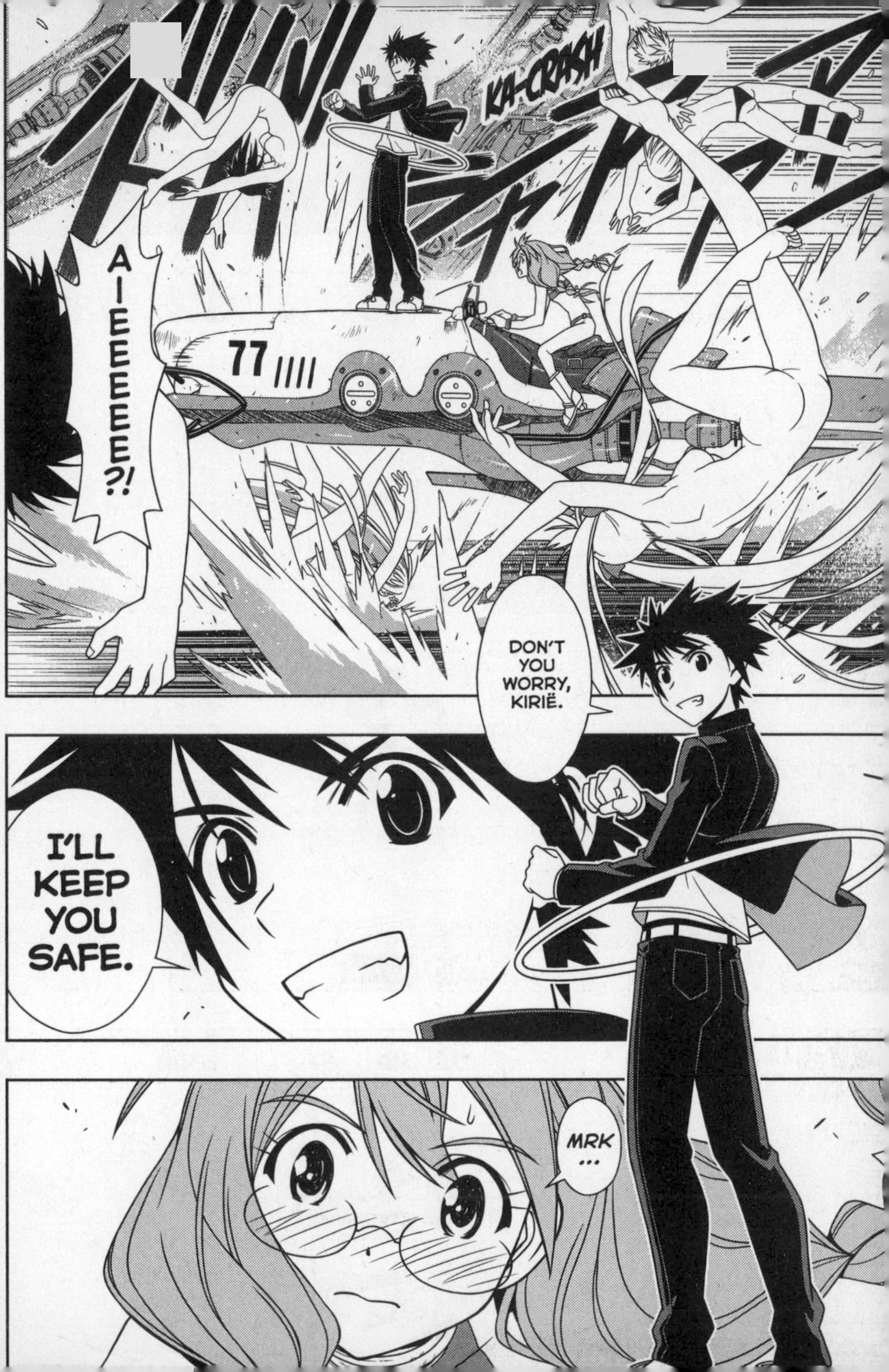
KA-CRASH
AIEEEEEE?!
DON'T YOU WORRY, KIRIË.
I'LL KEEP YOU SAFE.
MRK ...

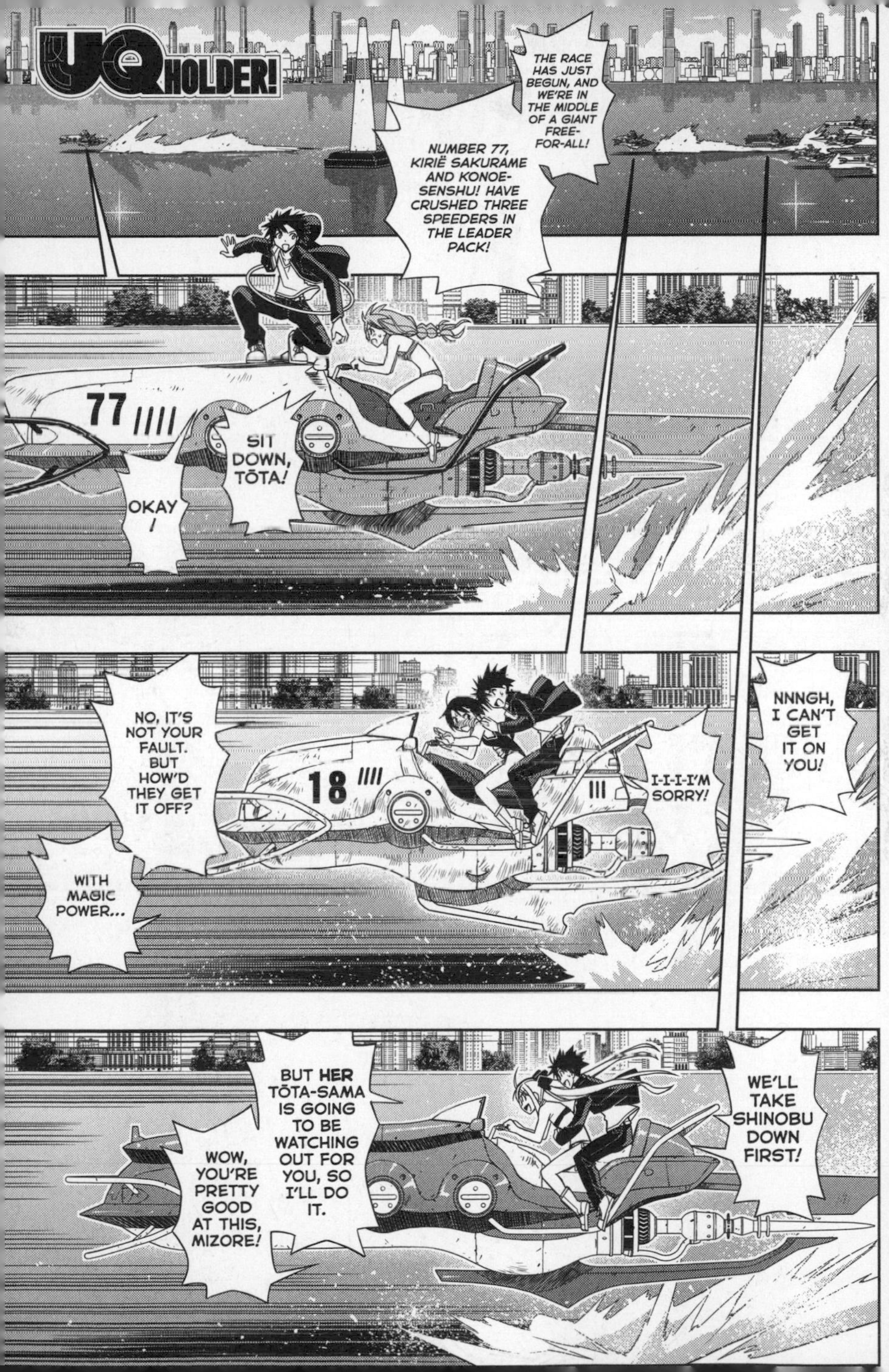
UQ HOLDER!
THE RACE HAS JUST BEGUN, AND WE'RE IN THE MIDDLE OF A GIANT FREE-FOR-ALL!
NUMBER 77, KIRIË SAKURAME AND KONOE-SENSHU! HAVE CRUSHED THREE SPEEDERS IN THE LEADER PACK!
77
SIT DOWN, TŌTA!
OKAY!
NNNGH, I CAN'T GET IT ON YOU!
I-I-I-I'M SORRY!
18
NO, IT'S NOT YOUR FAULT. BUT HOW'D THEY GET IT OFF?
WITH MAGIC POWER...
WE'LL TAKE SHINOBU DOWN FIRST!
BUT HER TŌTA-SAMA IS GOING TO BE WATCHING OUT FOR YOU, SO I'LL DO IT.
WOW, YOU'RE PRETTY GOOD AT THIS, MIZORE!

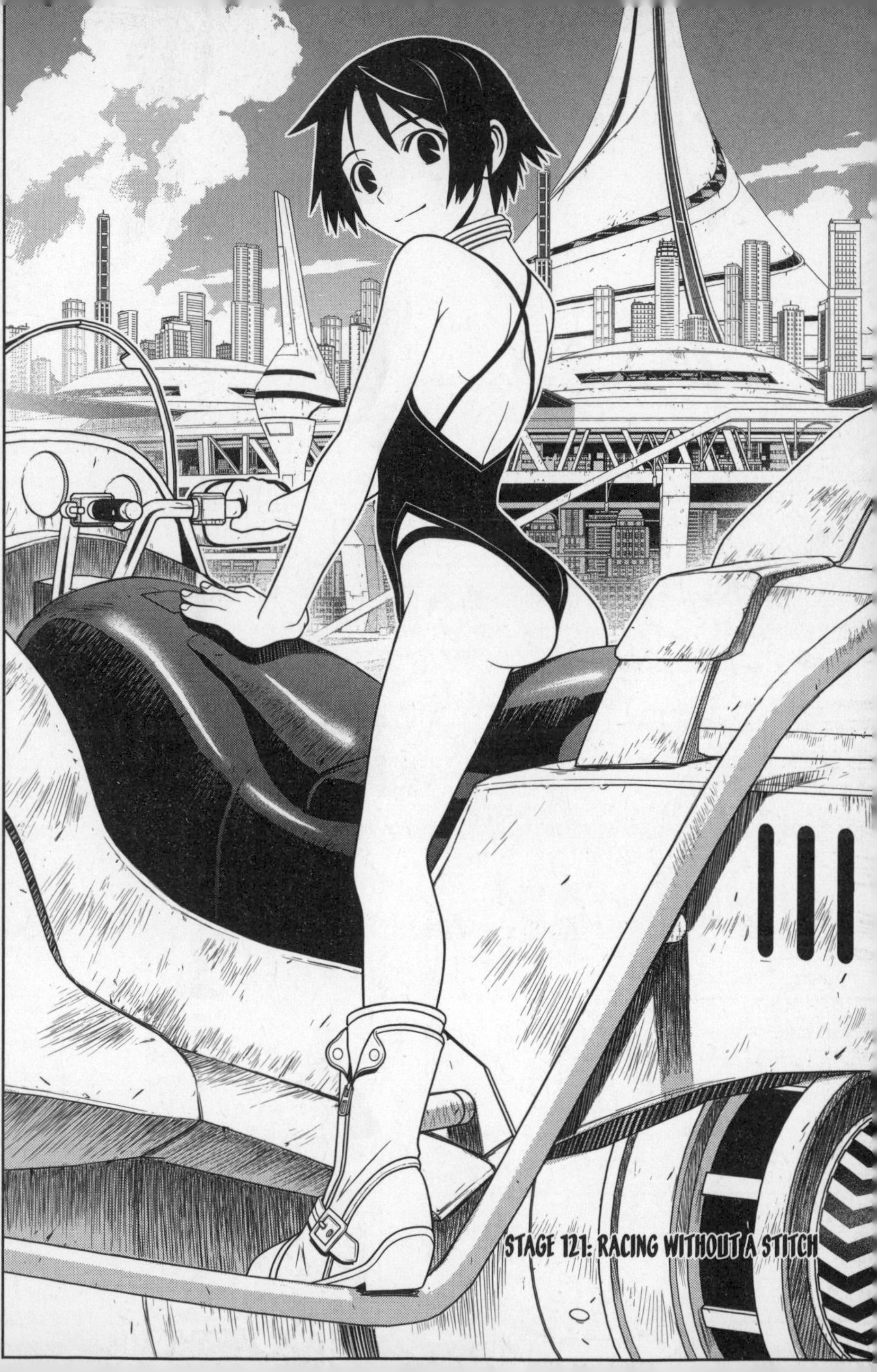
STAGE 121: RACING WITHOUT A STITCH

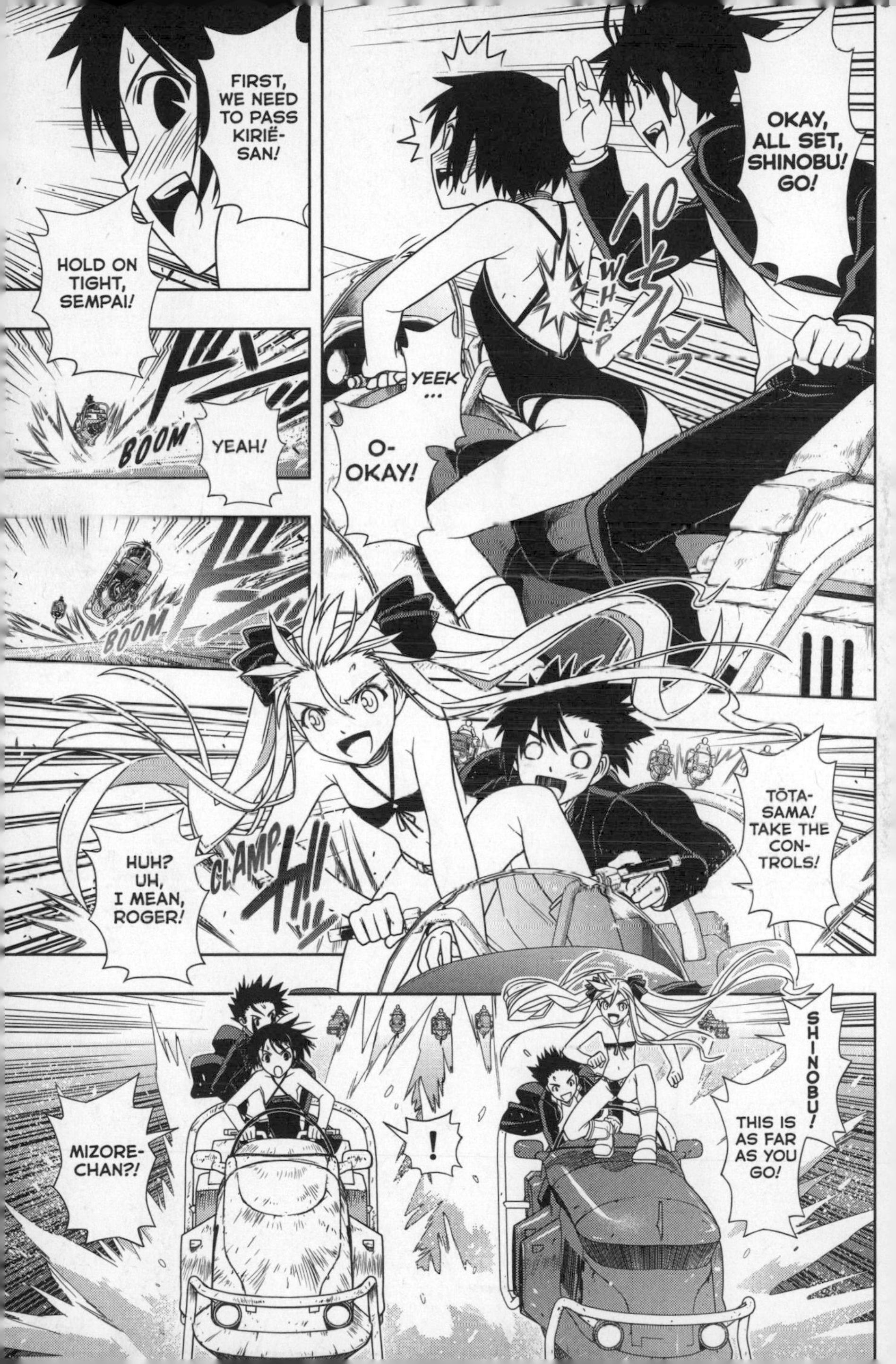
OKAY, ALL SET, SHINOBU! GO!
WHAP
YEEK ...
O-OKAY!
FIRST, WE NEED TO PASS KIRIË-SAN!
HOLD ON TIGHT, SEMPAI!
BOOM
YEAH!
BOOM
TŌTA-SAMA! TAKE THE CON-TROLS!
HUH? UH, I MEAN, ROGER!
CLAMP
SHINOBU! THIS IS AS FAR AS YOU GO!
!
MIZORE-CHAN?!

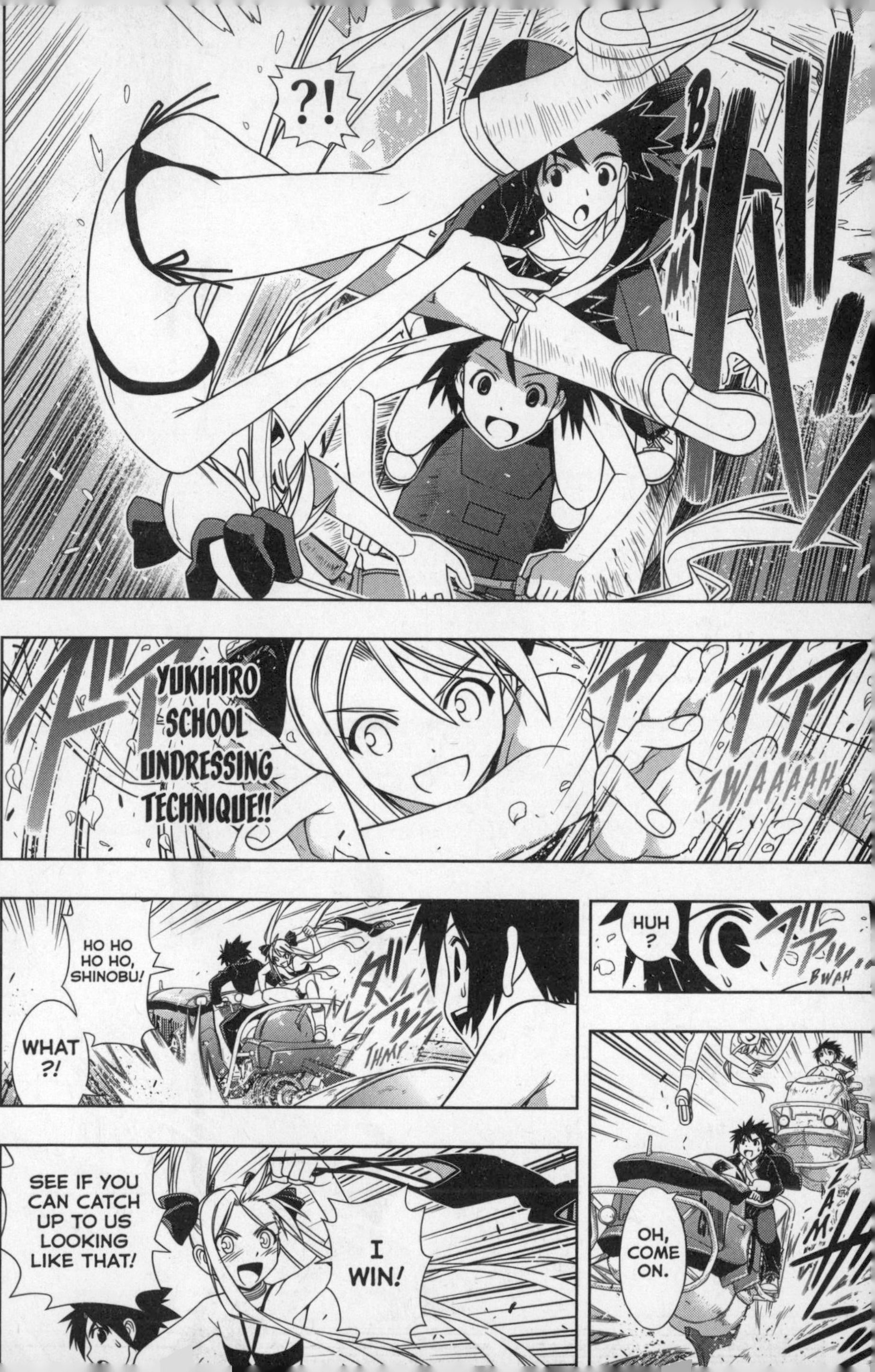
?!
BAM
YUKIHIRO SCHOOL UNDRESSING TECHNIQUE!!
ZWAAAAH
HUH ?
BWAH
OH, COME ON.
ZAM
HO HO HO HO, SHINOBU!
WHAT ?!
THMP
SEE IF YOU CAN CATCH UP TO US LOOKING LIKE THAT!
I WIN!

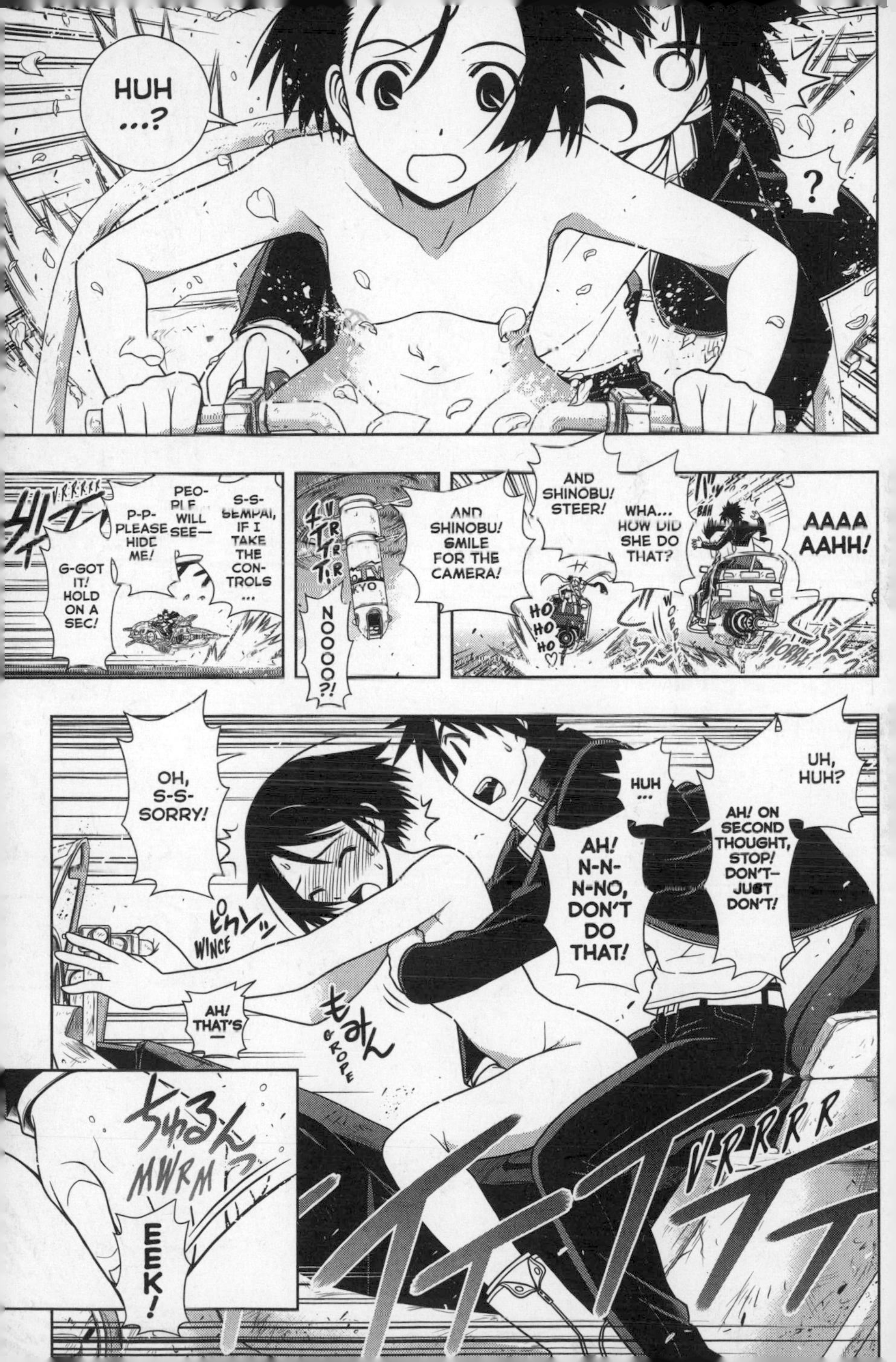
?
HUH ...?
AAAA AAHH!
WHA... HOW DID SHE DO THAT?
AND SHINOBU! STEER!
HO HO HO ♡
WOBBLE
AND SHINOBU! SMILE FOR THE CAMERA!
NOOOOO?!
S-S-SEMPAI, IF I TAKE THE CONTROLS ...
PEO-PLE WILL SEE—
P-P-PLEASE HIDE ME!
G-GOT IT! HOLD ON A SEC!
UH, HUH?
AH! ON SECOND THOUGHT, STOP! DON'T—JUST DON'T!
HUH ...
AH! N-N-N-NO, DON'T DO THAT!
OH, S-S-SORRY!
WINCE
AH! THAT'S—
GROPE
V-R-R-R-R
MWRM
EEK!

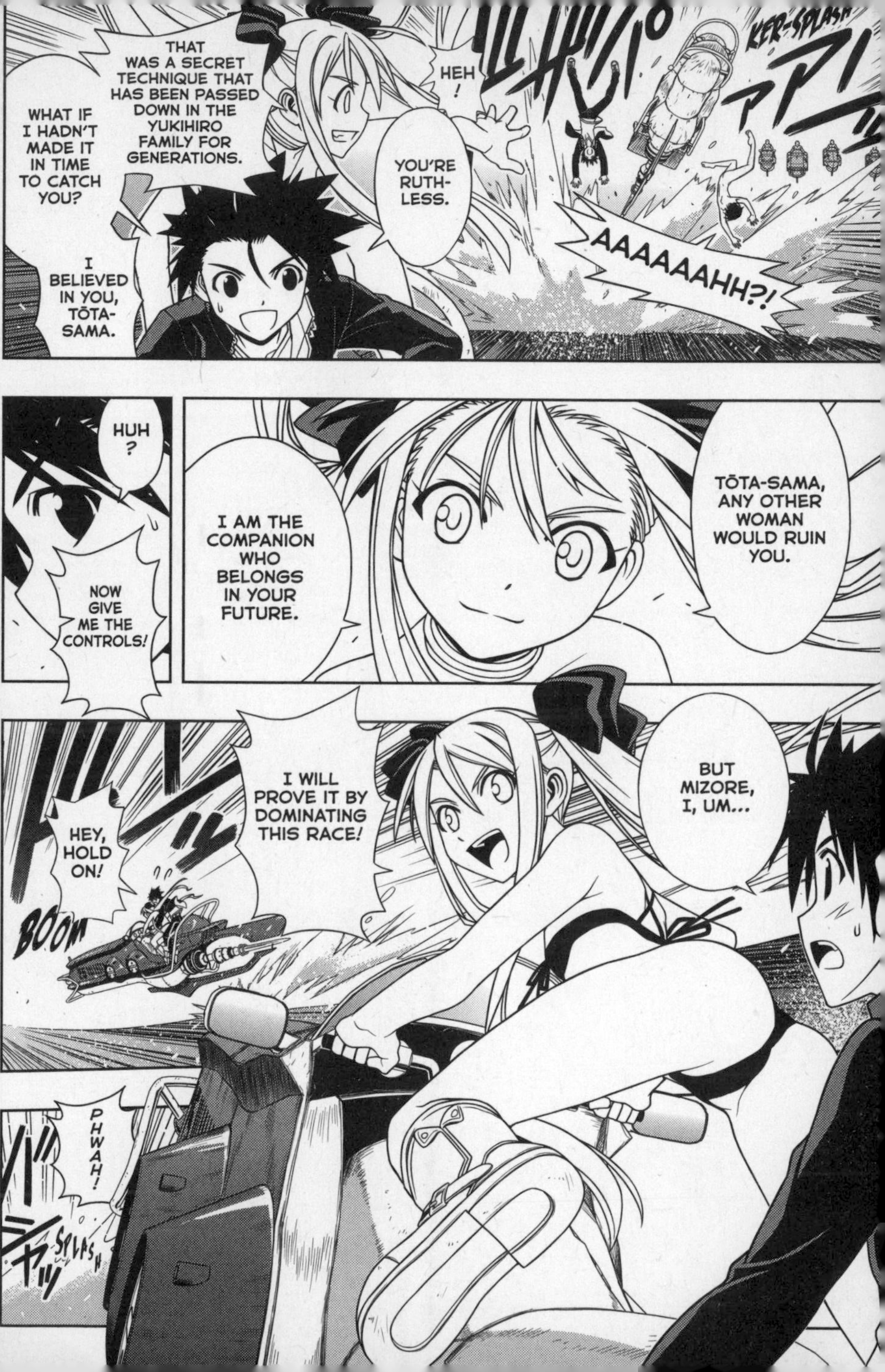
KER-SPLASH
AAAAAAAHH?!
HEH!
YOU'RE RUTHLESS.
THAT WAS A SECRET TECHNIQUE THAT HAS BEEN PASSED DOWN IN THE YUKIHIRO FAMILY FOR GENERATIONS.
WHAT IF I HADN'T MADE IT IN TIME TO CATCH YOU?
I BELIEVED IN YOU, TŌTA-SAMA.
TŌTA-SAMA, ANY OTHER WOMAN WOULD RUIN YOU.
I AM THE COMPANION WHO BELONGS IN YOUR FUTURE.
HUH?
NOW GIVE ME THE CONTROLS!
BUT MIZORE, I, UM...
I WILL PROVE IT BY DOMINATING THIS RACE!
HEY, HOLD ON!
BOOM
PHWAH!
SPLASH

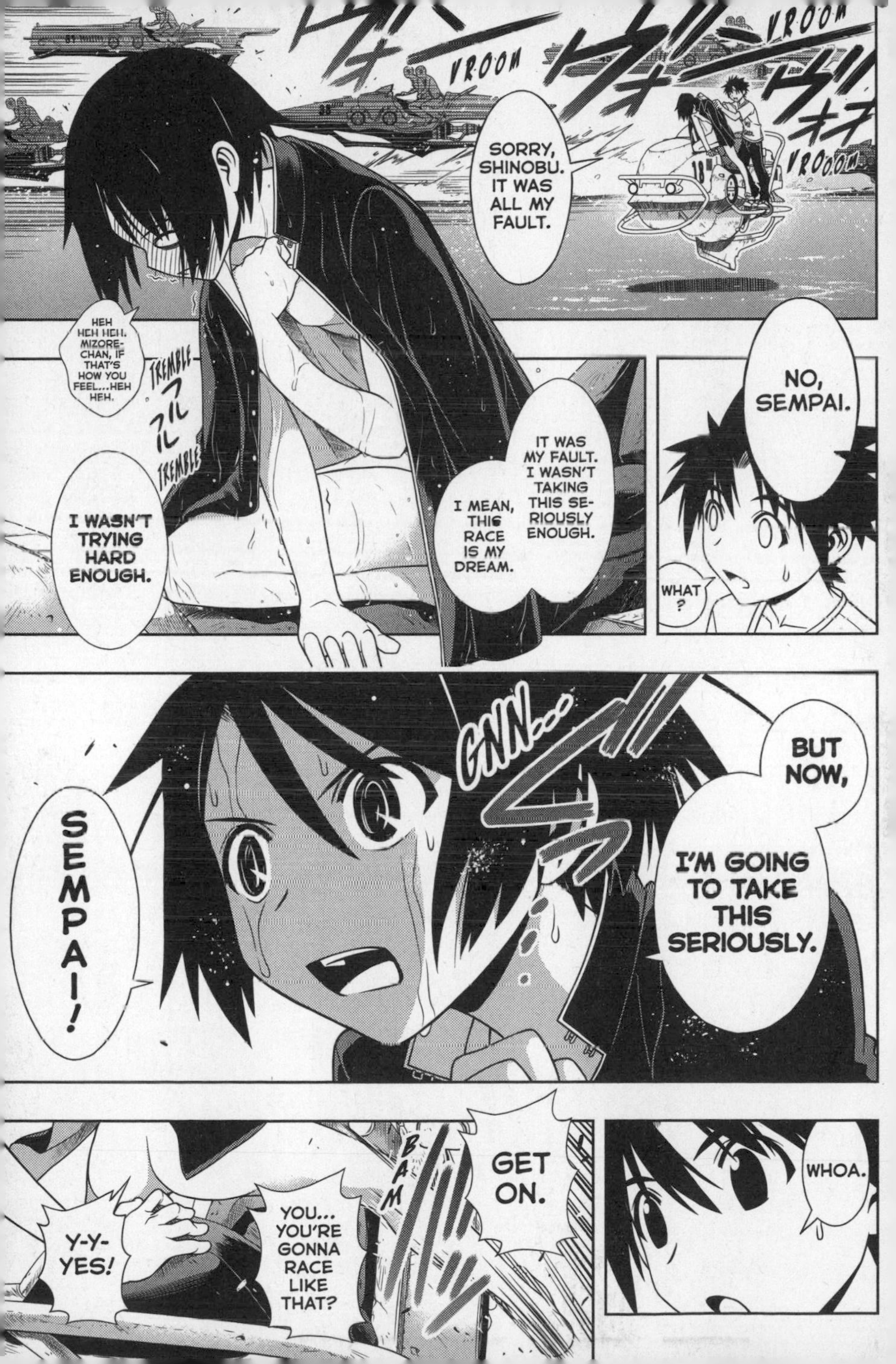
VROOM
VROOM
VROOM
SORRY, SHINOBU. IT WAS ALL MY FAULT.
NO, SEMPAI.
WHAT?
IT WAS MY FAULT. I WASN'T TAKING THIS SERIOUSLY ENOUGH.
I MEAN, THIS RACE IS MY DREAM.
I WASN'T TRYING HARD ENOUGH.
TREMBLE
TREMBLE
HEH HEH HEH. MIZORE-CHAN, IF THAT'S HOW YOU FEEL...HEH HEH.
BUT NOW, I'M GOING TO TAKE THIS SERIOUSLY.
GNN...
SEMPAI!
WHOA.
GET ON.
BAM
YOU... YOU'RE GONNA RACE LIKE THAT?
Y-Y-YES!

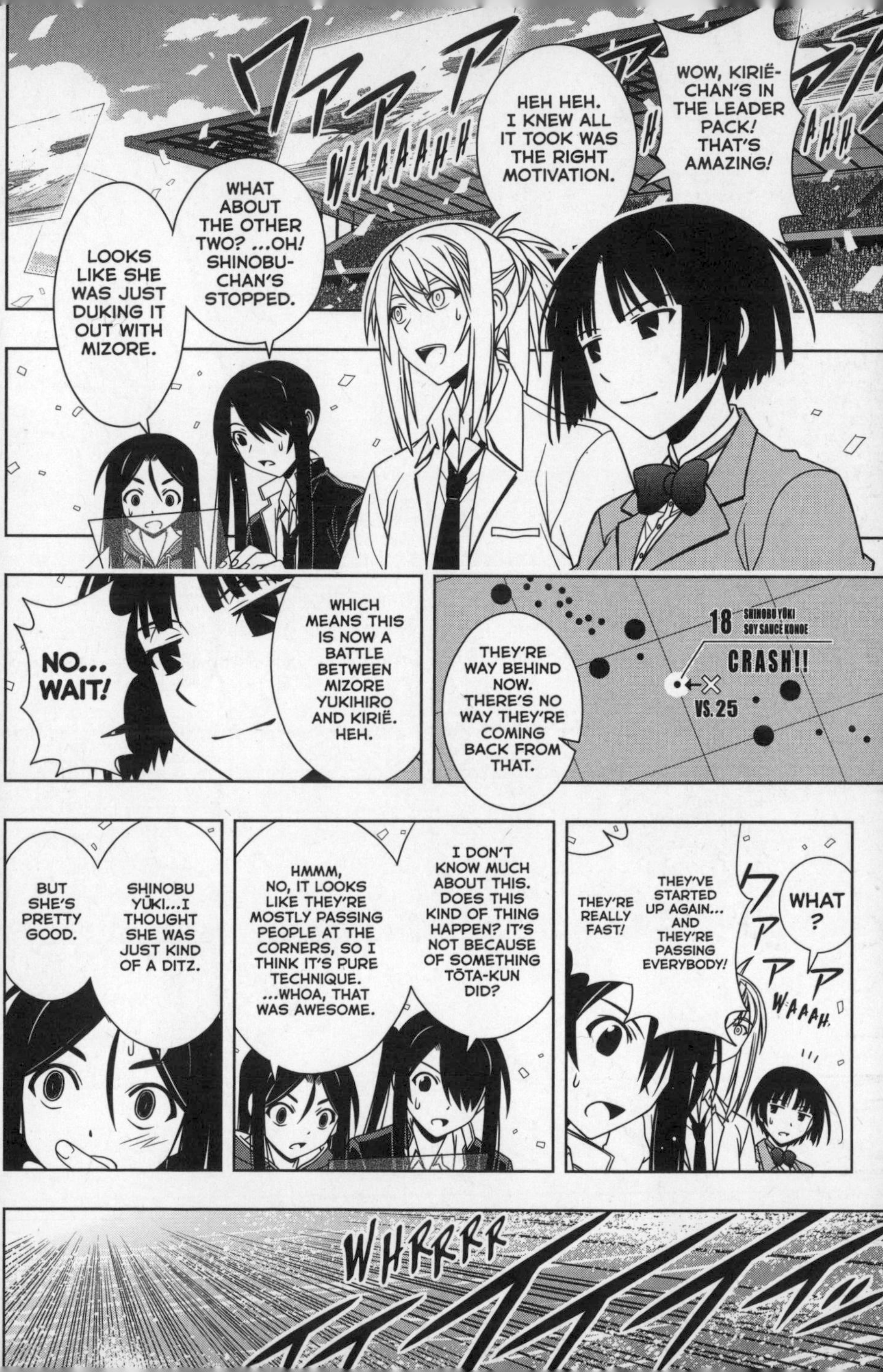
AHH
WOW, KIRIË-CHAN'S IN THE LEADER PACK! THAT'S AMAZING!
H
HEH HEH. I KNEW ALL IT TOOK WAS THE RIGHT MOTIVATION.
WAAAAHH
WHAT ABOUT THE OTHER TWO? ...OH! SHINOBU-CHAN'S STOPPED.
LOOKS LIKE SHE WAS JUST DUKING IT OUT WITH MIZORE.
18 SHINOBU YŪKI SOY SAUCE KONOE
CRASH!!
VS. 25
THEY'RE WAY BEHIND NOW. THERE'S NO WAY THEY'RE COMING BACK FROM THAT.
WHICH MEANS THIS IS NOW A BATTLE BETWEEN MIZORE YUKIHIRO AND KIRIË. HEH.
NO... WAIT!
WHAT?
WAAAH.
THEY'VE STARTED UP AGAIN... AND THEY'RE PASSING EVERYBODY!
THEY'RE REALLY FAST!
I DON'T KNOW MUCH ABOUT THIS. DOES THIS KIND OF THING HAPPEN? IT'S NOT BECAUSE OF SOMETHING TŌTA-KUN DID?
HMMM, NO, IT LOOKS LIKE THEY'RE MOSTLY PASSING PEOPLE AT THE CORNERS, SO I THINK IT'S PURE TECHNIQUE. ...WHOA, THAT WAS AWESOME.
SHINOBU YŪKI...I THOUGHT SHE WAS JUST KIND OF A DITZ.
BUT SHE'S PRETTY GOOD.
WHRRRR

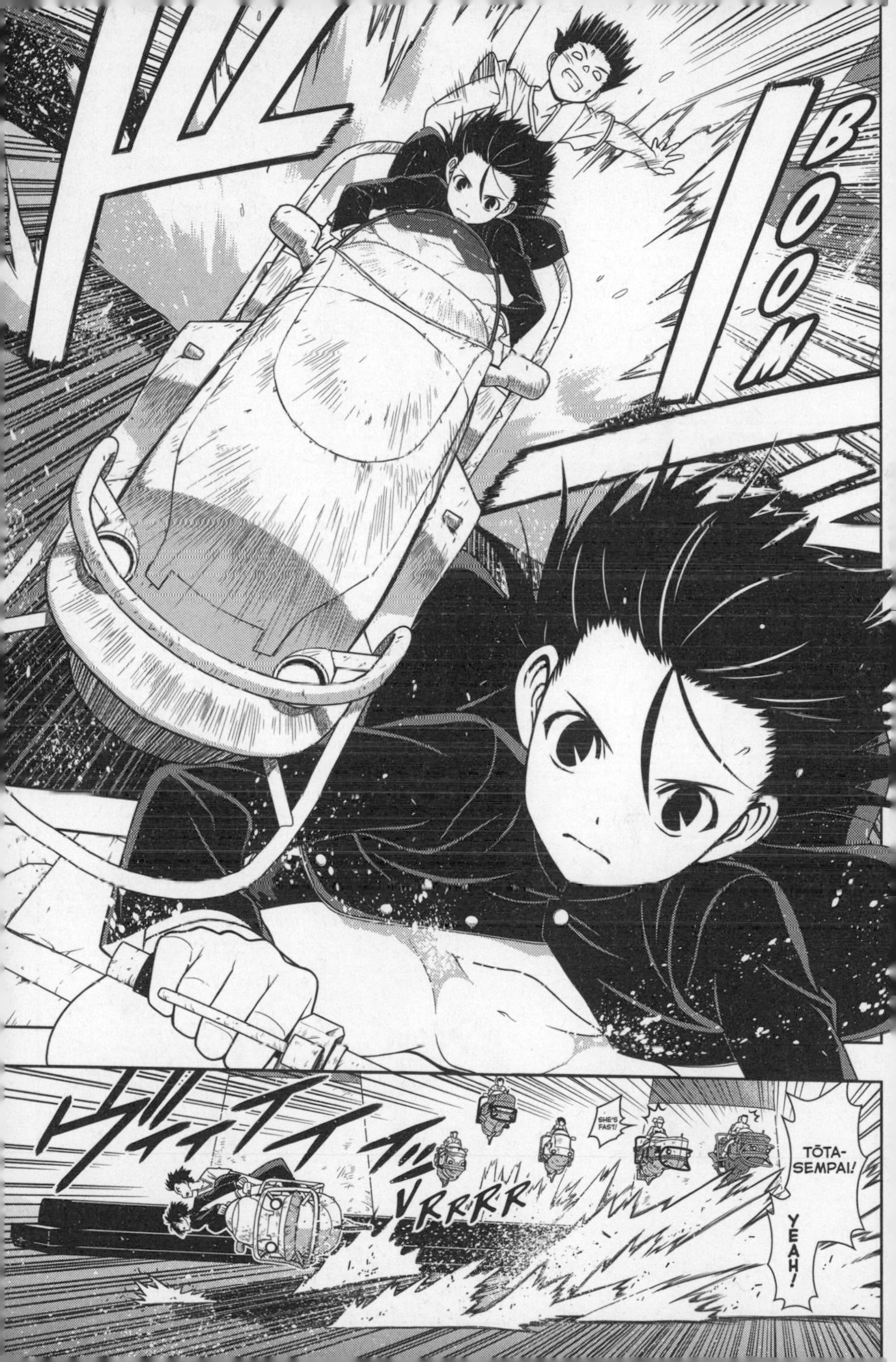
BOOM
TŌTA-SEMPAI!
YEAH!
SHE'S FAST!
VRRRR

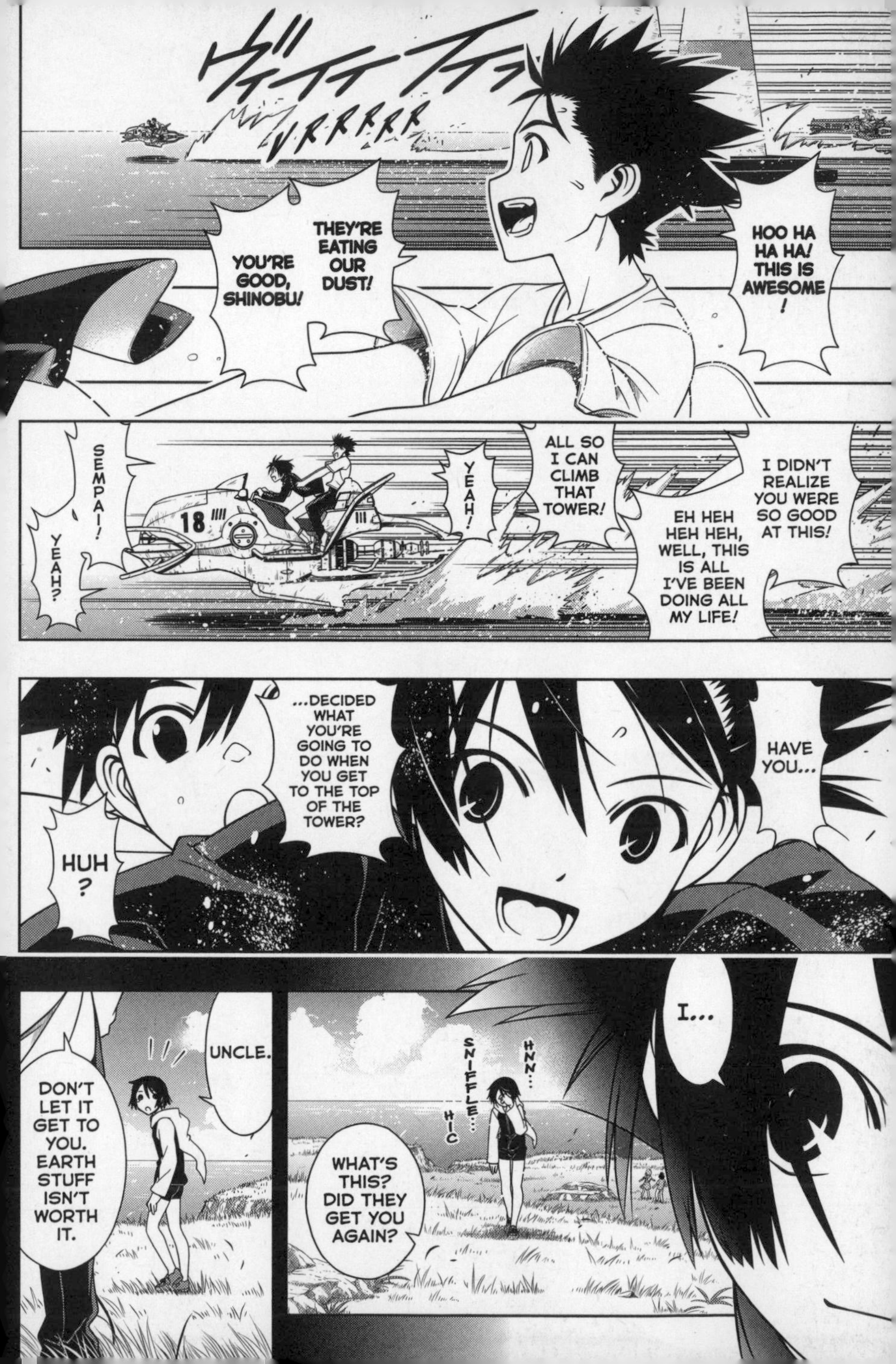
V-R-R-R-R-R
HOO HA HA HA! THIS IS AWESOME!
THEY'RE EATING OUR DUST!
YOU'RE GOOD, SHINOBU!
I DIDN'T REALIZE YOU WERE SO GOOD AT THIS!
EH HEH HEH HEH, WELL, THIS IS ALL I'VE BEEN DOING ALL MY LIFE!
ALL SO I CAN CLIMB THAT TOWER!
YEAH!
SEMPAI!
YEAH?
HAVE YOU...
...DECIDED WHAT YOU'RE GOING TO DO WHEN YOU GET TO THE TOP OF THE TOWER?
HUH?
I...
HNN...
SNIFFLE... HIC
WHAT'S THIS? DID THEY GET YOU AGAIN?
UNCLE.
DON'T LET IT GET TO YOU. EARTH STUFF ISN'T WORTH IT.

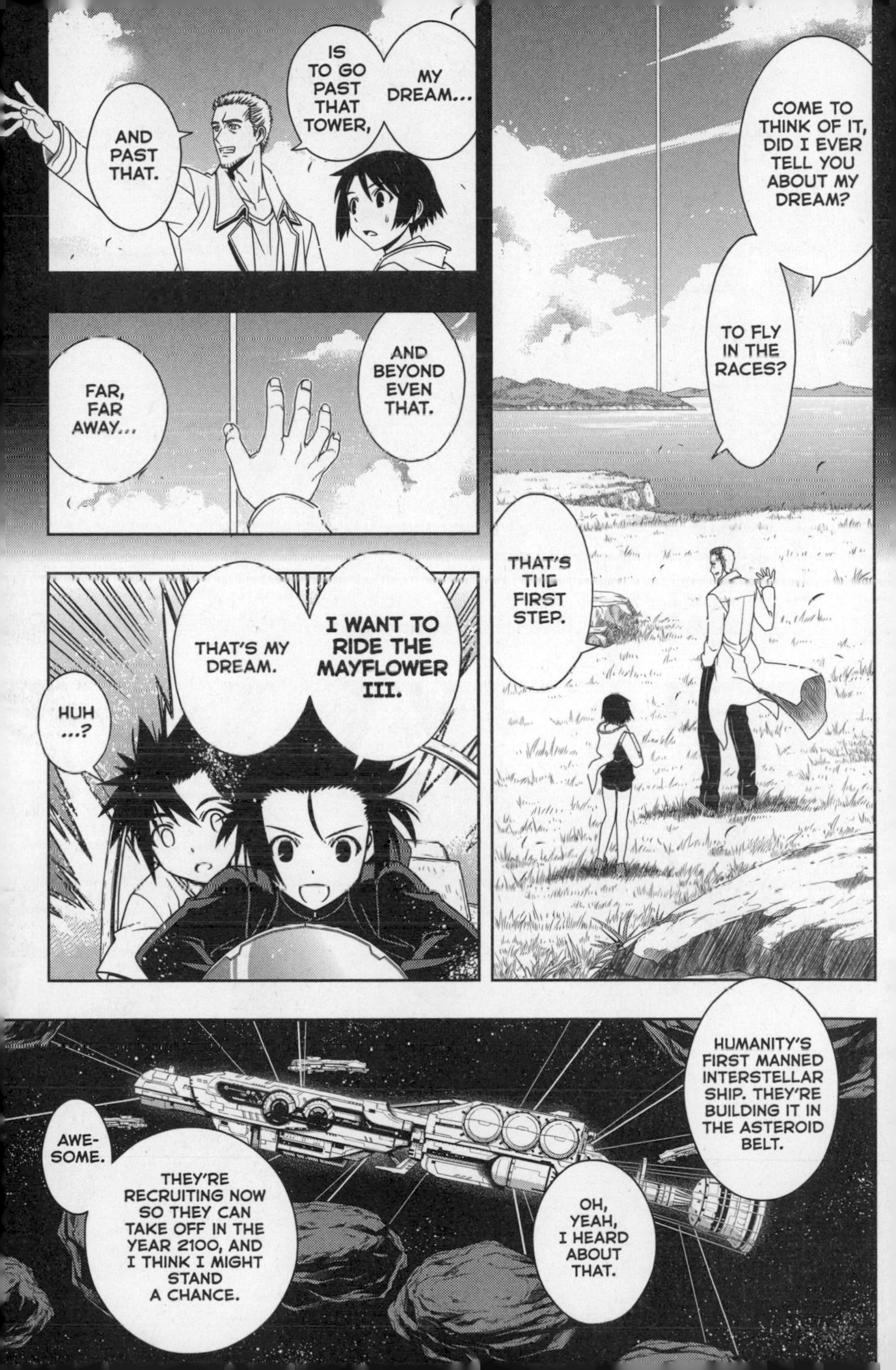
COME TO THINK OF IT, DID I EVER TELL YOU ABOUT MY DREAM?
TO FLY IN THE RACES?
THAT'S THE FIRST STEP.
MY DREAM...
IS TO GO PAST THAT TOWER,
AND PAST THAT.
AND BEYOND EVEN THAT.
FAR, FAR AWAY...
I WANT TO RIDE THE MAYFLOWER III.
THAT'S MY DREAM.
HUH ...?
HUMANITY'S FIRST MANNED INTERSTELLAR SHIP. THEY'RE BUILDING IT IN THE ASTEROID BELT.
OH, YEAH, I HEARD ABOUT THAT.
THEY'RE RECRUITING NOW SO THEY CAN TAKE OFF IN THE YEAR 2100, AND I THINK I MIGHT STAND A CHANCE.
AWE-SOME.

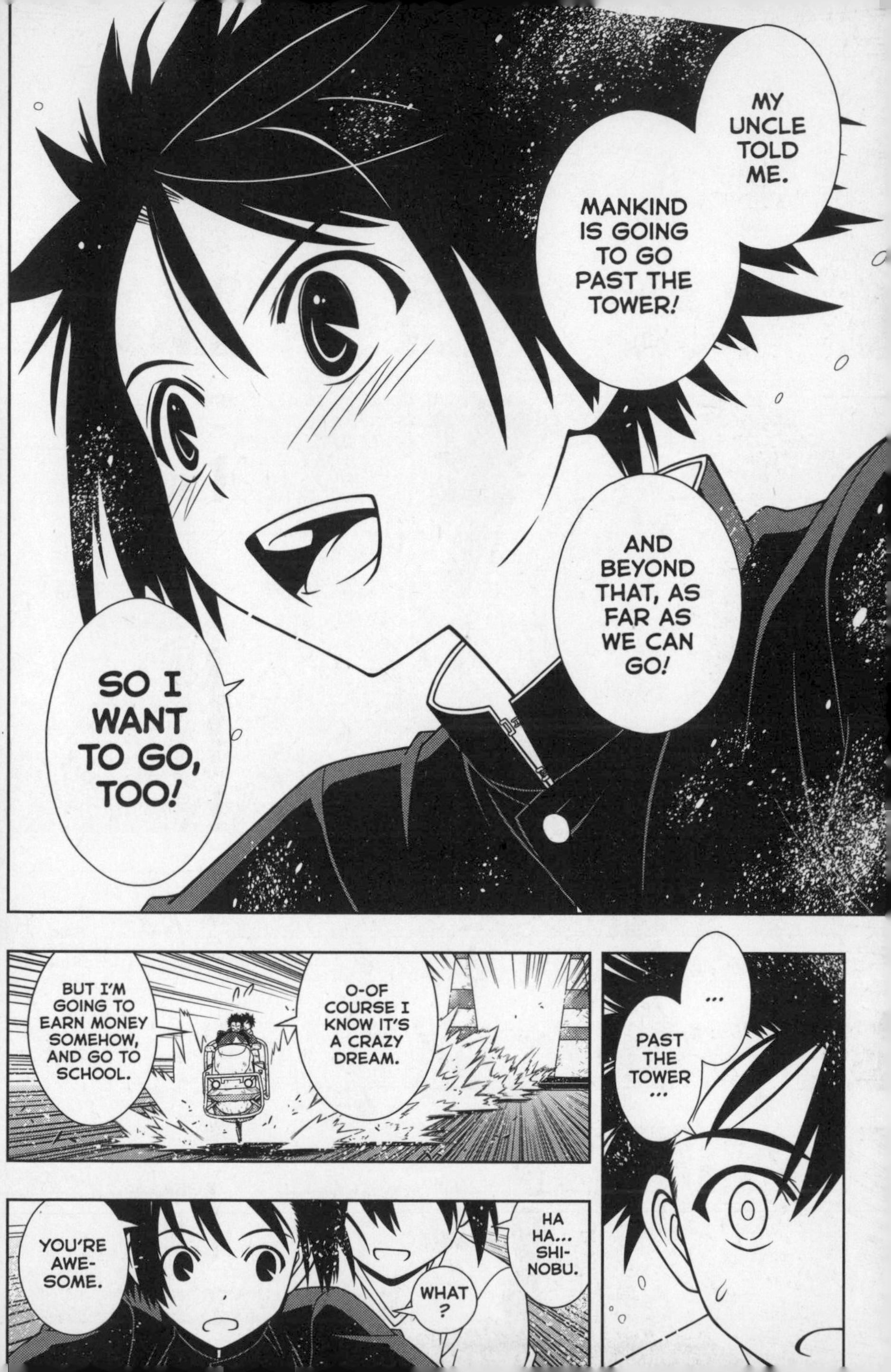
MY UNCLE TOLD ME.
MANKIND IS GOING TO GO PAST THE TOWER!
AND BEYOND THAT, AS FAR AS WE CAN GO!
SO I WANT TO GO, TOO!
... PAST THE TOWER ...
O-OF COURSE I KNOW IT'S A CRAZY DREAM.
BUT I'M GOING TO EARN MONEY SOMEHOW, AND GO TO SCHOOL.
HA HA... SHI-NOBU.
WHAT?
YOU'RE AWE-SOME.

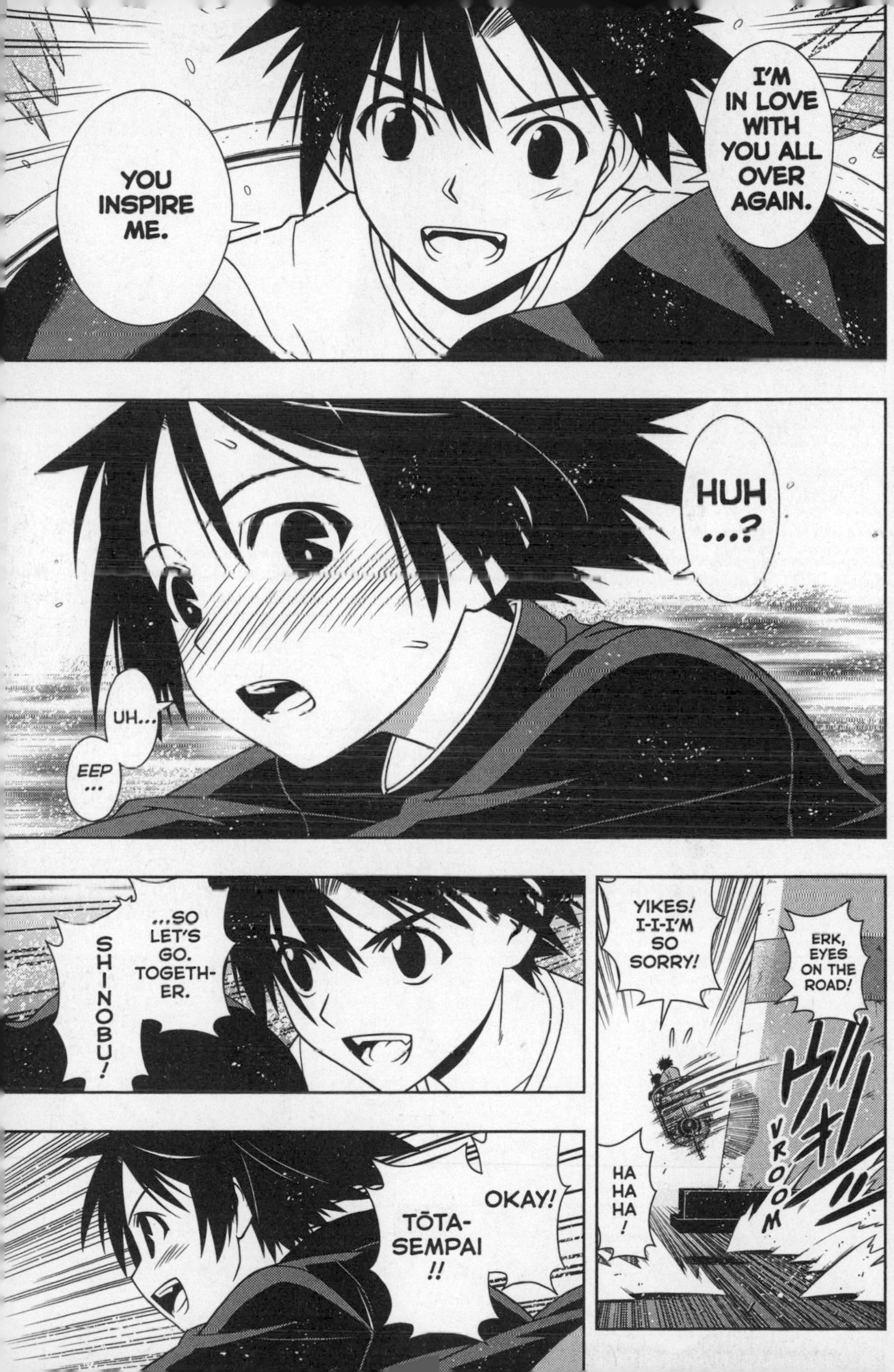
I'M IN LOVE WITH YOU ALL OVER AGAIN.
YOU INSPIRE ME.
HUH...?
UH...
EEP...
ERK, EYES ON THE ROAD!
YIKES! I-I-I'M SO SORRY!
VROOM
HA HA HA!
SHINOBU!
...SO LET'S GO. TOGETH-ER.
OKAY!
TŌTA-SEMPAI!!

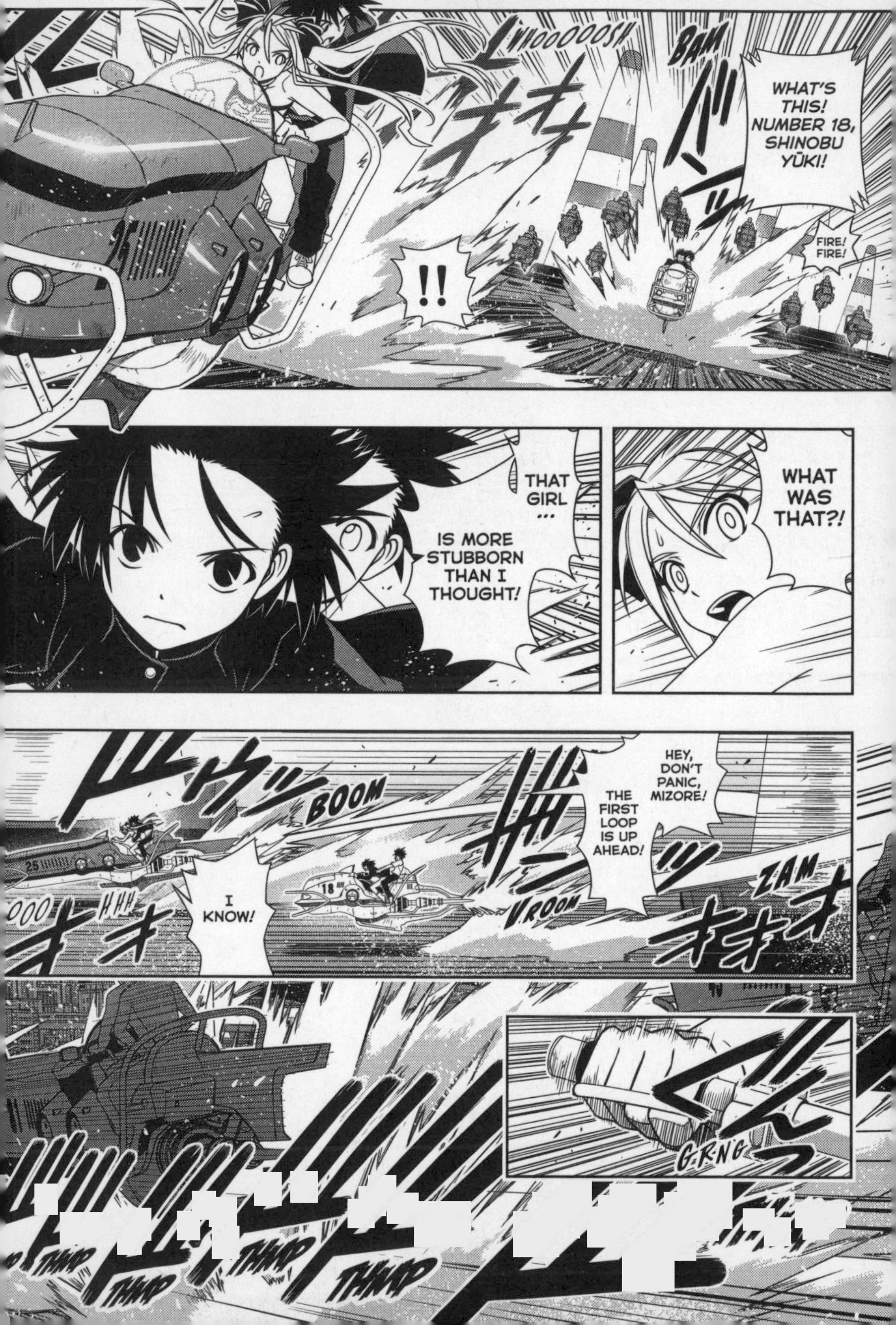
WHAT'S THIS! NUMBER 18, SHINOBU YŪKI!
BAM
FIRE! FIRE!
WHOOOOOSH
!!
WHAT WAS THAT?!
THAT GIRL ...
IS MORE STUBBORN THAN I THOUGHT!
HEY, DON'T PANIC, MIZORE!
THE FIRST LOOP IS UP AHEAD!
ZAM
VROOM
BOOM
I KNOW!
G-R-N-G
THMP
THMP
THMP
THMP

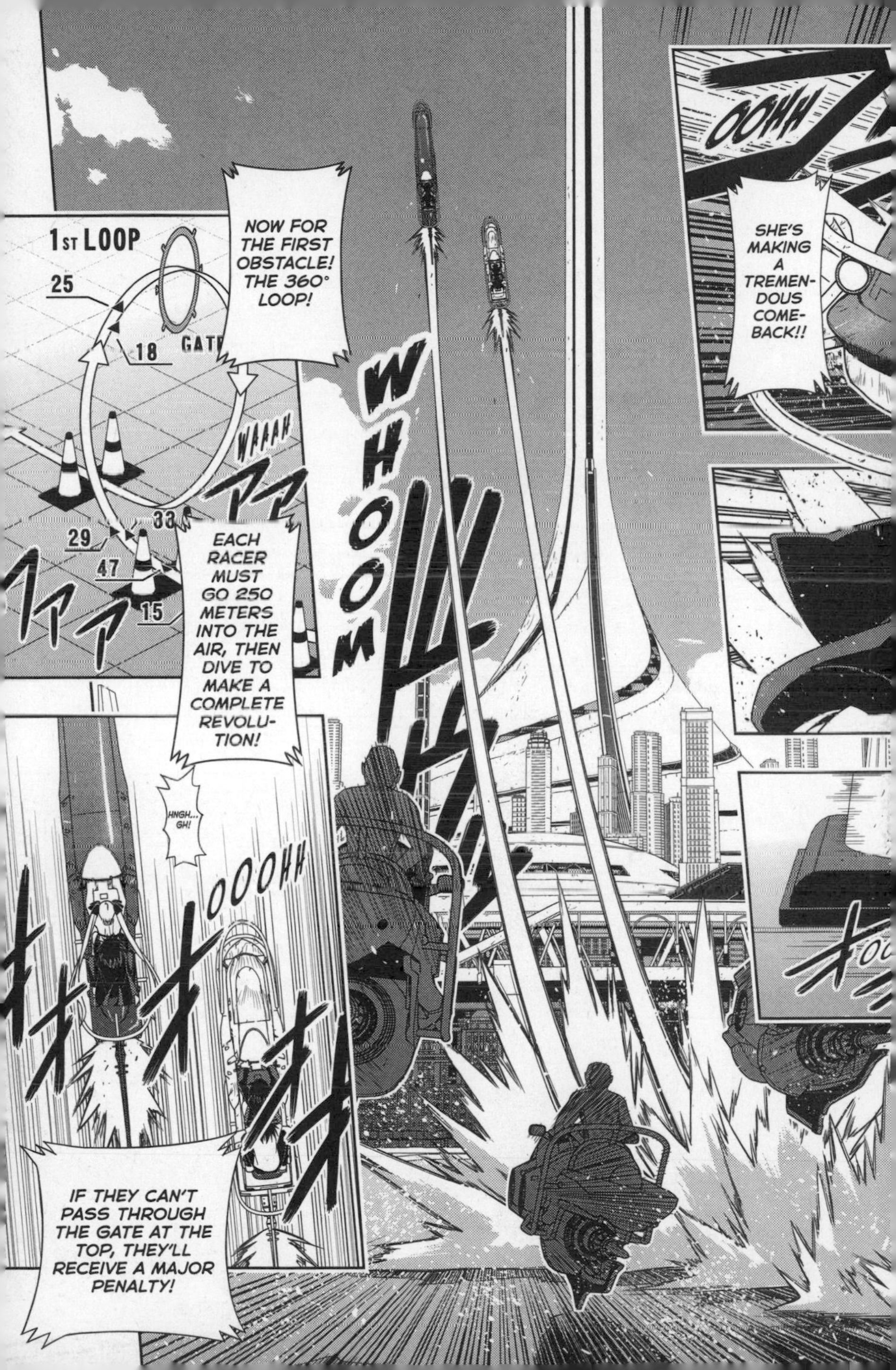
OOHH
SHE'S MAKING A TREMENDOUS COMEBACK!!
NOW FOR THE FIRST OBSTACLE! THE 360° LOOP!
WHOOM
1ST LOOP
25
18
GATE
WAAAH
33
29
47
15
EACH RACER MUST GO 250 METERS INTO THE AIR, THEN DIVE TO MAKE A COMPLETE REVOLUTION!
HNGH... GH!
OOOHH
IF THEY CAN'T PASS THROUGH THE GATE AT THE TOP, THEY'LL RECEIVE A MAJOR PENALTY!

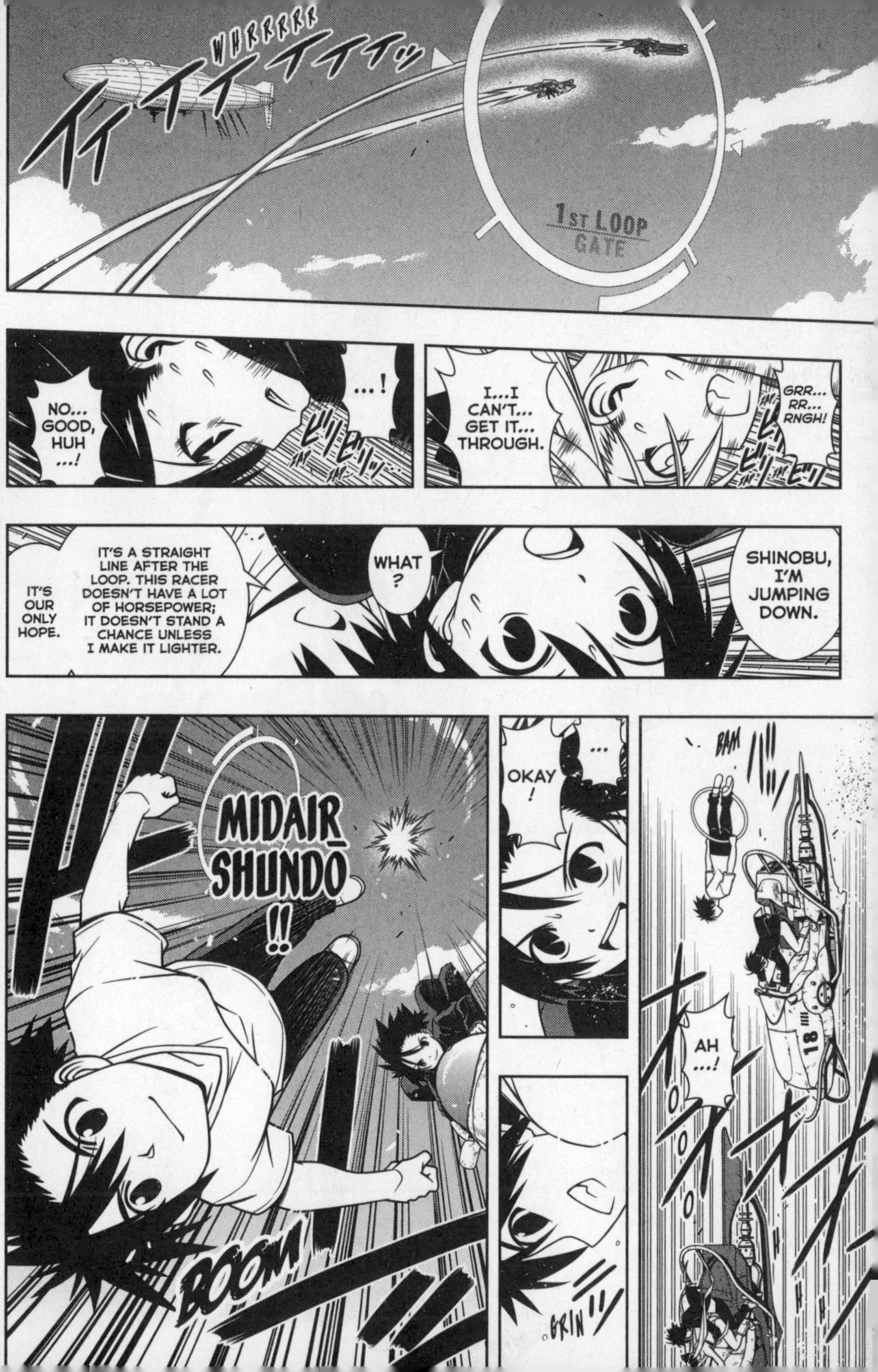
WHRRRRR
1ST LOOP GATE
I...I CAN'T... GET IT... THROUGH.
GRR... RR... RNGH!
...!
NO... GOOD, HUH ...!
SHINOBU, I'M JUMPING DOWN.
WHAT?
IT'S A STRAIGHT LINE AFTER THE LOOP. THIS RACER DOESN'T HAVE A LOT OF HORSEPOWER; IT DOESN'T STAND A CHANCE UNLESS I MAKE IT LIGHTER.
IT'S OUR ONLY HOPE.
BAM
AH ...!
... OKAY!
GRIN!!
MIDAIR SHUNDŌ!!
BOOM

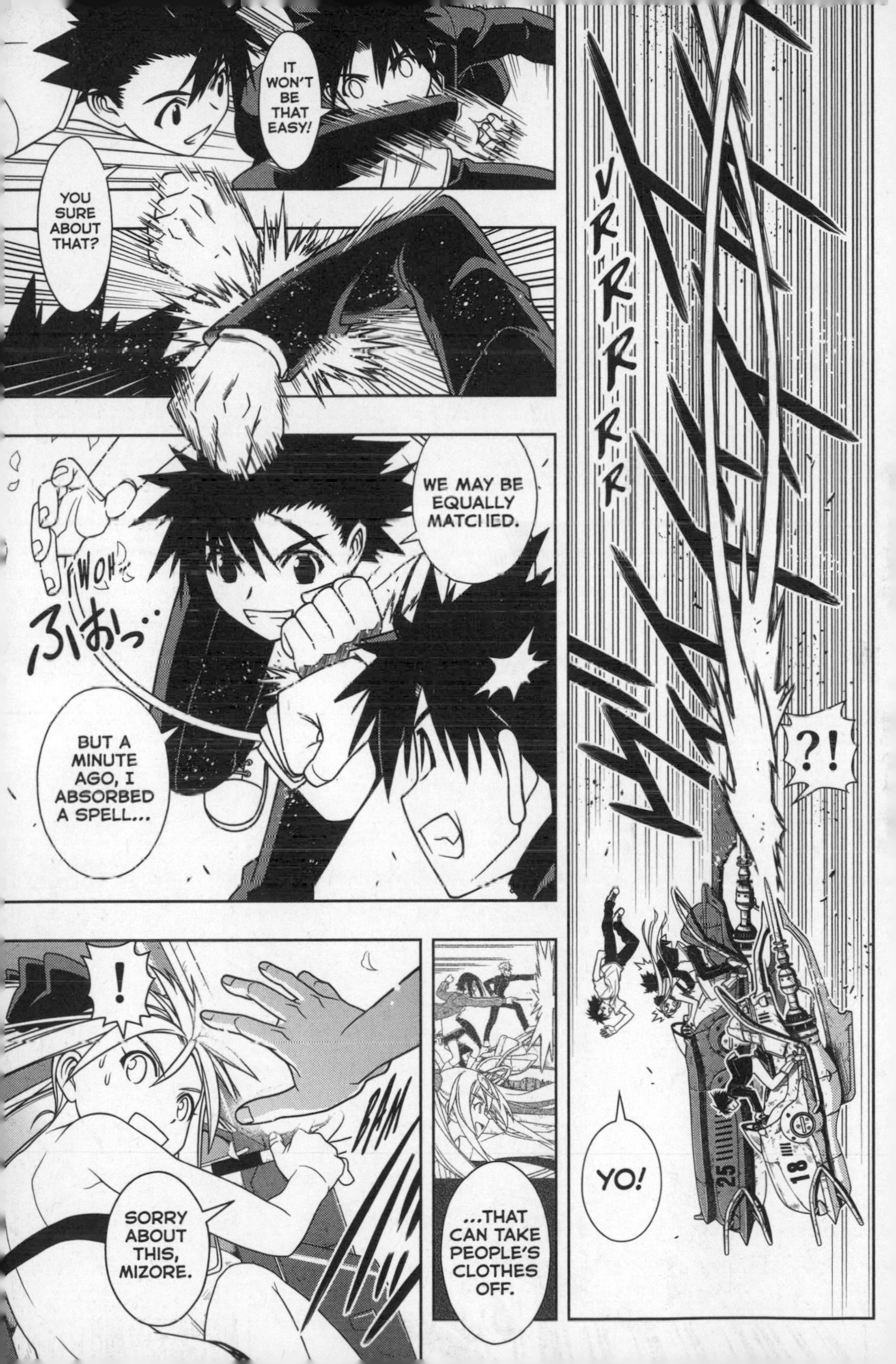
VRRRRRR
?!
YO!
IT WON'T BE THAT EASY!
YOU SURE ABOUT THAT?
WE MAY BE EQUALLY MATCHED.
FWOH
ふおっ
BUT A MINUTE AGO, I ABSORBED A SPELL...
...THAT CAN TAKE PEOPLE'S CLOTHES OFF.
!
SORRY ABOUT THIS, MIZORE.

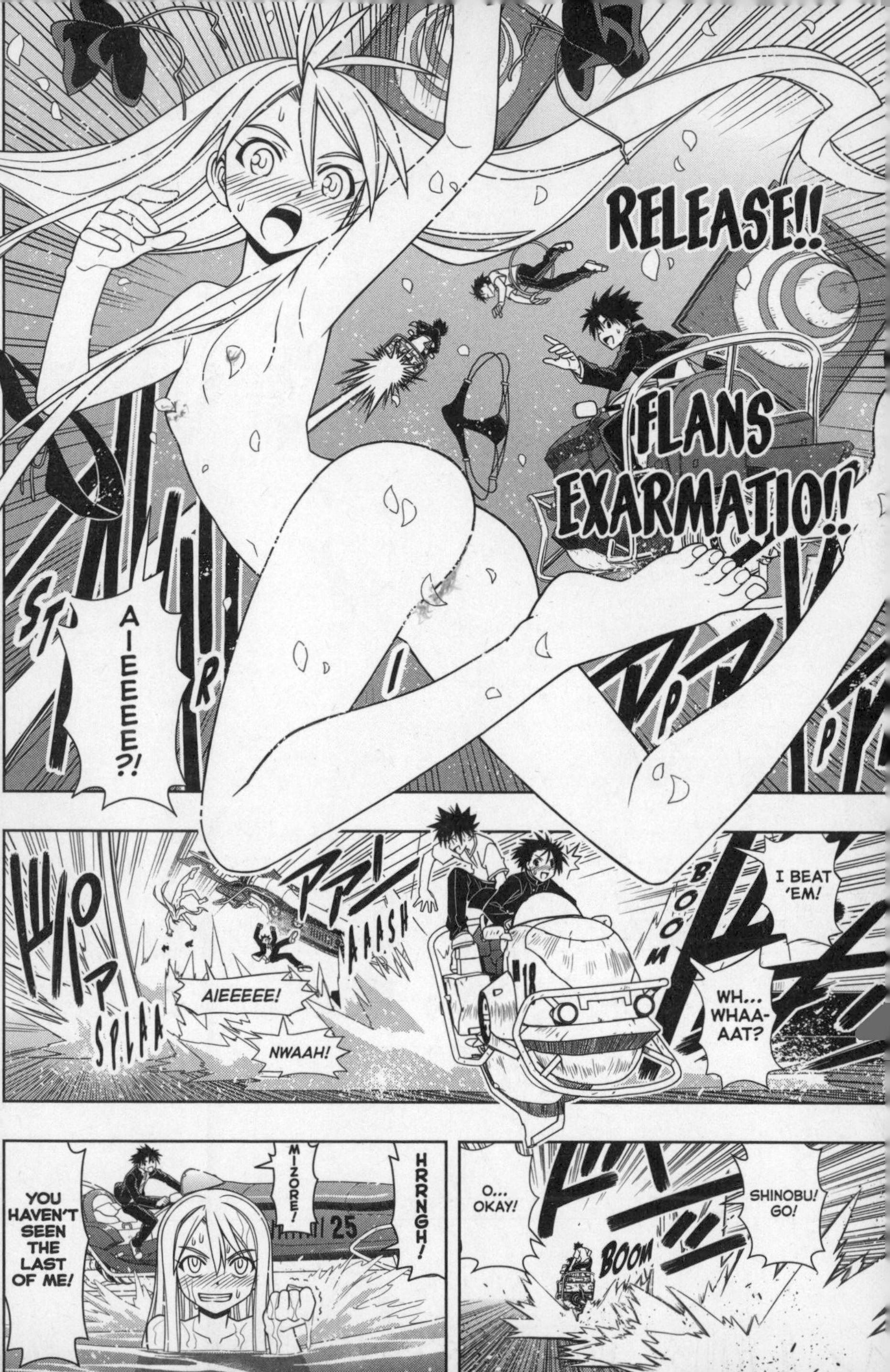

RELEASE!!
FLANS EXARMATIO!!
STRIP
AIEEEEE?!
I BEAT 'EM!
WH... WHAAAT?
BOOOOM
AAASH
AIEEEEE!
NWAAH!
SPLAA
SHINOBU! GO!
O... OKAY!
BOOM
HRRNGH!
MIZORE!
YOU HAVEN'T SEEN THE LAST OF ME!
25

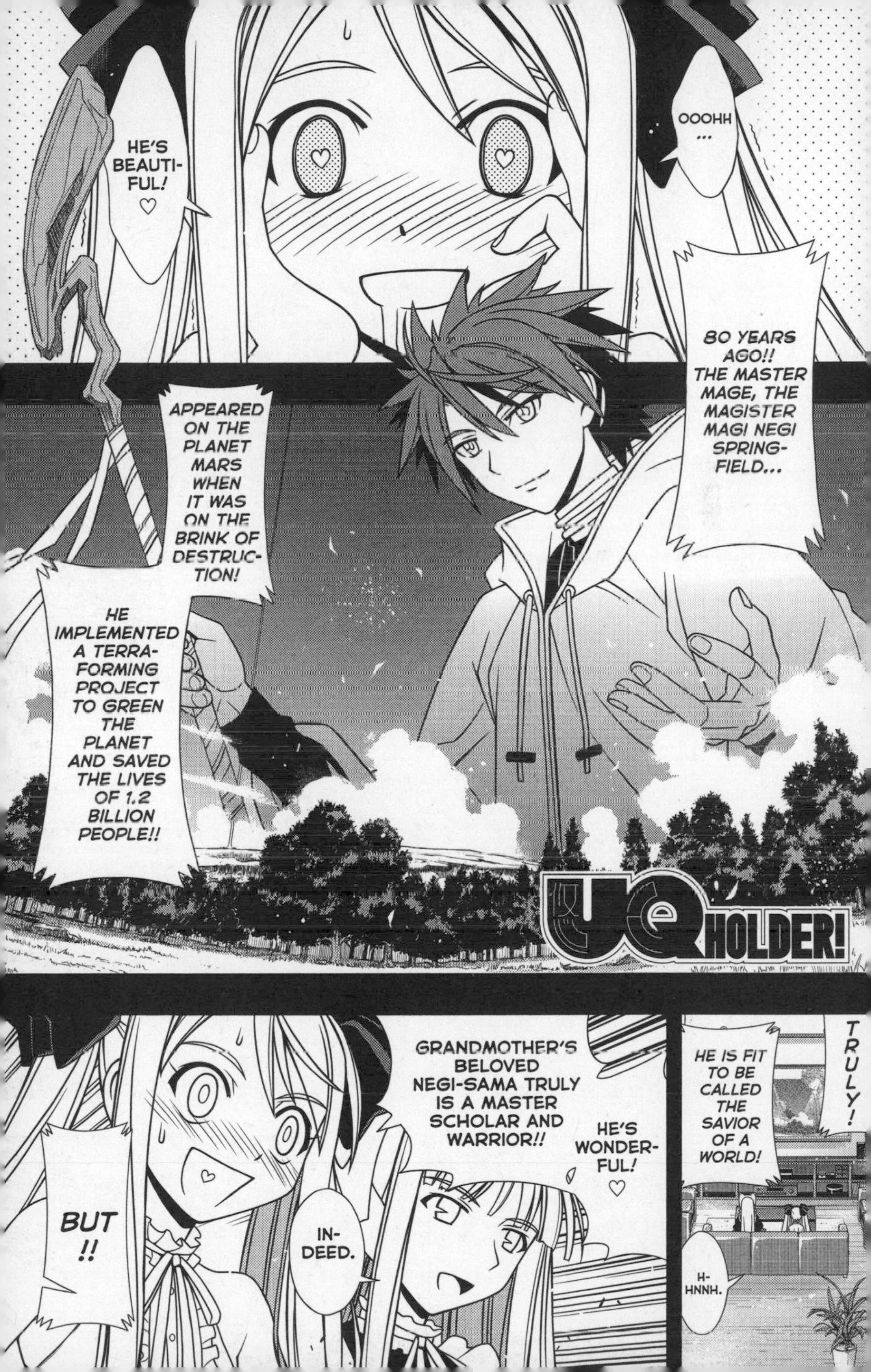
OOOHH ...
HE'S BEAUTIFUL! ♡
80 YEARS AGO!! THE MASTER MAGE, THE MAGISTER MAGI NEGI SPRINGFIELD...
APPEARED ON THE PLANET MARS WHEN IT WAS ON THE BRINK OF DESTRUCTION!
HE IMPLEMENTED A TERRAFORMING PROJECT TO GREEN THE PLANET AND SAVED THE LIVES OF 1.2 BILLION PEOPLE!!
UQ HOLDER!
TRULY!
HE IS FIT TO BE CALLED THE SAVIOR OF A WORLD!
H-HNNH.
GRANDMOTHER'S BELOVED NEGI-SAMA TRULY IS A MASTER SCHOLAR AND WARRIOR!!
HE'S WONDERFUL! ♡
IN-DEED.
BUT !!

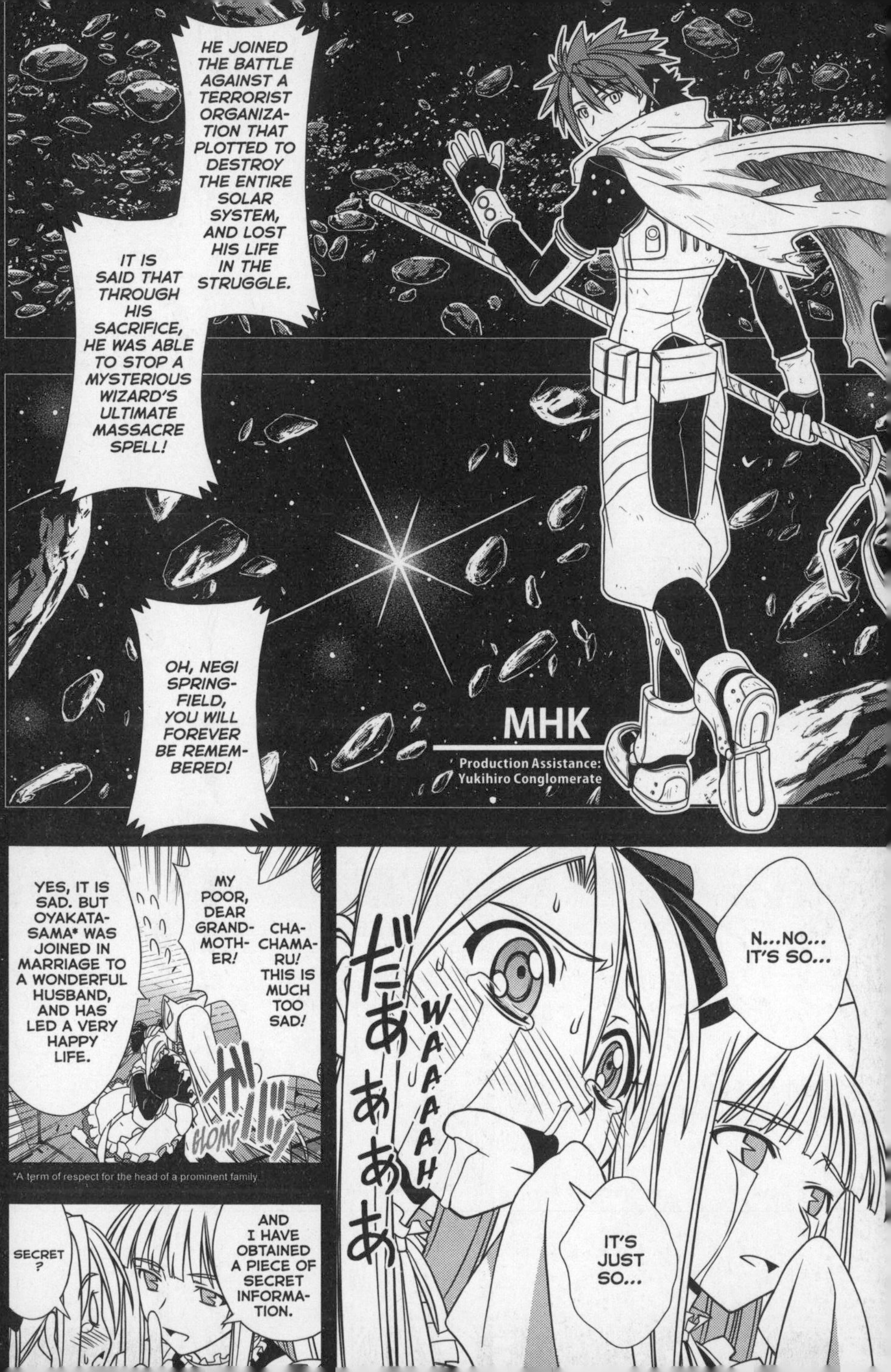
HE JOINED THE BATTLE AGAINST A TERRORIST ORGANIZATION THAT PLOTTED TO DESTROY THE ENTIRE SOLAR SYSTEM, AND LOST HIS LIFE IN THE STRUGGLE.
IT IS SAID THAT THROUGH HIS SACRIFICE, HE WAS ABLE TO STOP A MYSTERIOUS WIZARD'S ULTIMATE MASSACRE SPELL!
OH, NEGI SPRINGFIELD, YOU WILL FOREVER BE REMEMBERED!
MHK
Production Assistance: Yukihiro Conglomerate
N...NO... IT'S SO...
だあああ
WAAAAH
IT'S JUST SO...
CHACHAMARU! THIS IS MUCH TOO SAD!
MY POOR, DEAR GRANDMOTHER!
YES, IT IS SAD. BUT OYAKATA-SAMA* WAS JOINED IN MARRIAGE TO A WONDERFUL HUSBAND, AND HAS LED A VERY HAPPY LIFE.
ガバッ
GLOMP
AND I HAVE OBTAINED A PIECE OF SECRET INFORMATION.
SECRET?
*A term of respect for the head of a prominent family.

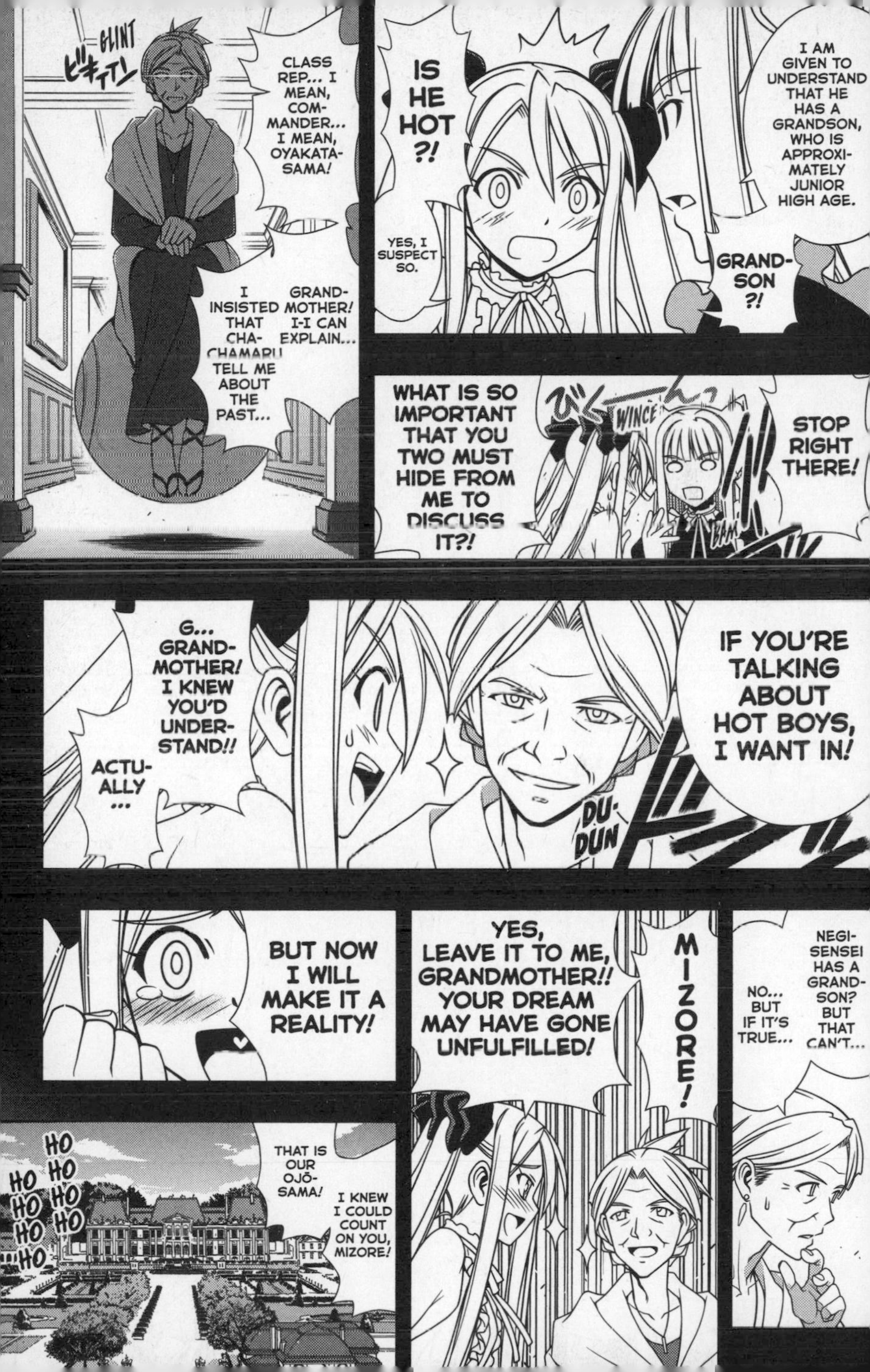
I AM GIVEN TO UNDERSTAND THAT HE HAS A GRANDSON, WHO IS APPROXIMATELY JUNIOR HIGH AGE.
GRAND-SON ?!
IS HE HOT ?!
YES, I SUSPECT SO.
STOP RIGHT THERE!
WINCE
BAM
WHAT IS SO IMPORTANT THAT YOU TWO MUST HIDE FROM ME TO DISCUSS IT?!
GLINT
CLASS REP... I MEAN, COM-MANDER... I MEAN, OYAKATA-SAMA!
GRAND-MOTHER! I-I CAN EXPLAIN...
I INSISTED THAT CHA-CHAMARU TELL ME ABOUT THE PAST...
IF YOU'RE TALKING ABOUT HOT BOYS, I WANT IN!
DU-DUN
G... GRAND-MOTHER! I KNEW YOU'D UNDER-STAND!!
ACTU-ALLY ...
NEGI-SENSEI HAS A GRAND-SON? BUT THAT CAN'T...
NO... BUT IF IT'S TRUE...
MIZORE!
YES, LEAVE IT TO ME, GRANDMOTHER!! YOUR DREAM MAY HAVE GONE UNFULFILLED!
BUT NOW I WILL MAKE IT A REALITY!
THAT IS OUR OJŌ-SAMA!
I KNEW I COULD COUNT ON YOU, MIZORE!
HO HO HO HO HO HO HO HO HO HO HO

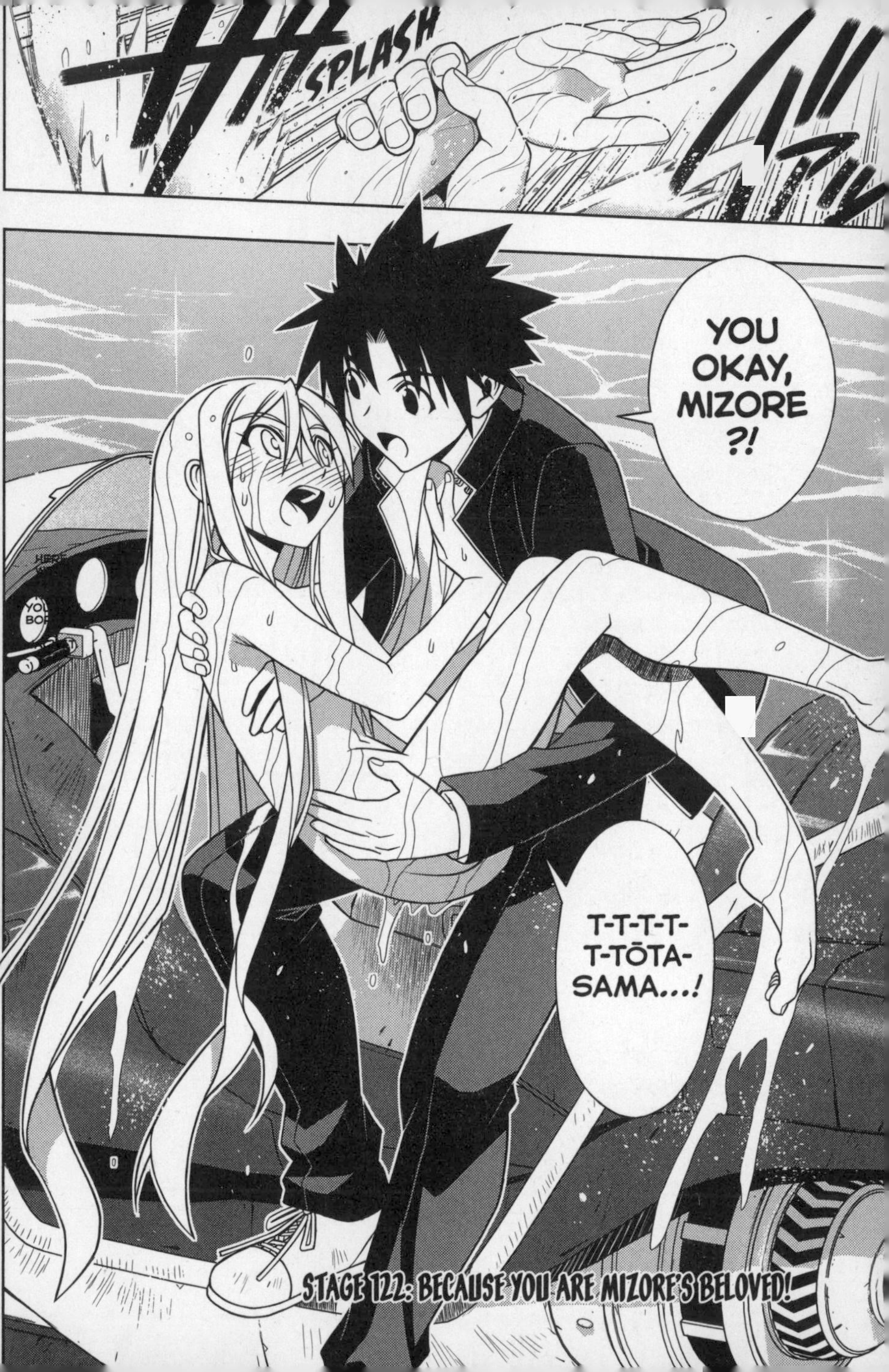
SPLASH
YOU OKAY, MIZORE ?!
T-T-T-T-T-TŌTA-SAMA...!
STAGE 122: BECAUSE YOU ARE MIZORE'S BELOVED!

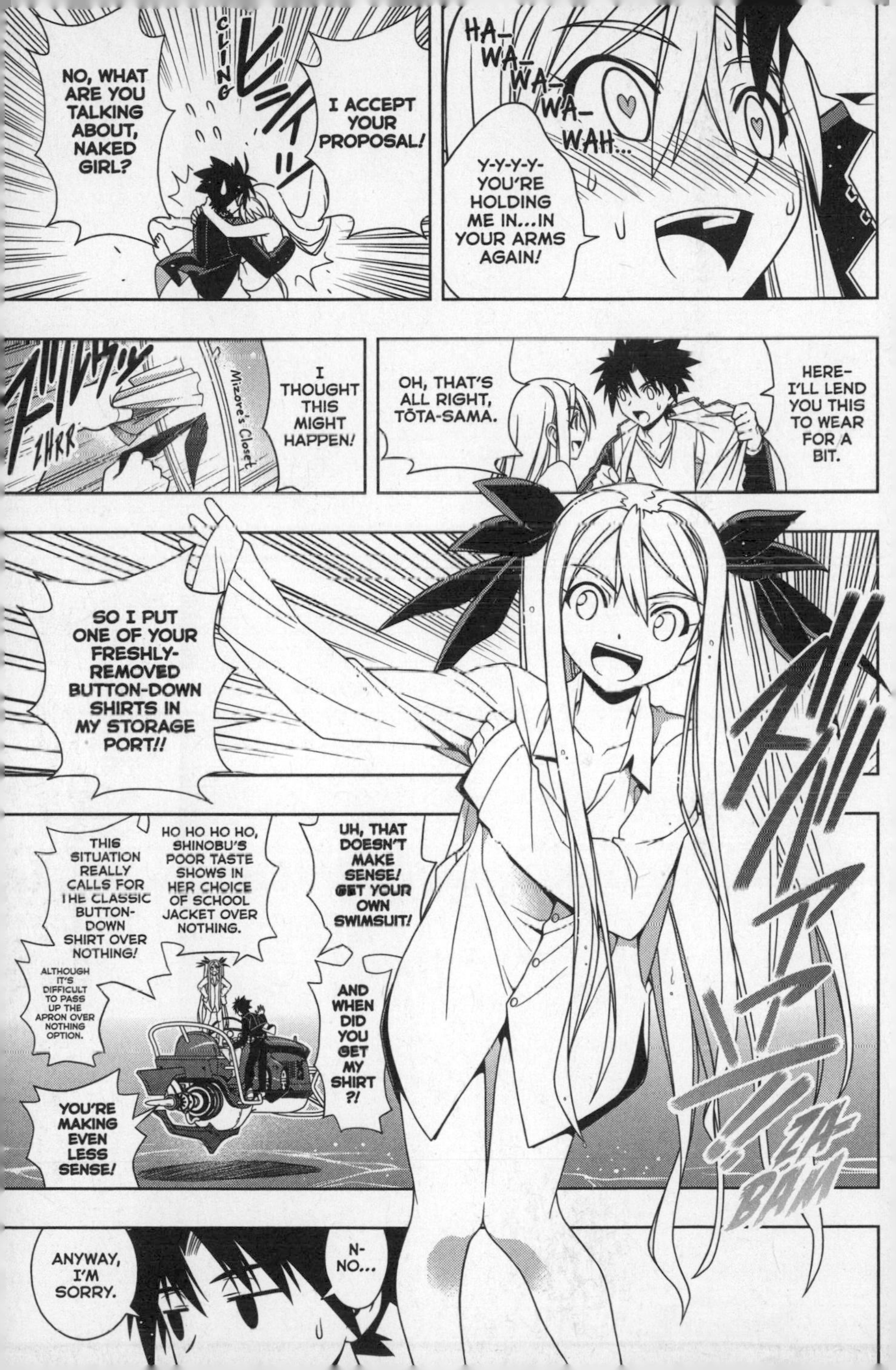
HA-WA-WA-WA-WAH...
Y-Y-Y-Y-YOU'RE HOLDING ME IN...IN YOUR ARMS AGAIN!
I ACCEPT YOUR PROPOSAL!
CLING
NO, WHAT ARE YOU TALKING ABOUT, NAKED GIRL?
HERE—I'LL LEND YOU THIS TO WEAR FOR A BIT.
OH, THAT'S ALL RIGHT, TŌTA-SAMA.
I THOUGHT THIS MIGHT HAPPEN!
Mizore's Closet
ZHRR
SO I PUT ONE OF YOUR FRESHLY-REMOVED BUTTON-DOWN SHIRTS IN MY STORAGE PORT!!
ZA-BAM
UH, THAT DOESN'T MAKE SENSE! GET YOUR OWN SWIMSUIT!
AND WHEN DID YOU GET MY SHIRT?!
HO HO HO HO, SHINOBU'S POOR TASTE SHOWS IN HER CHOICE OF SCHOOL JACKET OVER NOTHING.
THIS SITUATION REALLY CALLS FOR THE CLASSIC BUTTON-DOWN SHIRT OVER NOTHING!
ALTHOUGH IT'S DIFFICULT TO PASS UP THE APRON OVER NOTHING OPTION.
YOU'RE MAKING EVEN LESS SENSE!
N-NO...
ANYWAY, I'M SORRY.

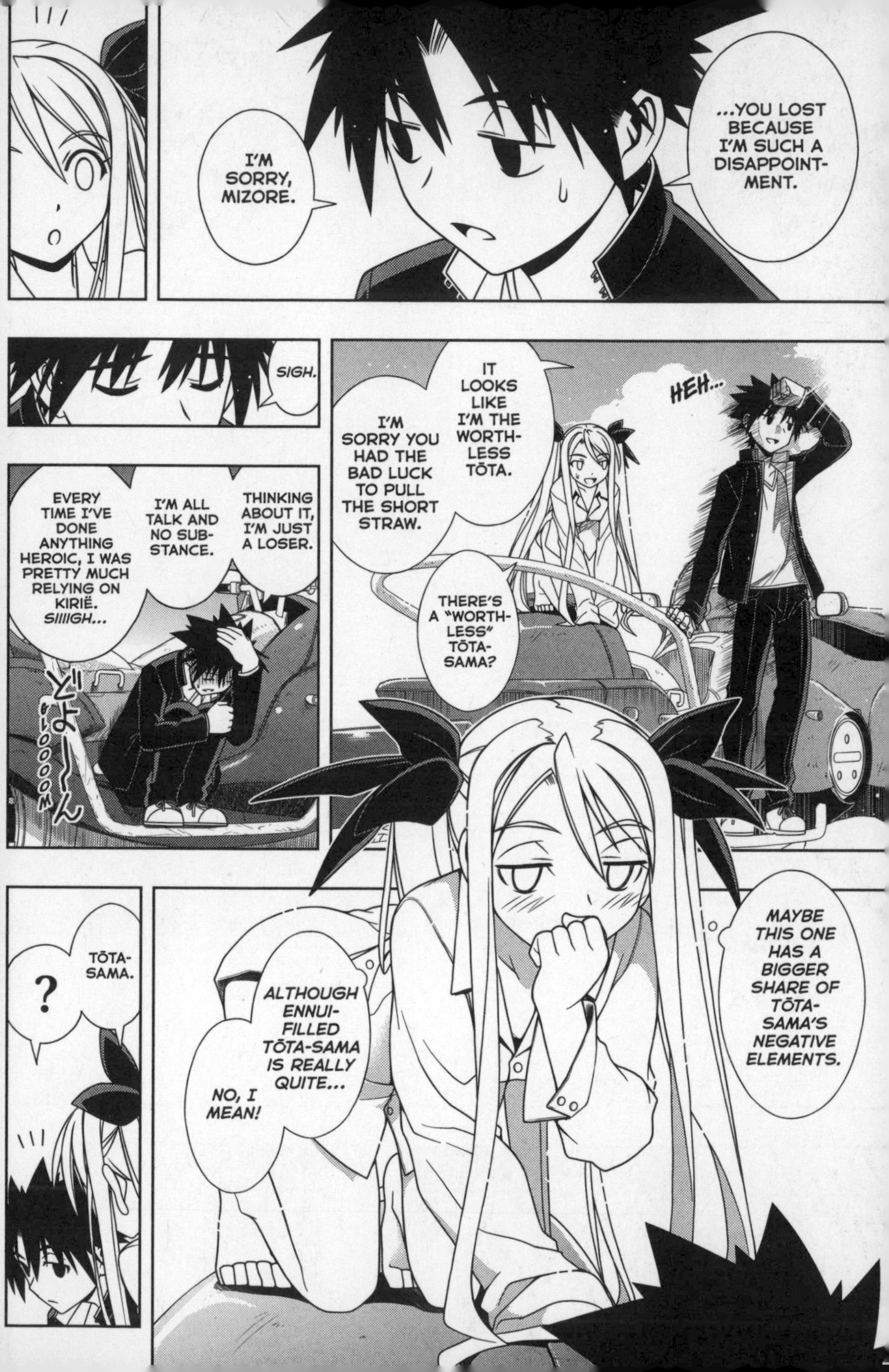
...YOU LOST BECAUSE I'M SUCH A DISAPPOINTMENT.
I'M SORRY, MIZORE.
HEH...
IT LOOKS LIKE I'M THE WORTHLESS TŌTA.
I'M SORRY YOU HAD THE BAD LUCK TO PULL THE SHORT STRAW.
THERE'S A "WORTHLESS" TŌTA-SAMA?
SIGH.
THINKING ABOUT IT, I'M JUST A LOSER.
I'M ALL TALK AND NO SUBSTANCE.
EVERY TIME I'VE DONE ANYTHING HEROIC, I WAS PRETTY MUCH RELYING ON KIRIË. SIIIGH...
どよ〜ん
DOOOOOM
MAYBE THIS ONE HAS A BIGGER SHARE OF TŌTA-SAMA'S NEGATIVE ELEMENTS.
ALTHOUGH ENNUI-FILLED TŌTA-SAMA IS REALLY QUITE...
NO, I MEAN!
TŌTA-SAMA.
?

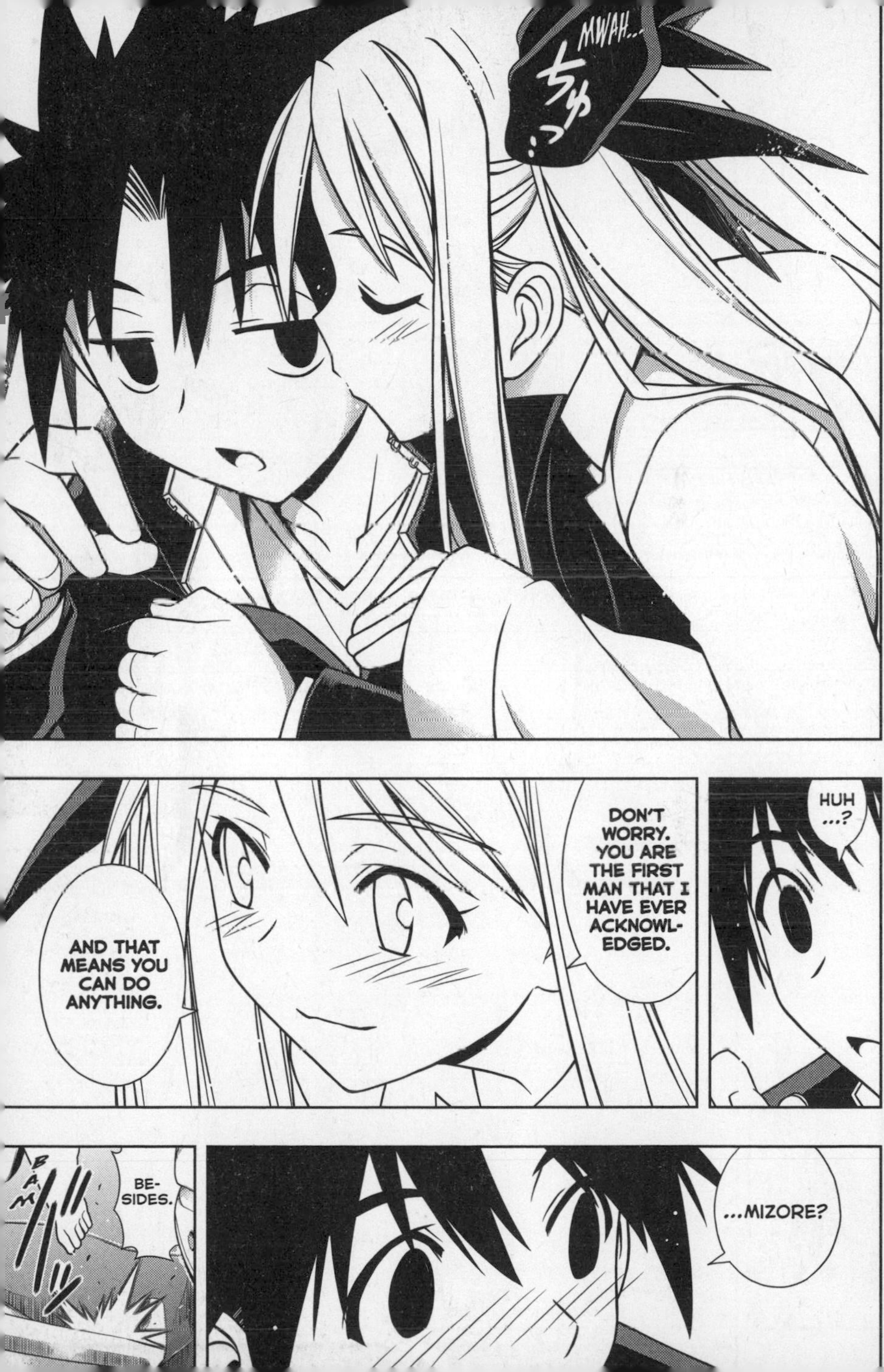
MWAH...
ちゅっ
HUH ...?
DON'T WORRY. YOU ARE THE FIRST MAN THAT I HAVE EVER ACKNOWL-EDGED.
AND THAT MEANS YOU CAN DO ANYTHING.
...MIZORE?
BE-SIDES.
BAM

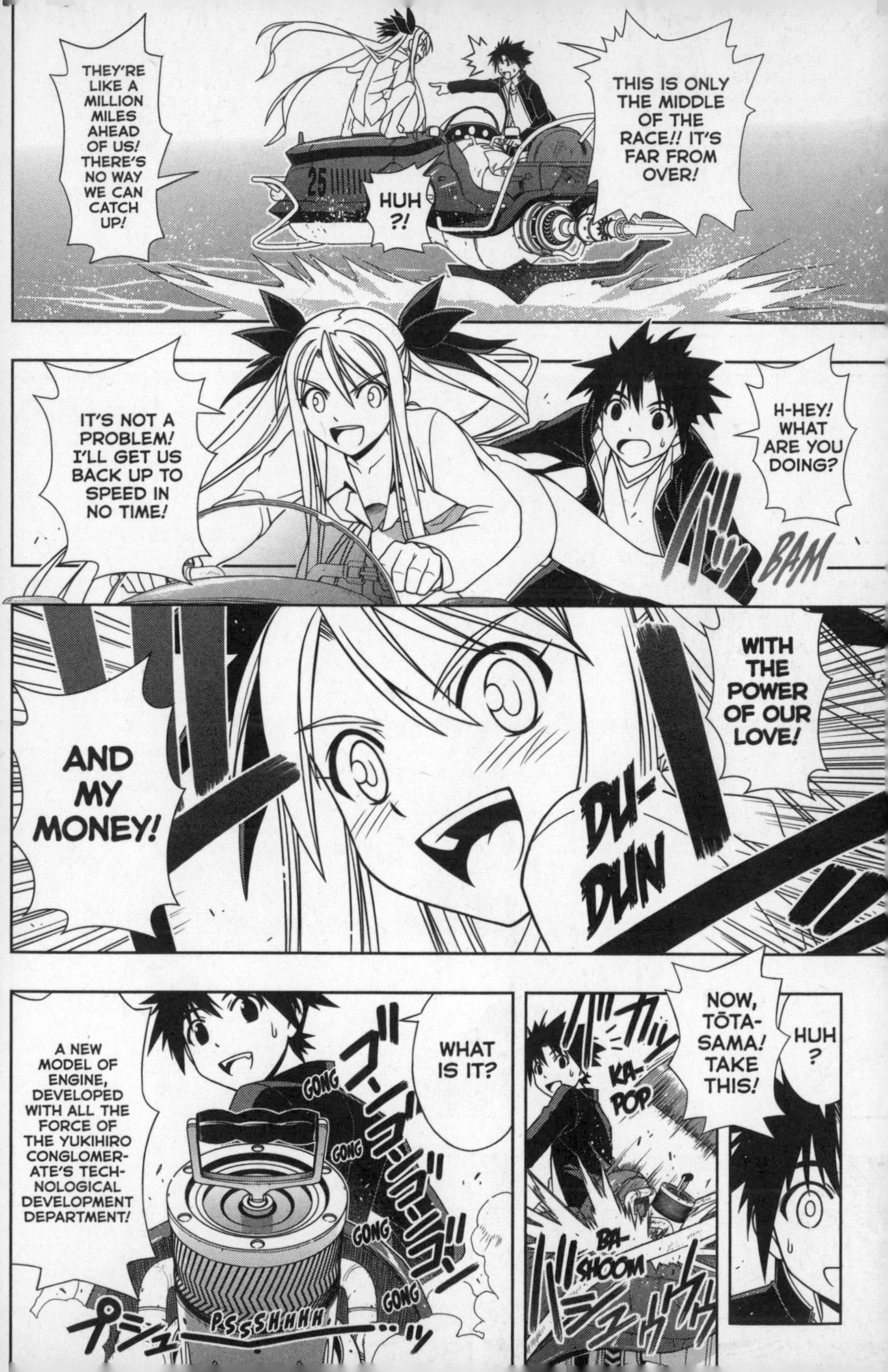
THIS IS ONLY THE MIDDLE OF THE RACE!! IT'S FAR FROM OVER!
HUH ?!
THEY'RE LIKE A MILLION MILES AHEAD OF US! THERE'S NO WAY WE CAN CATCH UP!
H-HEY! WHAT ARE YOU DOING?
BAM
IT'S NOT A PROBLEM! I'LL GET US BACK UP TO SPEED IN NO TIME!
WITH THE POWER OF OUR LOVE!
DU-DUN
AND MY MONEY!
HUH ?
NOW, TŌTA-SAMA! TAKE THIS!
KA-POP
BA-SHOOM
WHAT IS IT?
A NEW MODEL OF ENGINE, DEVELOPED WITH ALL THE FORCE OF THE YUKIHIRO CONGLOMERATE'S TECHNOLOGICAL DEVELOPMENT DEPARTMENT!
GONG
GONG
GONG
GONG
PSSSHHHH

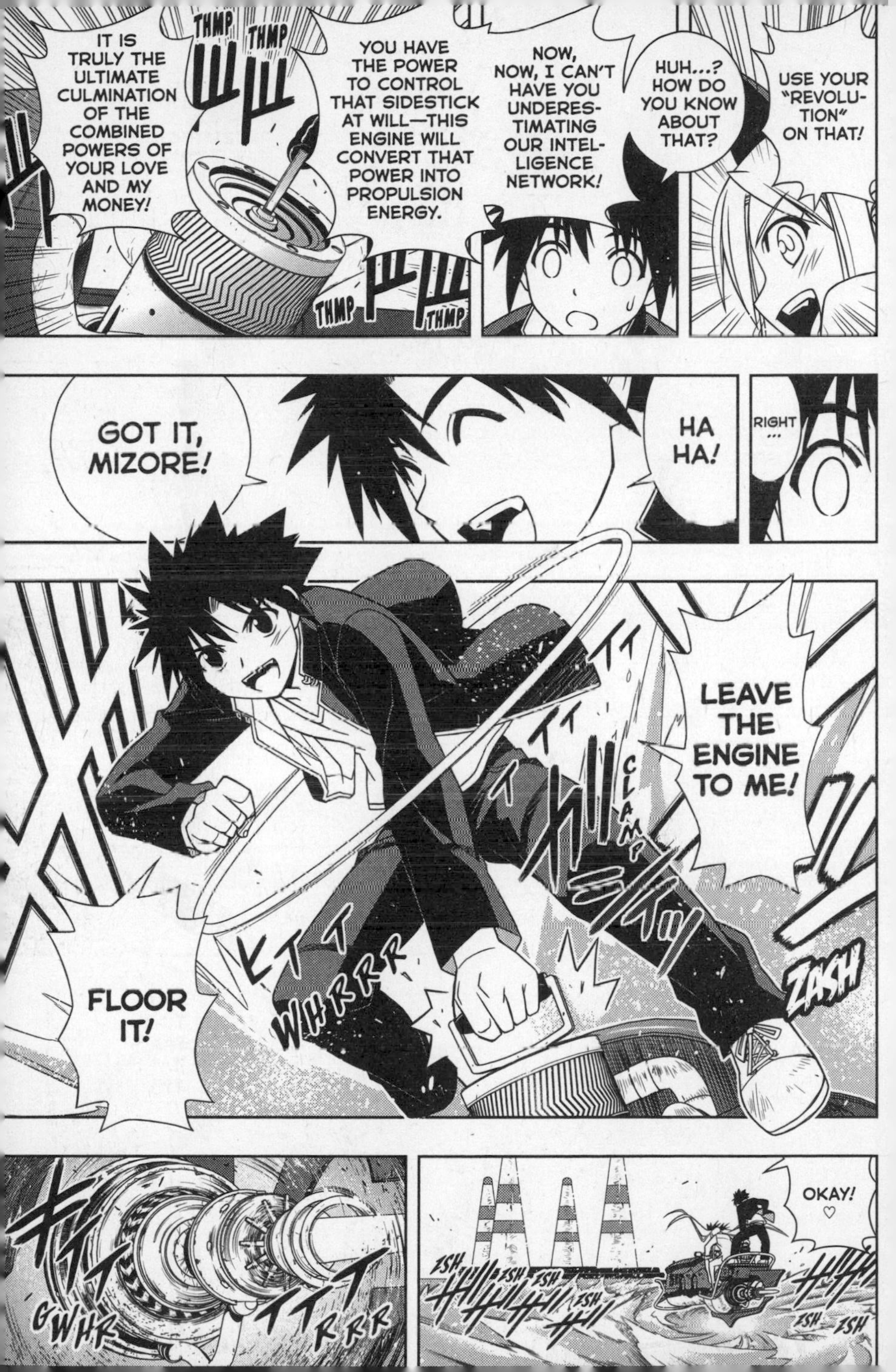
USE YOUR "REVOLUTION" ON THAT!
HUH...? HOW DO YOU KNOW ABOUT THAT?
NOW, NOW, I CAN'T HAVE YOU UNDERESTIMATING OUR INTELLIGENCE NETWORK!
YOU HAVE THE POWER TO CONTROL THAT SIDESTICK AT WILL—THIS ENGINE WILL CONVERT THAT POWER INTO PROPULSION ENERGY.
THMP THMP
IT IS TRULY THE ULTIMATE CULMINATION OF THE COMBINED POWERS OF YOUR LOVE AND MY MONEY!
THMP THMP
RIGHT...
HA HA!
GOT IT, MIZORE!
LEAVE THE ENGINE TO ME!
CLAMP
ZASH
WHRRRR
FLOOR IT!
OKAY! ♡
ZSH ZSH
ZSH ZSH ZSH ZSH
GWHRRRR

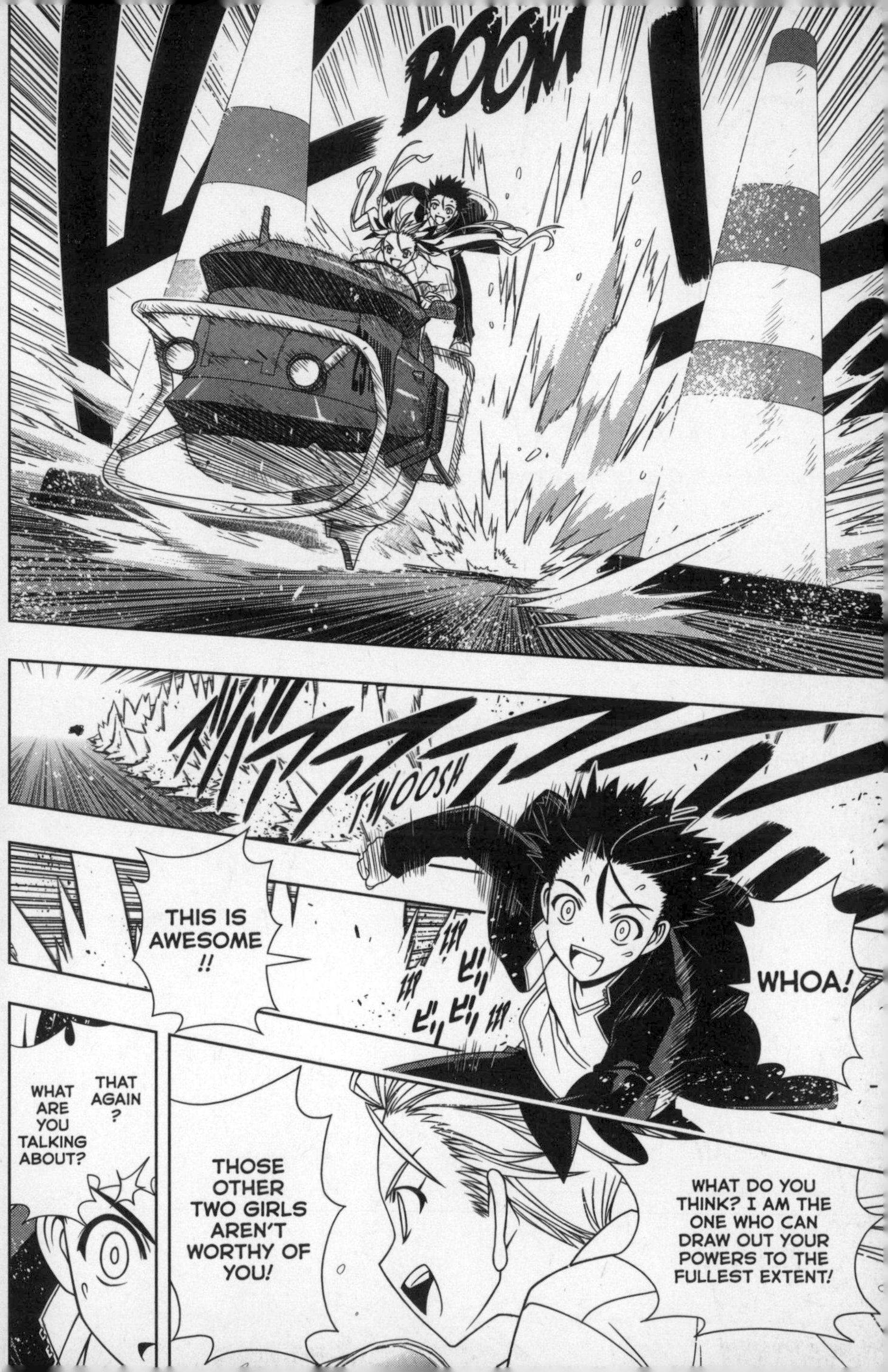
BOOM
FWOOSH
WHOA!
THIS IS AWESOME!!
WHAT DO YOU THINK? I AM THE ONE WHO CAN DRAW OUT YOUR POWERS TO THE FULLEST EXTENT!
THOSE OTHER TWO GIRLS AREN'T WORTHY OF YOU!
THAT AGAIN?
WHAT ARE YOU TALKING ABOUT?

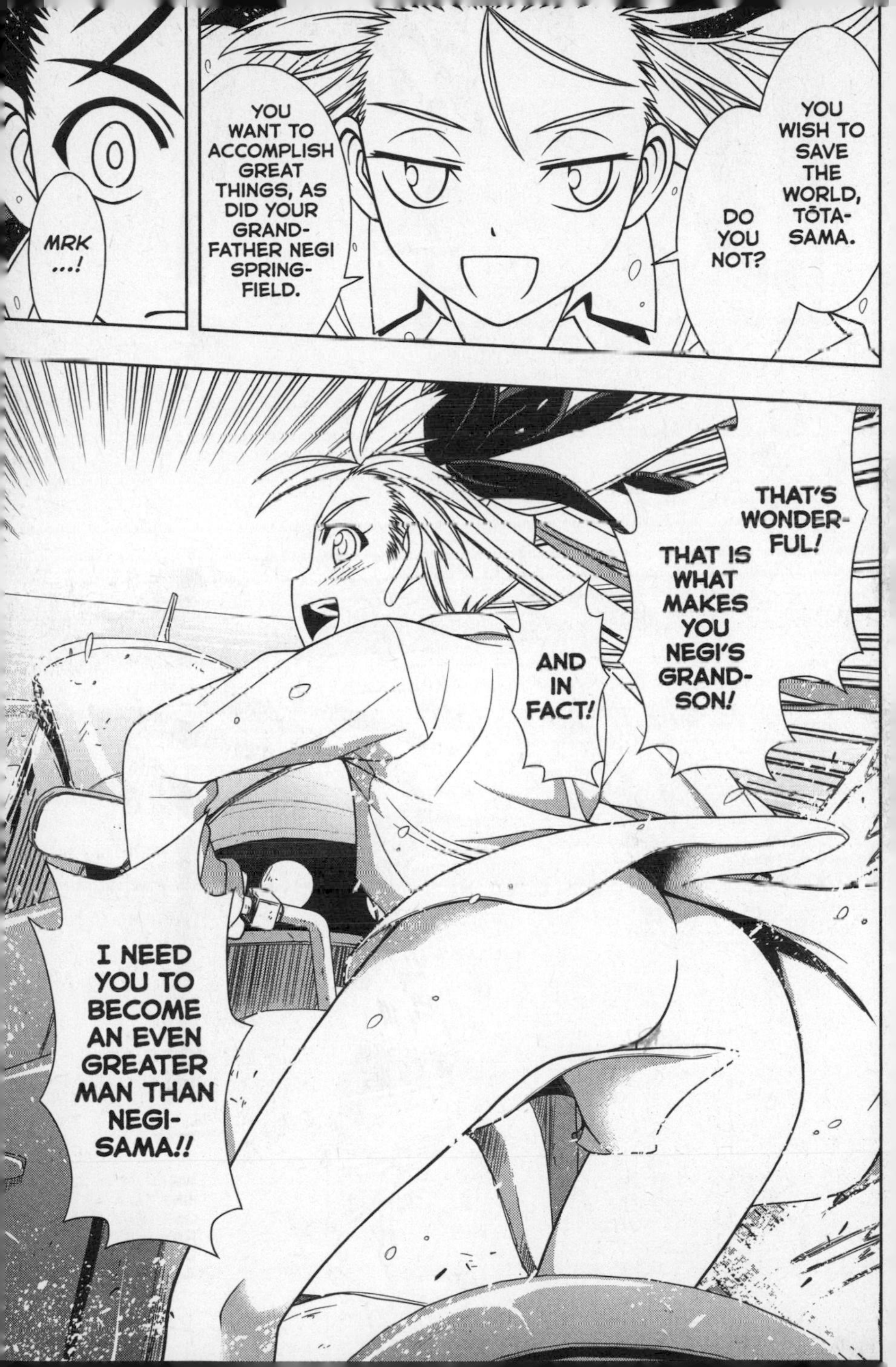
YOU WISH TO SAVE THE WORLD, TŌTA-SAMA.
DO YOU NOT?
YOU WANT TO ACCOMPLISH GREAT THINGS, AS DID YOUR GRANDFATHER NEGI SPRINGFIELD.
MRK ...!
THAT'S WONDERFUL!
THAT IS WHAT MAKES YOU NEGI'S GRANDSON!
AND IN FACT!
I NEED YOU TO BECOME AN EVEN GREATER MAN THAN NEGI-SAMA!!

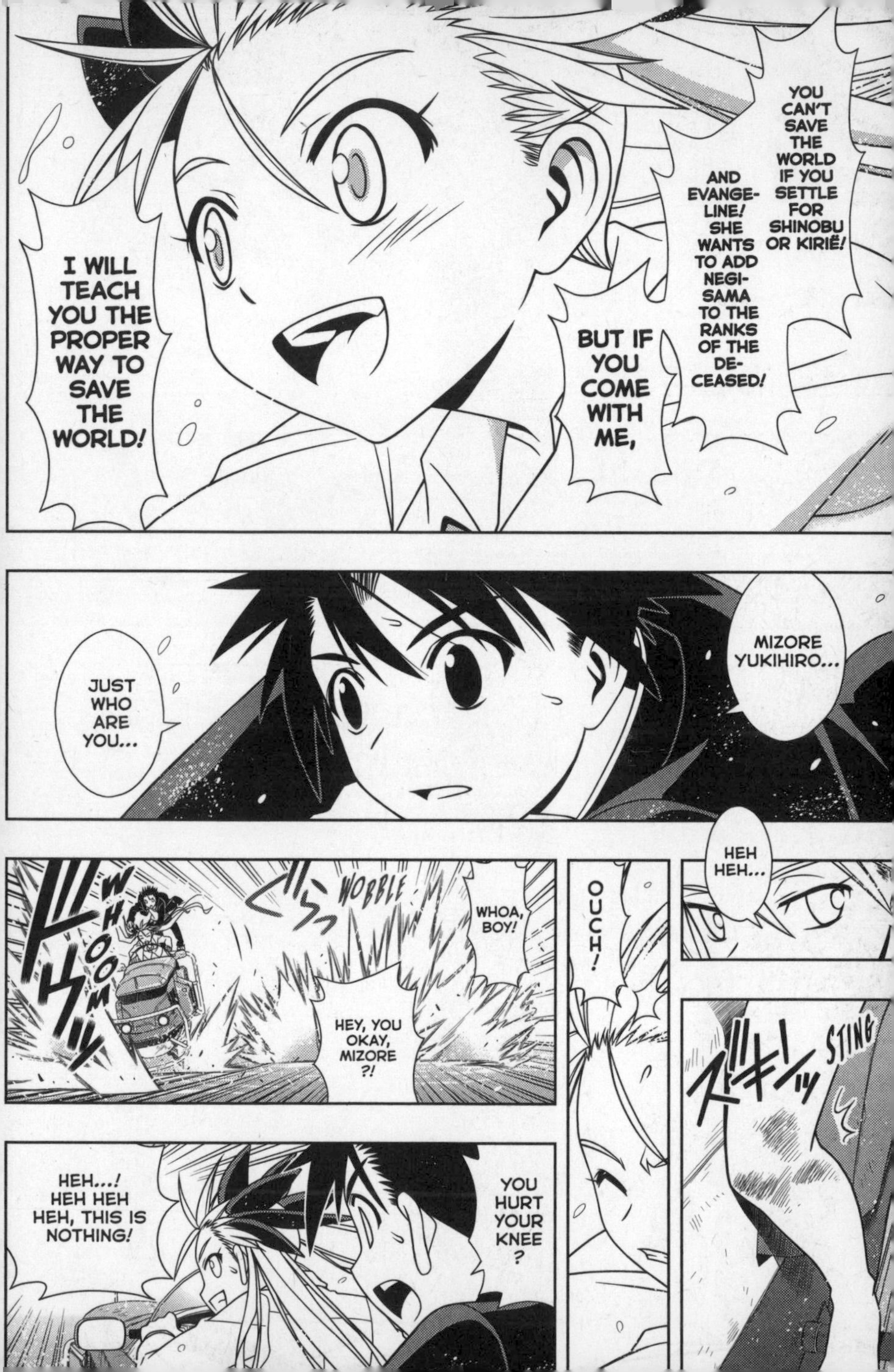
YOU CAN'T SAVE THE WORLD IF YOU SETTLE FOR SHINOBU OR KIRIË!
AND EVANGE-LINE! SHE WANTS TO ADD NEGI-SAMA TO THE RANKS OF THE DE-CEASED!
BUT IF YOU COME WITH ME,
I WILL TEACH YOU THE PROPER WAY TO SAVE THE WORLD!
MIZORE YUKIHIRO...
JUST WHO ARE YOU...
HEH HEH...
STING
OUCH!
WHOA, BOY!
WOBBLE
HEY, YOU OKAY, MIZORE?!
WHOOM
YOU HURT YOUR KNEE?
HEH...! HEH HEH HEH, THIS IS NOTHING!

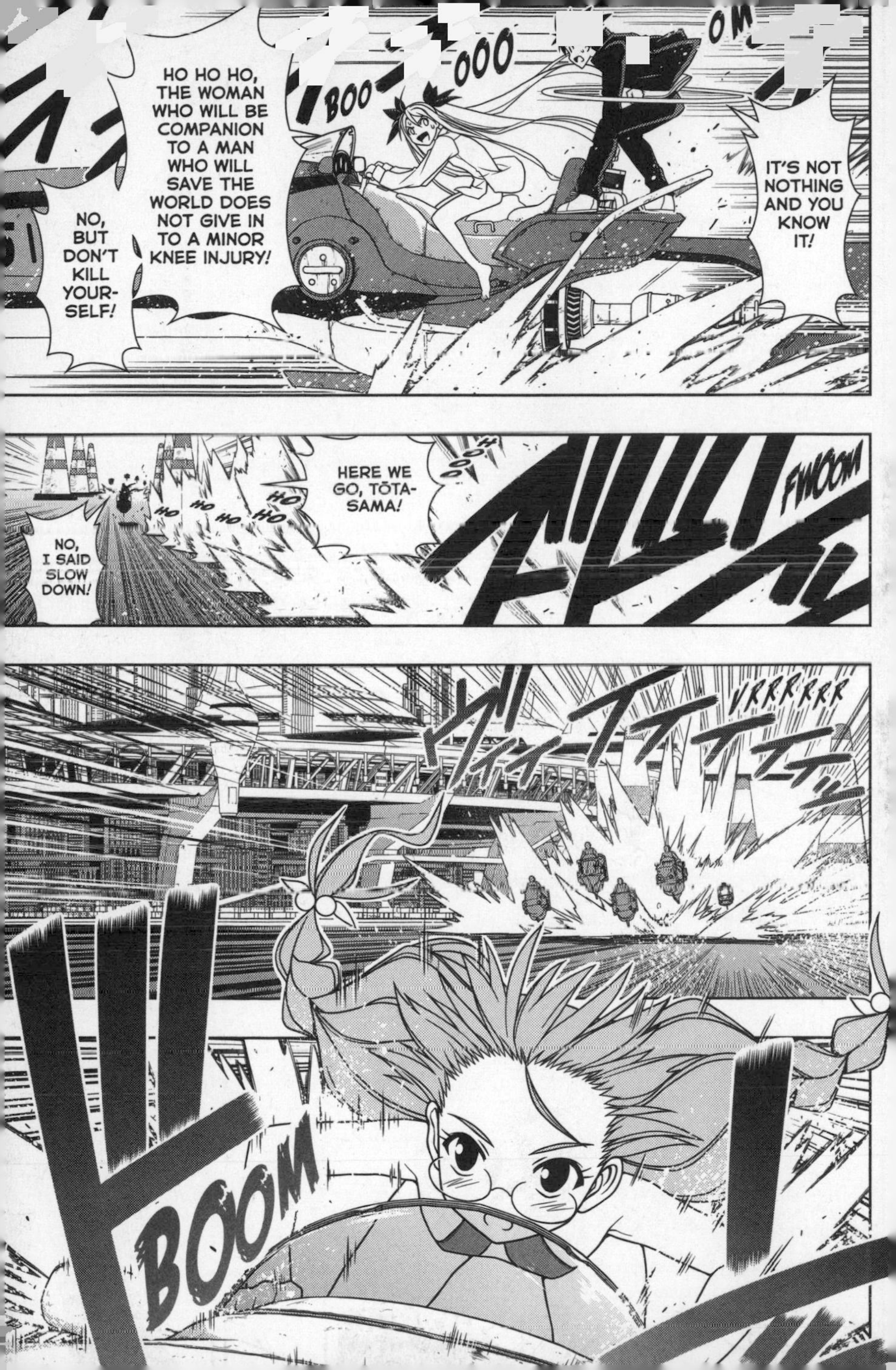
BOO
OOO
OM
IT'S NOT NOTHING AND YOU KNOW IT!
HO HO HO, THE WOMAN WHO WILL BE COMPANION TO A MAN WHO WILL SAVE THE WORLD DOES NOT GIVE IN TO A MINOR KNEE INJURY!
NO, BUT DON'T KILL YOURSELF!
FWOOM
HO HO HO
HERE WE GO, TŌTA-SAMA!
HO HO HO HO HO HO
NO, I SAID SLOW DOWN!
VRRRRRRR
BOOM

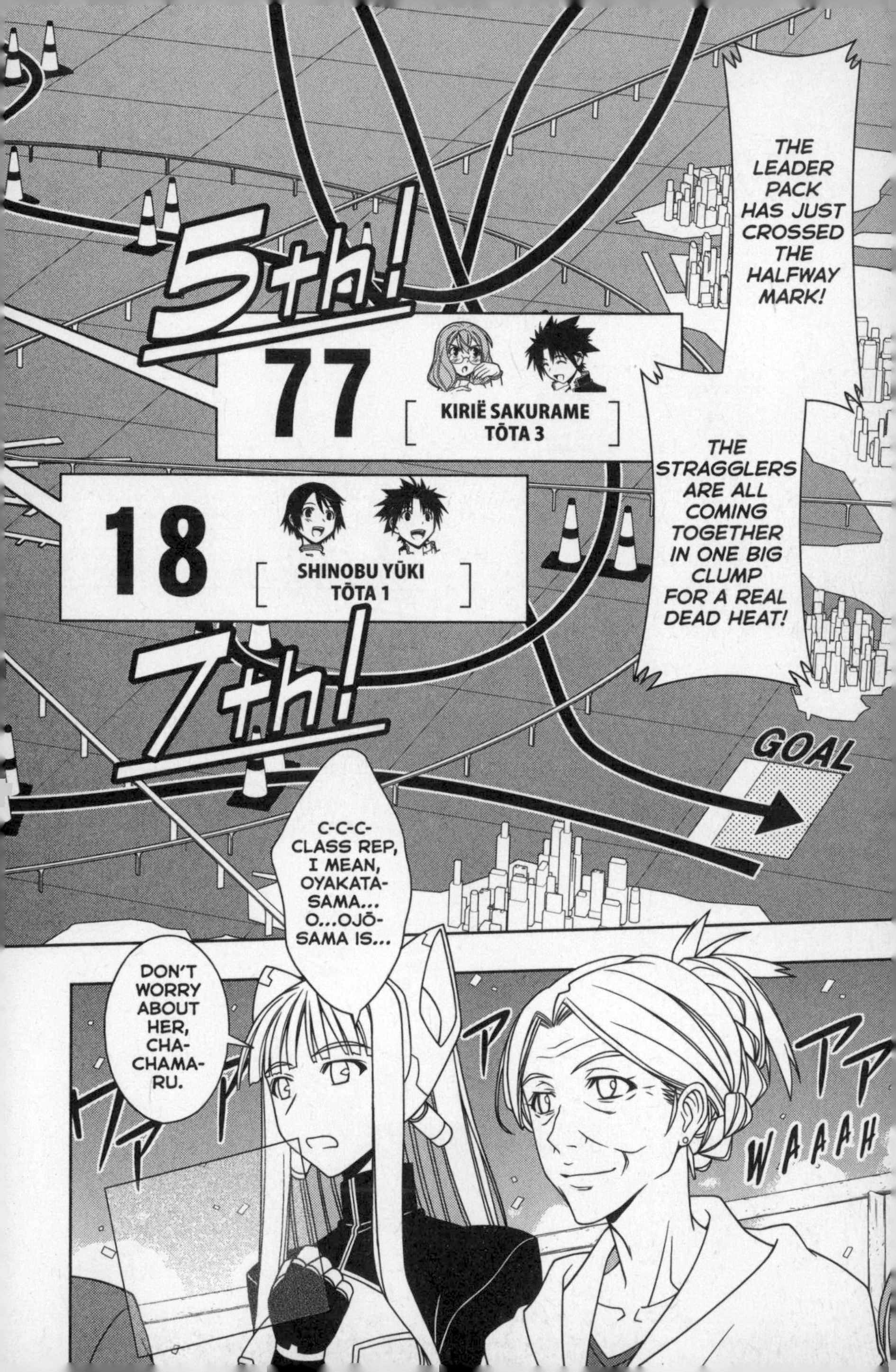
THE LEADER PACK HAS JUST CROSSED THE HALFWAY MARK!
THE STRAGGLERS ARE ALL COMING TOGETHER IN ONE BIG CLUMP FOR A REAL DEAD HEAT!
5th!
77
[KIRIË SAKURAME TŌTA 3]
18
[SHINOBU YŪKI TŌTA 1]
7th!
GOAL
C-C-C-CLASS REP, I MEAN, OYAKATA-SAMA... O...OJŌ-SAMA IS...
WAAAH
DON'T WORRY ABOUT HER, CHA-CHAMA-RU.

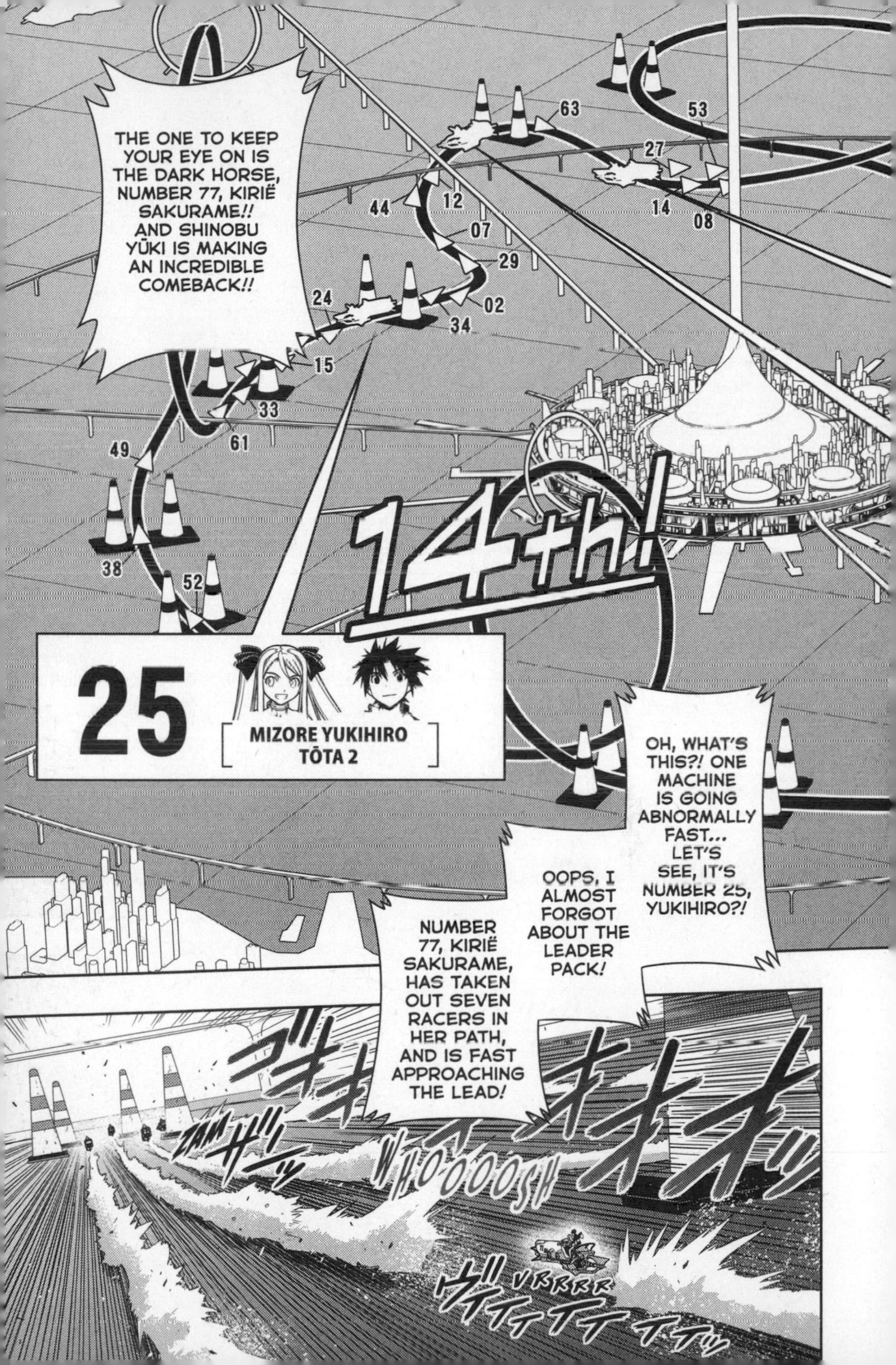

THE ONE TO KEEP YOUR EYE ON IS THE DARK HORSE, NUMBER 77, KIRIË SAKURAME!! AND SHINOBU YŪKI IS MAKING AN INCREDIBLE COMEBACK!!
63 53 27 14 08 44 12 07 29 02 24 34 15 33 61 49 38 52
14th!
25
MIZORE YUKIHIRO TŌTA 2
OH, WHAT'S THIS?! ONE MACHINE IS GOING ABNORMALLY FAST... LET'S SEE, IT'S NUMBER 25, YUKIHIRO?!
OOPS, I ALMOST FORGOT ABOUT THE LEADER PACK!
NUMBER 77, KIRIË SAKURAME, HAS TAKEN OUT SEVEN RACERS IN HER PATH, AND IS FAST APPROACHING THE LEAD!
WHOOOOSH
ZAM
VRRRRR

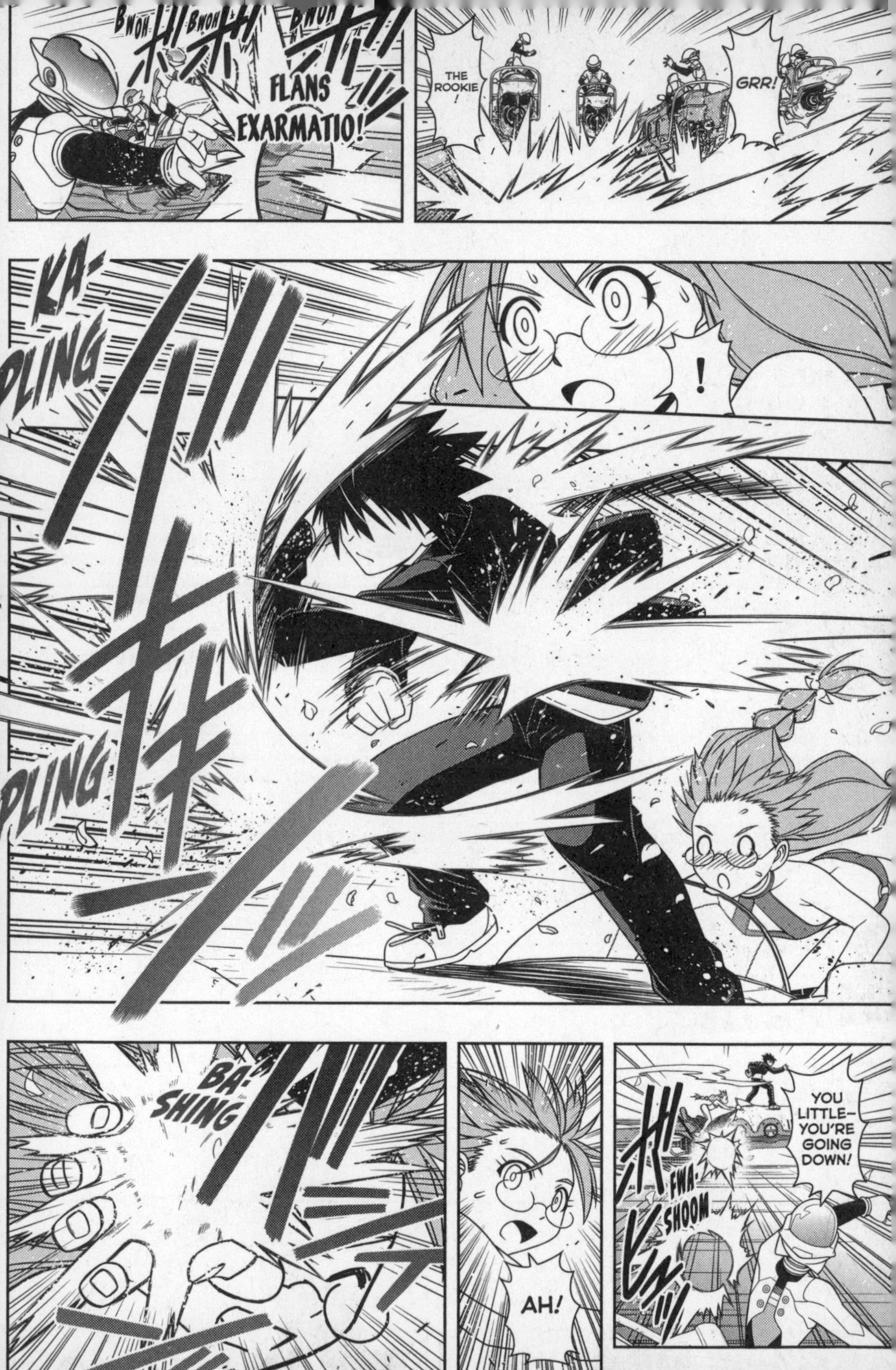
GRR!
THE ROOKIE!
BWOH
BWOH
BWOH
FLANS EXARMATIO!
!
KA-DLING
DLING
YOU LITTLE— YOU'RE GOING DOWN!
FWA-SHOOM
AH!
BA-SHING

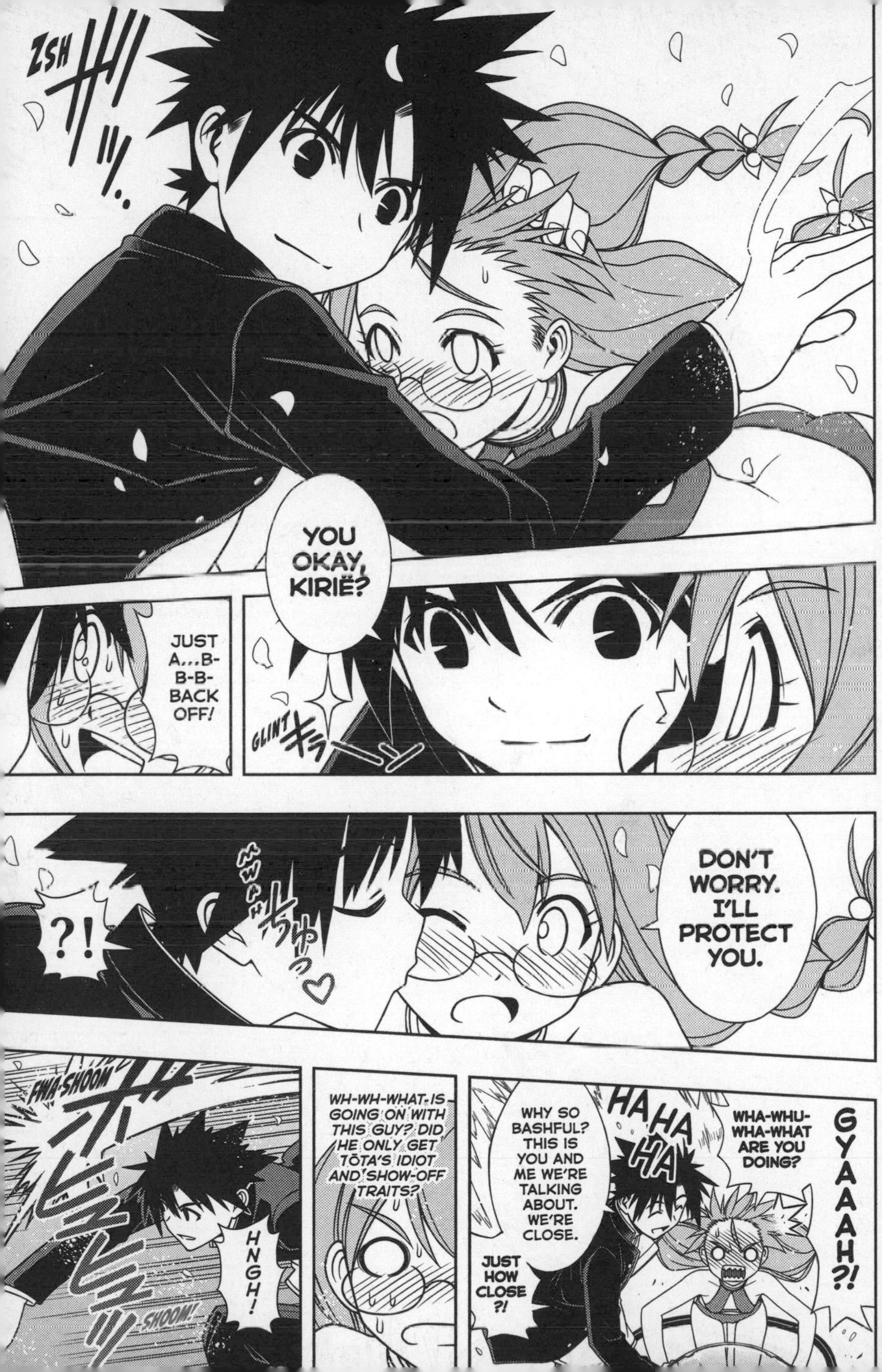
ZSH
YOU OKAY, KIRIË?
GLINT
JUST A...B-B-B-BACK OFF!
DON'T WORRY. I'LL PROTECT YOU.
MWAH
?!
GYAAAH?!
WHA-WHU-WHA-WHAT ARE YOU DOING?
HA HA HA
WHY SO BASHFUL? THIS IS YOU AND ME WE'RE TALKING ABOUT. WE'RE CLOSE.
JUST HOW CLOSE?!
WH-WH-WHAT IS GOING ON WITH THIS GUY? DID HE ONLY GET TŌTA'S IDIOT AND SHOW-OFF TRAITS?
FWA-SHOOM
HNGH!
SHOOM!

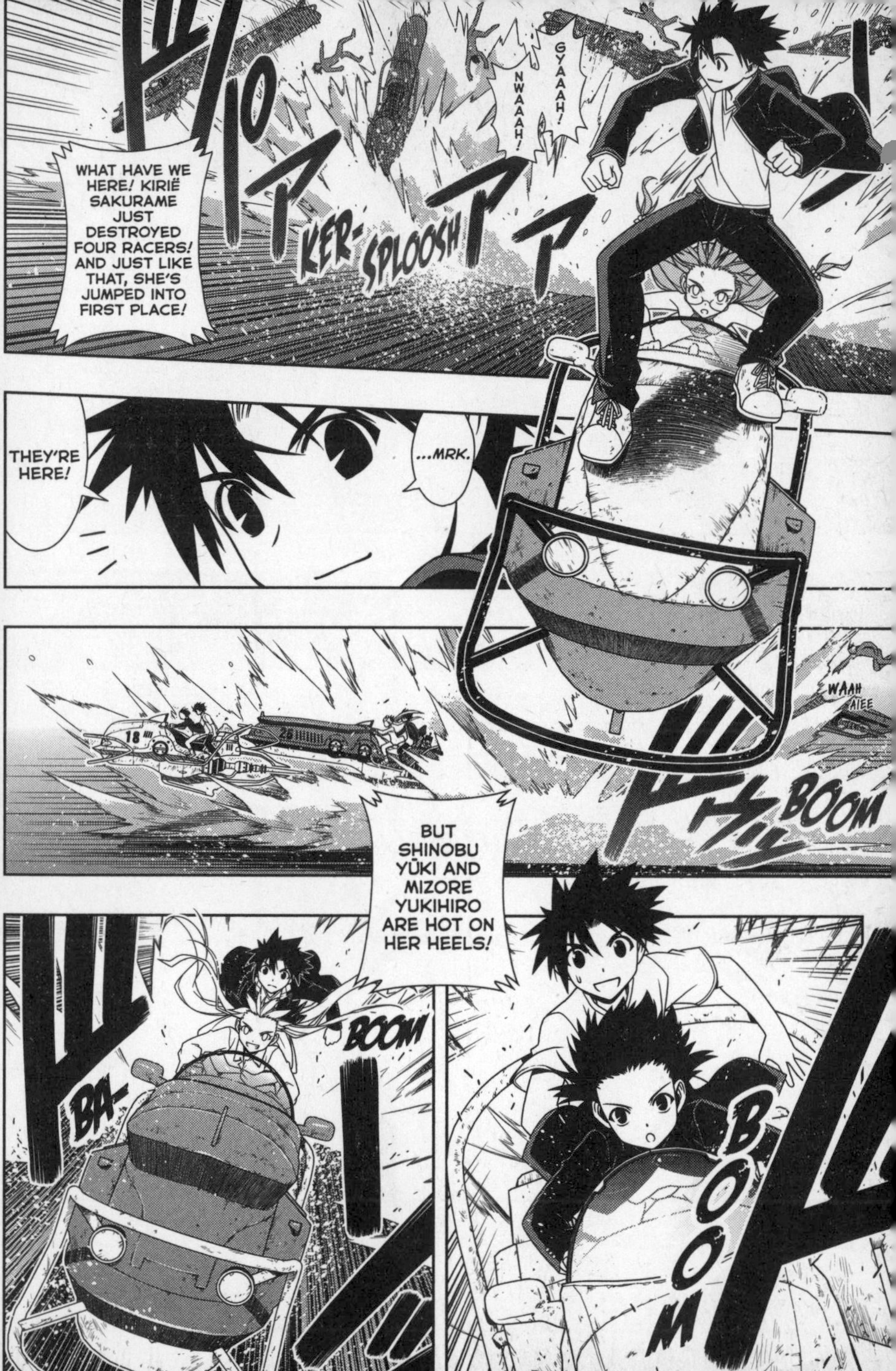
GYAAAH!
NWAAAH!
KER-SPLOOSH
WHAT HAVE WE HERE! KIRIË SAKURAME JUST DESTROYED FOUR RACERS! AND JUST LIKE THAT, SHE'S JUMPED INTO FIRST PLACE!
...MRK.
THEY'RE HERE!
WAAH
AIEE
BOOM
BUT SHINOBU YŪKI AND MIZORE YUKIHIRO ARE HOT ON HER HEELS!
BOOOOM
BOOM
BA-

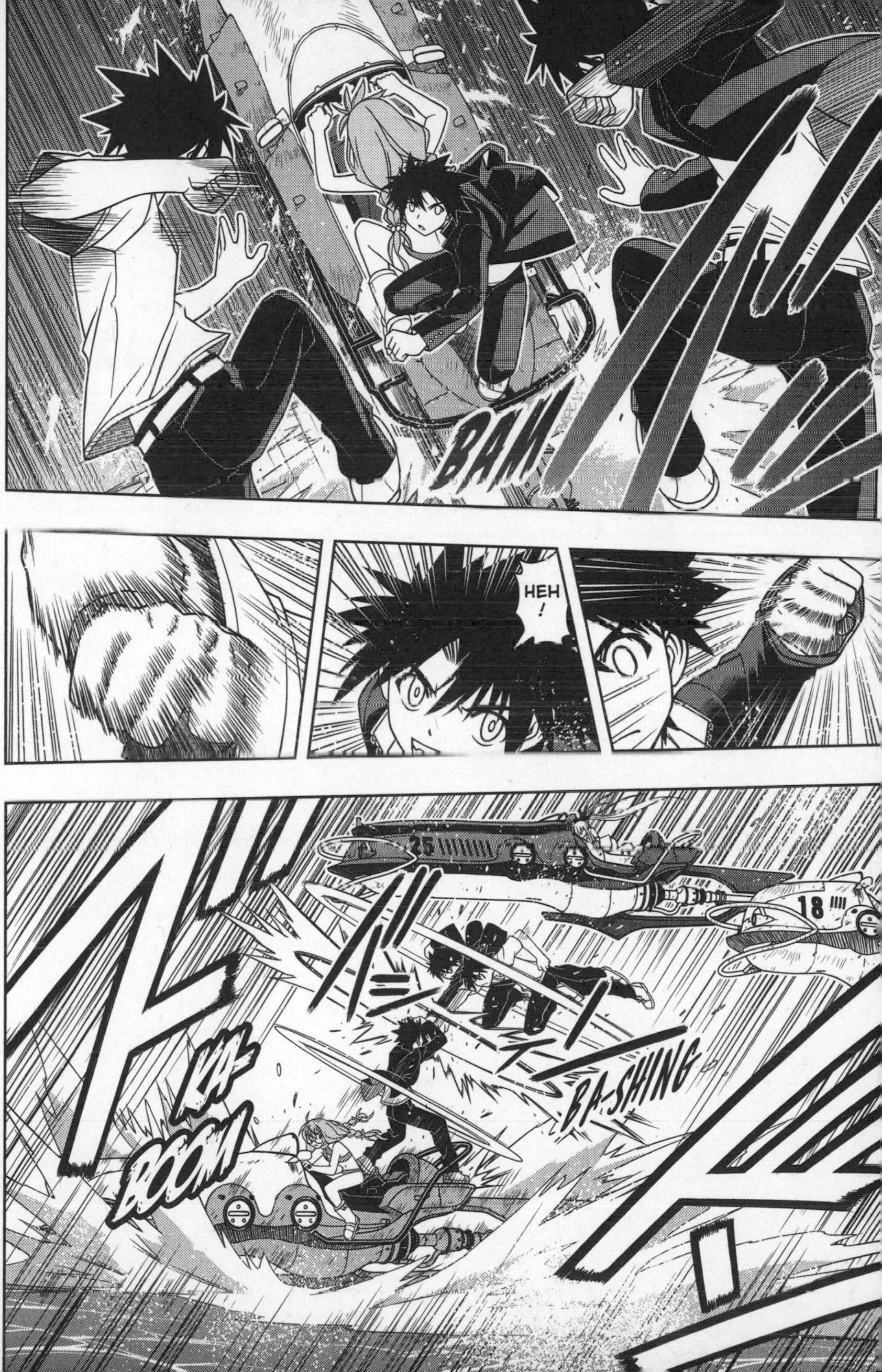
BAM
HEH
!
BA-SHING
KA
BOOM

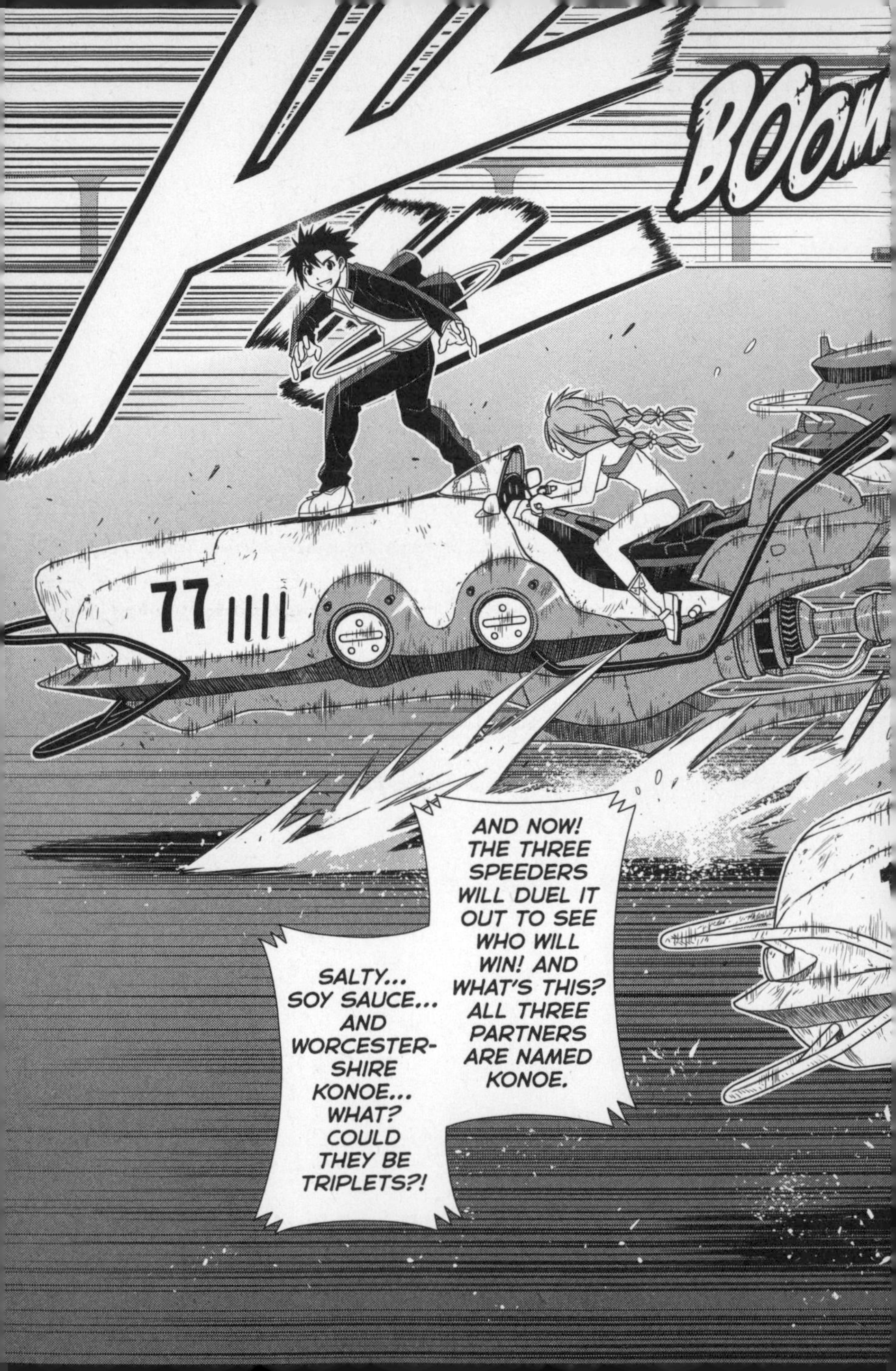
BOOM
AND NOW! THE THREE SPEEDERS WILL DUEL IT OUT TO SEE WHO WILL WIN! AND WHAT'S THIS? ALL THREE PARTNERS ARE NAMED KONOE.
SALTY... SOY SAUCE... AND WORCESTER-SHIRE KONOE... WHAT? COULD THEY BE TRIPLETS?!

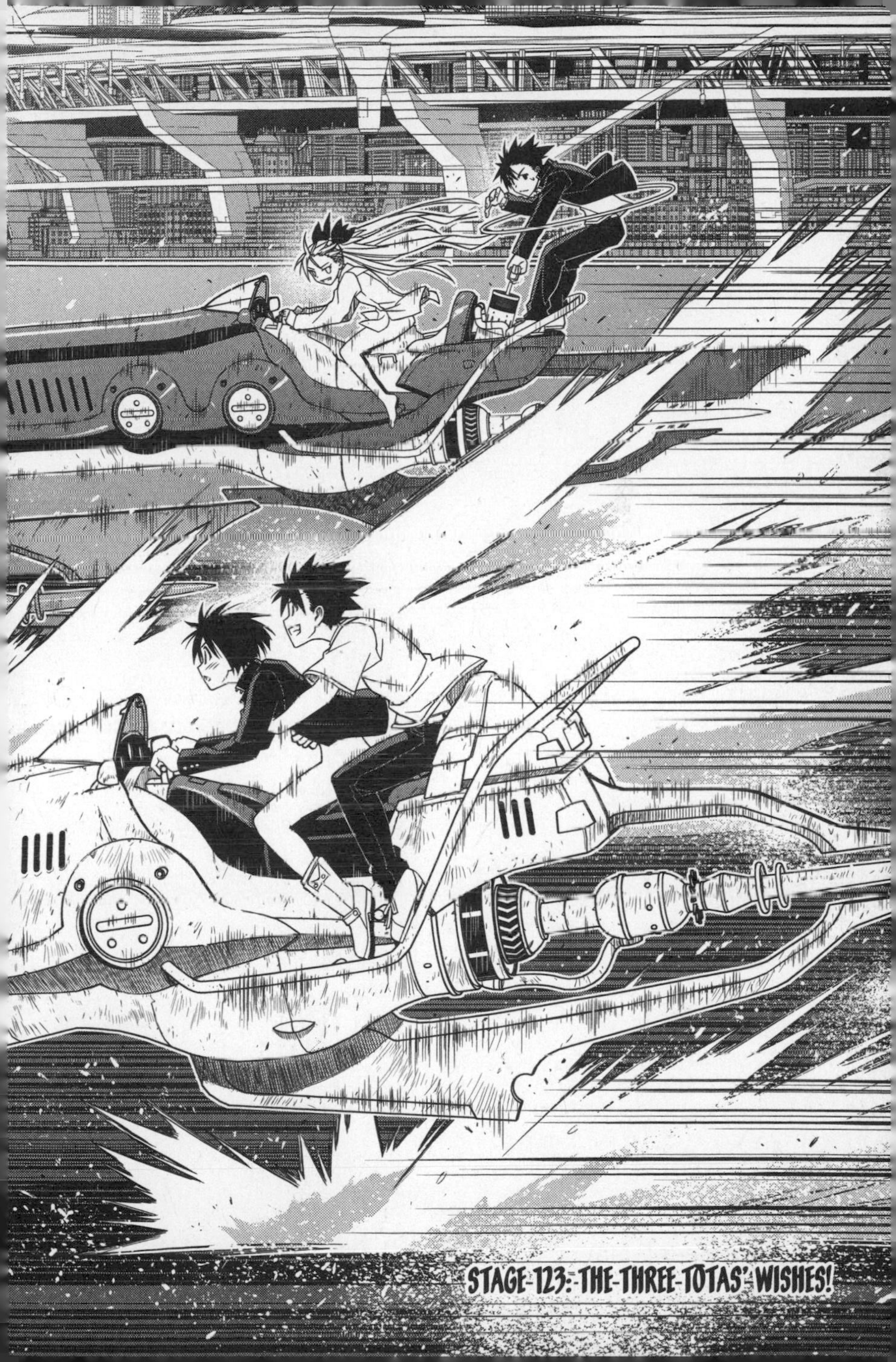
STAGE 123: THE THREE TOTAS' WISHES!

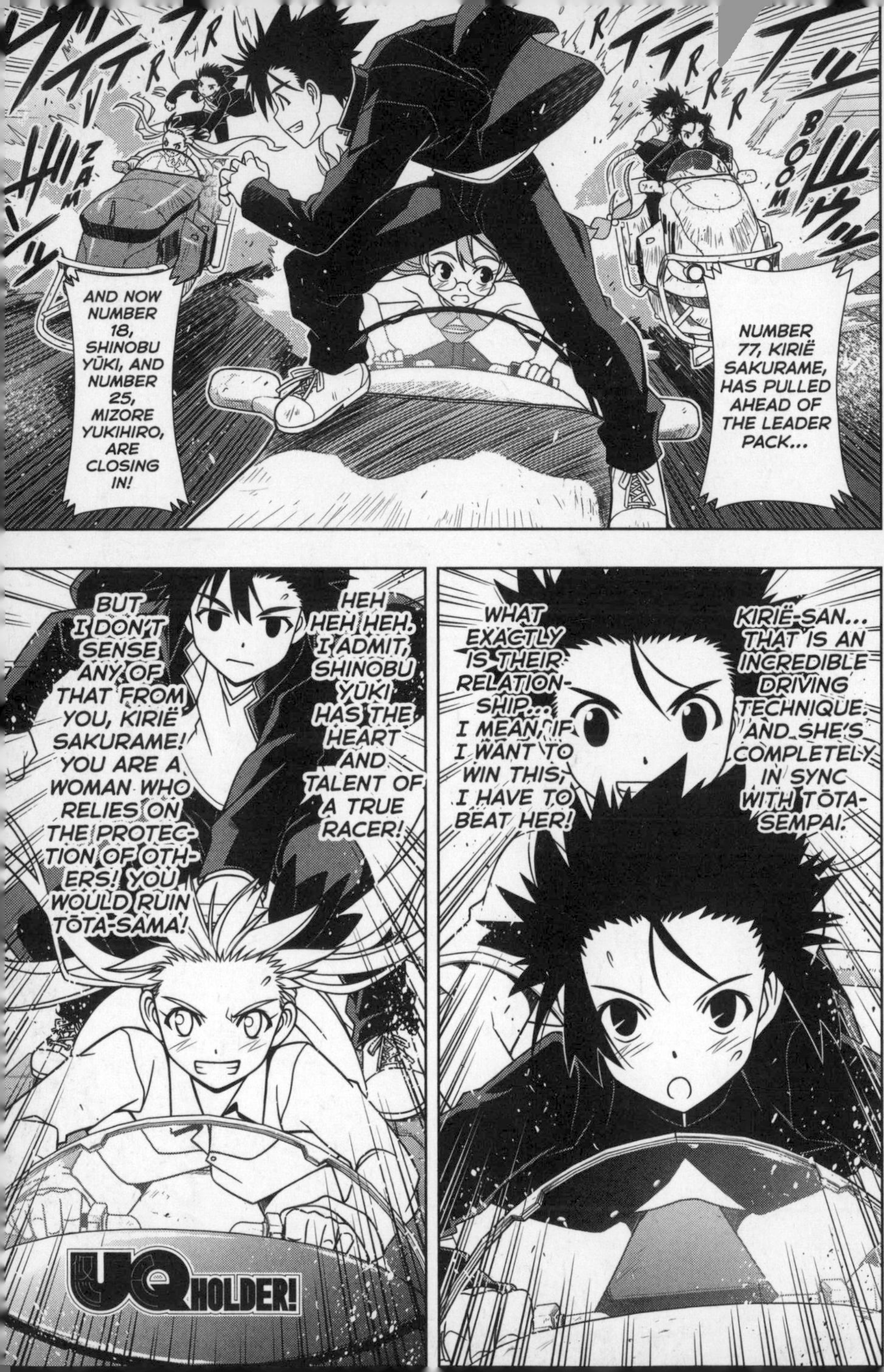
BOOM
NUMBER 77, KIRIË SAKURAME, HAS PULLED AHEAD OF THE LEADER PACK...
ZAM
AND NOW NUMBER 18, SHINOBU YŪKI, AND NUMBER 25, MIZORE YUKIHIRO, ARE CLOSING IN!
KIRIË-SAN... THAT IS AN INCREDIBLE DRIVING TECHNIQUE, AND SHE'S COMPLETELY IN SYNC WITH TŌTA-SEMPAI.
WHAT EXACTLY IS THEIR RELATIONSHIP...? I MEAN, IF I WANT TO WIN THIS, I HAVE TO BEAT HER!
HEH HEH HEH. I ADMIT, SHINOBU YŪKI HAS THE HEART AND TALENT OF A TRUE RACER!
BUT I DON'T SENSE ANY OF THAT FROM YOU, KIRIË SAKURAME! YOU ARE A WOMAN WHO RELIES ON THE PROTECTION OF OTHERS! YOU WOULD RUIN TŌTA-SAMA!
UQ HOLDER!

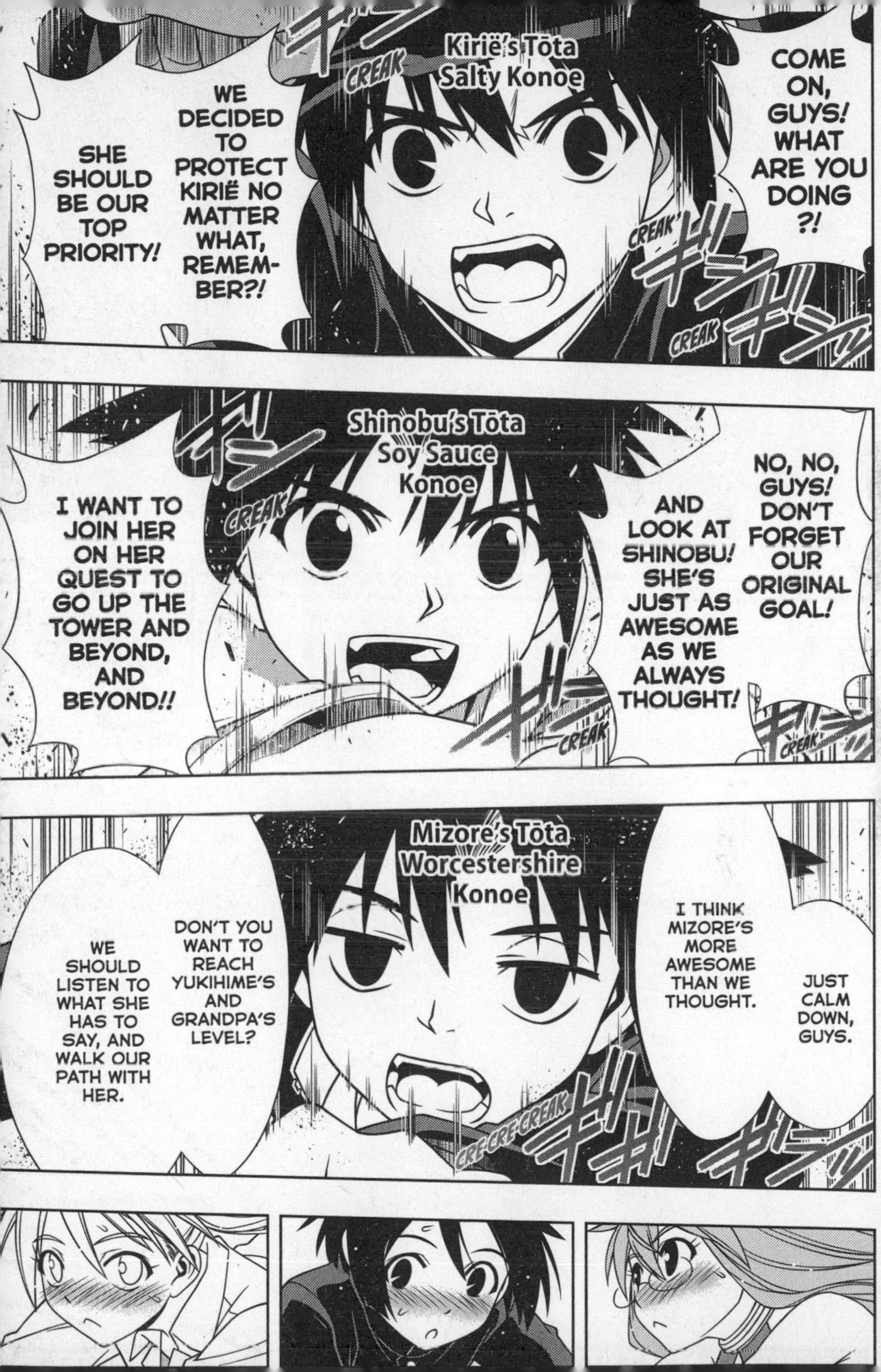
COME ON, GUYS! WHAT ARE YOU DOING?!
CREAK
Kiriё's Tōta Salty Konoe
CREAK
WE DECIDED TO PROTECT KIRIË NO MATTER WHAT, REMEMBER?!
SHE SHOULD BE OUR TOP PRIORITY!
CREAK
NO, NO, GUYS! DON'T FORGET OUR ORIGINAL GOAL!
CREAK
AND LOOK AT SHINOBU! SHE'S JUST AS AWESOME AS WE ALWAYS THOUGHT!
CREAK
Shinobu's Tōta Soy Sauce Konoe
CREAK
I WANT TO JOIN HER ON HER QUEST TO GO UP THE TOWER AND BEYOND, AND BEYOND!!
JUST CALM DOWN, GUYS.
I THINK MIZORE'S MORE AWESOME THAN WE THOUGHT.
CRE-CRE-CREAK
Mizore's Tōta Worcestershire Konoe
DON'T YOU WANT TO REACH YUKIHIME'S AND GRANDPA'S LEVEL?
WE SHOULD LISTEN TO WHAT SHE HAS TO SAY, AND WALK OUR PATH WITH HER.

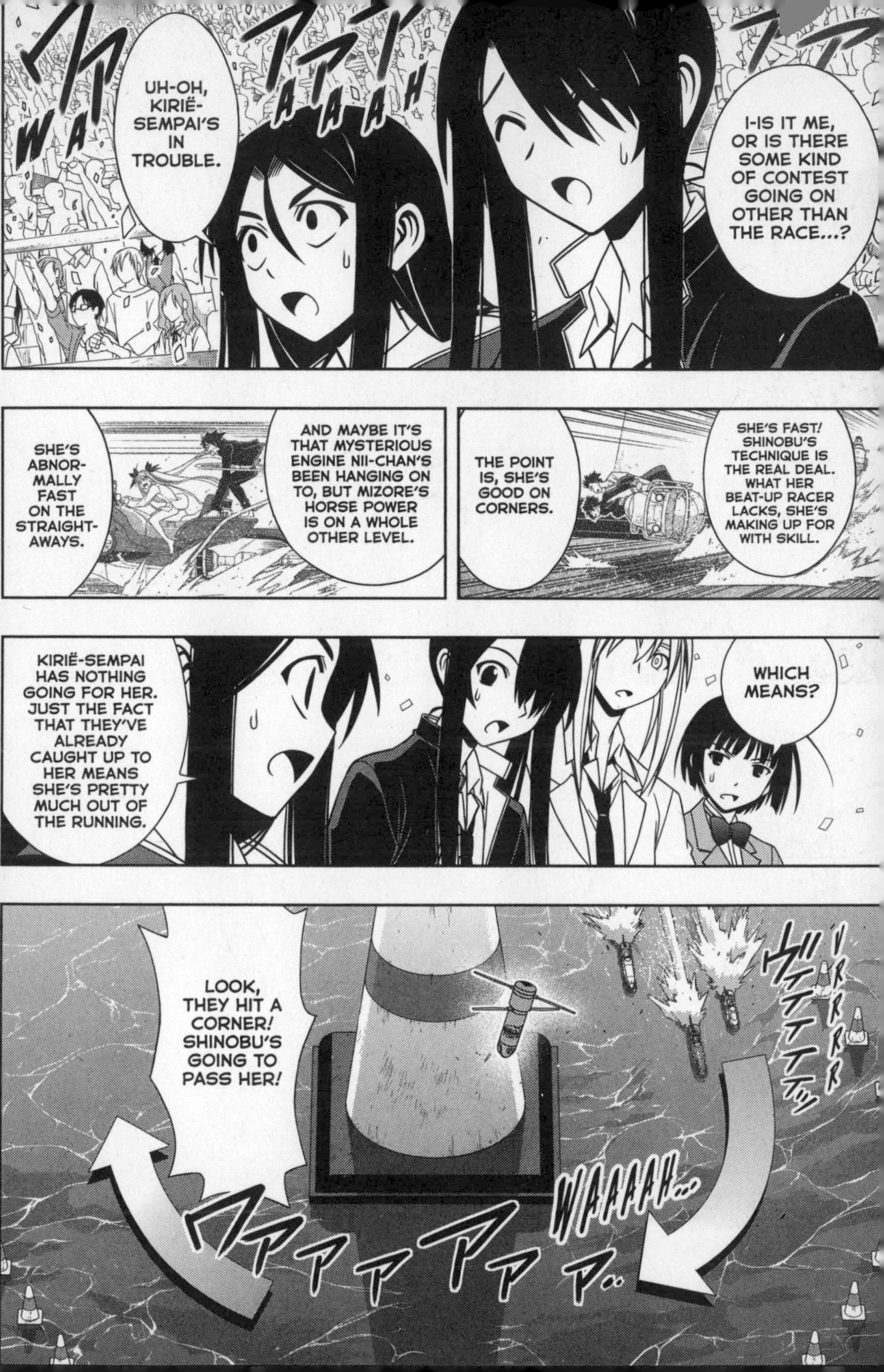
WAAAAH
I-IS IT ME, OR IS THERE SOME KIND OF CONTEST GOING ON OTHER THAN THE RACE...?
UH-OH, KIRIË-SEMPAI'S IN TROUBLE.
SHE'S FAST! SHINOBU'S TECHNIQUE IS THE REAL DEAL. WHAT HER BEAT-UP RACER LACKS, SHE'S MAKING UP FOR WITH SKILL.
THE POINT IS, SHE'S GOOD ON CORNERS.
AND MAYBE IT'S THAT MYSTERIOUS ENGINE NII-CHAN'S BEEN HANGING ON TO, BUT MIZORE'S HORSE POWER IS ON A WHOLE OTHER LEVEL.
SHE'S ABNORMALLY FAST ON THE STRAIGHTAWAYS.
WHICH MEANS?
KIRIË-SEMPAI HAS NOTHING GOING FOR HER. JUST THE FACT THAT THEY'VE ALREADY CAUGHT UP TO HER MEANS SHE'S PRETTY MUCH OUT OF THE RUNNING.
VRRRRR
LOOK, THEY HIT A CORNER! SHINOBU'S GOING TO PASS HER!
WAAAAH...

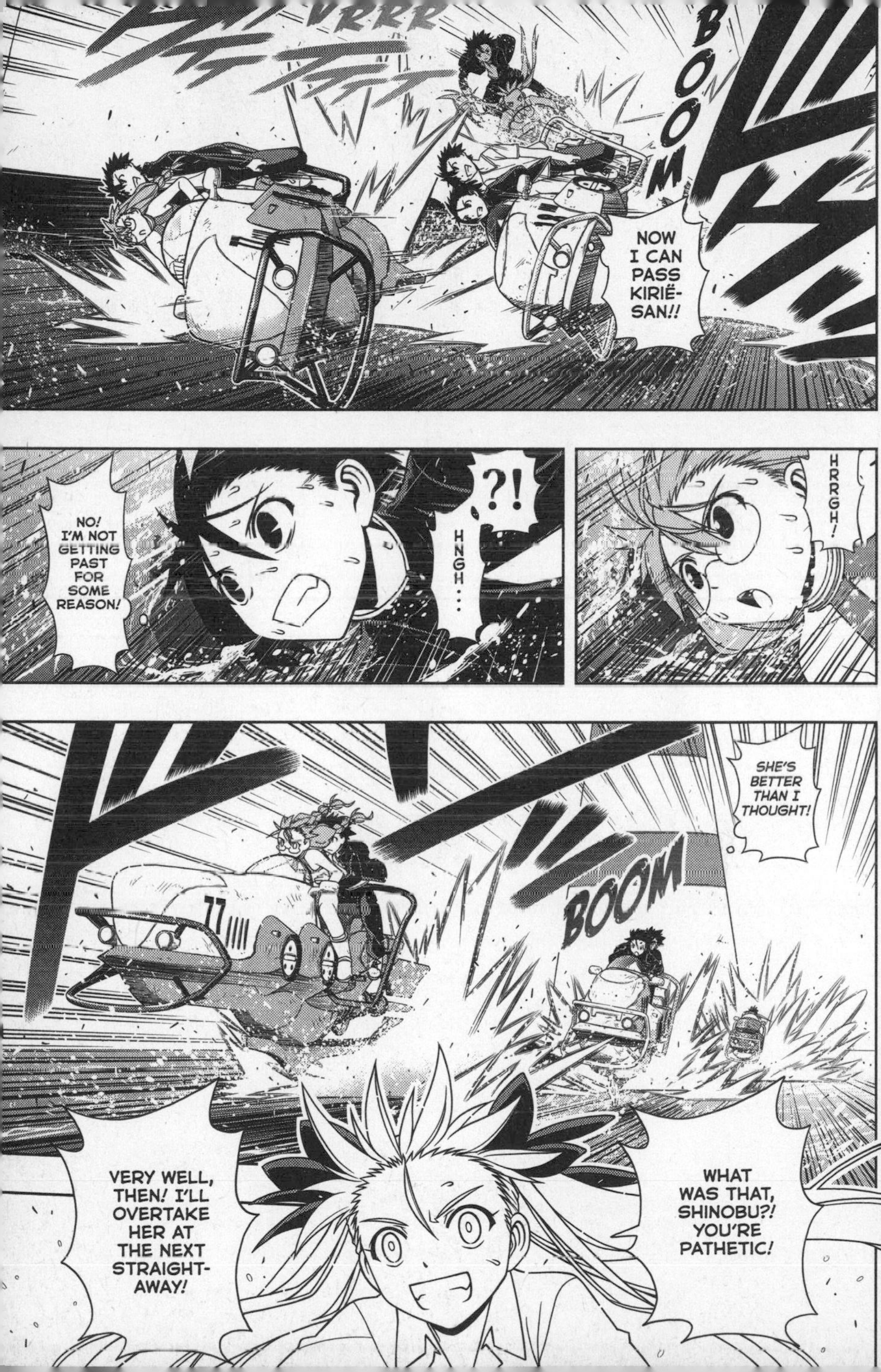
BOOM
NOW I CAN PASS KIRIË-SAN!!
VRRR
HRRGH!
?!
HNGH...
NO! I'M NOT GETTING PAST FOR SOME REASON!
SHE'S BETTER THAN I THOUGHT!
BOOM
WHAT WAS THAT, SHINOBU?! YOU'RE PATHETIC!
VERY WELL, THEN! I'LL OVERTAKE HER AT THE NEXT STRAIGHT-AWAY!

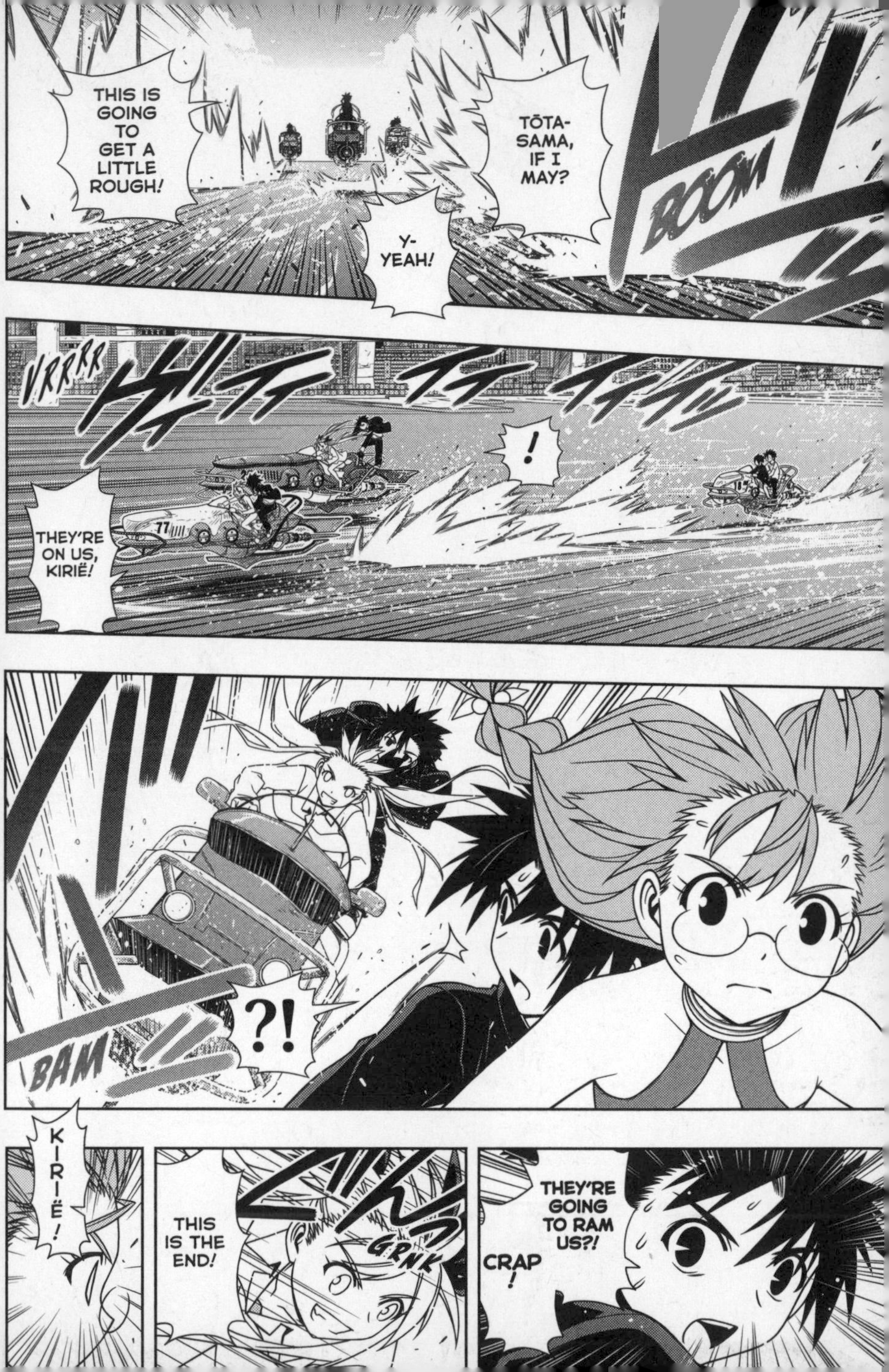
BOOM
TŌTA-SAMA, IF I MAY?
THIS IS GOING TO GET A LITTLE ROUGH!
Y-YEAH!
!
VRRRR
THEY'RE ON US, KIRIË!
?!
BAM
THEY'RE GOING TO RAM US?!
CRAP!
GRNK
THIS IS THE END!
KIRIË!

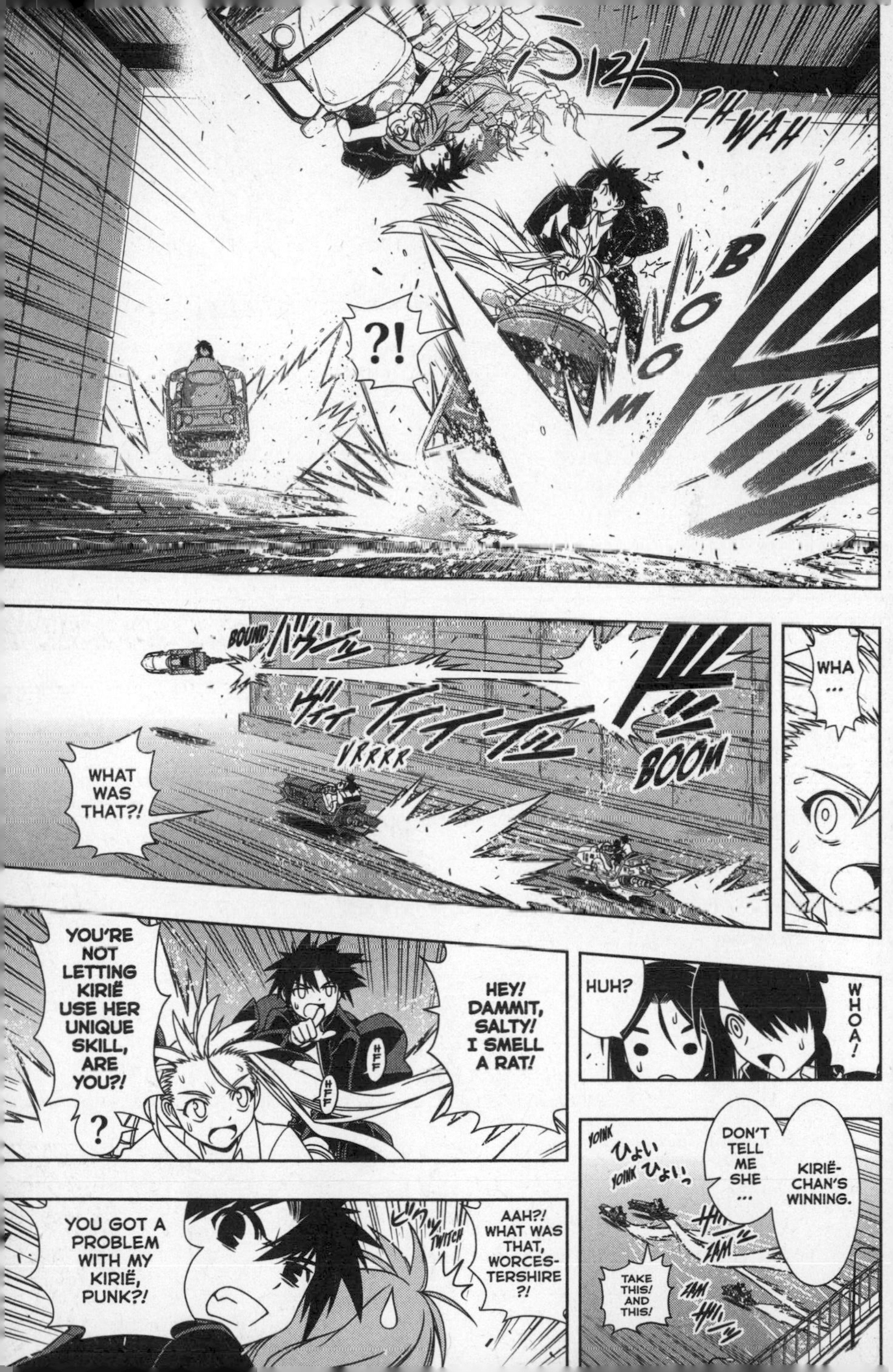
ふわっ
PHWAH
?!
BOOM
WHA ...
BOUND
VRRRR
BOOM
WHAT WAS THAT?!
WHOA!
HUH?
KIRIË-CHAN'S WINNING.
DON'T TELL ME SHE ...
YOINK ひょい
YOINK ひょいっ
ZAM
TAKE THIS! AND THIS!
ZAM
HEY! DAMMIT, SALTY! I SMELL A RAT!
HFF
HFF
YOU'RE NOT LETTING KIRIË USE HER UNIQUE SKILL, ARE YOU?!
?
AAH?! WHAT WAS THAT, WORCES-TERSHIRE ?!
TWITCH
YOU GOT A PROBLEM WITH MY KIRIË, PUNK?!

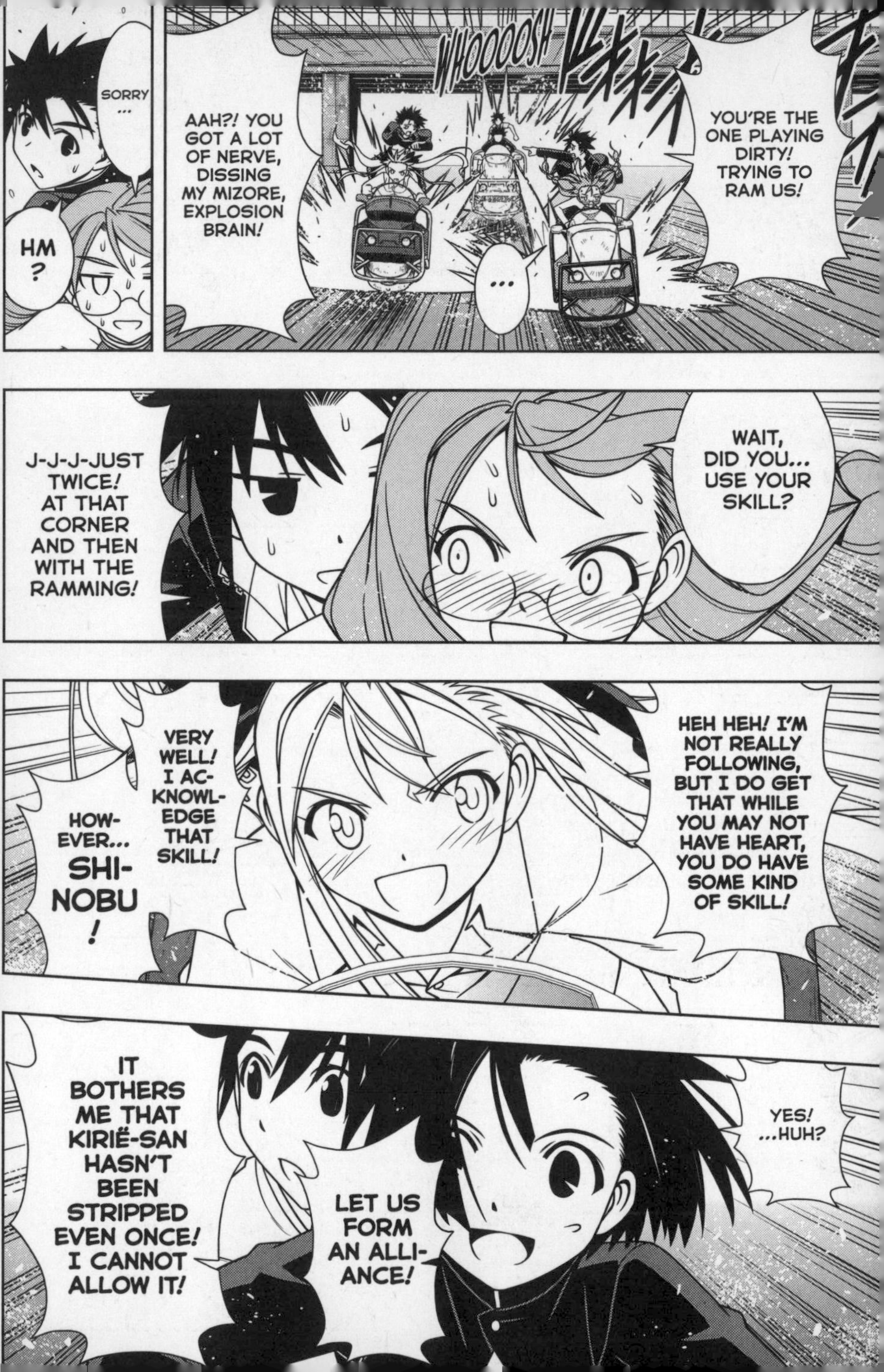
WHOOOOSH
YOU'RE THE ONE PLAYING DIRTY! TRYING TO RAM US!
AAH?! YOU GOT A LOT OF NERVE, DISSING MY MIZORE, EXPLOSION BRAIN!
...
SORRY ...
HM ?
WAIT, DID YOU... USE YOUR SKILL?
J-J-J-JUST TWICE! AT THAT CORNER AND THEN WITH THE RAMMING!
HEH HEH! I'M NOT REALLY FOLLOWING, BUT I DO GET THAT WHILE YOU MAY NOT HAVE HEART, YOU DO HAVE SOME KIND OF SKILL!
VERY WELL! I ACKNOWLEDGE THAT SKILL!
HOWEVER... SHINOBU!
IT BOTHERS ME THAT KIRIË-SAN HASN'T BEEN STRIPPED EVEN ONCE! I CANNOT ALLOW IT!
LET US FORM AN ALLIANCE!
YES! ...HUH?

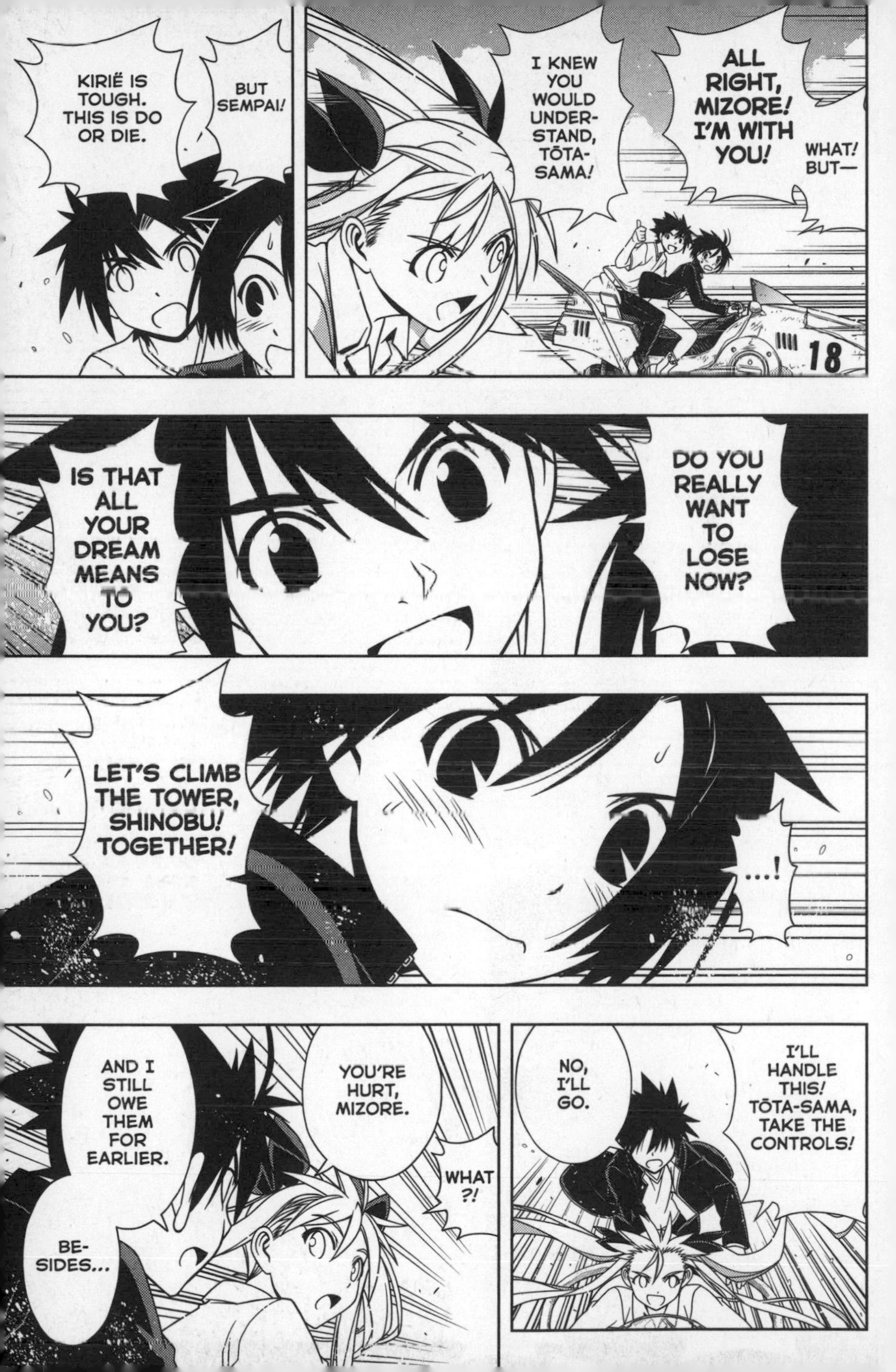
ALL RIGHT, MIZORE! I'M WITH YOU!
WHAT! BUT—
I KNEW YOU WOULD UNDERSTAND, TŌTA-SAMA!
18
BUT SEMPAI!
KIRIË IS TOUGH. THIS IS DO OR DIE.
DO YOU REALLY WANT TO LOSE NOW?
IS THAT ALL YOUR DREAM MEANS TO YOU?
LET'S CLIMB THE TOWER, SHINOBU! TOGETHER!
...!
I'LL HANDLE THIS! TŌTA-SAMA, TAKE THE CONTROLS!
NO, I'LL GO.
WHAT?!
YOU'RE HURT, MIZORE.
AND I STILL OWE THEM FOR EARLIER.
BE-SIDES...

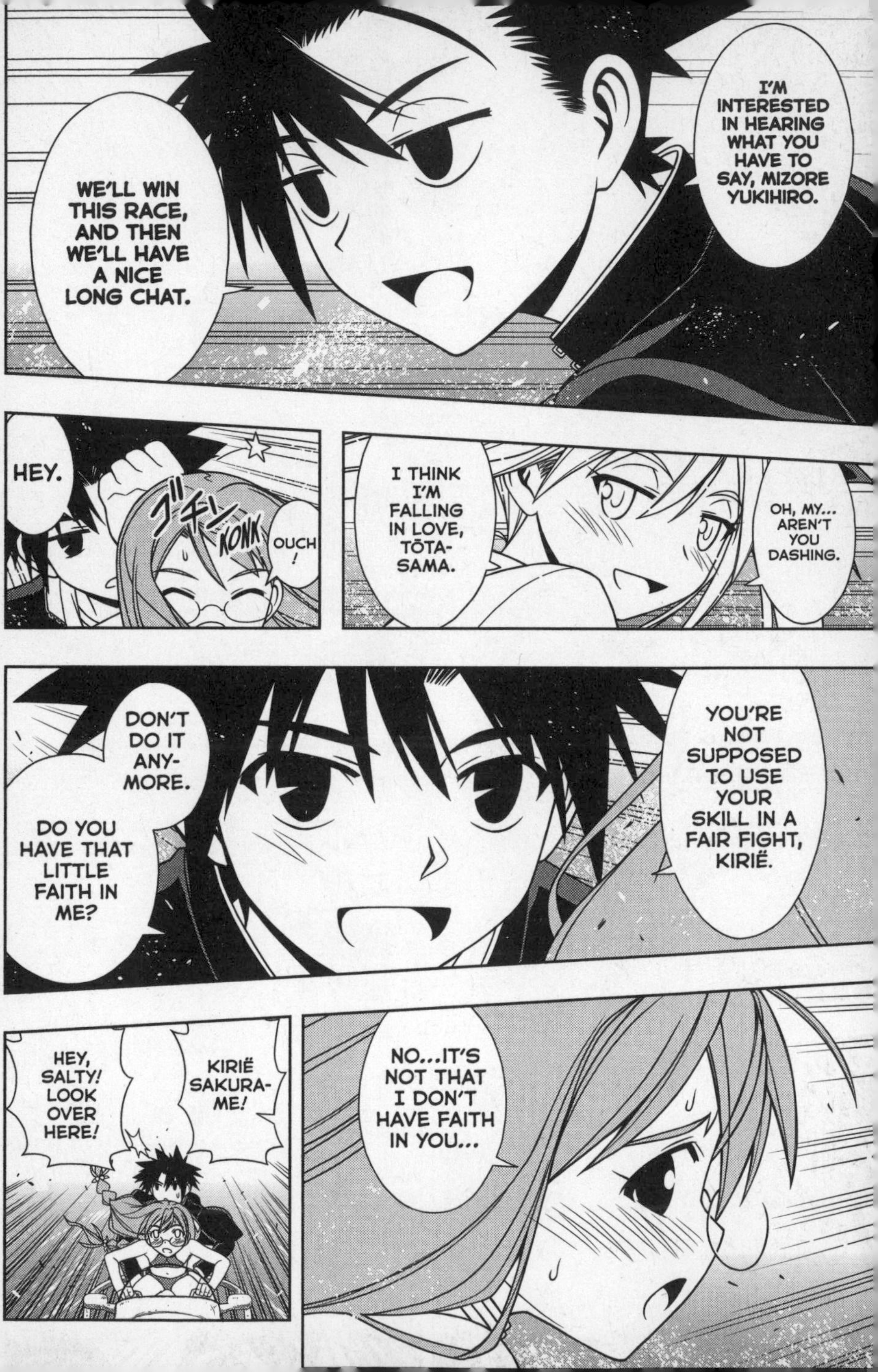
I'M INTERESTED IN HEARING WHAT YOU HAVE TO SAY, MIZORE YUKIHIRO.
WE'LL WIN THIS RACE, AND THEN WE'LL HAVE A NICE LONG CHAT.
OH, MY... AREN'T YOU DASHING.
I THINK I'M FALLING IN LOVE, TŌTA-SAMA.
HEY.
ゴチン
KONK
OUCH!
YOU'RE NOT SUPPOSED TO USE YOUR SKILL IN A FAIR FIGHT, KIRIË.
DON'T DO IT ANYMORE.
DO YOU HAVE THAT LITTLE FAITH IN ME?
NO...IT'S NOT THAT I DON'T HAVE FAITH IN YOU...
KIRIË SAKURA-ME!
HEY, SALTY! LOOK OVER HERE!

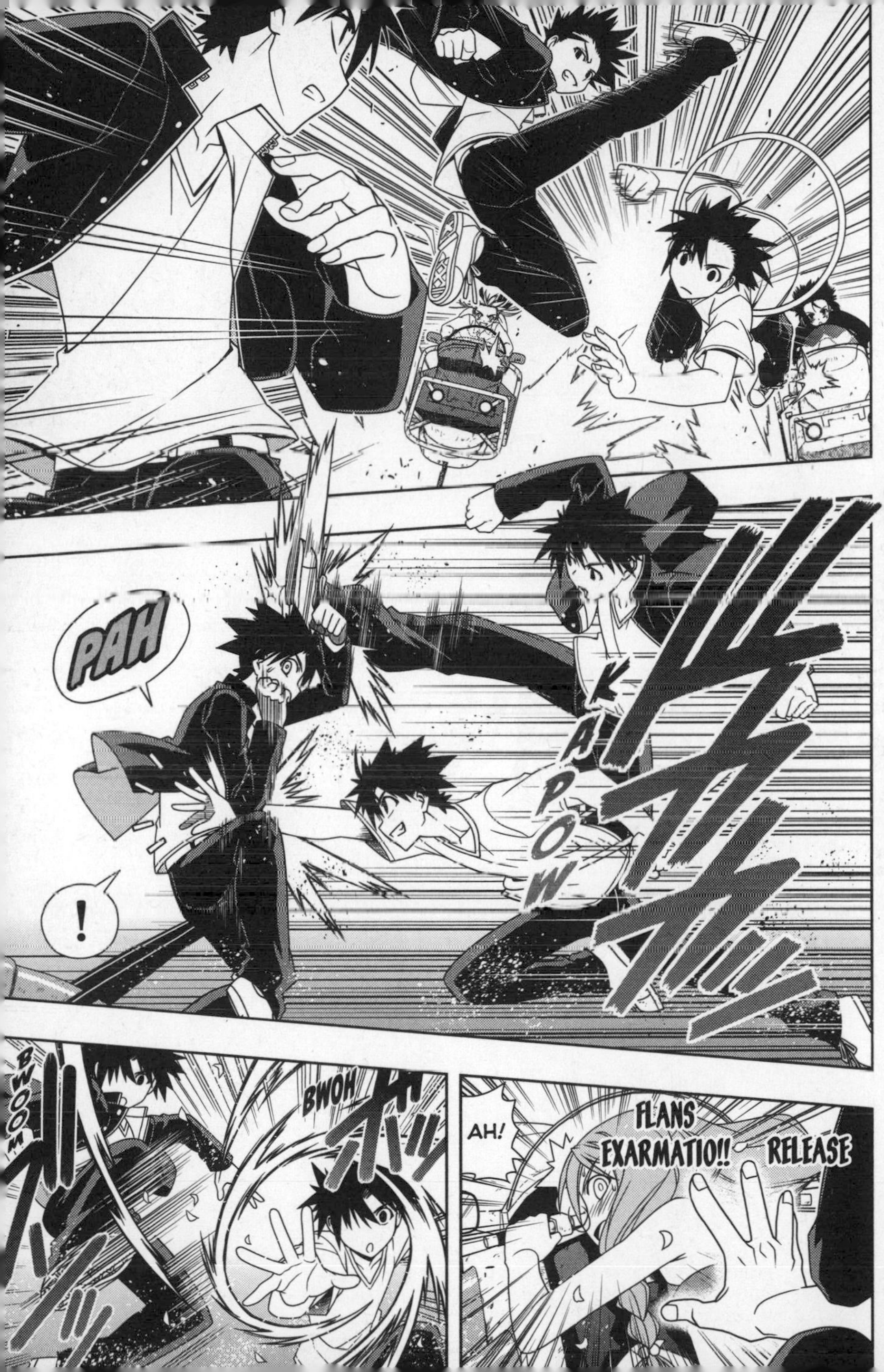
KAPOW
PAH
!
RELEASE
FLANS EXARMATIO!!
AH!
BWOH
BWOOM

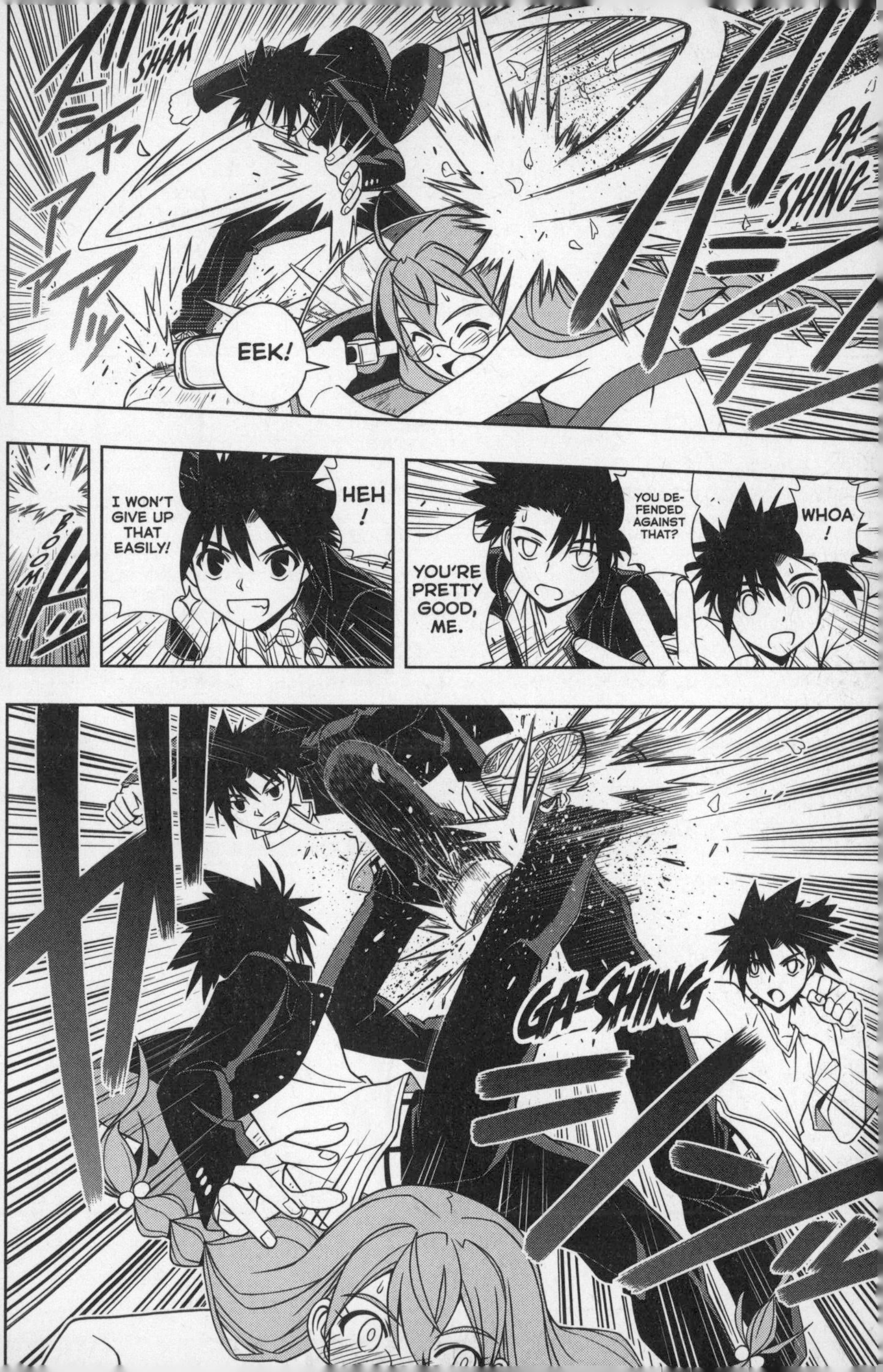
BA-SHING
ZA-SHAM
EEK!
WHOA!
YOU DE-FENDED AGAINST THAT?
YOU'RE PRETTY GOOD, ME.
HEH!
I WON'T GIVE UP THAT EASILY!
BOOM
GA-SHING

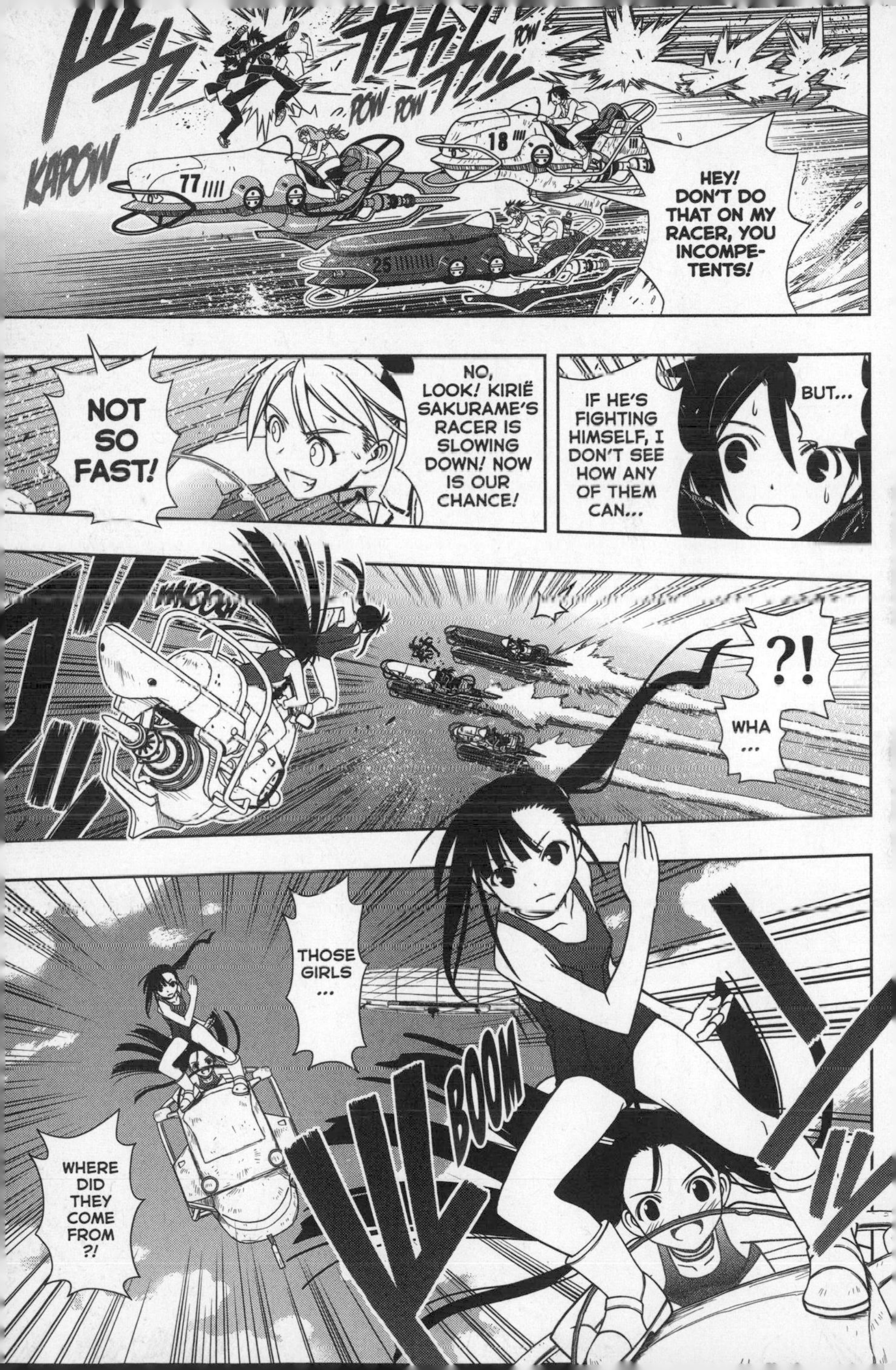
POW
HEY! DON'T DO THAT ON MY RACER, YOU INCOMPETENTS!
POW POW
KAPOW
BUT...
IF HE'S FIGHTING HIMSELF, I DON'T SEE HOW ANY OF THEM CAN...
NO, LOOK! KIRIË SAKURAME'S RACER IS SLOWING DOWN! NOW IS OUR CHANCE!
NOT SO FAST!
?!
WHA ...
THOSE GIRLS ...
BOOM
WHERE DID THEY COME FROM ?!

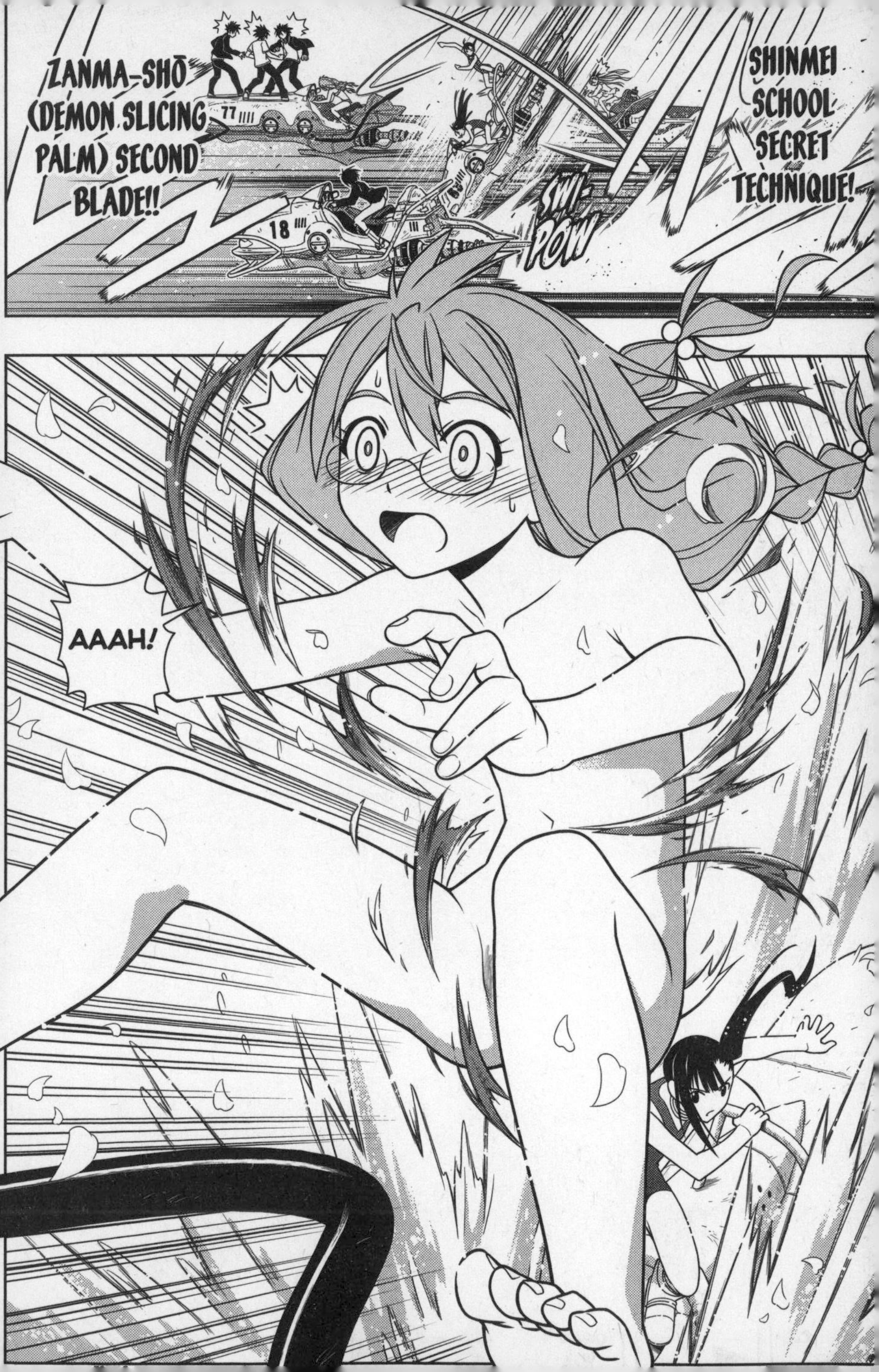
SHINMEI SCHOOL SECRET TECHNIQUE!
ZANMA-SHŌ (DEMON SLICING PALM) SECOND BLADE!!
SWI-POW
AAAH!

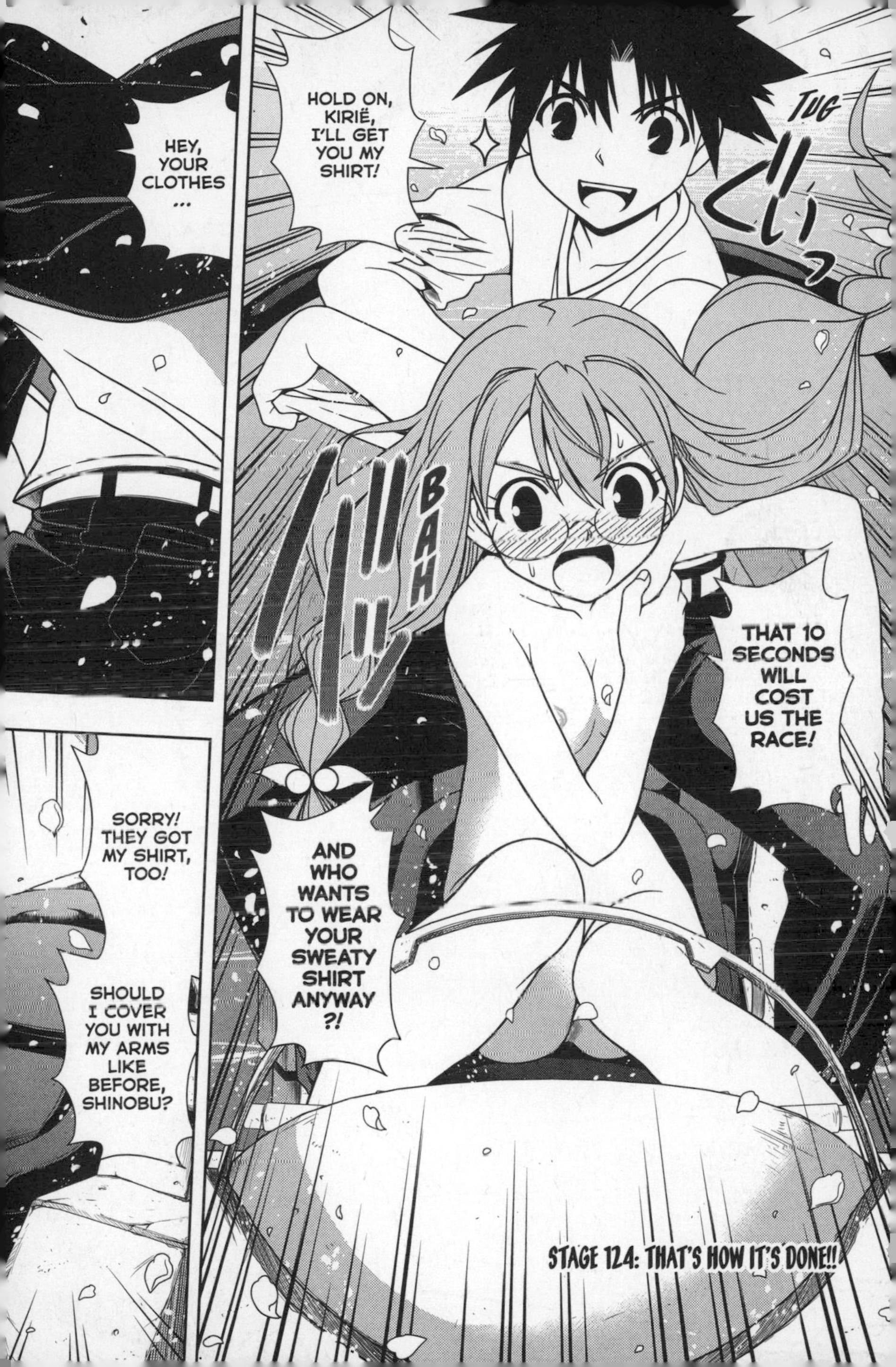
TUG
ぐいっ
HOLD ON, KIRIË, I'LL GET YOU MY SHIRT!
BAH
THAT 10 SECONDS WILL COST US THE RACE!
AND WHO WANTS TO WEAR YOUR SWEATY SHIRT ANYWAY?!
STAGE 124: THAT'S HOW IT'S DONE!!
HEY, YOUR CLOTHES...
SORRY! THEY GOT MY SHIRT, TOO!
SHOULD I COVER YOU WITH MY ARMS LIKE BEFORE, SHINOBU?

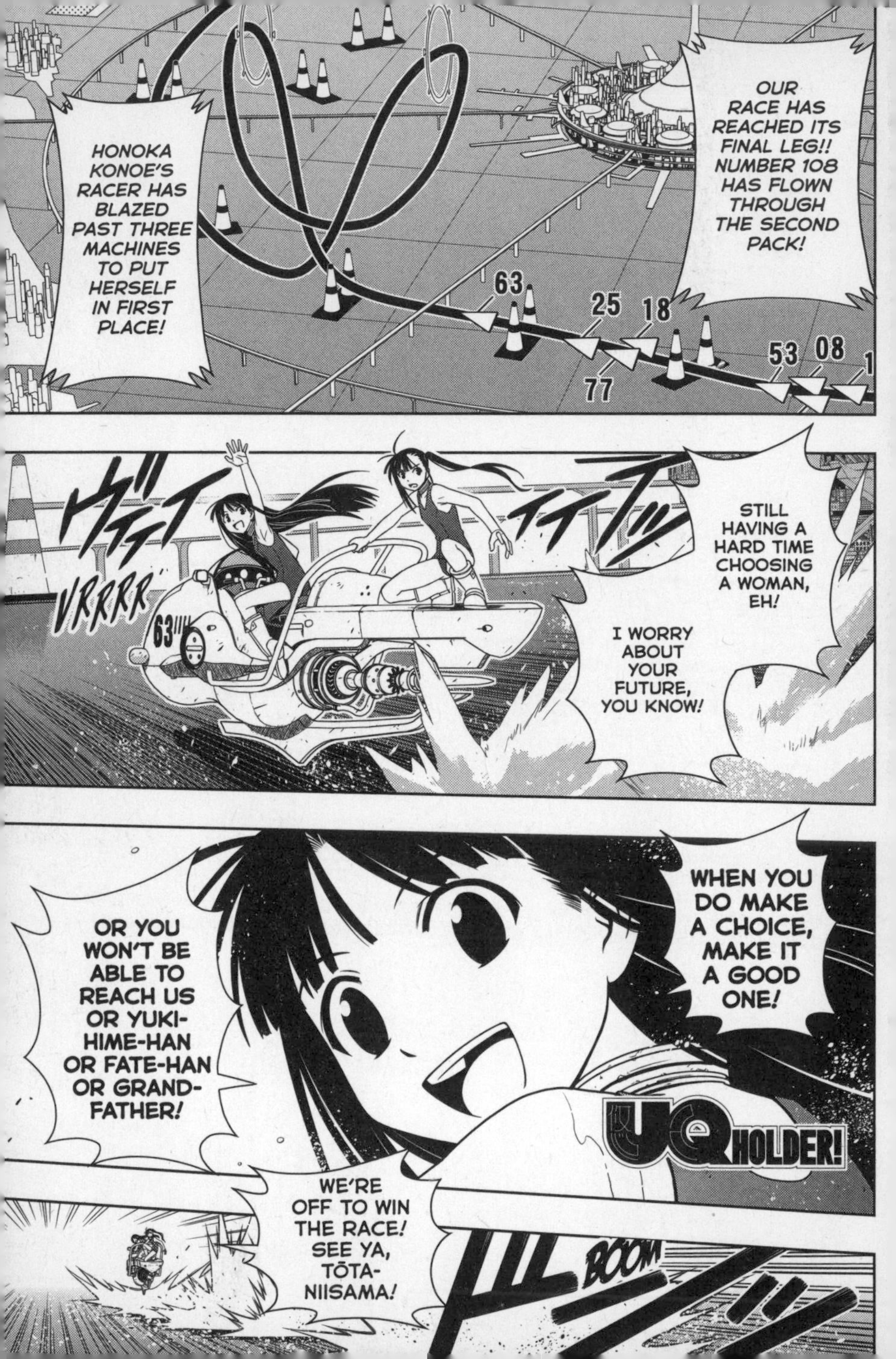

OUR RACE HAS REACHED ITS FINAL LEG!! NUMBER 108 HAS FLOWN THROUGH THE SECOND PACK!
HONOKA KONOE'S RACER HAS BLAZED PAST THREE MACHINES TO PUT HERSELF IN FIRST PLACE!
63
25
18
77
53
08
STILL HAVING A HARD TIME CHOOSING A WOMAN, EH!
I WORRY ABOUT YOUR FUTURE, YOU KNOW!
VRRRR
63
WHEN YOU DO MAKE A CHOICE, MAKE IT A GOOD ONE!
OR YOU WON'T BE ABLE TO REACH US OR YUKI-HIME-HAN OR FATE-HAN OR GRAND-FATHER!
UQ HOLDER!
BOOM
WE'RE OFF TO WIN THE RACE! SEE YA, TŌTA-NIISAMA!

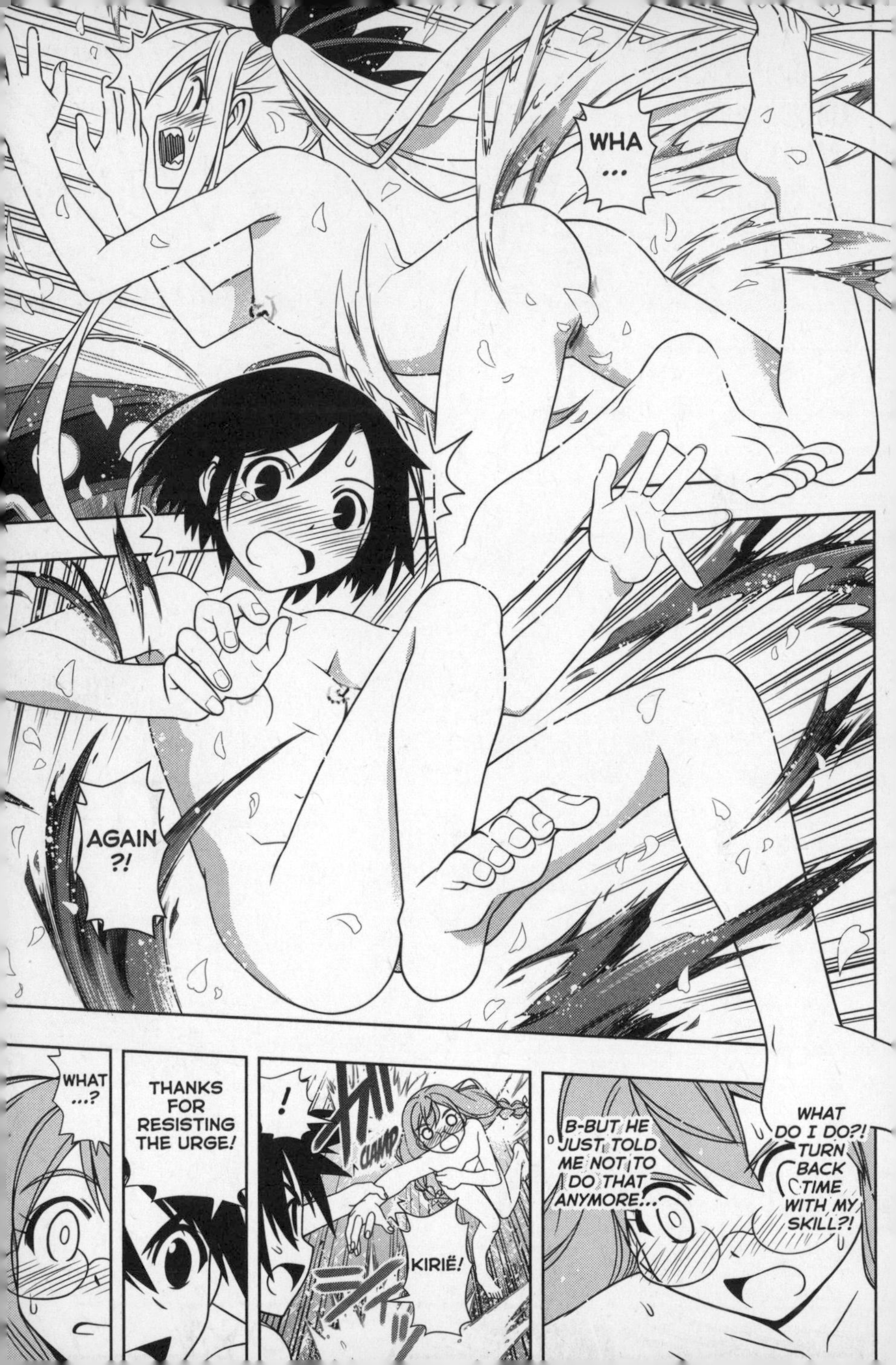
WHA...
AGAIN?!
WHAT DO I DO?! TURN BACK TIME WITH MY SKILL?!
B-BUT HE JUST TOLD ME NOT TO DO THAT ANYMORE...
!
CLAMP
KIRIË!
THANKS FOR RESISTING THE URGE!
WHAT...?

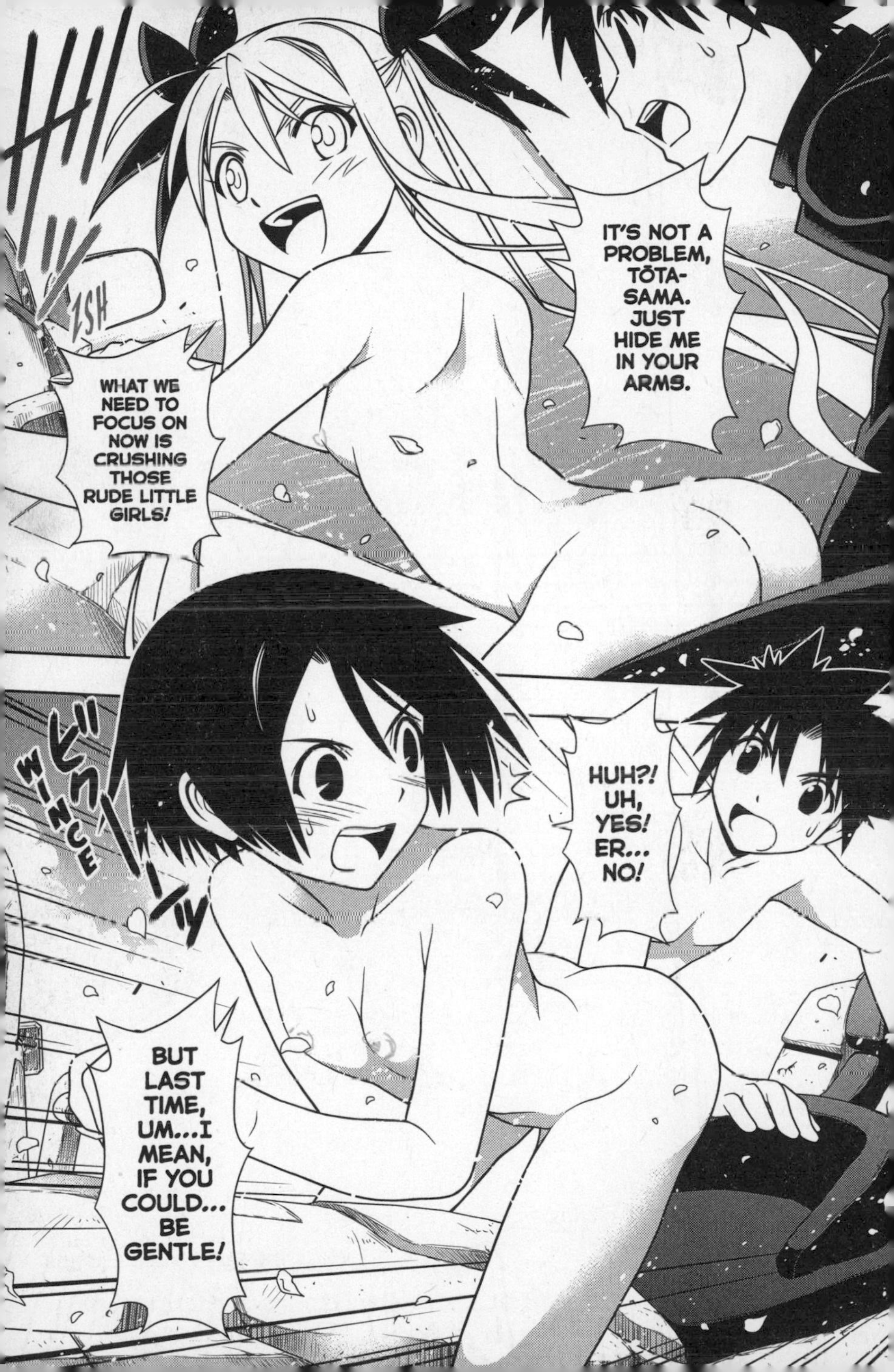
IT'S NOT A PROBLEM, TŌTA-SAMA. JUST HIDE ME IN YOUR ARMS.
WHAT WE NEED TO FOCUS ON NOW IS CRUSHING THOSE RUDE LITTLE GIRLS!
ZSH
HUH?! UH, YES! ER... NO!
WINCE
BUT LAST TIME, UM...I MEAN, IF YOU COULD... BE GENTLE!

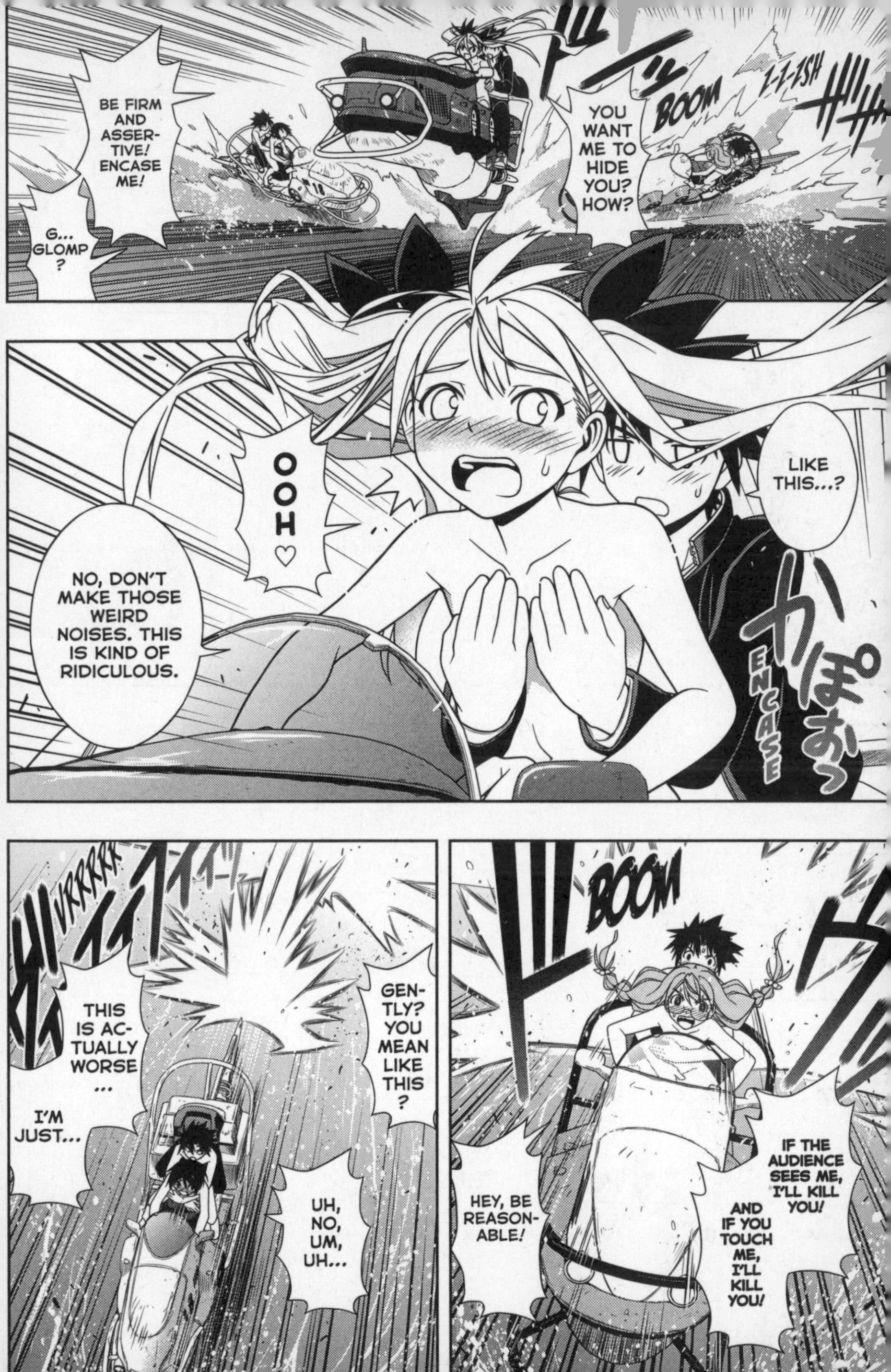
BOOM
YOU WANT ME TO HIDE YOU? HOW?
BE FIRM AND ASSERTIVE! ENCASE ME!
G... GLOMP?
LIKE THIS...?
ENCASE
OOH ♡
NO, DON'T MAKE THOSE WEIRD NOISES. THIS IS KIND OF RIDICULOUS.
BOOM
IF THE AUDIENCE SEES ME, I'LL KILL YOU!
AND IF YOU TOUCH ME, I'LL KILL YOU!
HEY, BE REASONABLE!
VRRRRR
GENTLY? YOU MEAN LIKE THIS?
UH, NO, UM, UH...
THIS IS ACTUALLY WORSE...
I'M JUST...

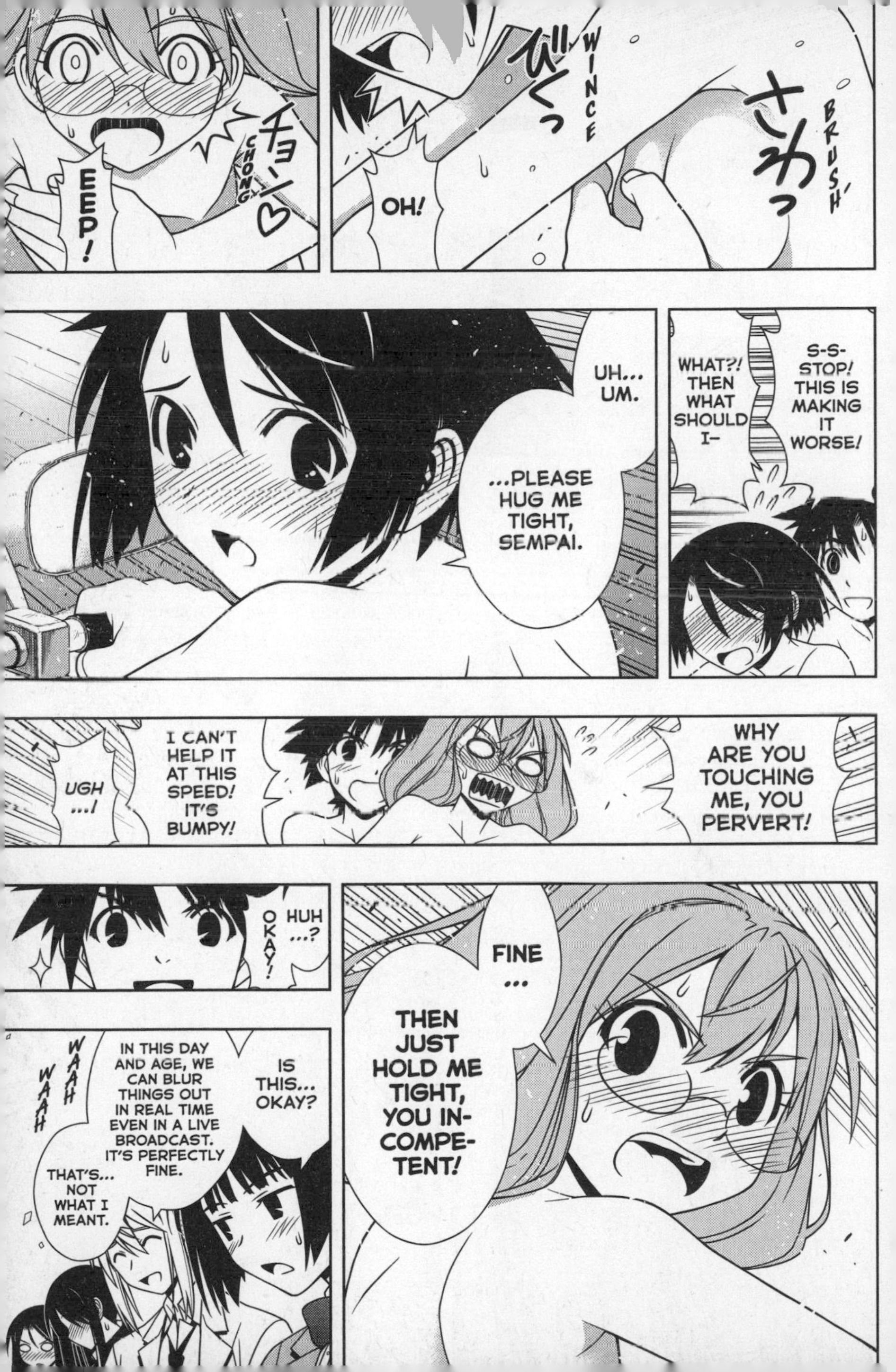
さわっ
BRUSH
びくっ
WINCE
OH!
チョン♡
CHONG
EEP!
S-S-STOP! THIS IS MAKING IT WORSE!
WHAT?! THEN WHAT SHOULD I–
UH... UM.
...PLEASE HUG ME TIGHT, SEMPAI.
WHY ARE YOU TOUCHING ME, YOU PERVERT!
I CAN'T HELP IT AT THIS SPEED! IT'S BUMPY!
UGH ...!
FINE ...
THEN JUST HOLD ME TIGHT, YOU IN-COMPE-TENT!
HUH ...?
OKAY!
IS THIS... OKAY?
IN THIS DAY AND AGE, WE CAN BLUR THINGS OUT IN REAL TIME EVEN IN A LIVE BROADCAST. IT'S PERFECTLY FINE.
WAAH
WAAH
THAT'S... NOT WHAT I MEANT.

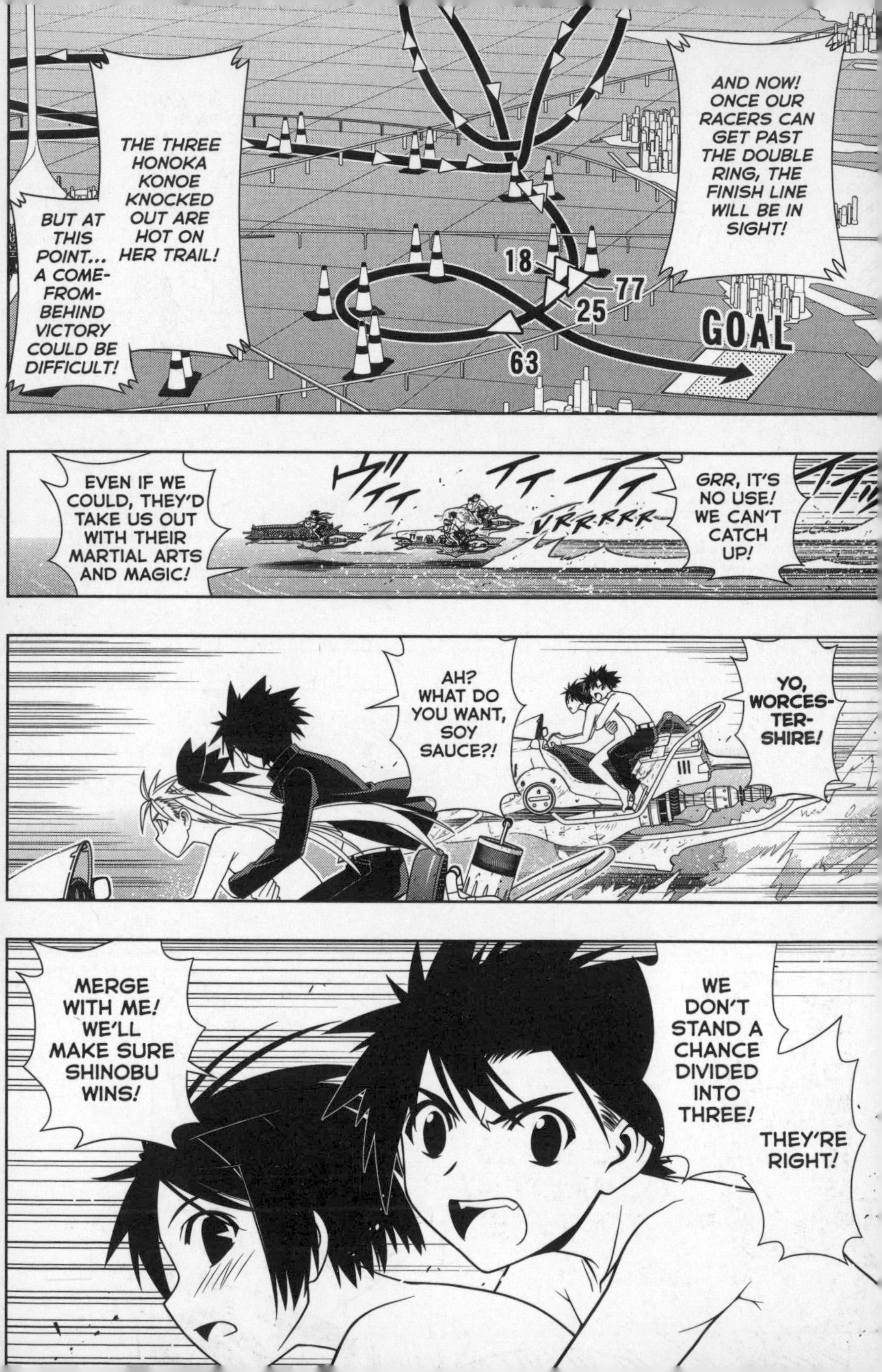
AND NOW! ONCE OUR RACERS CAN GET PAST THE DOUBLE RING, THE FINISH LINE WILL BE IN SIGHT!
THE THREE HONOKA KONOE KNOCKED OUT ARE HOT ON HER TRAIL!
BUT AT THIS POINT... A COME-FROM-BEHIND VICTORY COULD BE DIFFICULT!
18
77
25
63
GOAL
GRR, IT'S NO USE! WE CAN'T CATCH UP!
VRRRRR
EVEN IF WE COULD, THEY'D TAKE US OUT WITH THEIR MARTIAL ARTS AND MAGIC!
YO, WORCESTERSHIRE!
AH? WHAT DO YOU WANT, SOY SAUCE?!
WE DON'T STAND A CHANCE DIVIDED INTO THREE!
THEY'RE RIGHT!
MERGE WITH ME! WE'LL MAKE SURE SHINOBU WINS!

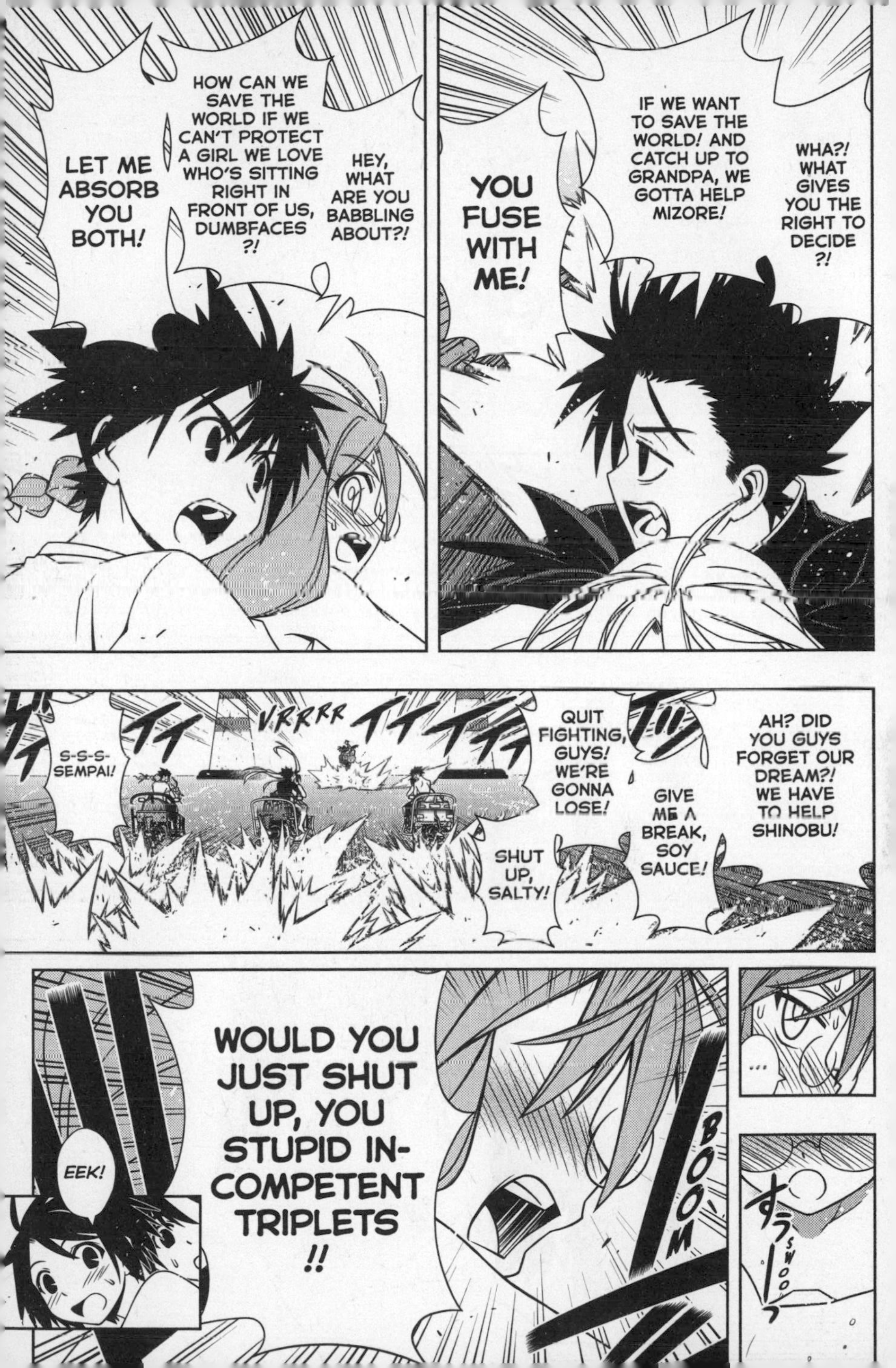
WHA?! WHAT GIVES YOU THE RIGHT TO DECIDE ?!
IF WE WANT TO SAVE THE WORLD! AND CATCH UP TO GRANDPA, WE GOTTA HELP MIZORE!
YOU FUSE WITH ME!
HEY, WHAT ARE YOU BABBLING ABOUT?!
HOW CAN WE SAVE THE WORLD IF WE CAN'T PROTECT A GIRL WE LOVE WHO'S SITTING RIGHT IN FRONT OF US, DUMBFACES ?!
LET ME ABSORB YOU BOTH!
AH? DID YOU GUYS FORGET OUR DREAM?! WE HAVE TO HELP SHINOBU!
GIVE ME A BREAK, SOY SAUCE!
QUIT FIGHTING, GUYS! WE'RE GONNA LOSE!
SHUT UP, SALTY!
VRRRR
S-S-S-SEMPAI!
...
SWOOO
WOULD YOU JUST SHUT UP, YOU STUPID IN-COMPETENT TRIPLETS !!
BOOM
EEK!

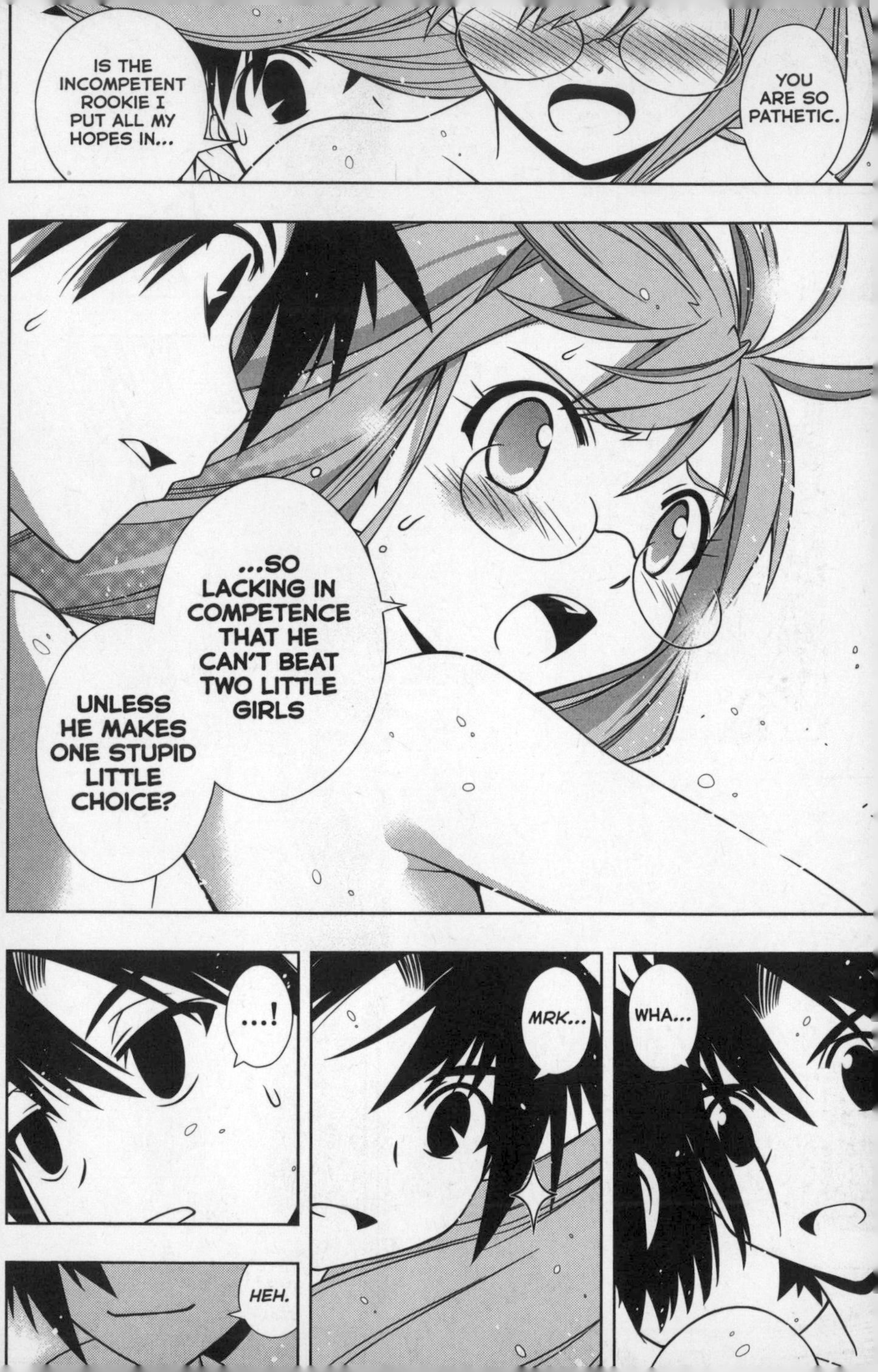
YOU ARE SO PATHETIC.
IS THE INCOMPETENT ROOKIE I PUT ALL MY HOPES IN...
...SO LACKING IN COMPETENCE THAT HE CAN'T BEAT TWO LITTLE GIRLS
UNLESS HE MAKES ONE STUPID LITTLE CHOICE?
WHA...
MRK...
...!
HEH.

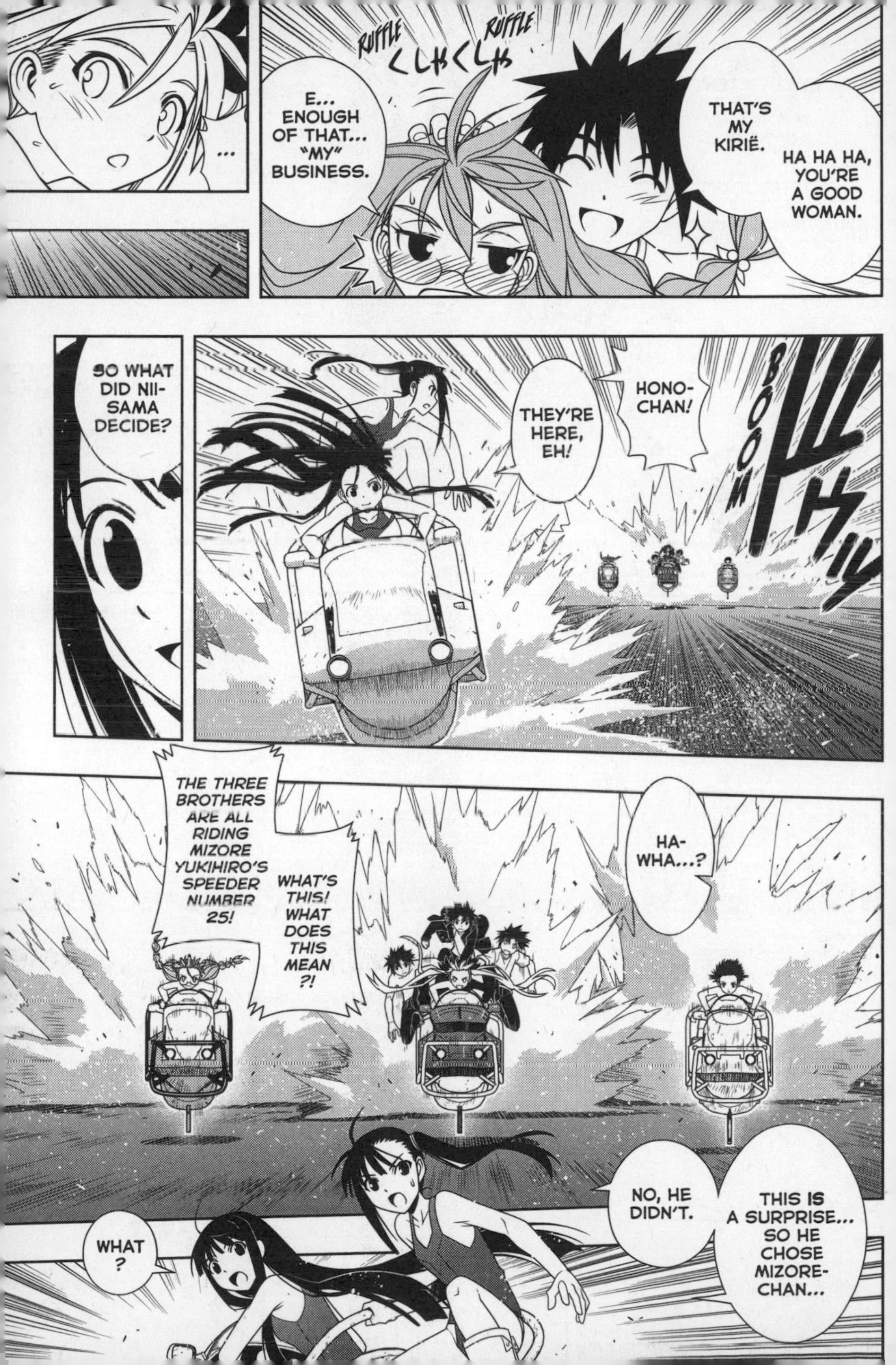
RUFFLE RUFFLE
くしゃくしゃ
THAT'S MY KIRIË.
HA HA HA, YOU'RE A GOOD WOMAN.
E... ENOUGH OF THAT... "MY" BUSINESS.
...
BOOOM
HONO-CHAN!
THEY'RE HERE, EH!
SO WHAT DID NII-SAMA DECIDE?
HA-WHA...?
WHAT'S THIS! WHAT DOES THIS MEAN?!
THE THREE BROTHERS ARE ALL RIDING MIZORE YUKIHIRO'S SPEEDER NUMBER 25!
THIS IS A SURPRISE... SO HE CHOSE MIZORE-CHAN...
NO, HE DIDN'T.
WHAT?

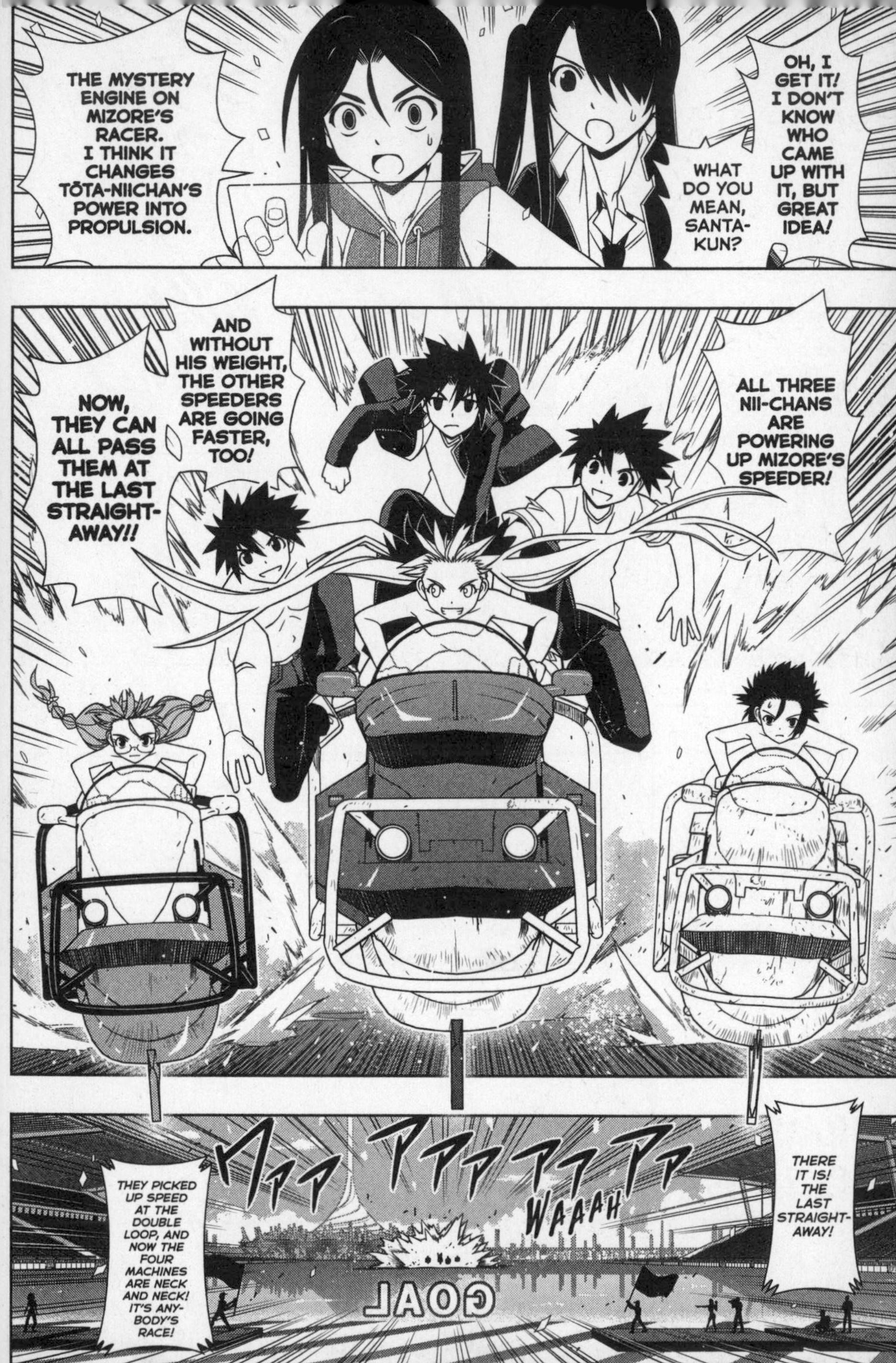
OH, I GET IT! I DON'T KNOW WHO CAME UP WITH IT, BUT GREAT IDEA!
WHAT DO YOU MEAN, SANTA-KUN?
THE MYSTERY ENGINE ON MIZORE'S RACER. I THINK IT CHANGES TŌTA-NIICHAN'S POWER INTO PROPULSION.
ALL THREE NII-CHANS ARE POWERING UP MIZORE'S SPEEDER!
AND WITHOUT HIS WEIGHT, THE OTHER SPEEDERS ARE GOING FASTER, TOO!
NOW, THEY CAN ALL PASS THEM AT THE LAST STRAIGHT-AWAY!!
THERE IT IS! THE LAST STRAIGHT-AWAY!
WAAAH
THEY PICKED UP SPEED AT THE DOUBLE LOOP, AND NOW THE FOUR MACHINES ARE NECK AND NECK! IT'S ANY-BODY'S RACE!

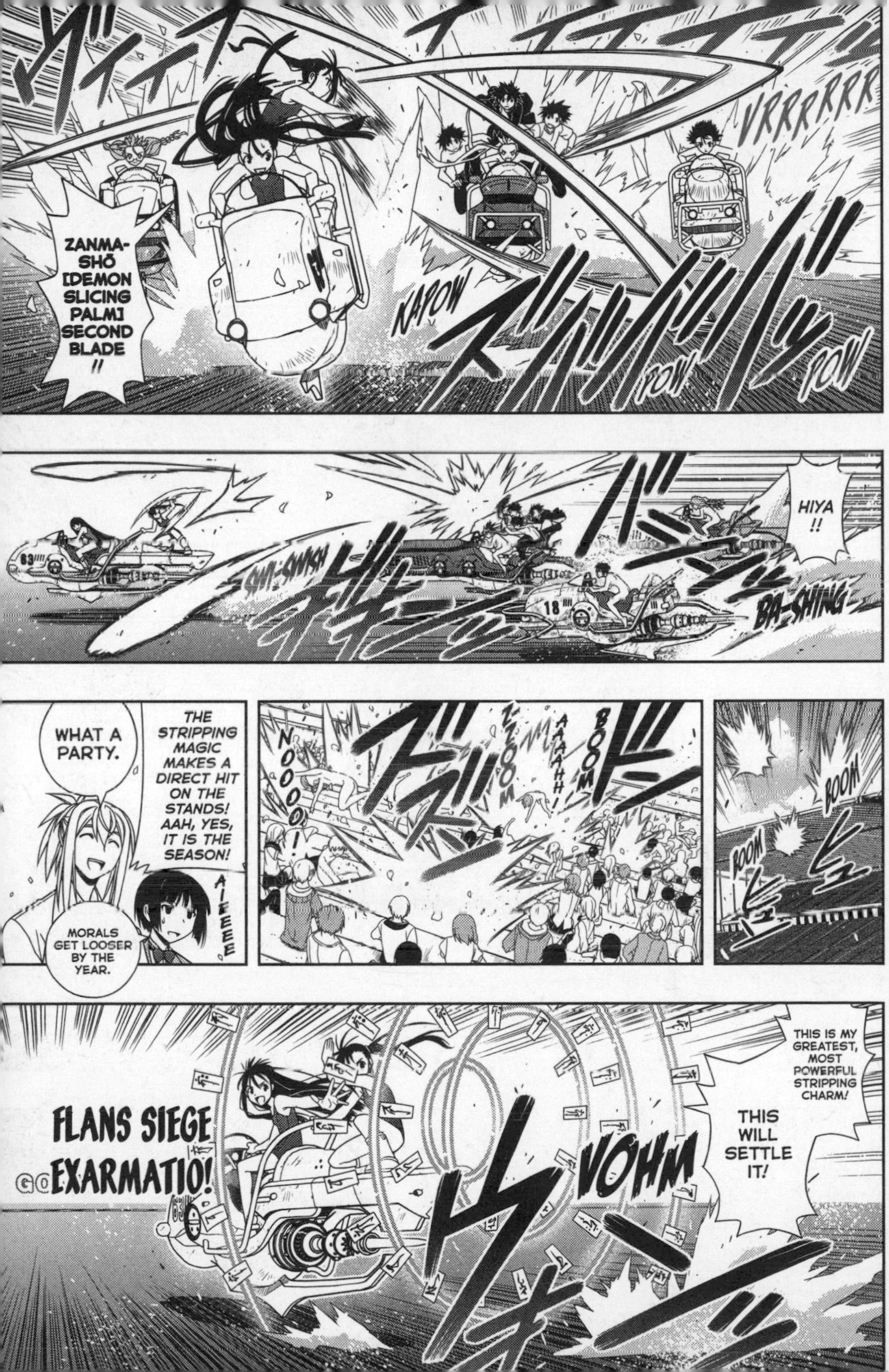

VRRRRRR
POW
ZANMA-SHŌ [DEMON SLICING PALM] SECOND BLADE !!
KAPOW
POW
HIYA !!
BA-SHING
SWI-SWISH
BOOM
BOOM
BOOM
AAAAHH!
ZZOOM
NOOOOO!
THE STRIPPING MAGIC MAKES A DIRECT HIT ON THE STANDS! AAH, YES, IT IS THE SEASON!
WHAT A PARTY.
AIEEEE
MORALS GET LOOSER BY THE YEAR.
THIS IS MY GREATEST, MOST POWERFUL STRIPPING CHARM!
THIS WILL SETTLE IT!
VOHM
FLANS SIEGE EXARMATIO!

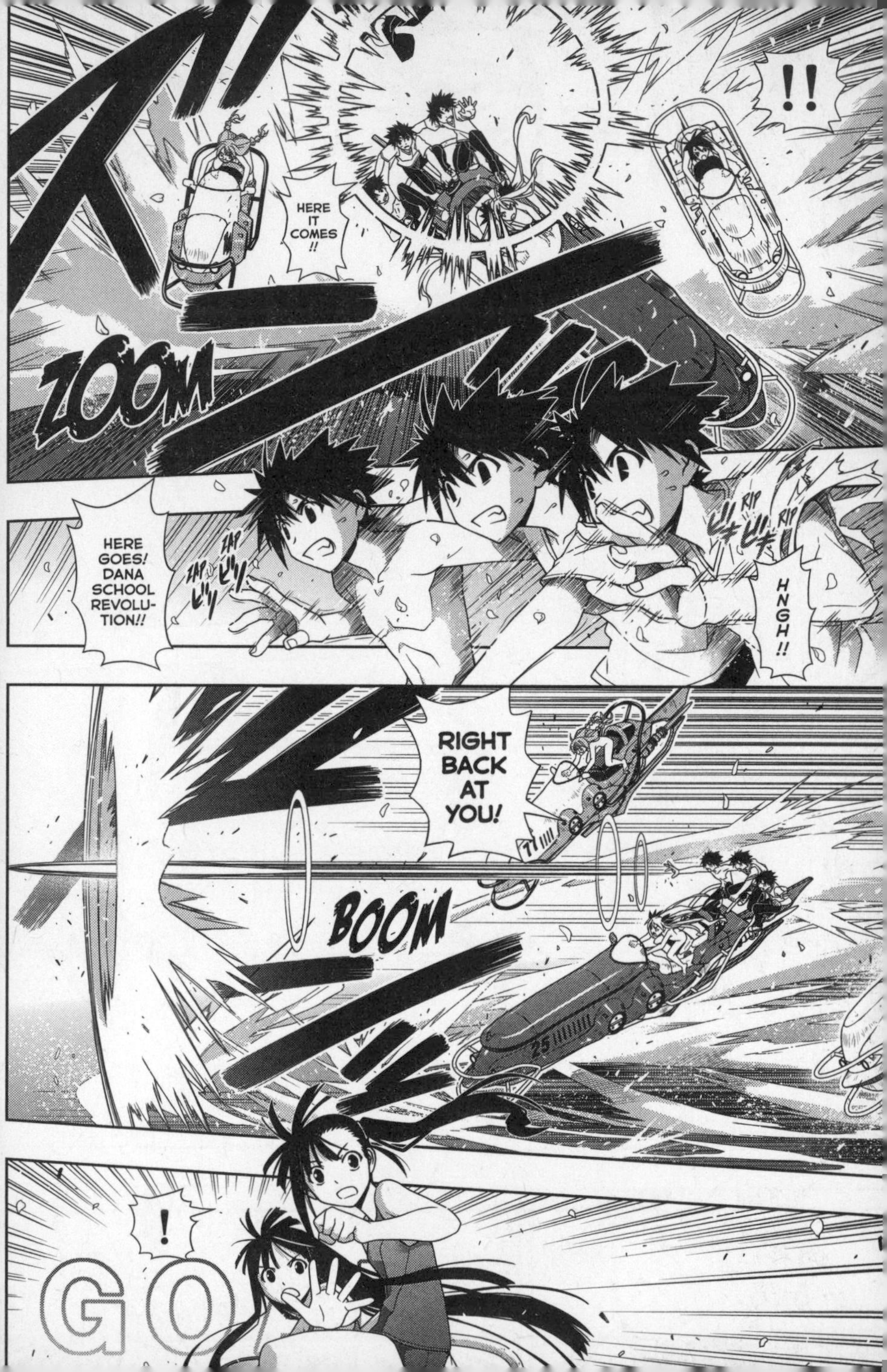

!!
HERE IT COMES!!
ZOOM
RIP RIP
HNGH!!
HERE GOES! DANA SCHOOL REVOLUTION!!
ZAP ZAP
RIGHT BACK AT YOU!
BOOM
!
GO

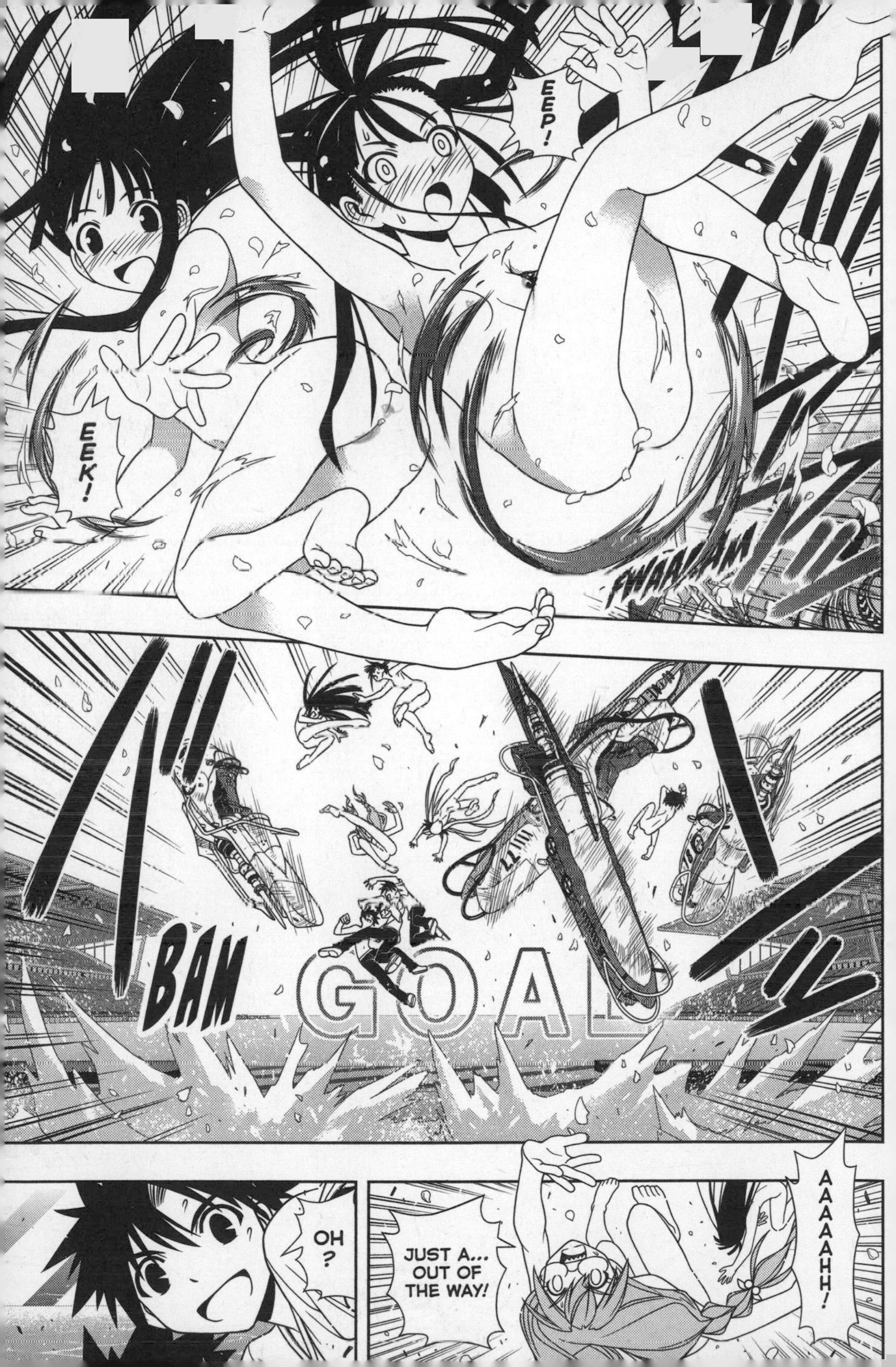
EEP!
EEK!
FWAAAAM
BAM
GOAL
AAAAAAHH!
JUST A... OUT OF THE WAY!
OH?

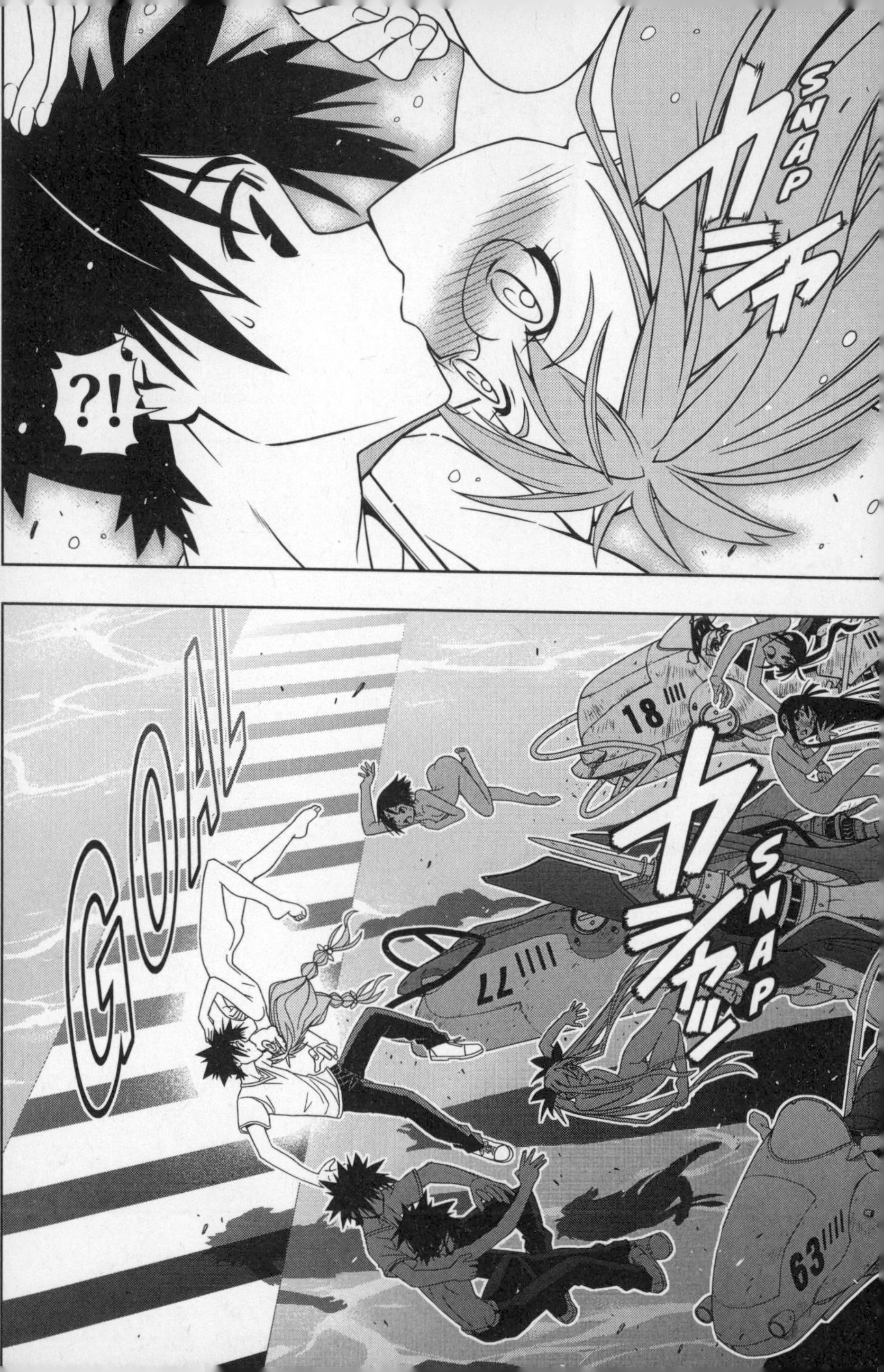
SNAP
?!
GOAL
SNAP

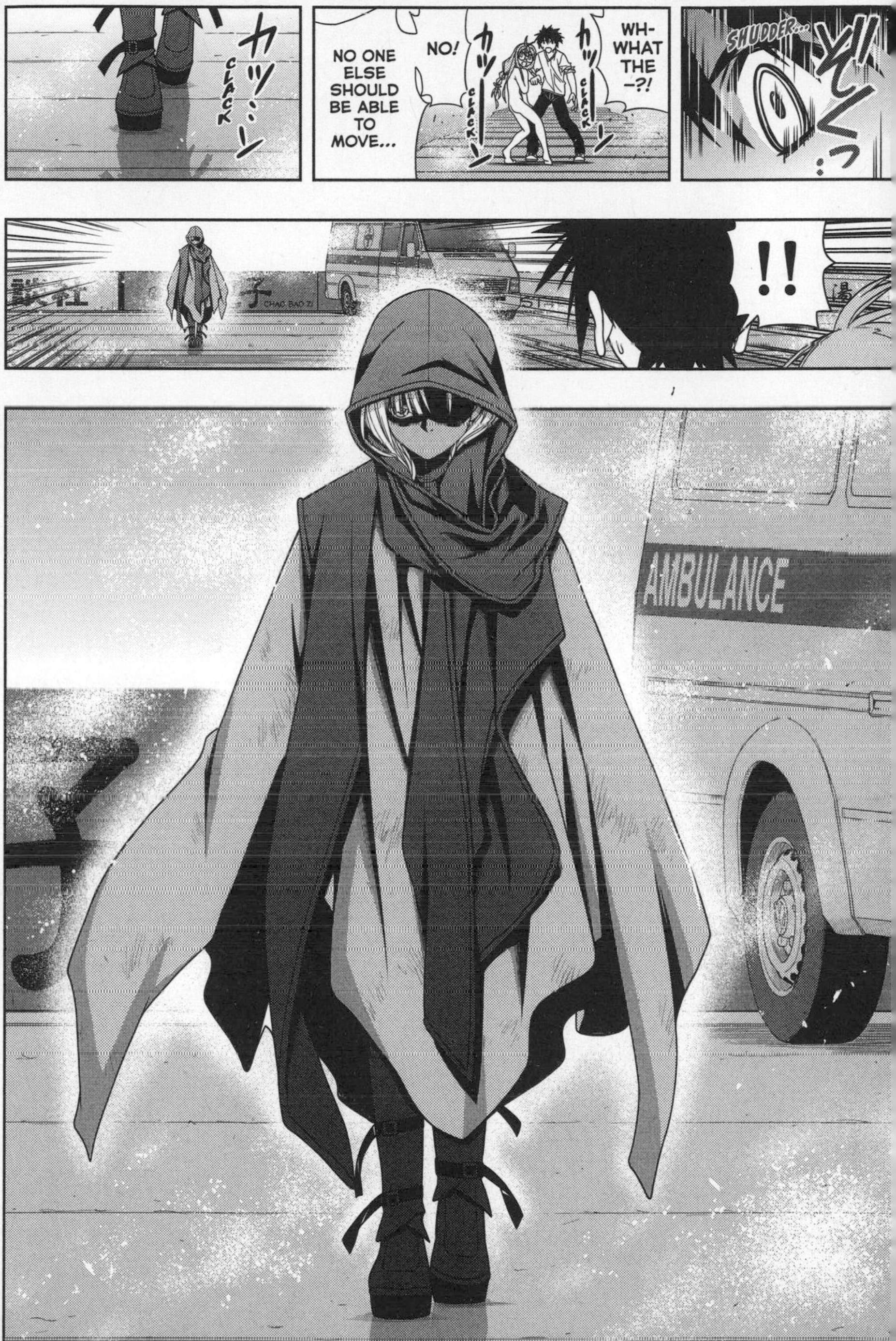
SHUDDER...
ぞくっ…
WH-WHAT THE—?!
カッ
CLACK
NO!
カッ
CLACK
NO ONE ELSE SHOULD BE ABLE TO MOVE...
カツ…
CLACK
!!
CHAO BAO ZI
AMBULANCE

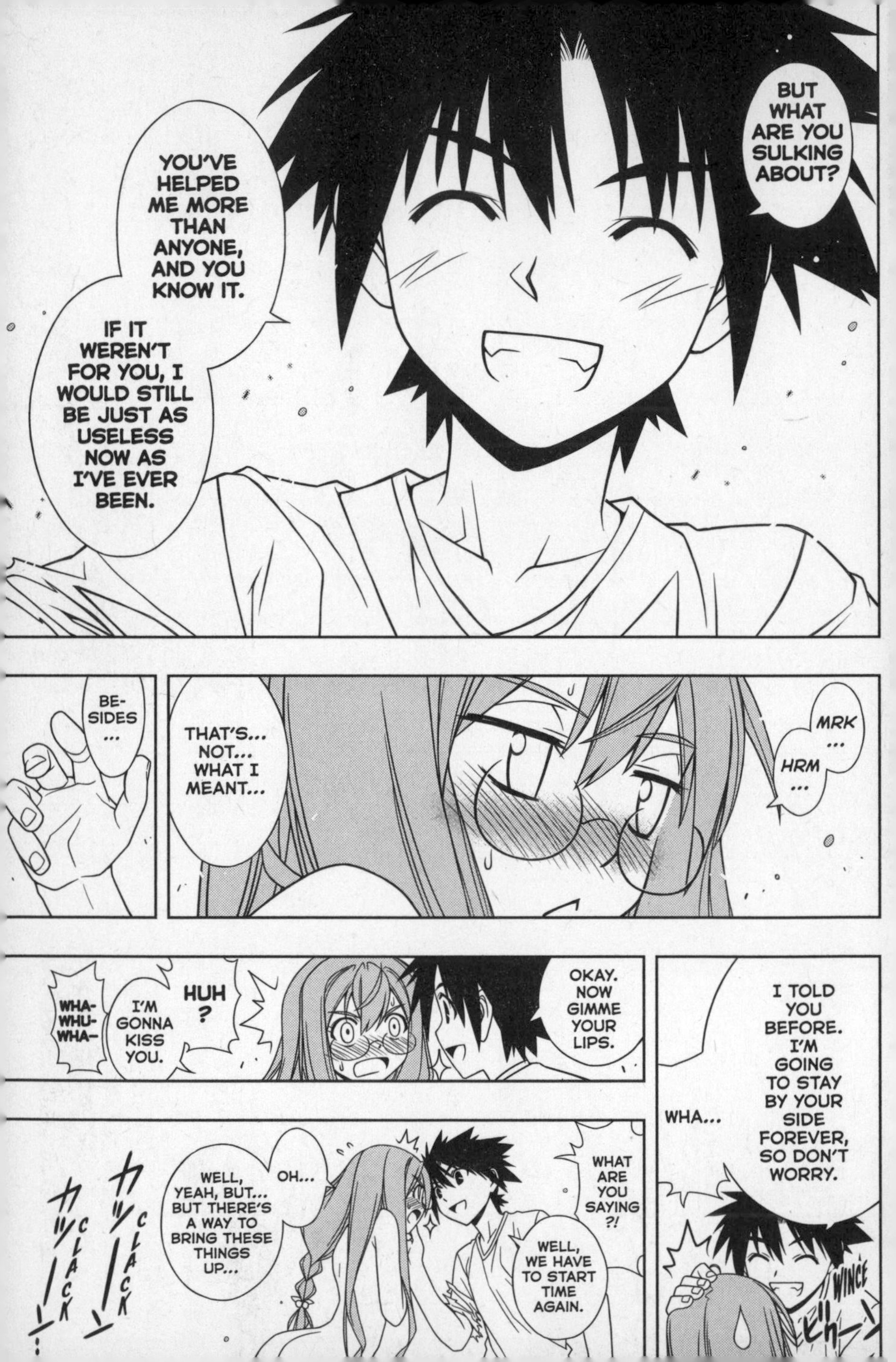
BUT WHAT ARE YOU SULKING ABOUT?
YOU'VE HELPED ME MORE THAN ANYONE, AND YOU KNOW IT.
IF IT WEREN'T FOR YOU, I WOULD STILL BE JUST AS USELESS NOW AS I'VE EVER BEEN.
MRK... HRM...
THAT'S... NOT... WHAT I MEANT...
BE-SIDES...
I TOLD YOU BEFORE. I'M GOING TO STAY BY YOUR SIDE FOREVER, SO DON'T WORRY.
WHA...
WINCE
OKAY. NOW GIMME YOUR LIPS.
HUH?
I'M GONNA KISS YOU.
WHA-WHU-WHA-
WHAT ARE YOU SAYING?!
WELL, WE HAVE TO START TIME AGAIN.
OH...
WELL, YEAH, BUT... BUT THERE'S A WAY TO BRING THESE THINGS UP...
CLACK
CLACK

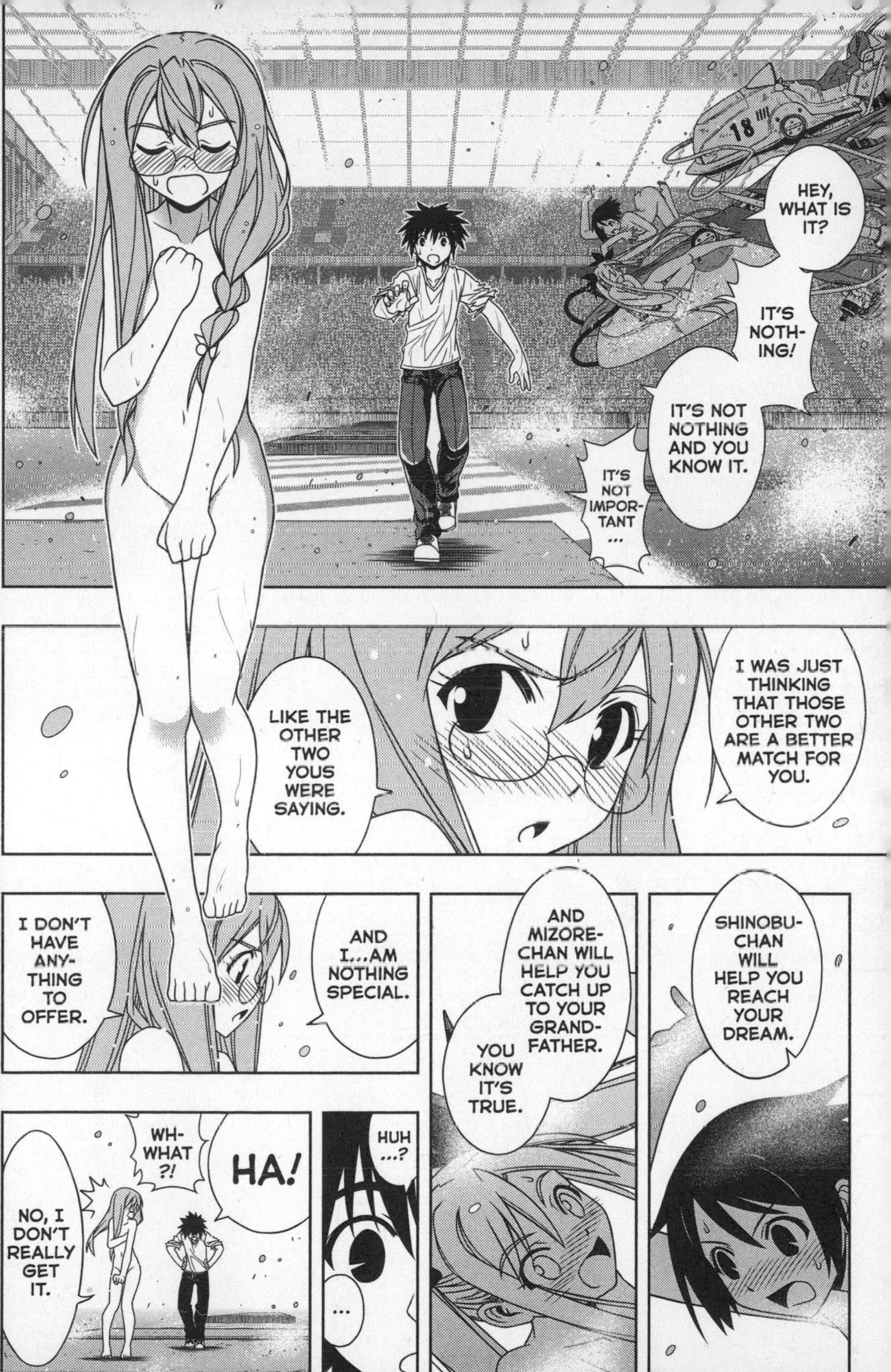
HEY, WHAT IS IT?
IT'S NOTHING!
IT'S NOT NOTHING AND YOU KNOW IT.
IT'S NOT IMPORTANT...
I WAS JUST THINKING THAT THOSE OTHER TWO ARE A BETTER MATCH FOR YOU.
LIKE THE OTHER TWO YOUS WERE SAYING.
SHINOBU-CHAN WILL HELP YOU REACH YOUR DREAM.
AND MIZORE-CHAN WILL HELP YOU CATCH UP TO YOUR GRAND-FATHER.
YOU KNOW IT'S TRUE.
AND I...AM NOTHING SPECIAL.
I DON'T HAVE ANY-THING TO OFFER.
HUH...?
...
HA!
WH-WHAT?!
NO, I DON'T REALLY GET IT.

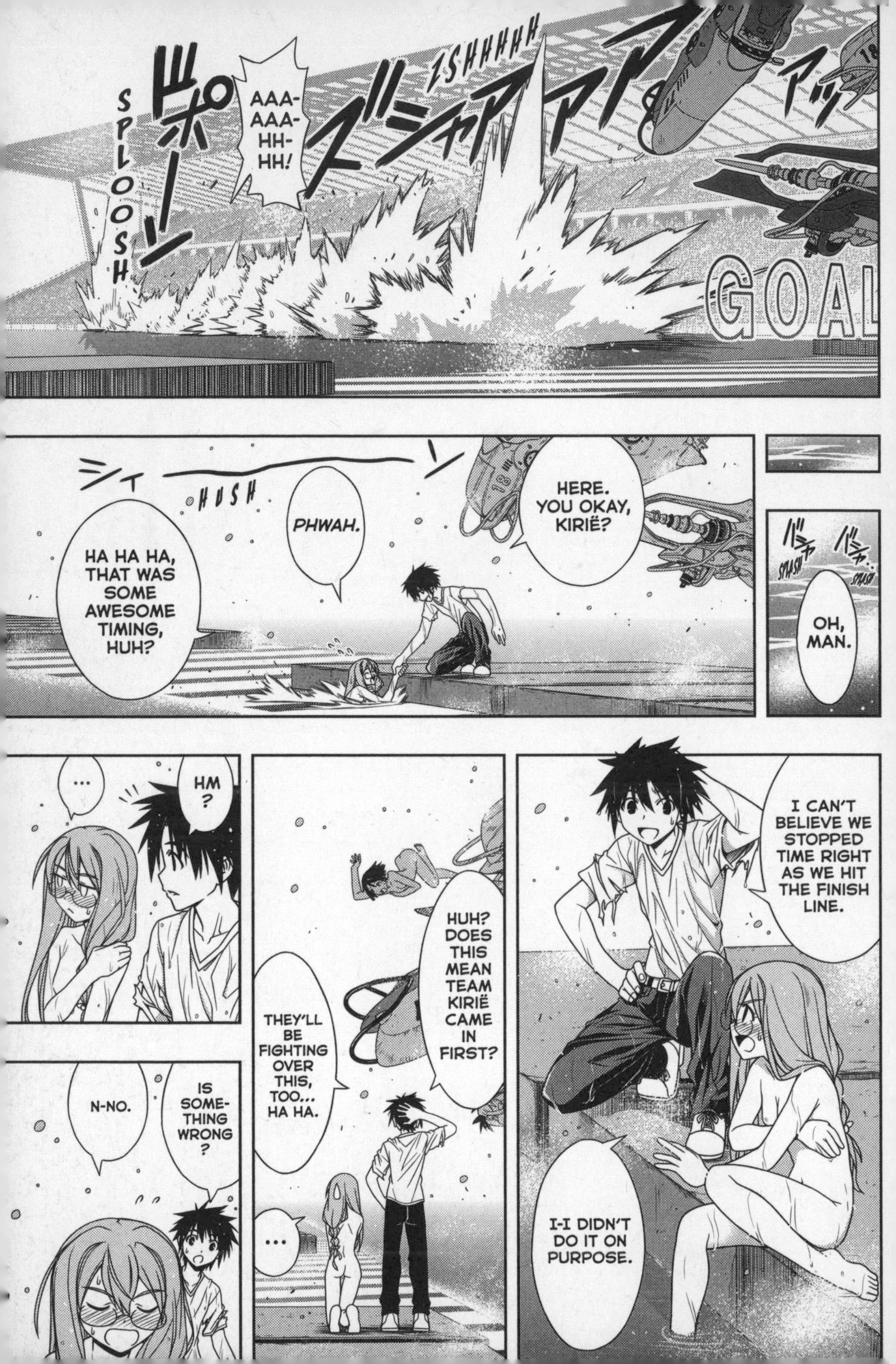
GOAL
ZSHHHHH
AAA-AAA-HH-HH!
SPLOOSH
SPLASH
SPLASH
OH, MAN.
HERE. YOU OKAY, KIRIË?
PHWAH.
HUSH
HA HA HA, THAT WAS SOME AWESOME TIMING, HUH?
I CAN'T BELIEVE WE STOPPED TIME RIGHT AS WE HIT THE FINISH LINE.
I-I DIDN'T DO IT ON PURPOSE.
HUH? DOES THIS MEAN TEAM KIRIË CAME IN FIRST?
THEY'LL BE FIGHTING OVER THIS, TOO... HA HA.
...
HM?
...
IS SOMETHING WRONG?
N-NO.

悠久 UQ HOLDER!

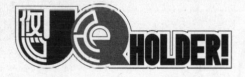

UQ
HOLDER!

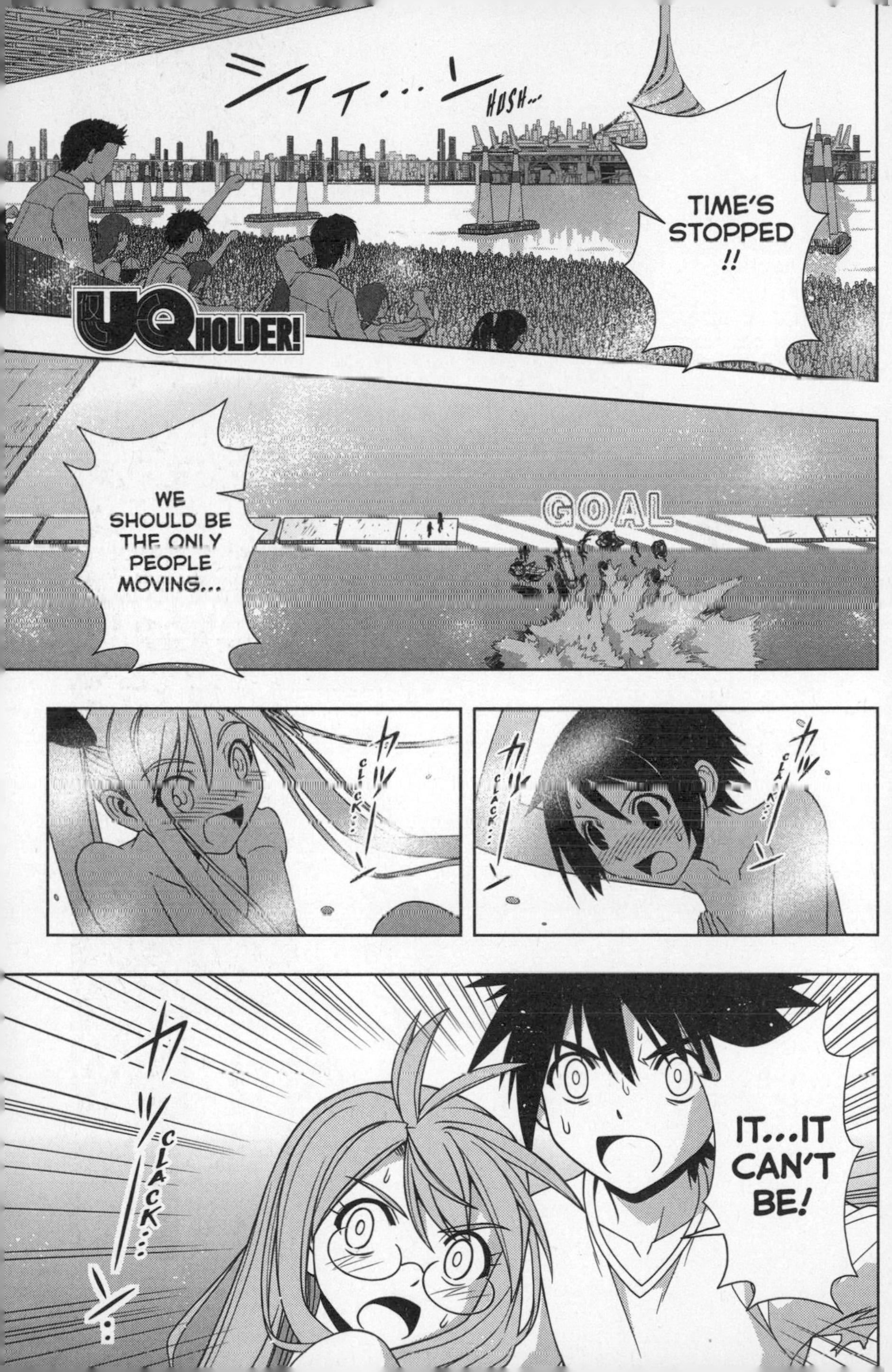
シイイ…ン
HUSH...
TIME'S STOPPED!!
UQ HOLDER!
WE SHOULD BE THE ONLY PEOPLE MOVING...
GOAL
CLACK...
CLACK...
CLACK...
CLACK...
IT...IT CAN'T BE!

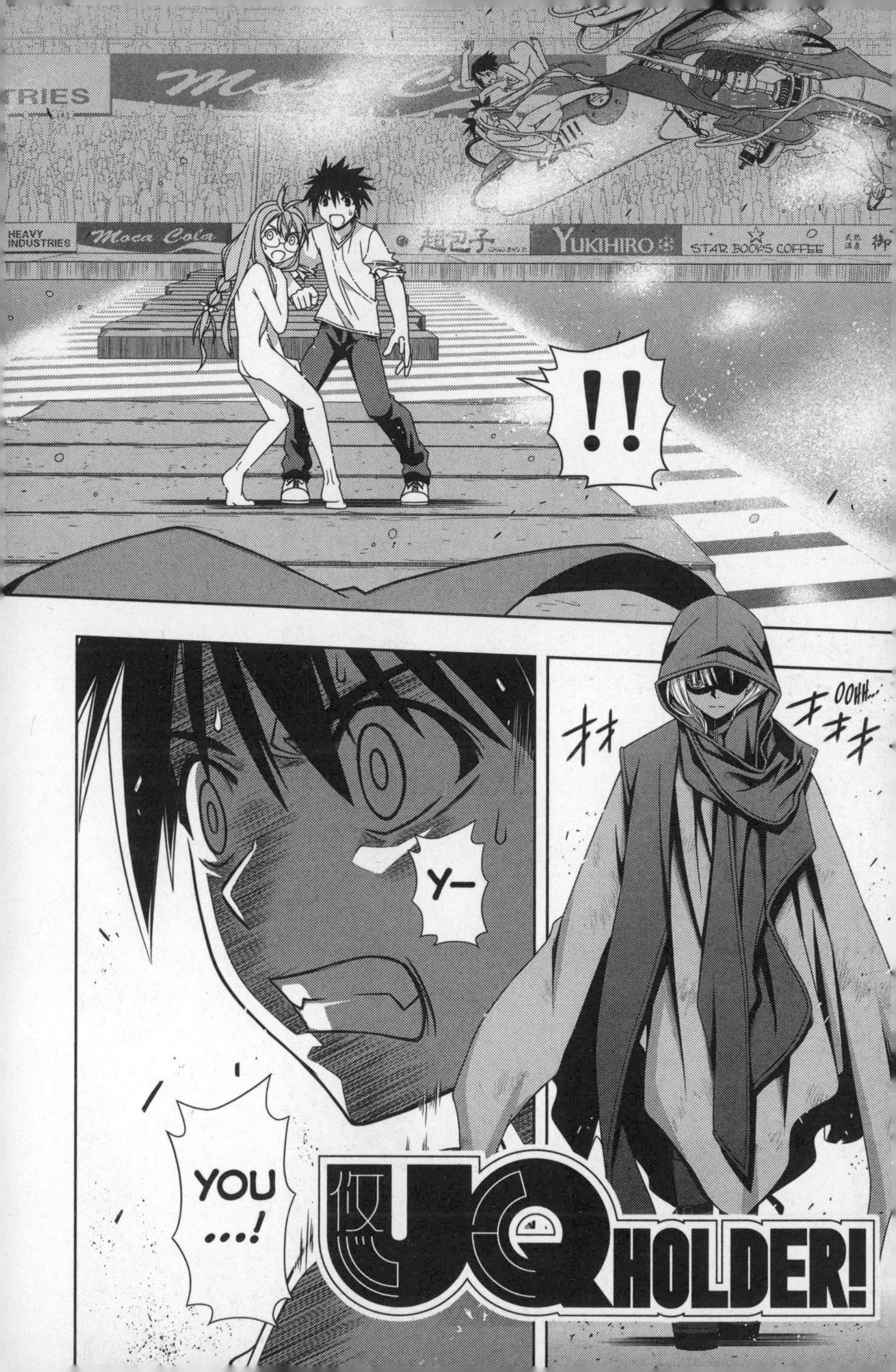
TRIES
HEAVY INDUSTRIES
Moca Cola
超包子
YUKIHIRO
STAR BOOKS COFFEE
!!
オオ
OOHH...
オオオ
Y—
YOU ...!
UQ HOLDER!

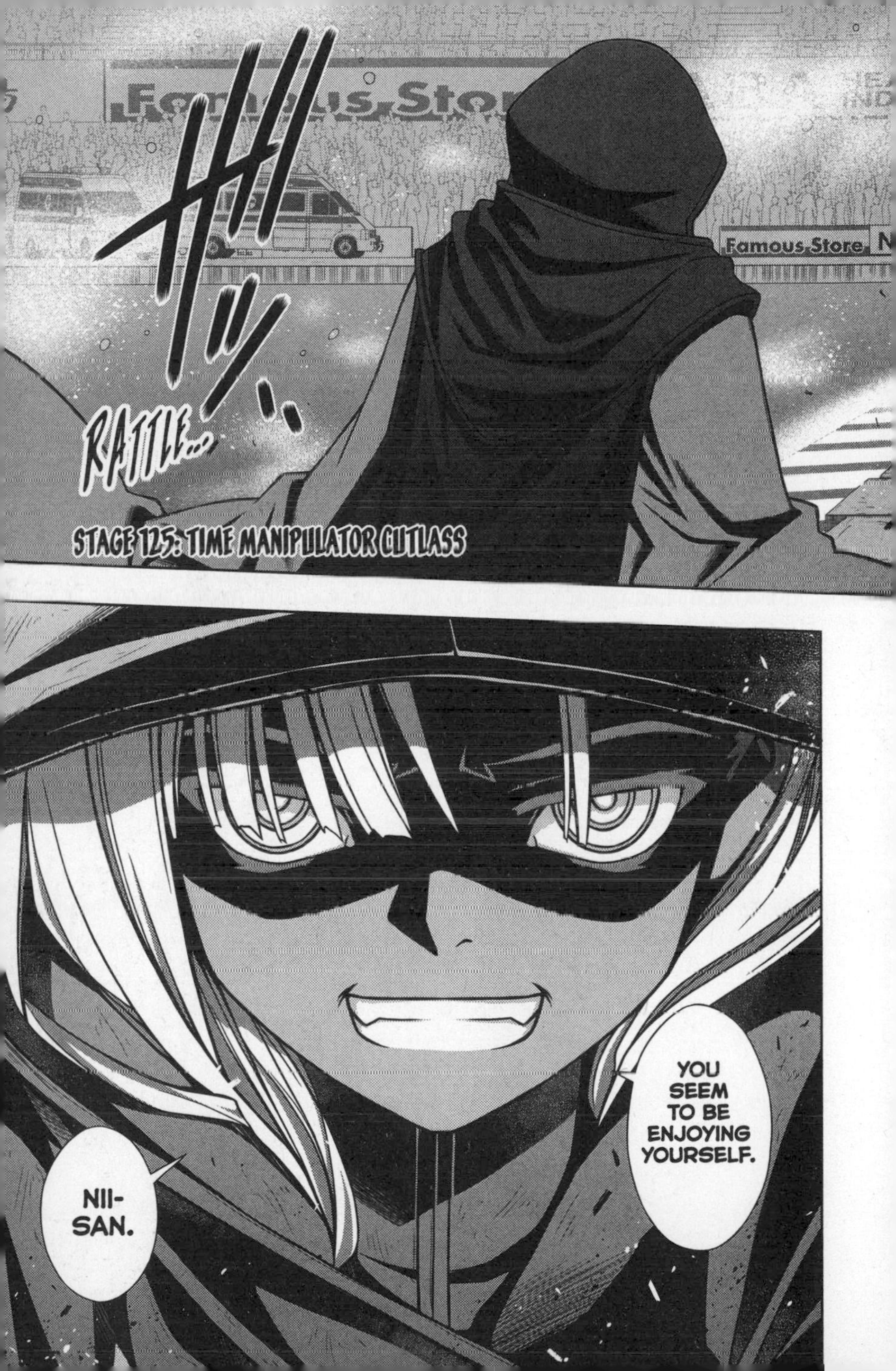
Famous Store
Famous Store
RATTLE...
STAGE 125: TIME MANIPULATOR CUTLASS
YOU SEEM TO BE ENJOYING YOURSELF.
NII-SAN.

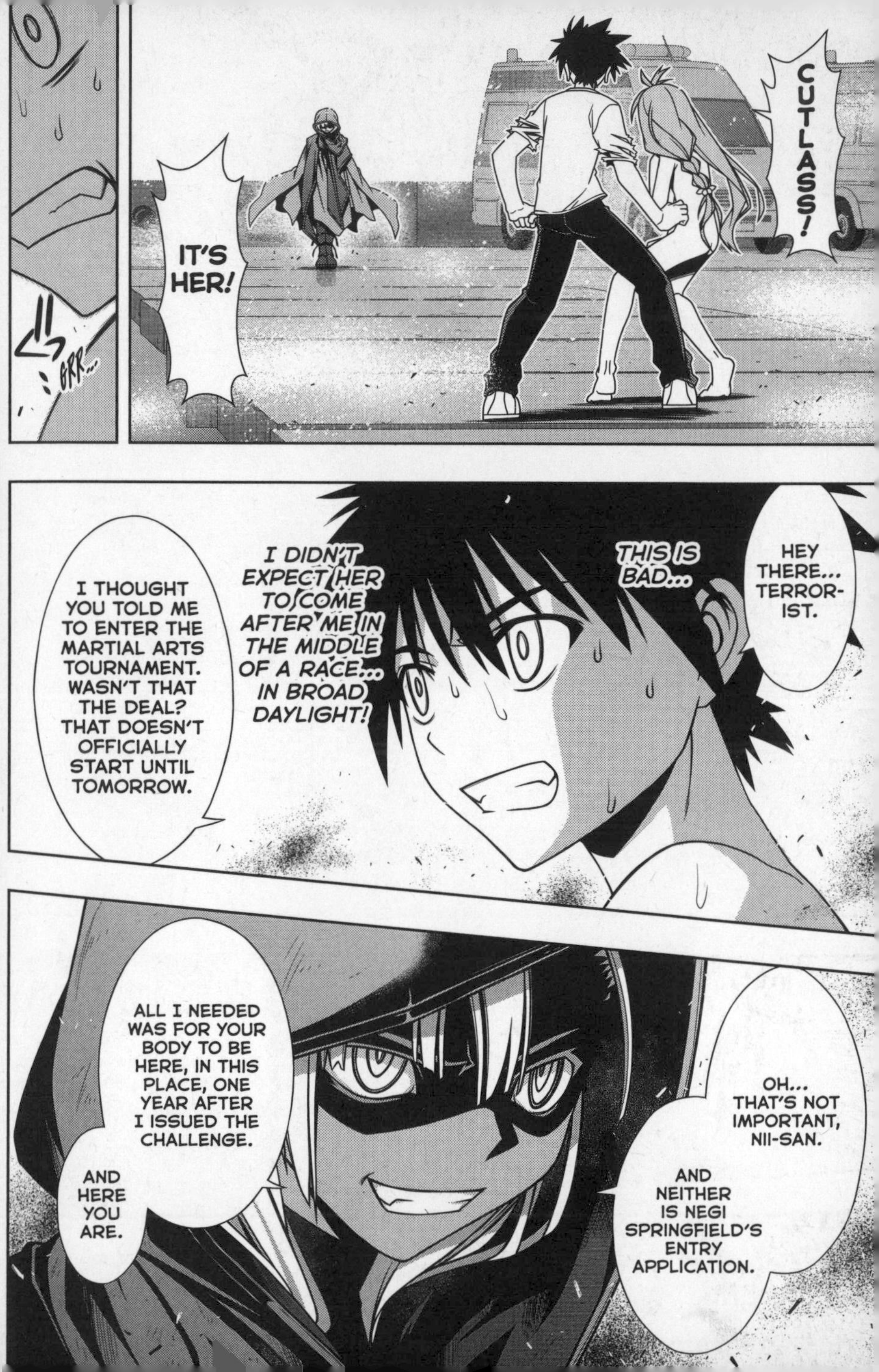
CUTLASS!
IT'S HER!
GRR...
HEY THERE... TERROR-IST.
THIS IS BAD...
I DIDN'T EXPECT HER TO COME AFTER ME IN THE MIDDLE OF A RACE... IN BROAD DAYLIGHT!
I THOUGHT YOU TOLD ME TO ENTER THE MARTIAL ARTS TOURNAMENT. WASN'T THAT THE DEAL? THAT DOESN'T OFFICIALLY START UNTIL TOMORROW.
OH... THAT'S NOT IMPORTANT, NII-SAN.
AND NEITHER IS NEGI SPRINGFIELD'S ENTRY APPLICATION.
ALL I NEEDED WAS FOR YOUR BODY TO BE HERE, IN THIS PLACE, ONE YEAR AFTER I ISSUED THE CHALLENGE.
AND HERE YOU ARE.

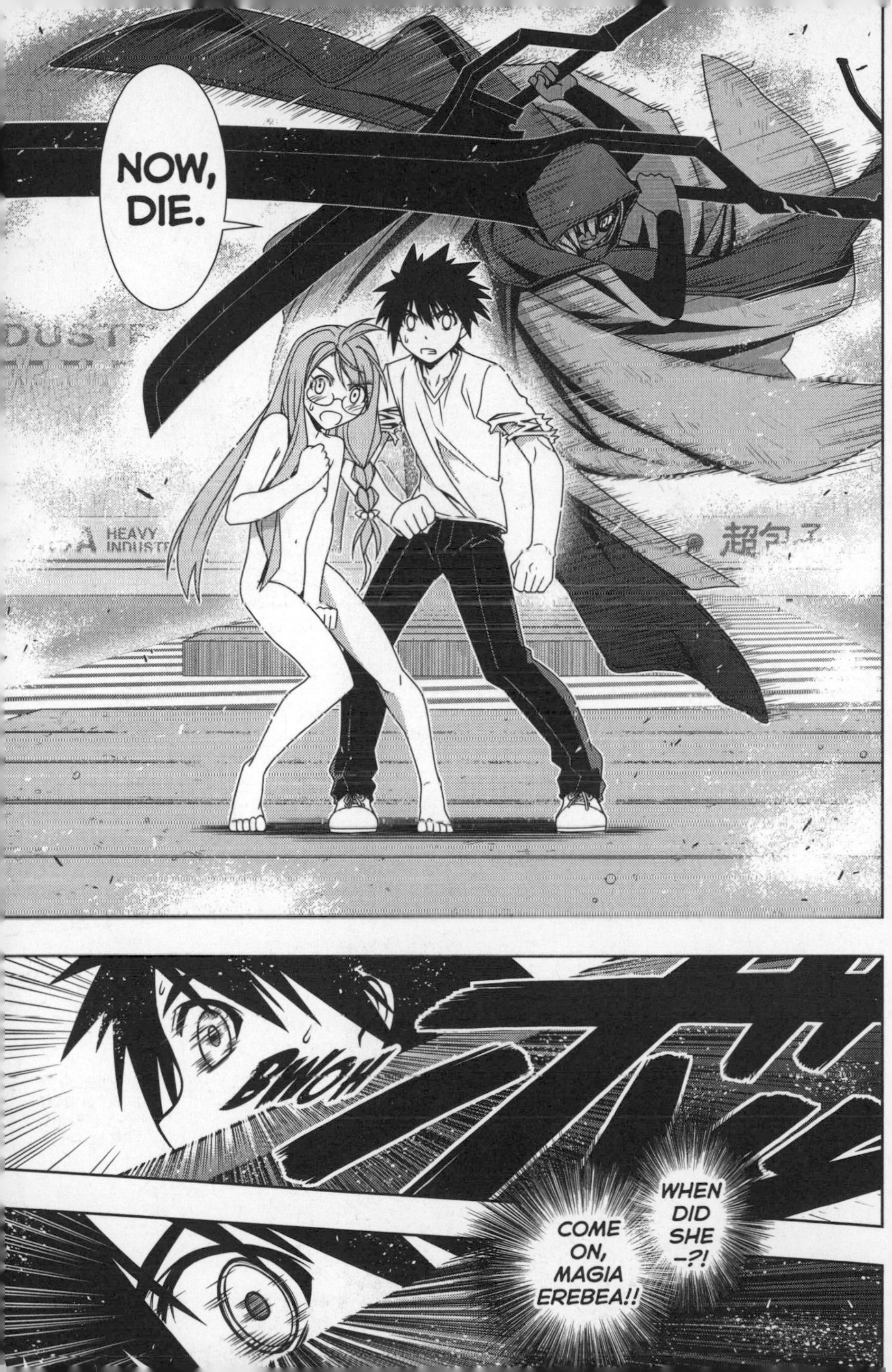
NOW, DIE.
BWOH!
WHEN DID SHE -?!
COME ON, MAGIA EREBEA!!

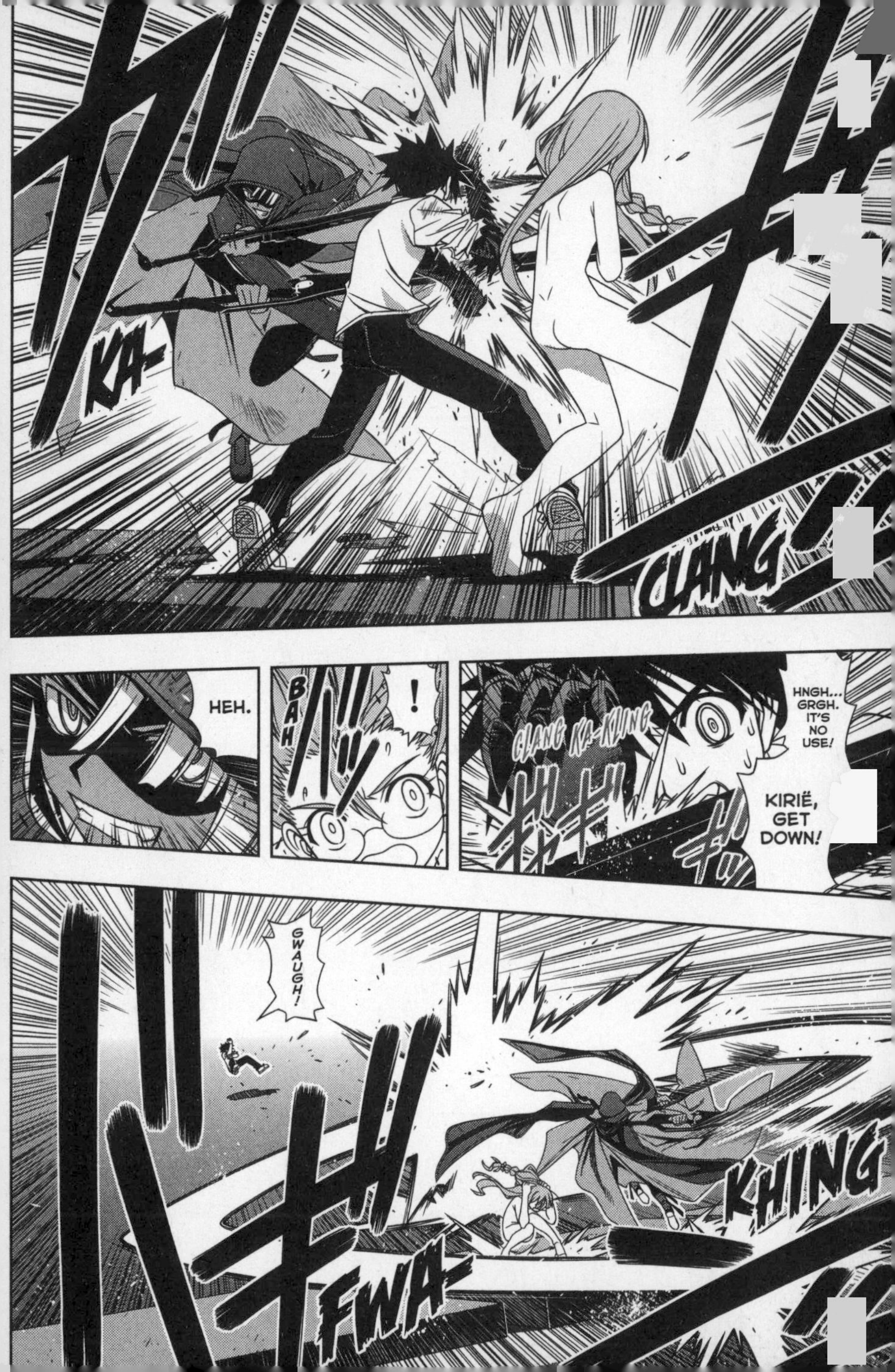
KA-
CLANG
HNGH... GRGH. IT'S NO USE!
CLANG KA-KLING
KIRIË, GET DOWN!
!
BAH
HEH.
GWAUGH!
KHING
FWA

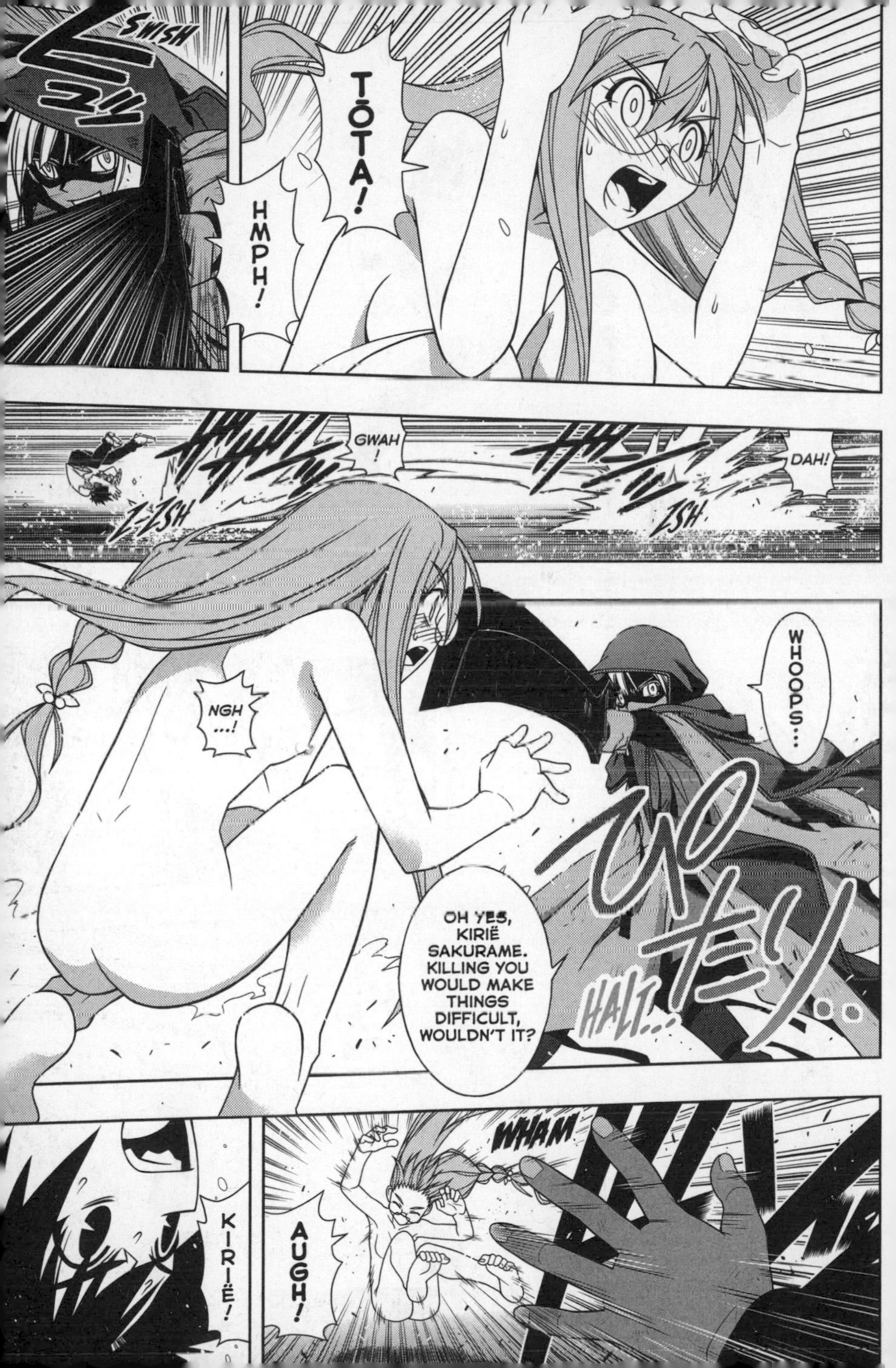
TŌTA!
HMPH!
SWISH
DAH!
ZSH
GWAH!
Z-ZSH
WHOOPS...
HALT...
OH YES, KIRIË SAKURAME. KILLING YOU WOULD MAKE THINGS DIFFICULT, WOULDN'T IT?
NGH ...!
WHAM
AUGH!
KIRIË!

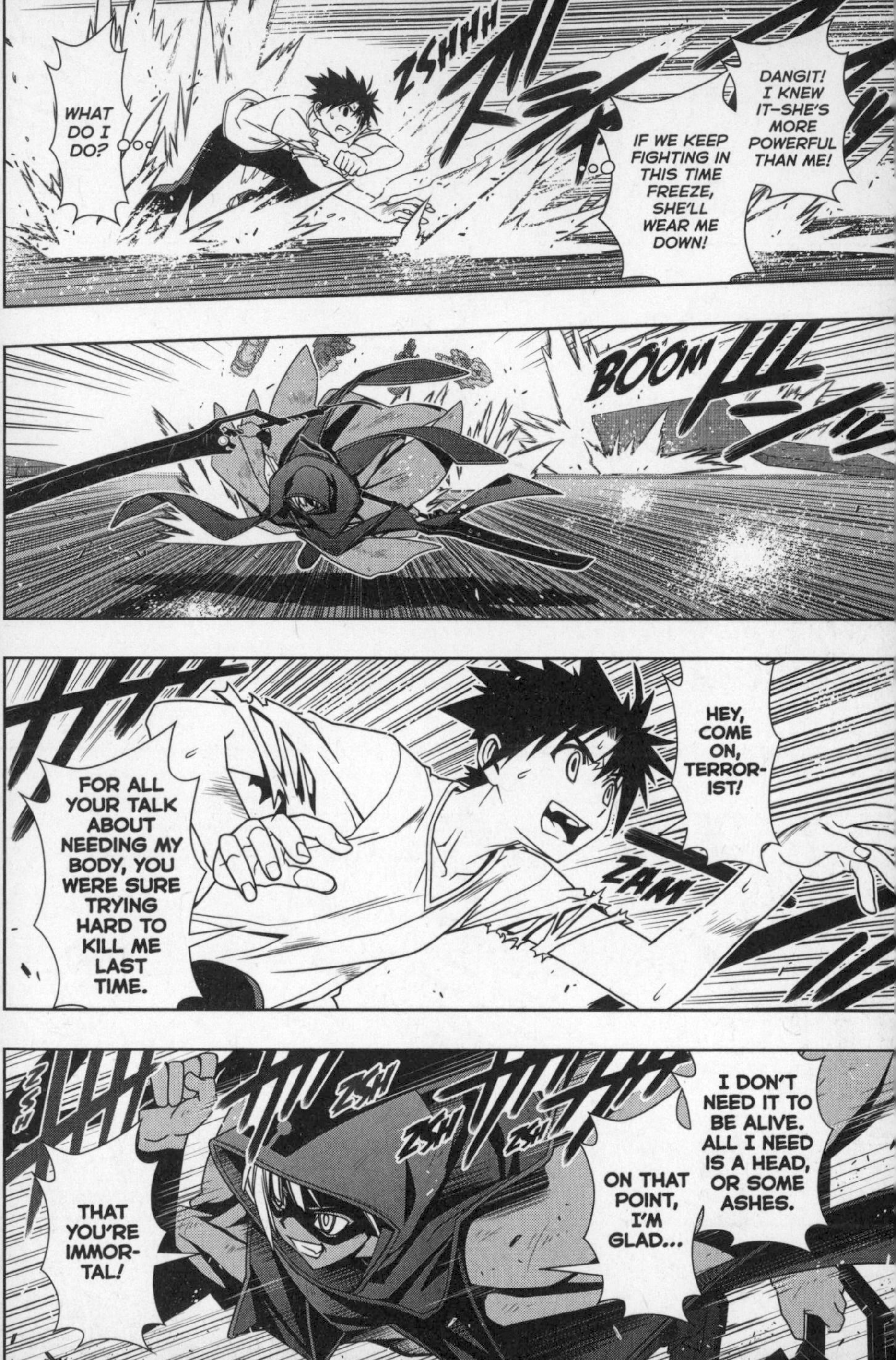
ZSHHH
DANGIT! I KNEW IT—SHE'S MORE POWERFUL THAN ME!
IF WE KEEP FIGHTING IN THIS TIME FREEZE, SHE'LL WEAR ME DOWN!
WHAT DO I DO?
BOOM
HEY, COME ON, TERROR-IST!
ZAM
FOR ALL YOUR TALK ABOUT NEEDING MY BODY, YOU WERE SURE TRYING HARD TO KILL ME LAST TIME.
ZSH
ZSH
ZSH
I DON'T NEED IT TO BE ALIVE. ALL I NEED IS A HEAD, OR SOME ASHES.
ON THAT POINT, I'M GLAD...
THAT YOU'RE IMMORTAL!

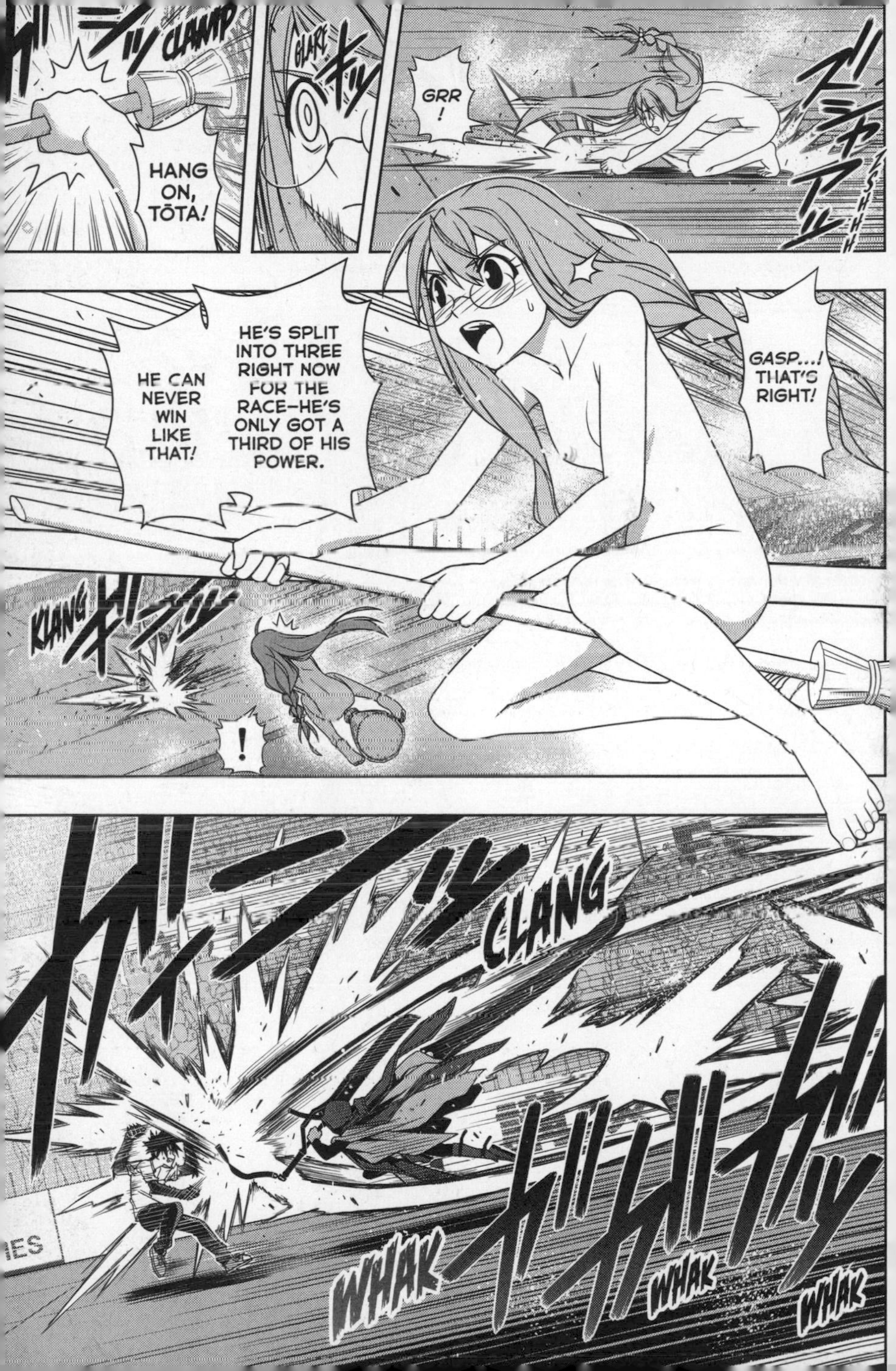
TSHHHH
GRR!
GLARE
CLAMP
HANG ON, TŌTA!
GASP...! THAT'S RIGHT!
HE'S SPLIT INTO THREE RIGHT NOW FOR THE RACE—HE'S ONLY GOT A THIRD OF HIS POWER.
HE CAN NEVER WIN LIKE THAT!
KLANG
!
CLANG
WHAK
WHAK
WHAK

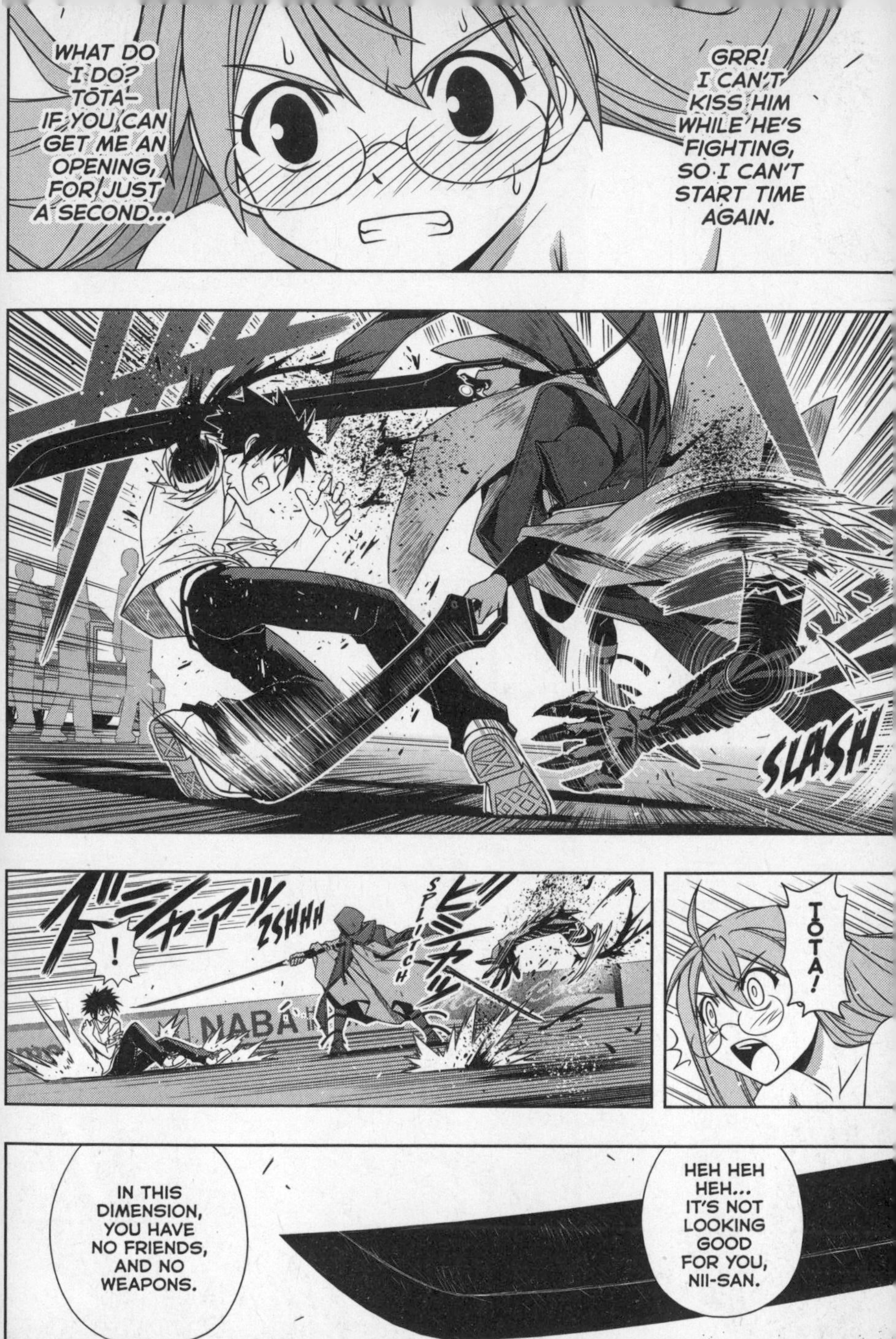
GRR! I CAN'T KISS HIM WHILE HE'S FIGHTING, SO I CAN'T START TIME AGAIN.
WHAT DO I DO? TOTA– IF YOU CAN GET ME AN OPENING, FOR JUST A SECOND...
SLASH
TOTA!
SPLITCH
ZSHHH
!
NABA
HEH HEH HEH... IT'S NOT LOOKING GOOD FOR YOU, NII-SAN.
IN THIS DIMENSION, YOU HAVE NO FRIENDS, AND NO WEAPONS.

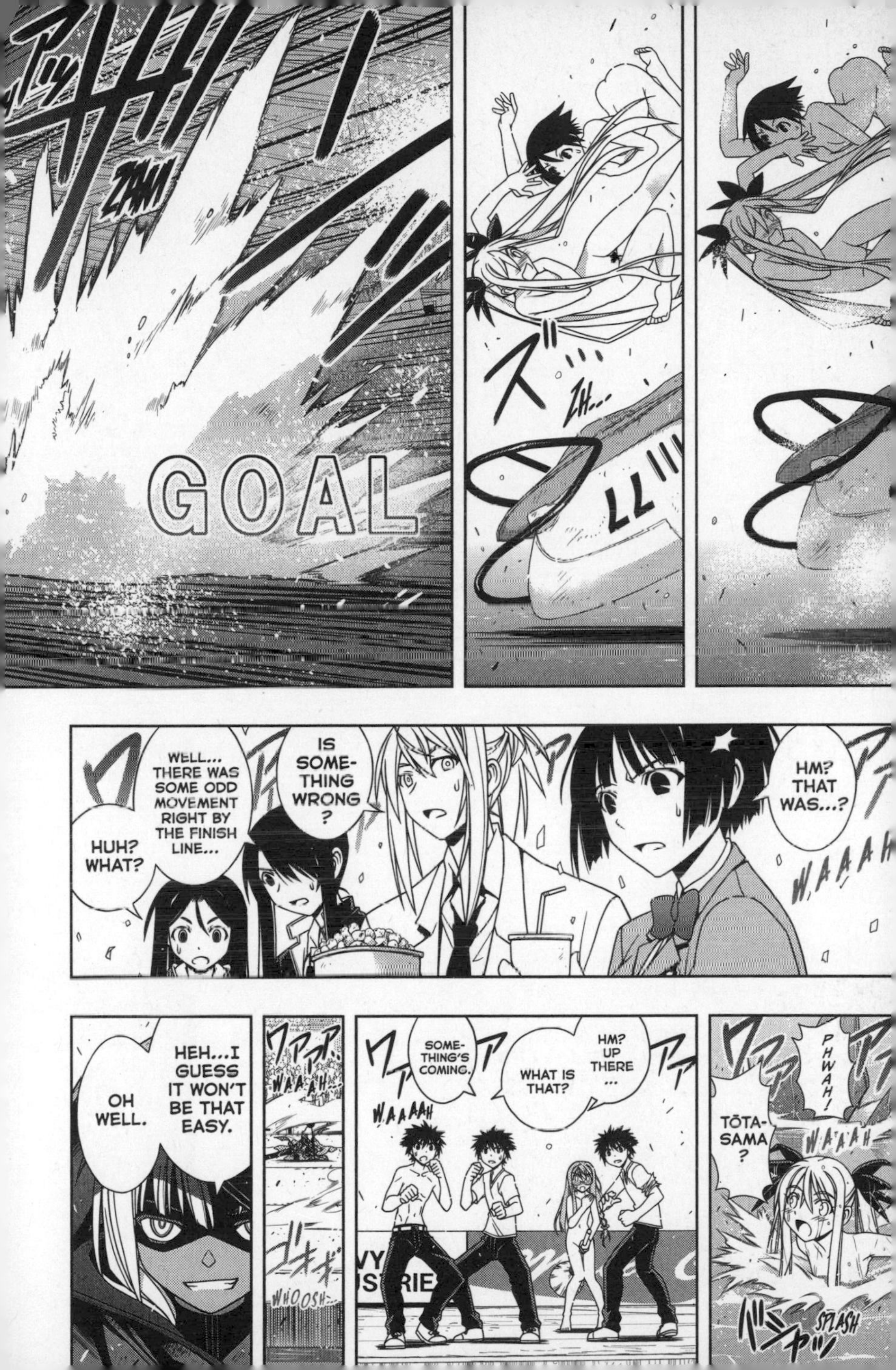
ZH...
ZHAN
GOAL
HM? THAT WAS...?
WAAAH
IS SOMETHING WRONG?
WELL... THERE WAS SOME ODD MOVEMENT RIGHT BY THE FINISH LINE...
HUH? WHAT?
PHWAH!
TŌTA-SAMA?
WAAAH
SPLASH
HM? UP THERE ...
WHAT IS THAT?
SOMETHING'S COMING.
WAAAAH
WAAAH...
WHOOSH...
HEH...I GUESS IT WON'T BE THAT EASY.
OH WELL.

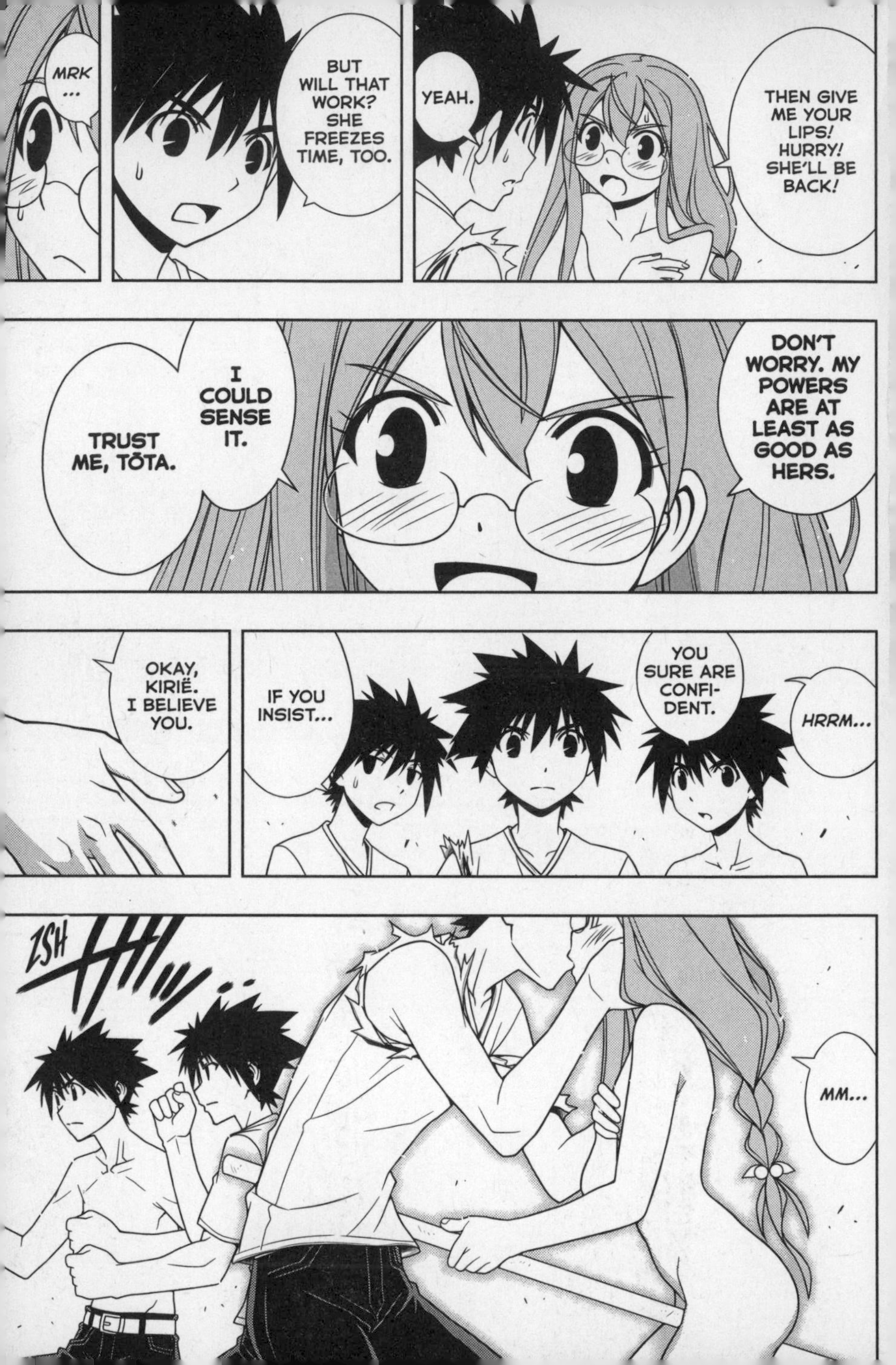
THEN GIVE ME YOUR LIPS! HURRY! SHE'LL BE BACK!
YEAH.
BUT WILL THAT WORK? SHE FREEZES TIME, TOO.
MRK ...
DON'T WORRY. MY POWERS ARE AT LEAST AS GOOD AS HERS.
I COULD SENSE IT.
TRUST ME, TŌTA.
HRRM...
YOU SURE ARE CONFI-DENT.
IF YOU INSIST...
OKAY, KIRIË. I BELIEVE YOU.
MM...
ZSH

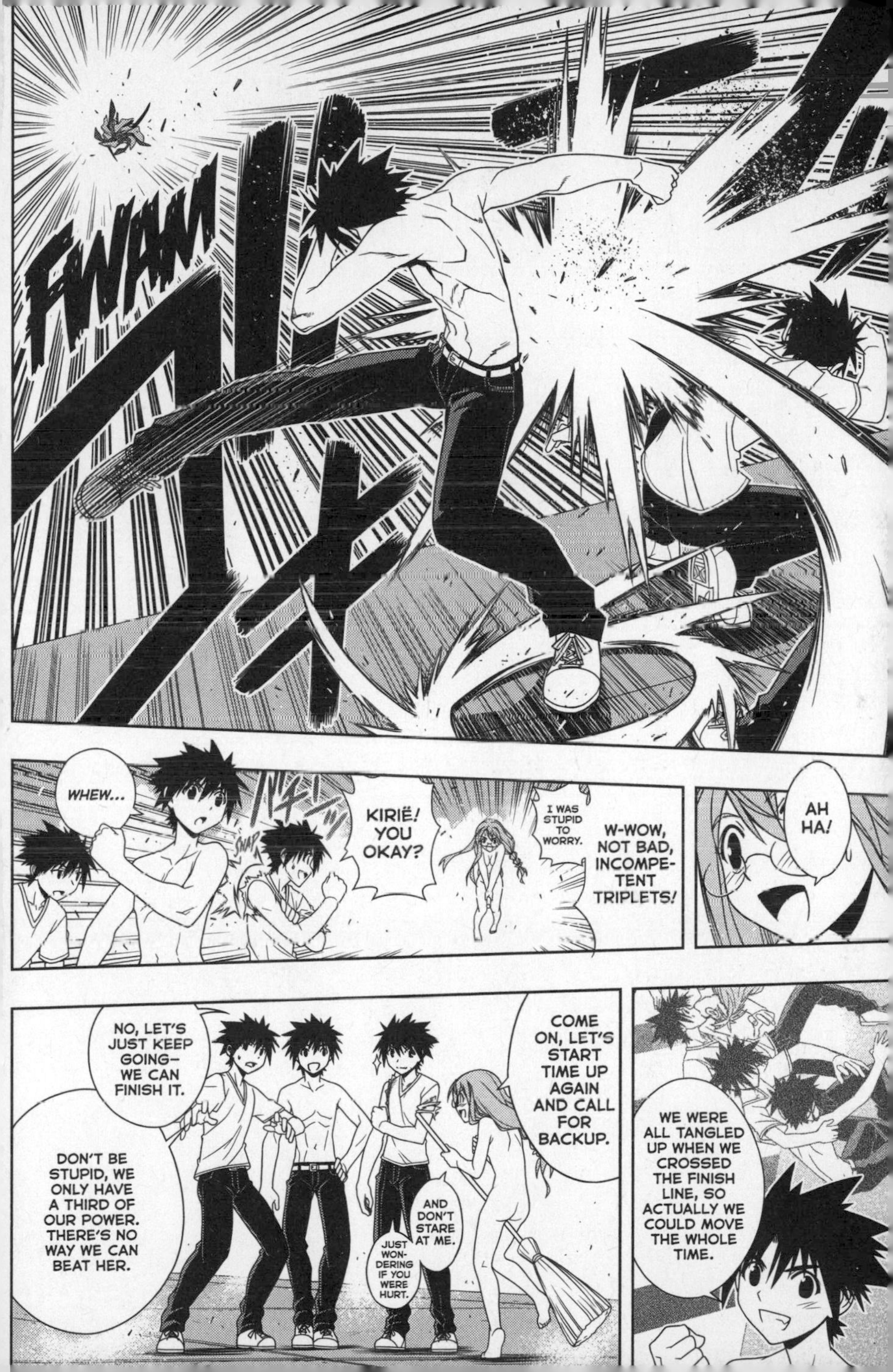
FWAM
AH HA!
W-WOW, NOT BAD, INCOMPETENT TRIPLETS!
I WAS STUPID TO WORRY.
KIRIË! YOU OKAY?
SNAP
WHEW...
WE WERE ALL TANGLED UP WHEN WE CROSSED THE FINISH LINE, SO ACTUALLY WE COULD MOVE THE WHOLE TIME.
COME ON, LET'S START TIME UP AGAIN AND CALL FOR BACKUP.
NO, LET'S JUST KEEP GOING— WE CAN FINISH IT.
DON'T BE STUPID, WE ONLY HAVE A THIRD OF OUR POWER. THERE'S NO WAY WE CAN BEAT HER.
AND DON'T STARE AT ME.
JUST WONDERING IF YOU WERE HURT.

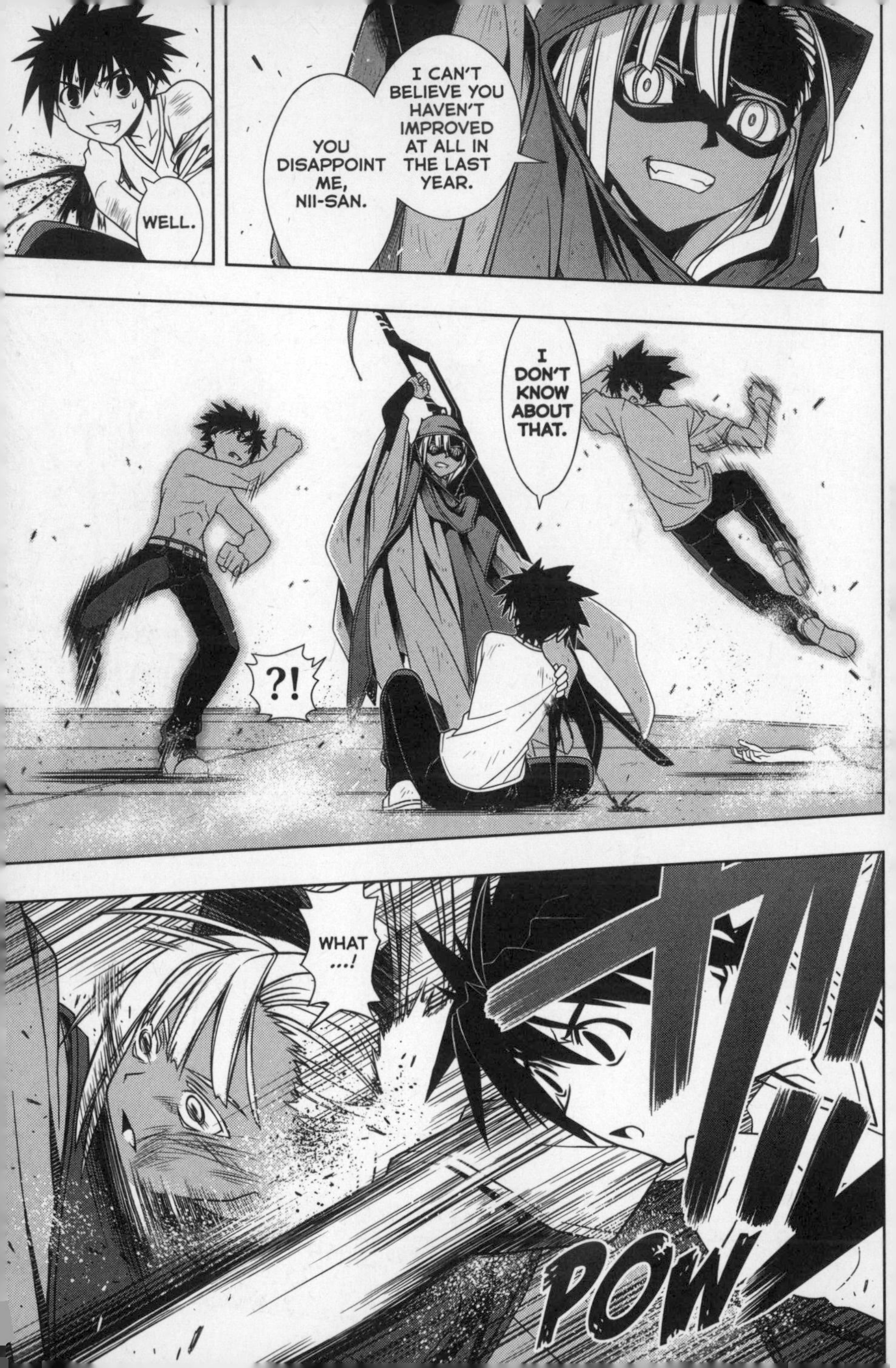
I CAN'T BELIEVE YOU HAVEN'T IMPROVED AT ALL IN THE LAST YEAR.
YOU DISAPPOINT ME, NII-SAN.
WELL.
I DON'T KNOW ABOUT THAT.
?!
WHAT ...!
POW

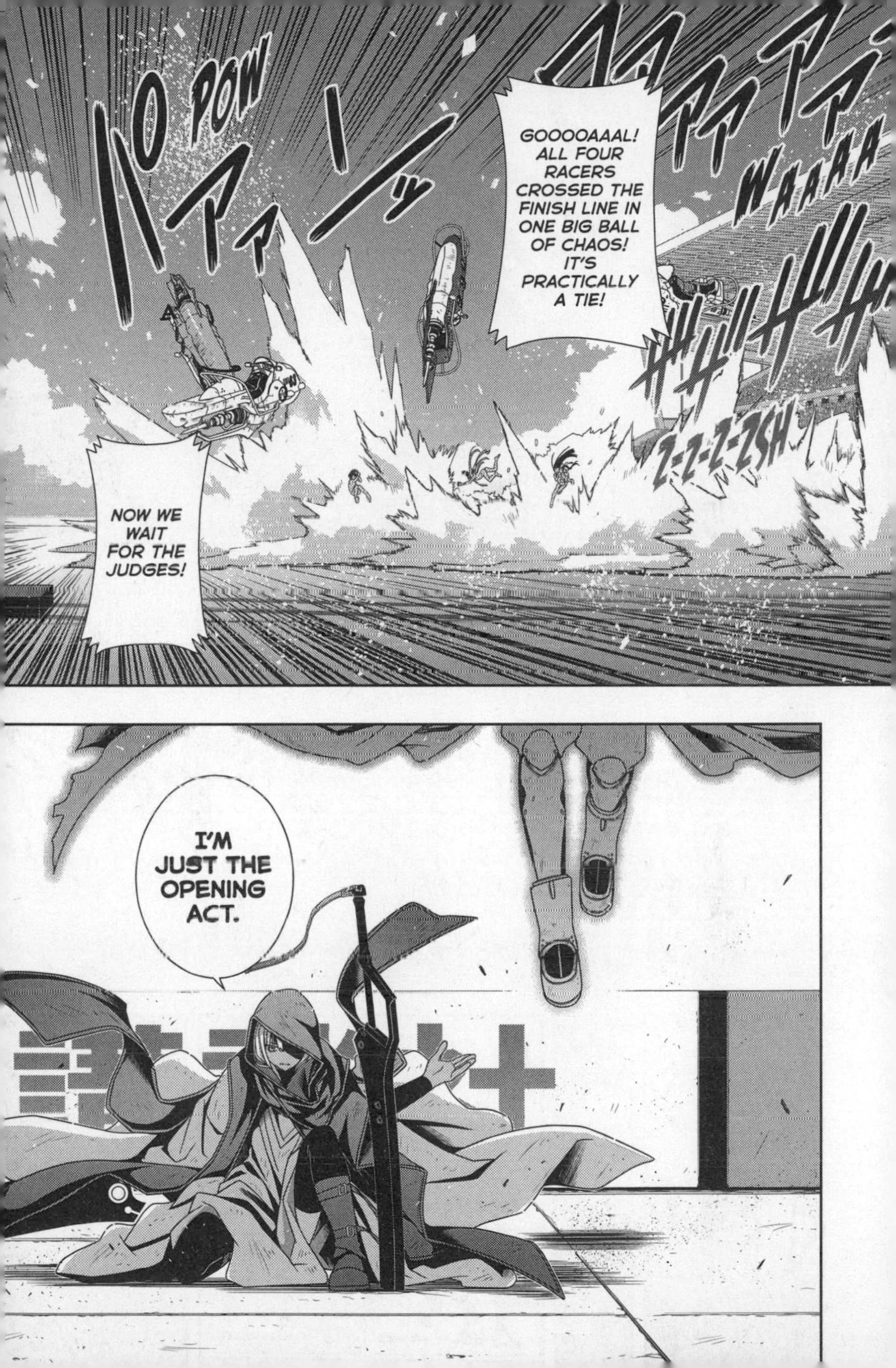
WAAAA
GOOOOAAAL! ALL FOUR RACERS CROSSED THE FINISH LINE IN ONE BIG BALL OF CHAOS! IT'S PRACTICALLY A TIE!
POW
Z-Z-Z-ZSH
NOW WE WAIT FOR THE JUDGES!
I'M JUST THE OPENING ACT.

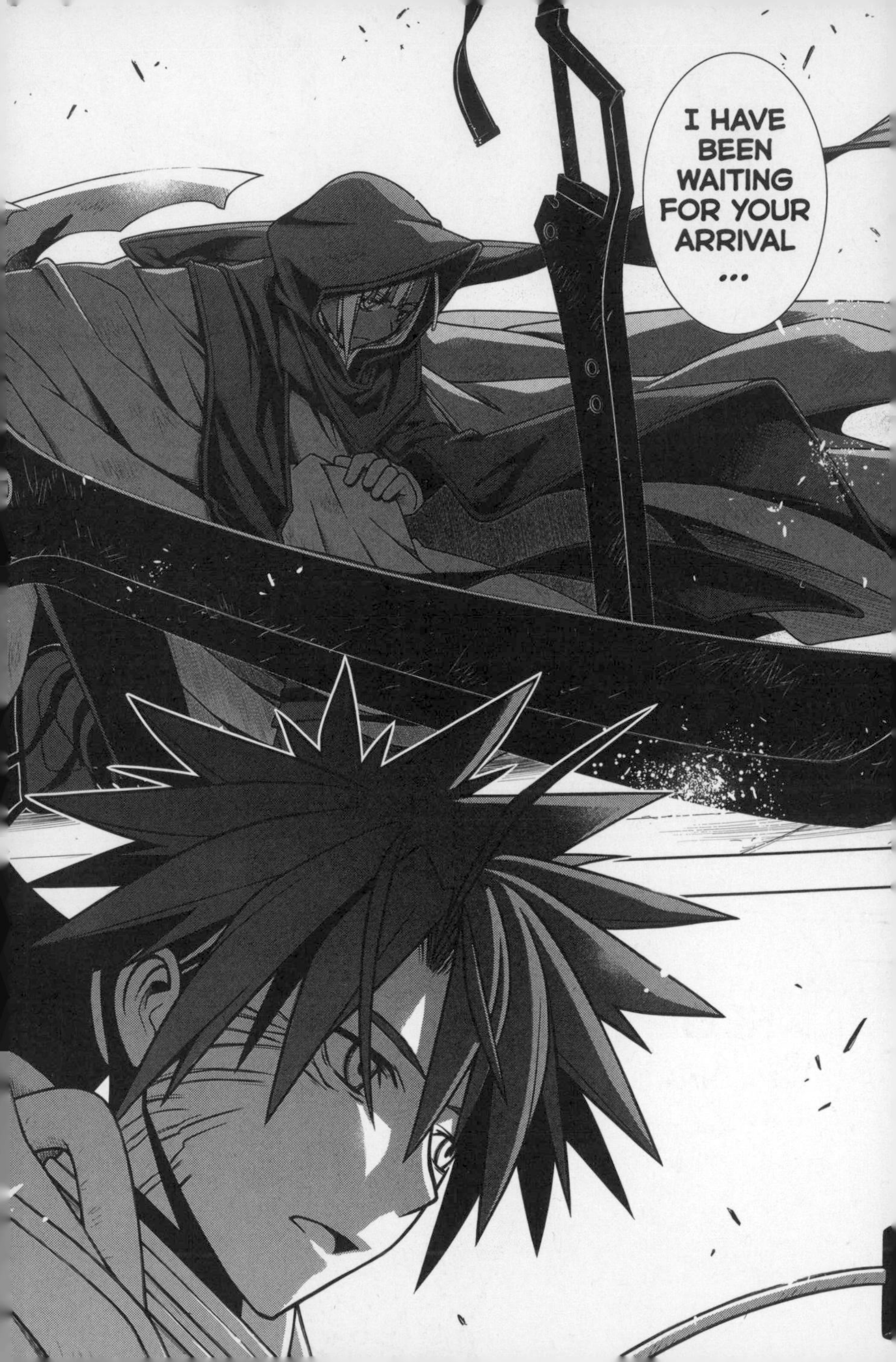
I HAVE BEEN WAITING FOR YOUR ARRIVAL ...

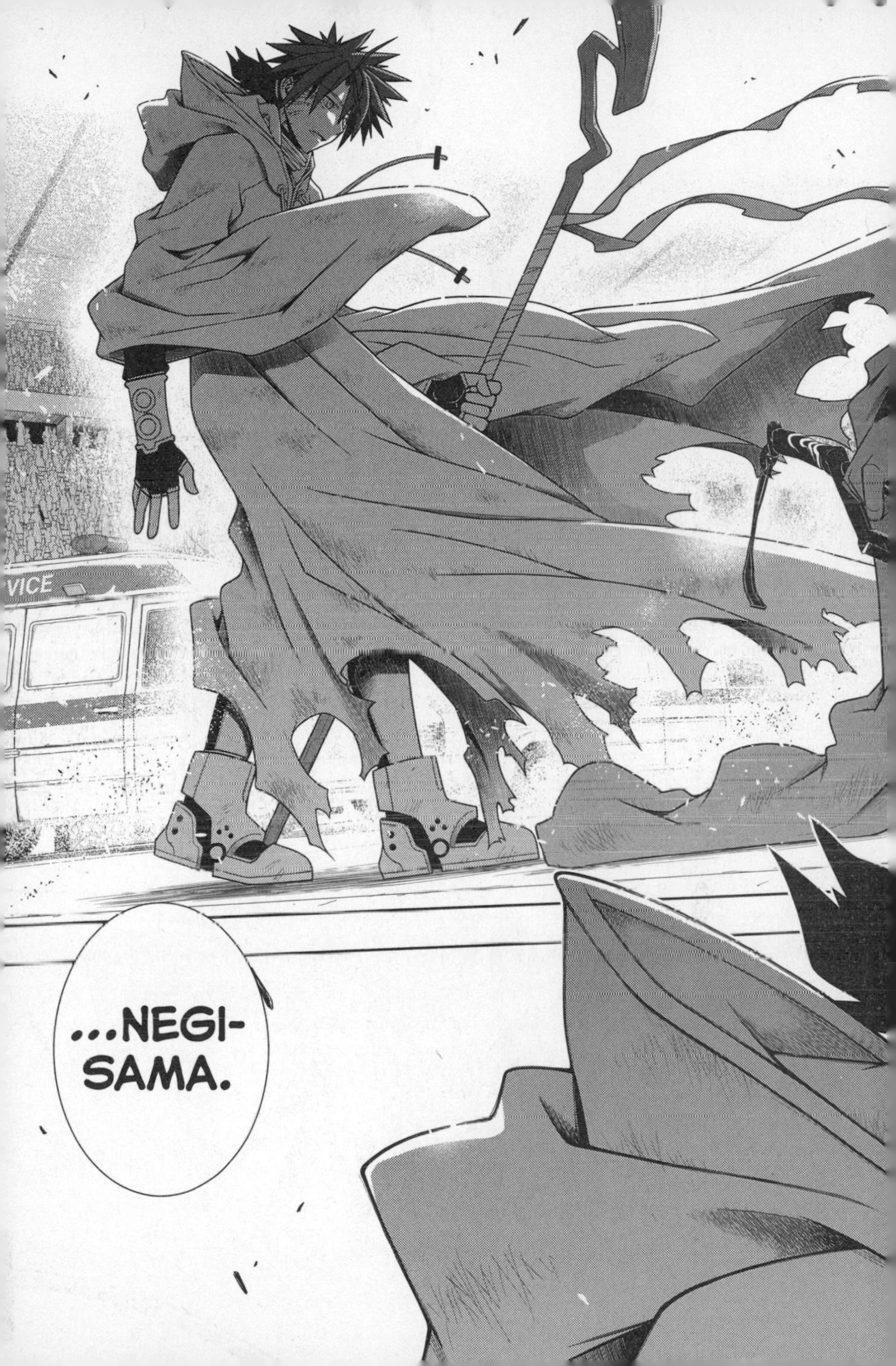
VICE
...NEGI-SAMA.

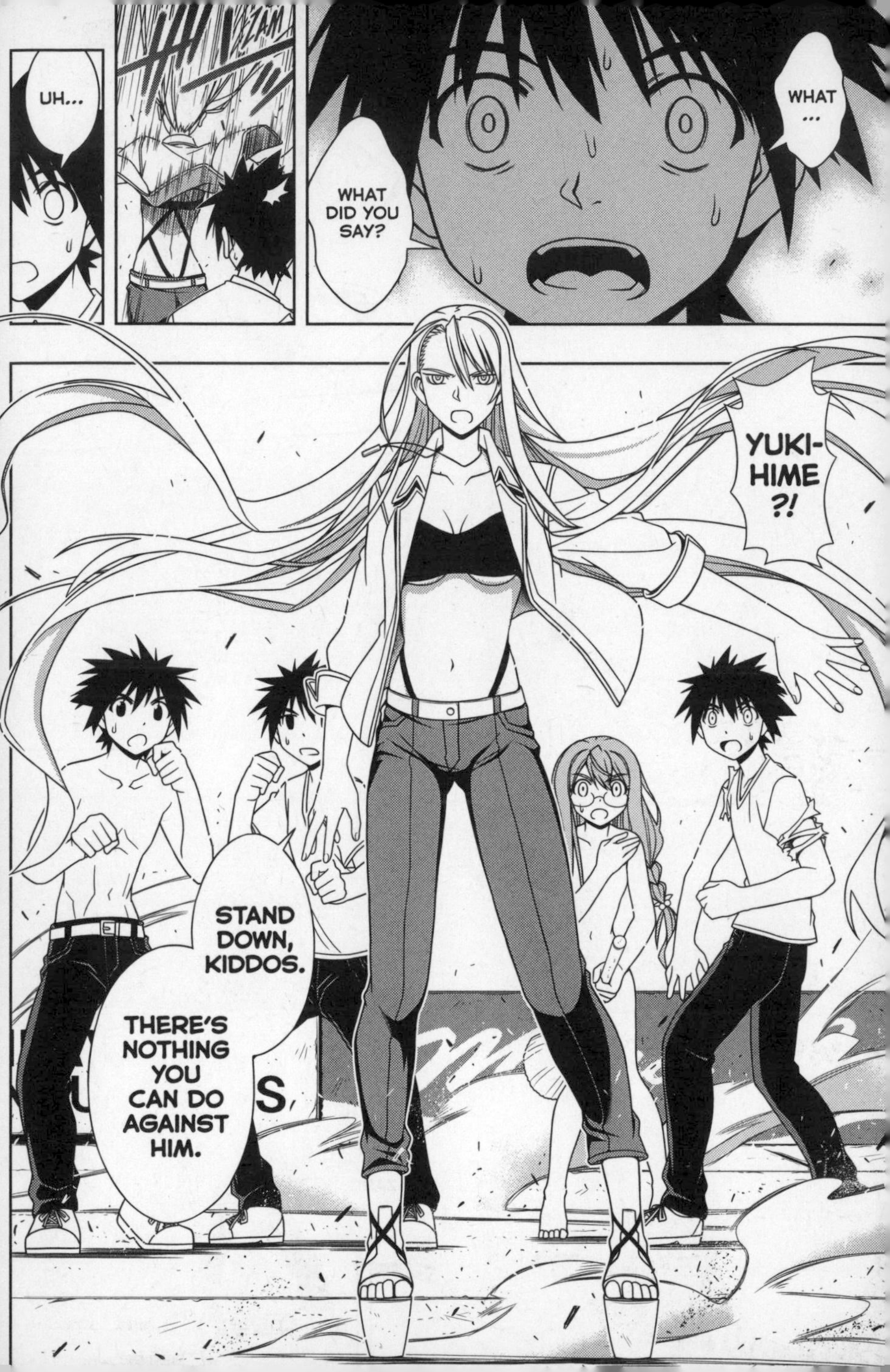
WHAT ...
WHAT DID YOU SAY?
UH...
YUKI-HIME ?!
STAND DOWN, KIDDOS.
THERE'S NOTHING YOU CAN DO AGAINST HIM.

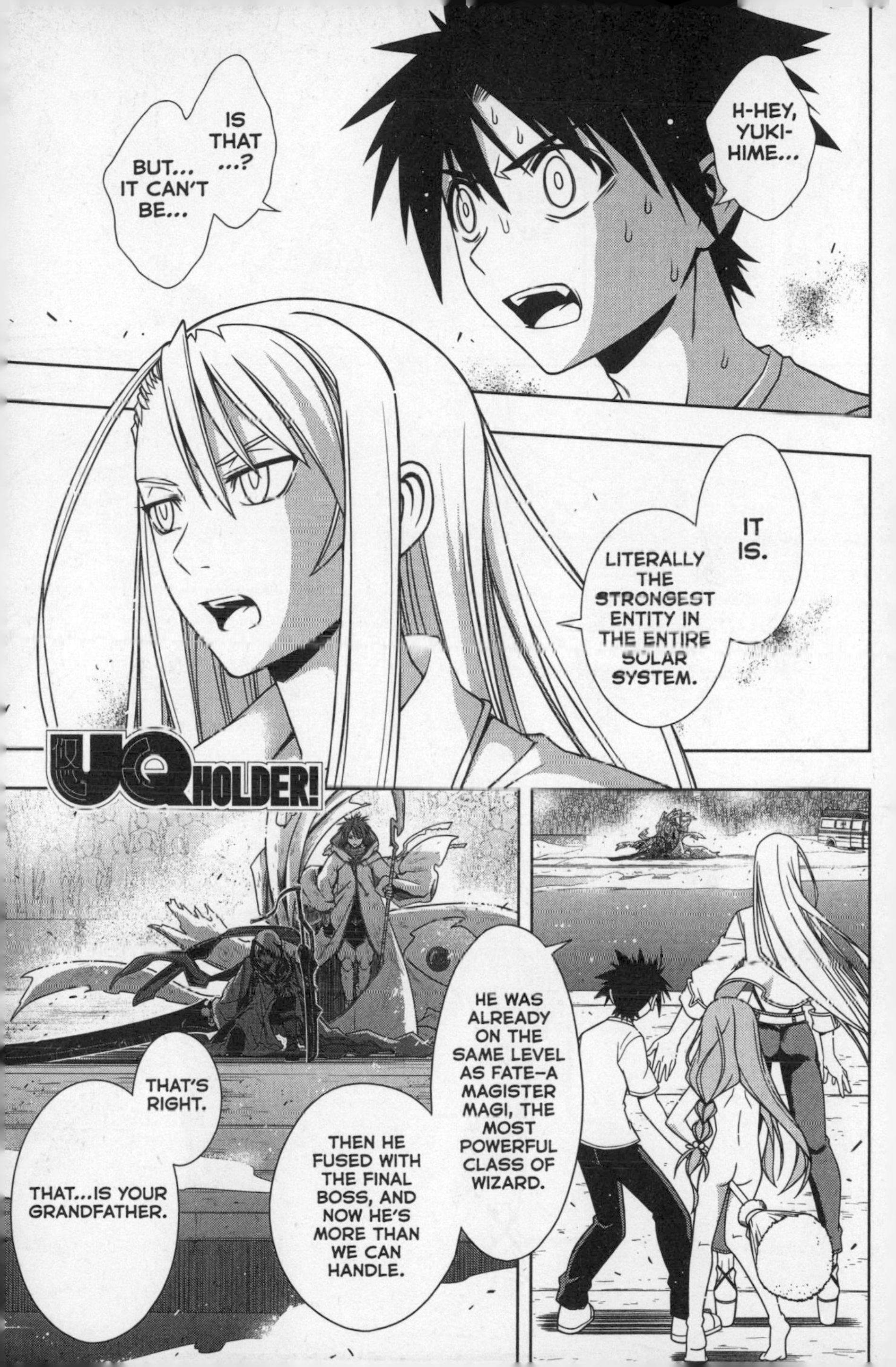
H-HEY, YUKI-HIME...
IS THAT ...?
BUT... IT CAN'T BE...
IT IS.
LITERALLY THE STRONGEST ENTITY IN THE ENTIRE SOLAR SYSTEM.
UQ HOLDER!
HE WAS ALREADY ON THE SAME LEVEL AS FATE—A MAGISTER MAGI, THE MOST POWERFUL CLASS OF WIZARD.
THEN HE FUSED WITH THE FINAL BOSS, AND NOW HE'S MORE THAN WE CAN HANDLE.
THAT'S RIGHT.
THAT...IS YOUR GRANDFATHER.

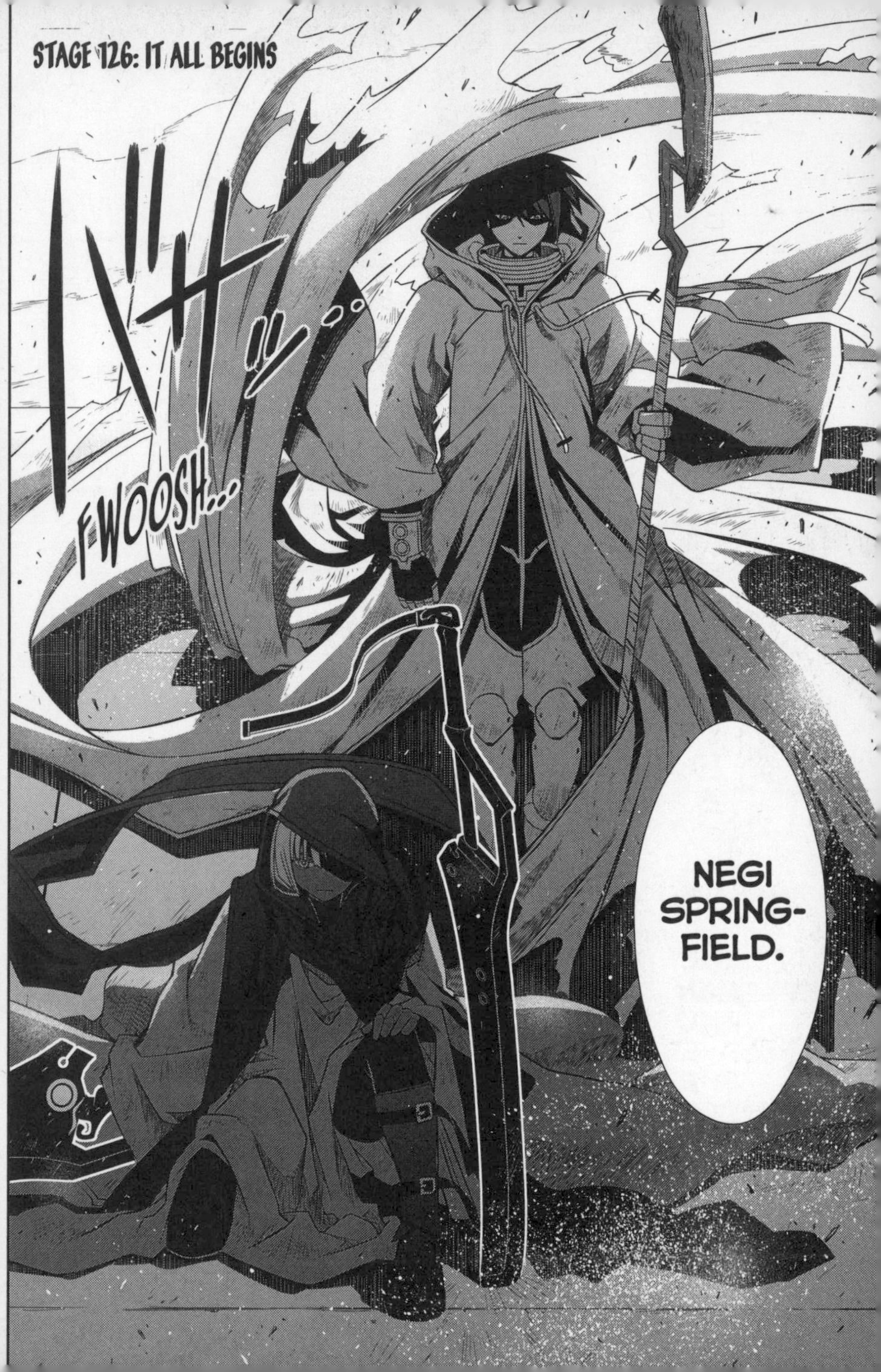
STAGE 126: IT ALL BEGINS
F-WOOSH...
NEGI SPRING-FIELD.

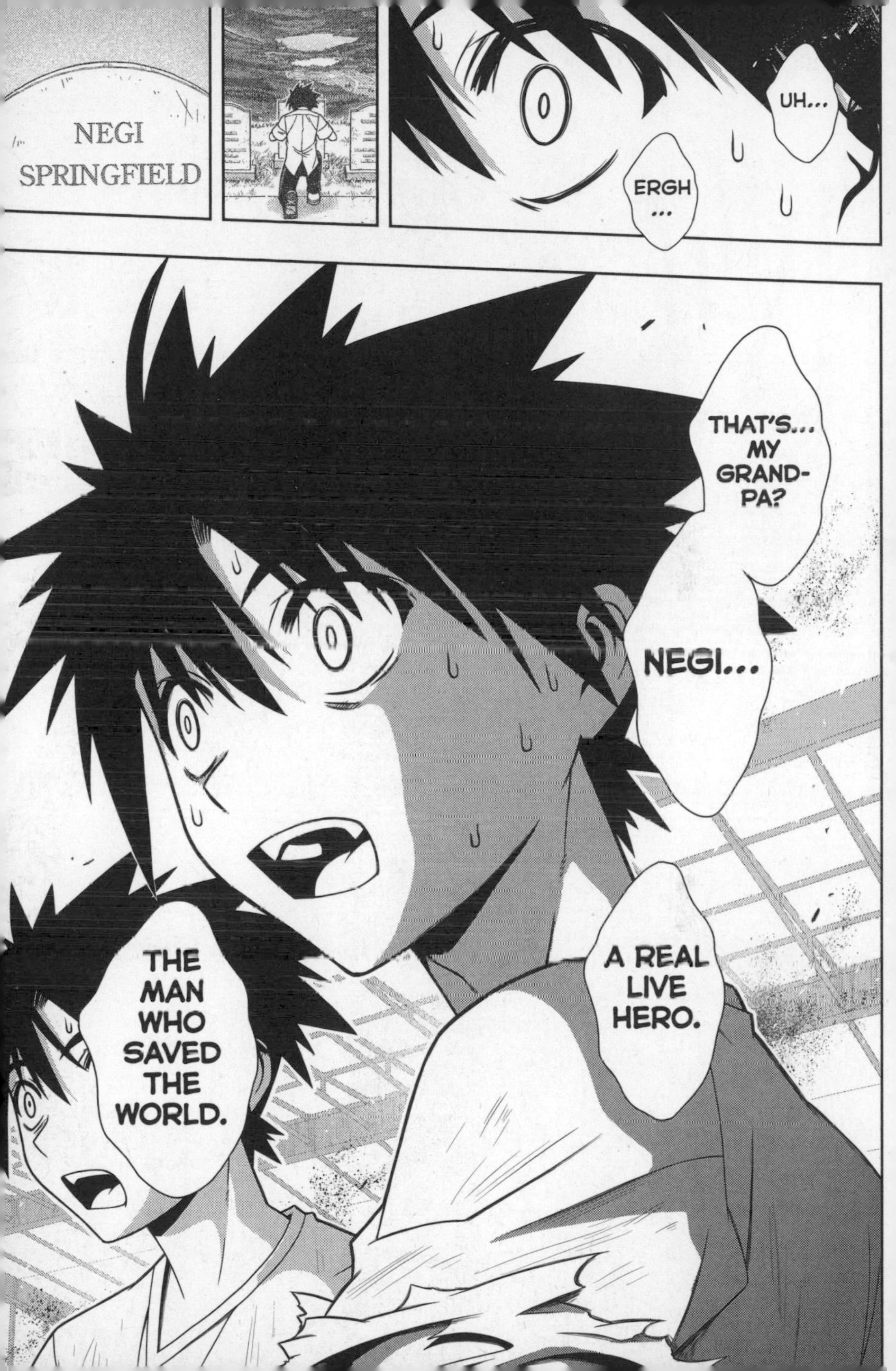
UH...
ERGH...
NEGI SPRINGFIELD
THAT'S... MY GRANDPA?
NEGI...
A REAL LIVE HERO.
THE MAN WHO SAVED THE WORLD.

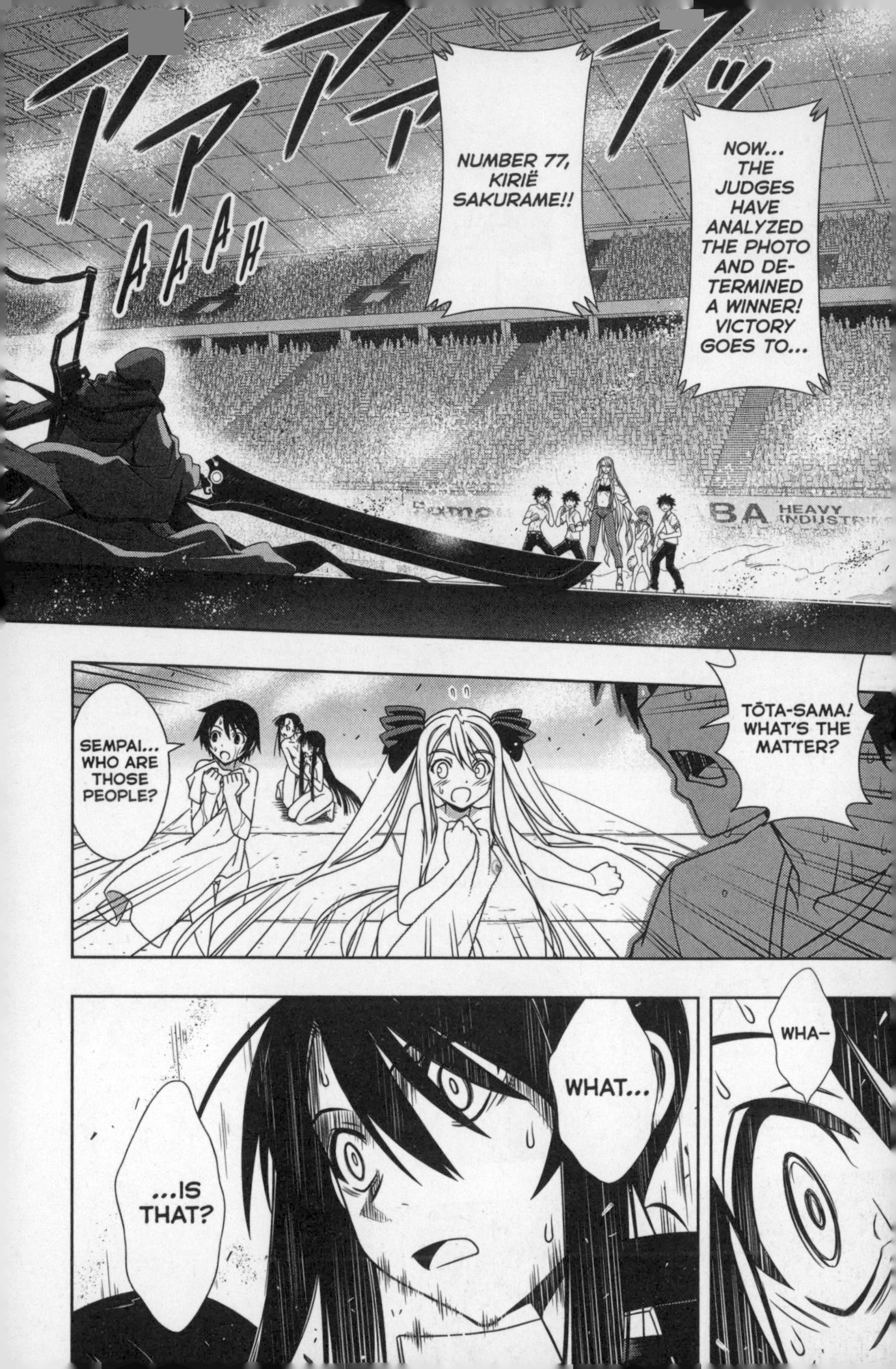
AAAH
NOW... THE JUDGES HAVE ANALYZED THE PHOTO AND DE-TERMINED A WINNER! VICTORY GOES TO...
NUMBER 77, KIRIË SAKURAME!!
TŌTA-SAMA! WHAT'S THE MATTER?
SEMPAI... WHO ARE THOSE PEOPLE?
WHA-
WHAT...
...IS THAT?

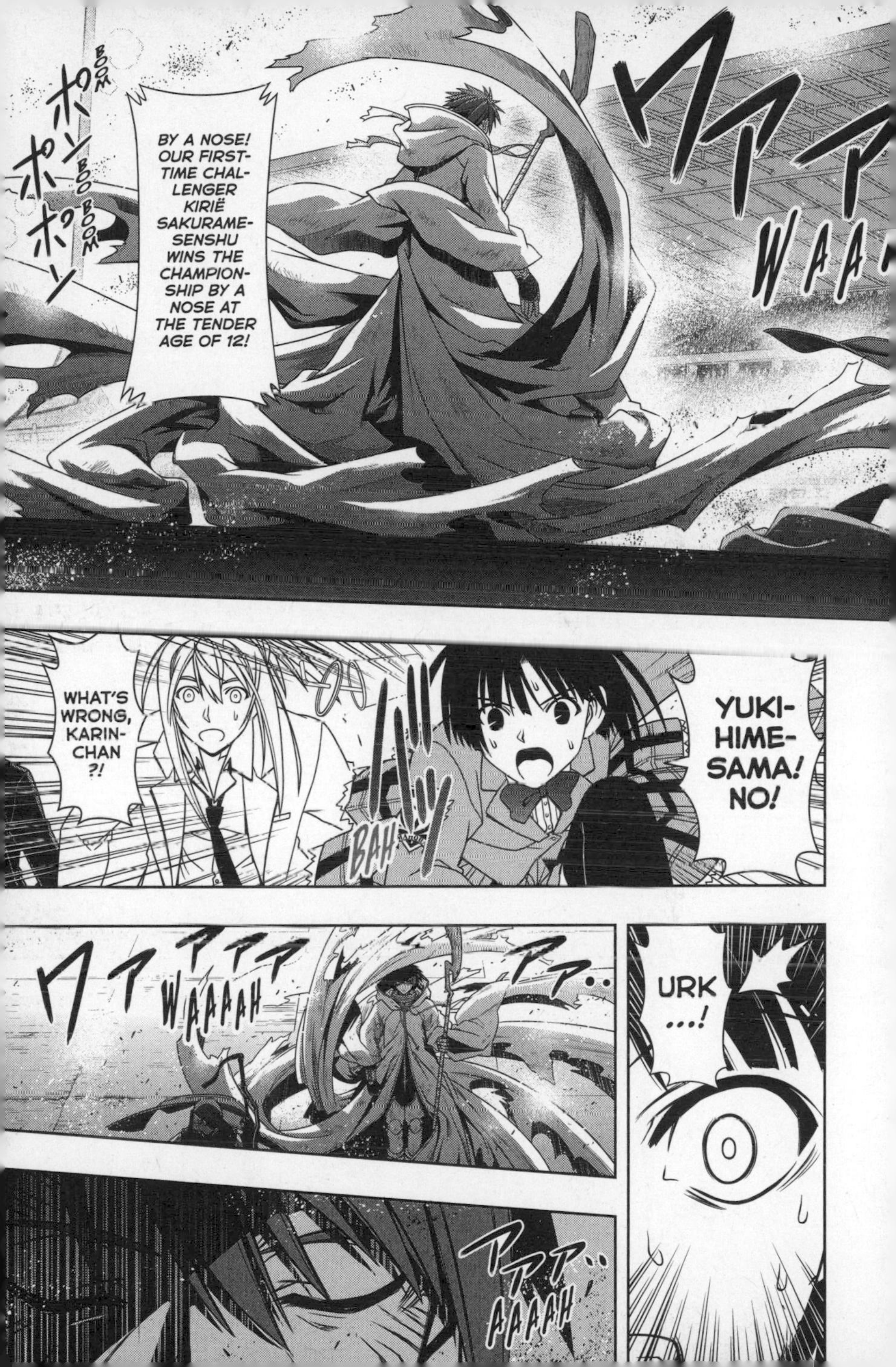
WAAA
BY A NOSE! OUR FIRST-TIME CHALLENGER KIRIË SAKURAME-SENSHU WINS THE CHAMPIONSHIP BY A NOSE AT THE TENDER AGE OF 12!
BOOM BOO BOOM
YUKI-HIME-SAMA! NO!
BAH
WHAT'S WRONG, KARIN-CHAN?!
URK ...!
WAAAAH
AAAAH

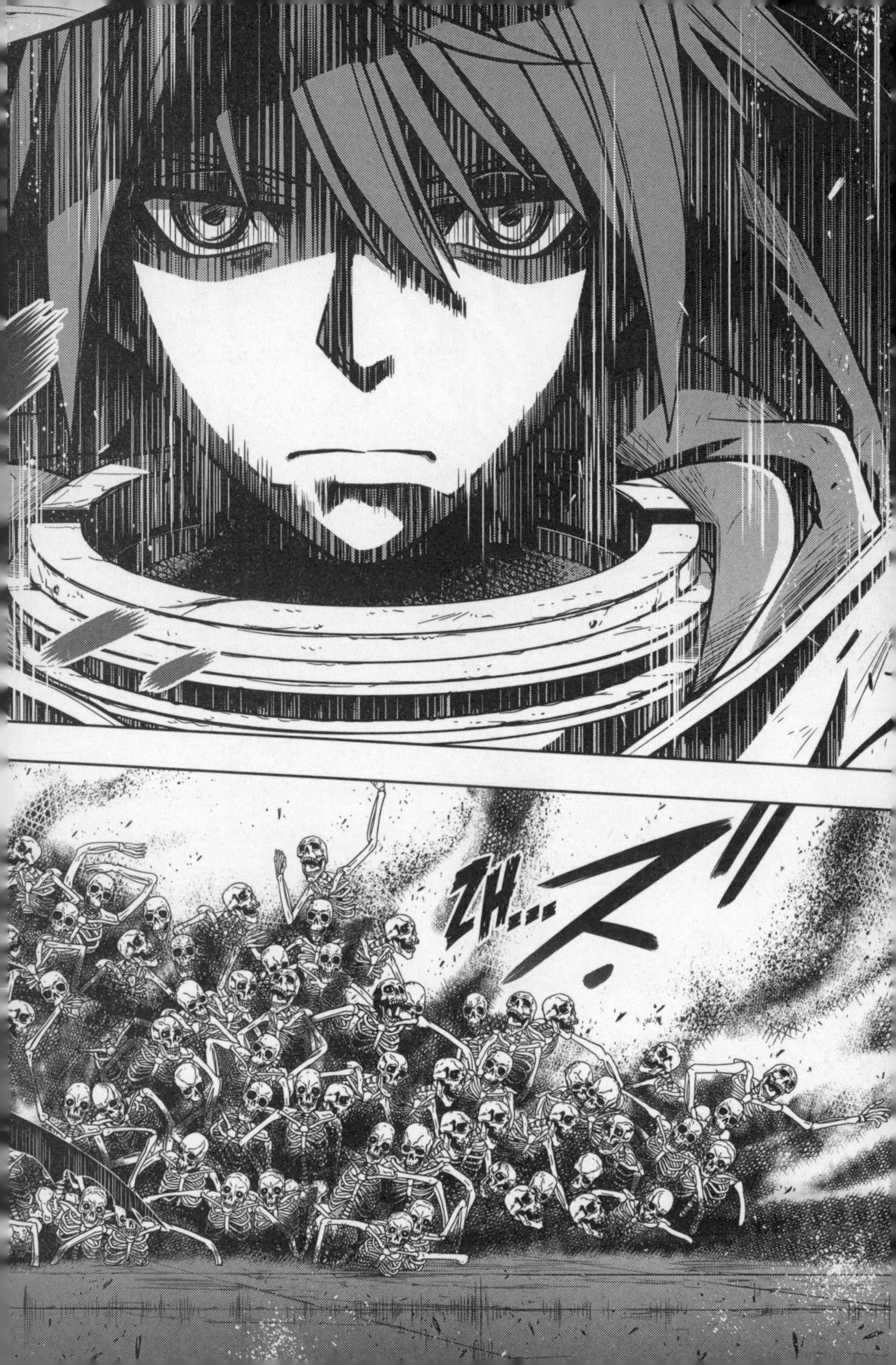
ZH...

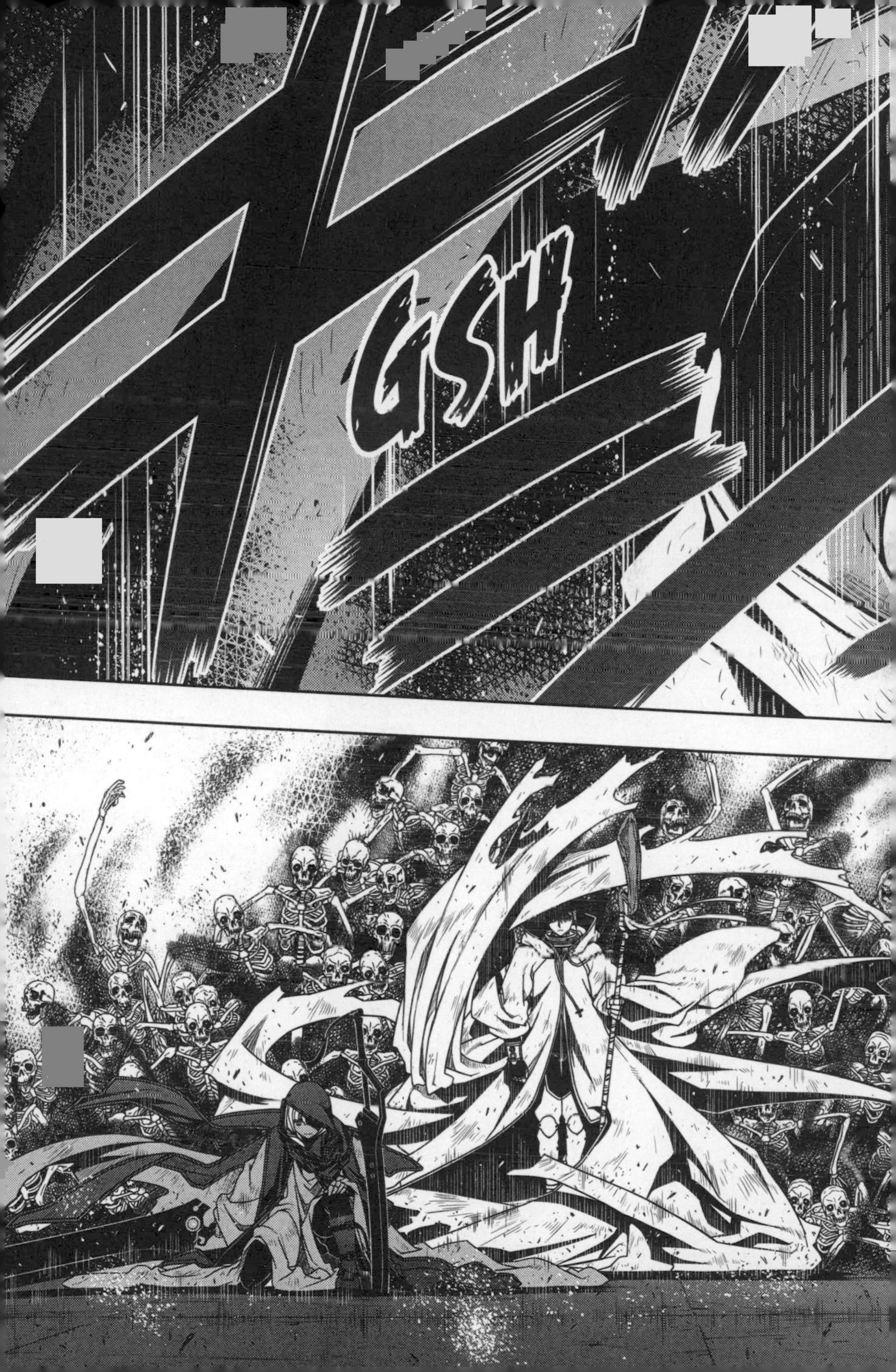
GSH

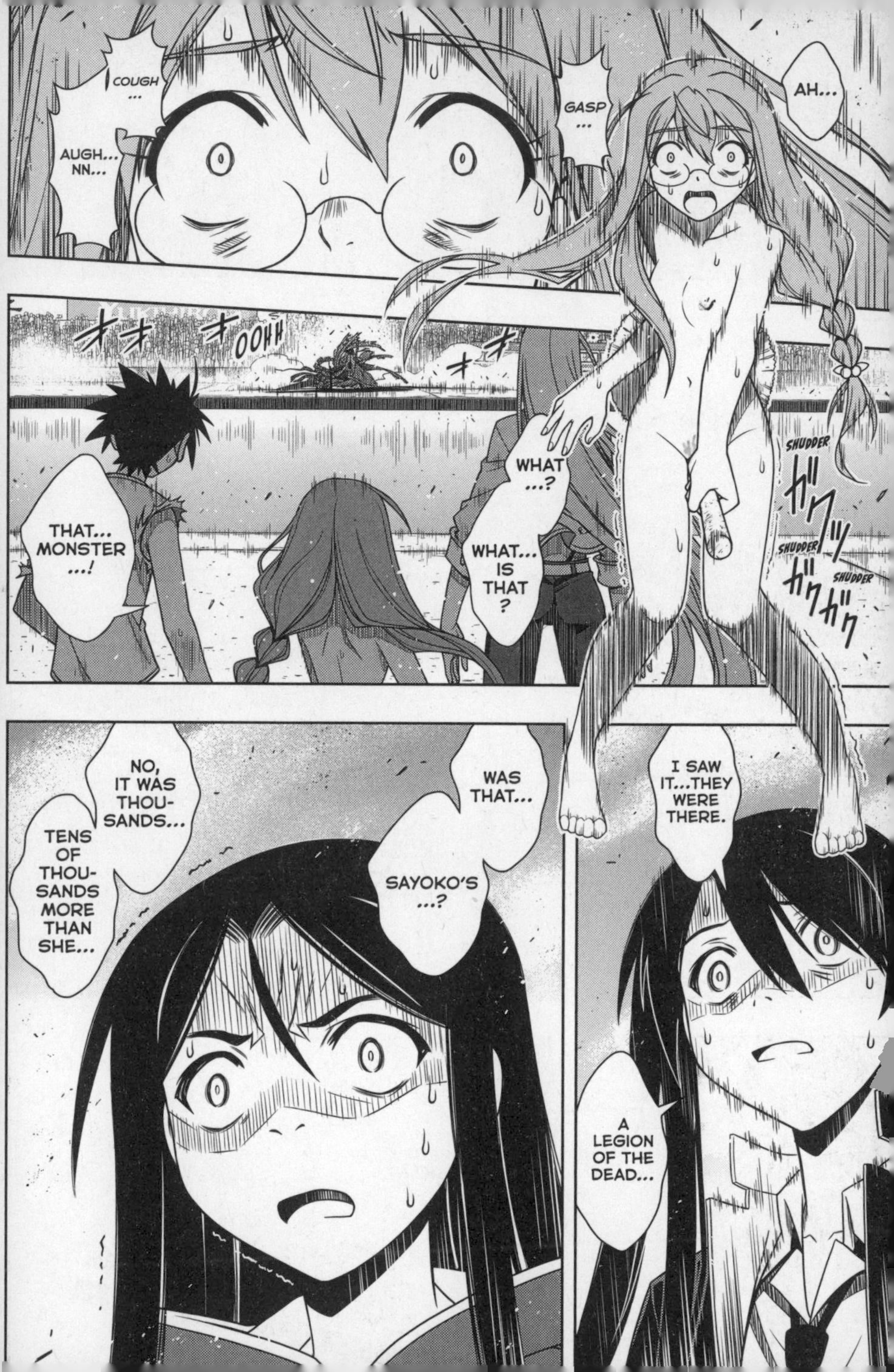
AH...
GASP ...
COUGH ...
AUGH... NN...
SHUDDER
SHUDDER
SHUDDER
OOHH
WHAT ...?
WHAT... IS THAT ?
THAT... MONSTER ...!
I SAW IT...THEY WERE THERE.
A LEGION OF THE DEAD...
WAS THAT...
SAYOKO'S ...?
NO, IT WAS THOUSANDS...
TENS OF THOUSANDS MORE THAN SHE...

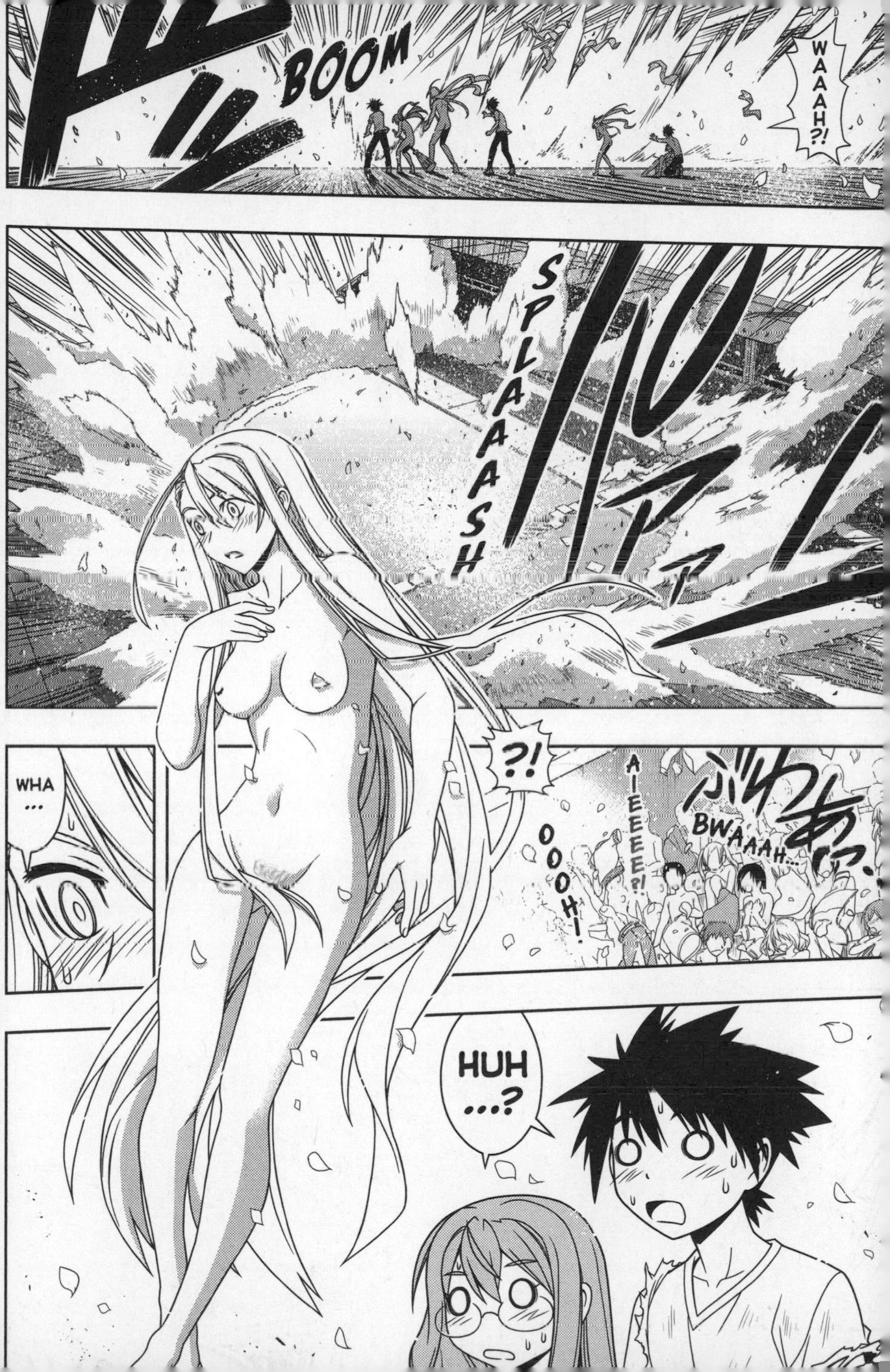
WAAAAH?!
BOOM
SPLAAAASH
?!
BWAAAAH...
AIEEEEE?!
OOOOH!
WHA ...
HUH ...?

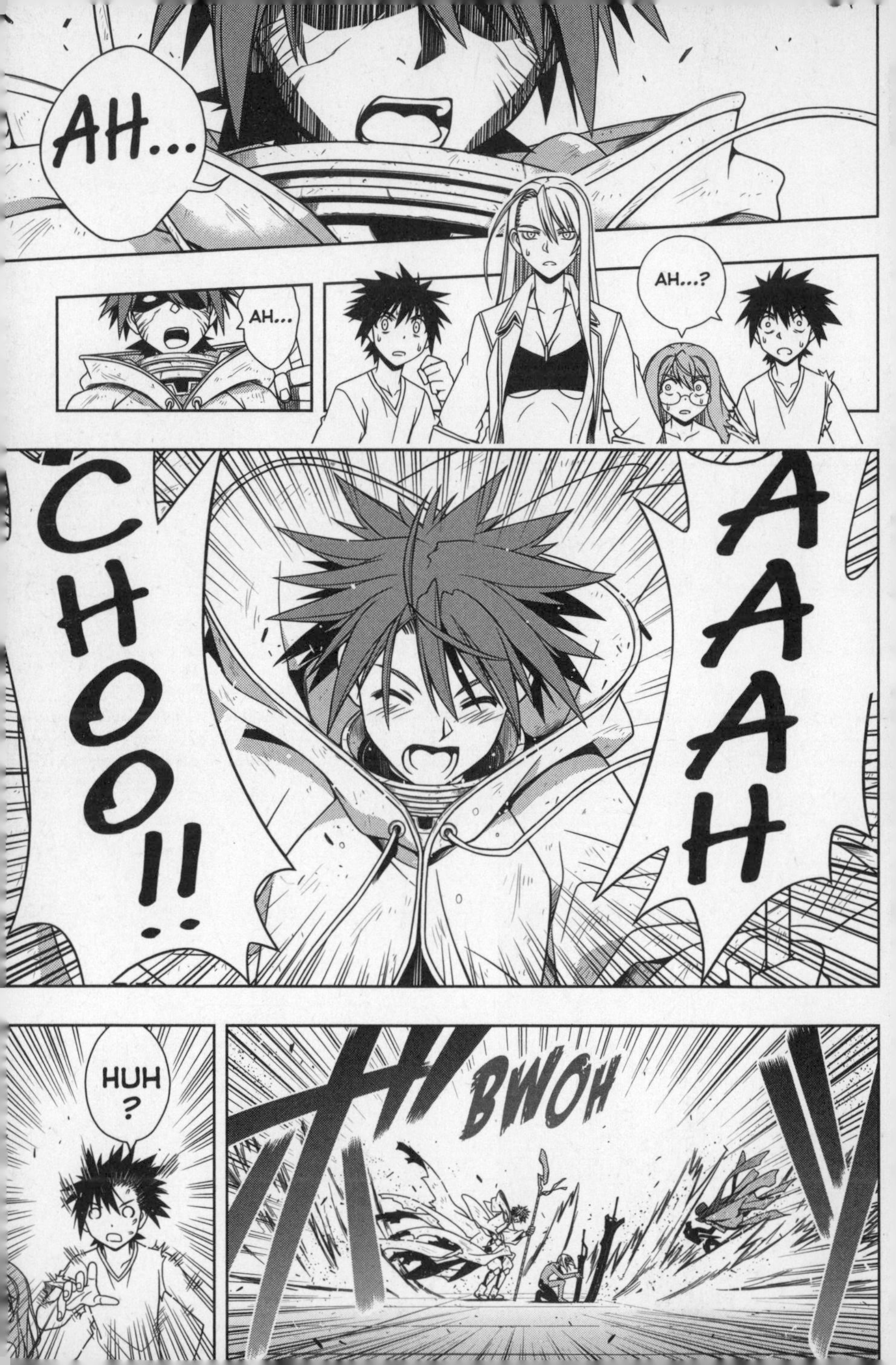
AH...
AH...?
AH...
AAAH
CHOO!!
BWOH
HUH ?

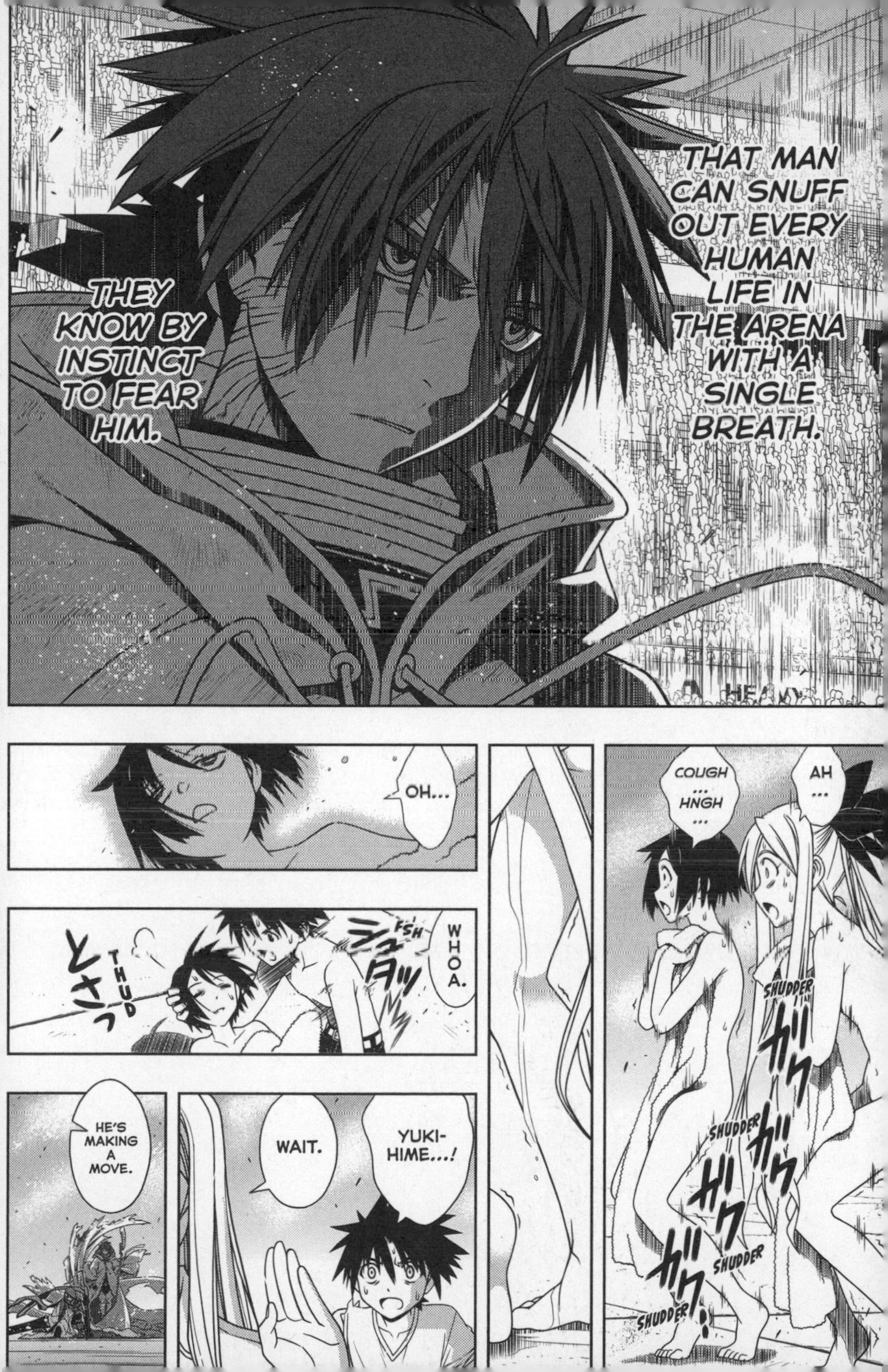

THAT MAN CAN SNUFF OUT EVERY HUMAN LIFE IN THE ARENA WITH A SINGLE BREATH.
THEY KNOW BY INSTINCT TO FEAR HIM.
A HEAVY
AH ...
COUGH ... HNGH ...
SHUDDER
SHUDDER
SHUDDER
SHUDDER
OH...
WHOA.
FSH
THUD
YUKI-HIME...!
WAIT.
HE'S MAKING A MOVE.

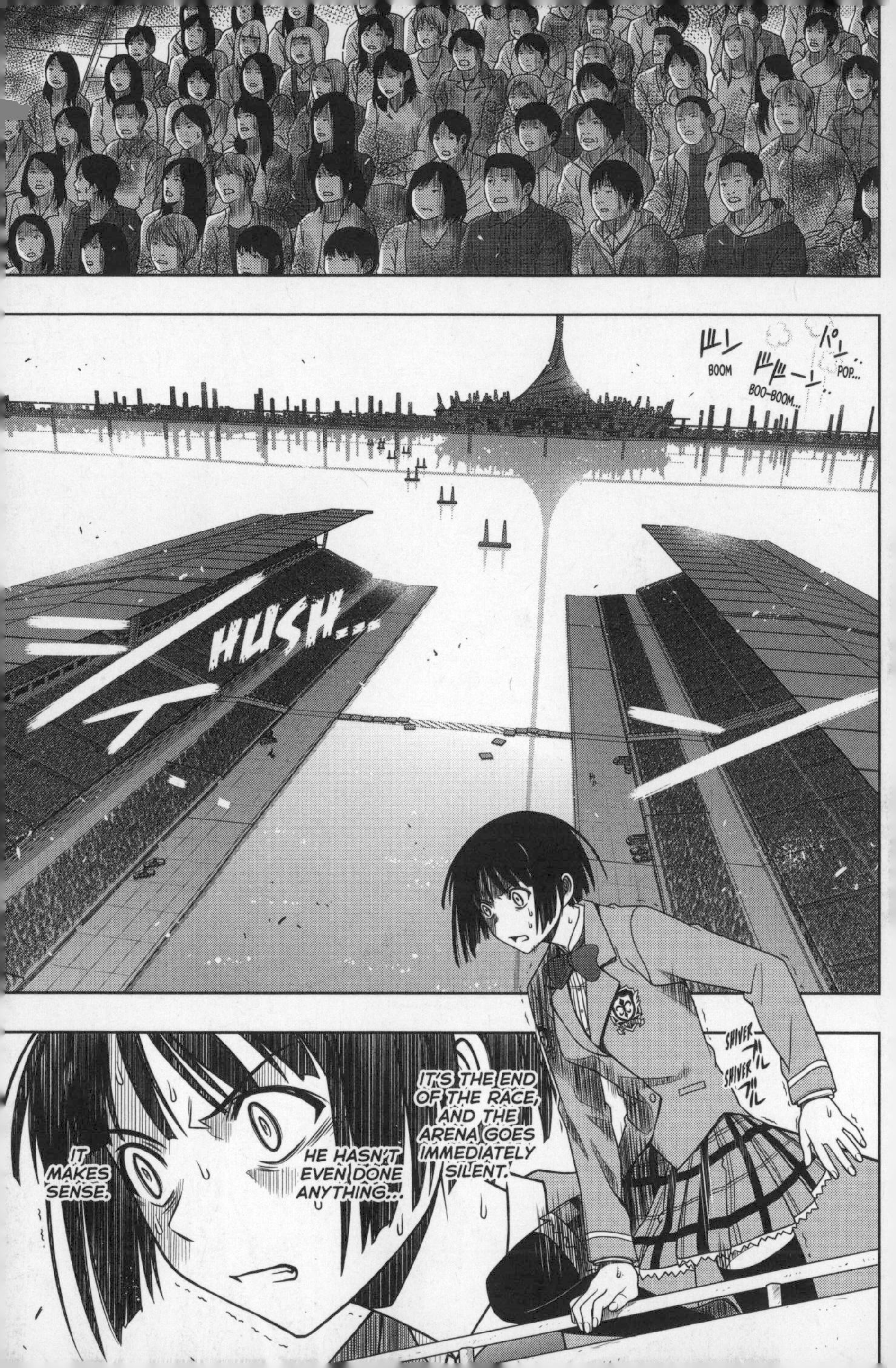
POP...
BOOM
BOO-BOOM...
HUSH...
SHIVER
SHIVER
IT'S THE END OF THE RACE, AND THE ARENA GOES IMMEDIATELY SILENT.
HE HASN'T EVEN DONE ANYTHING...
IT MAKES SENSE.

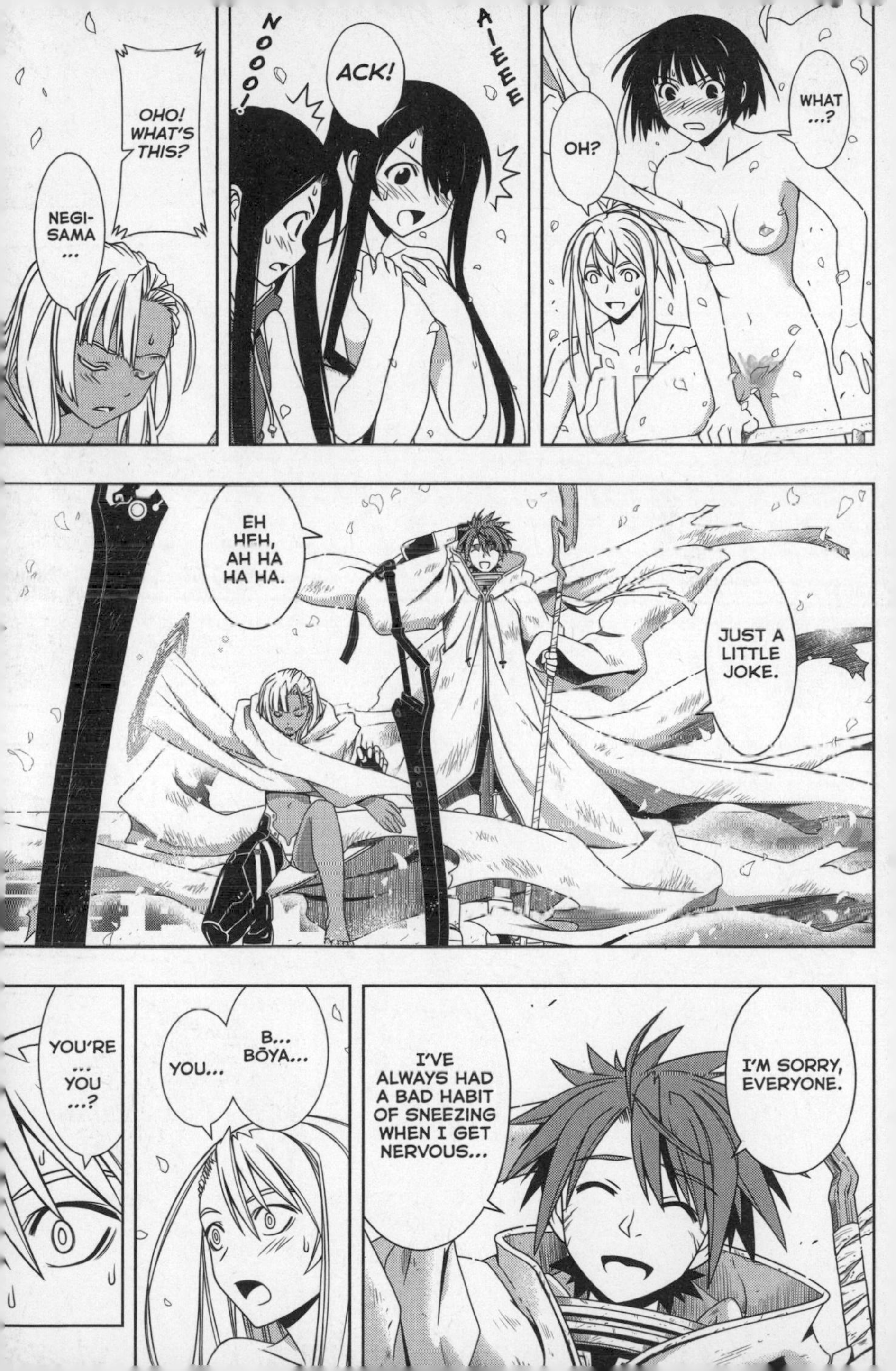
WHAT ...?
OH?
AIEEE
ACK!
NOOOO!
OHO! WHAT'S THIS?
NEGI-SAMA ...
EH HEH, AH HA HA HA.
JUST A LITTLE JOKE.
I'M SORRY, EVERYONE.
I'VE ALWAYS HAD A BAD HABIT OF SNEEZING WHEN I GET NERVOUS...
B... BŌYA...
YOU...
YOU'RE ... YOU ...?

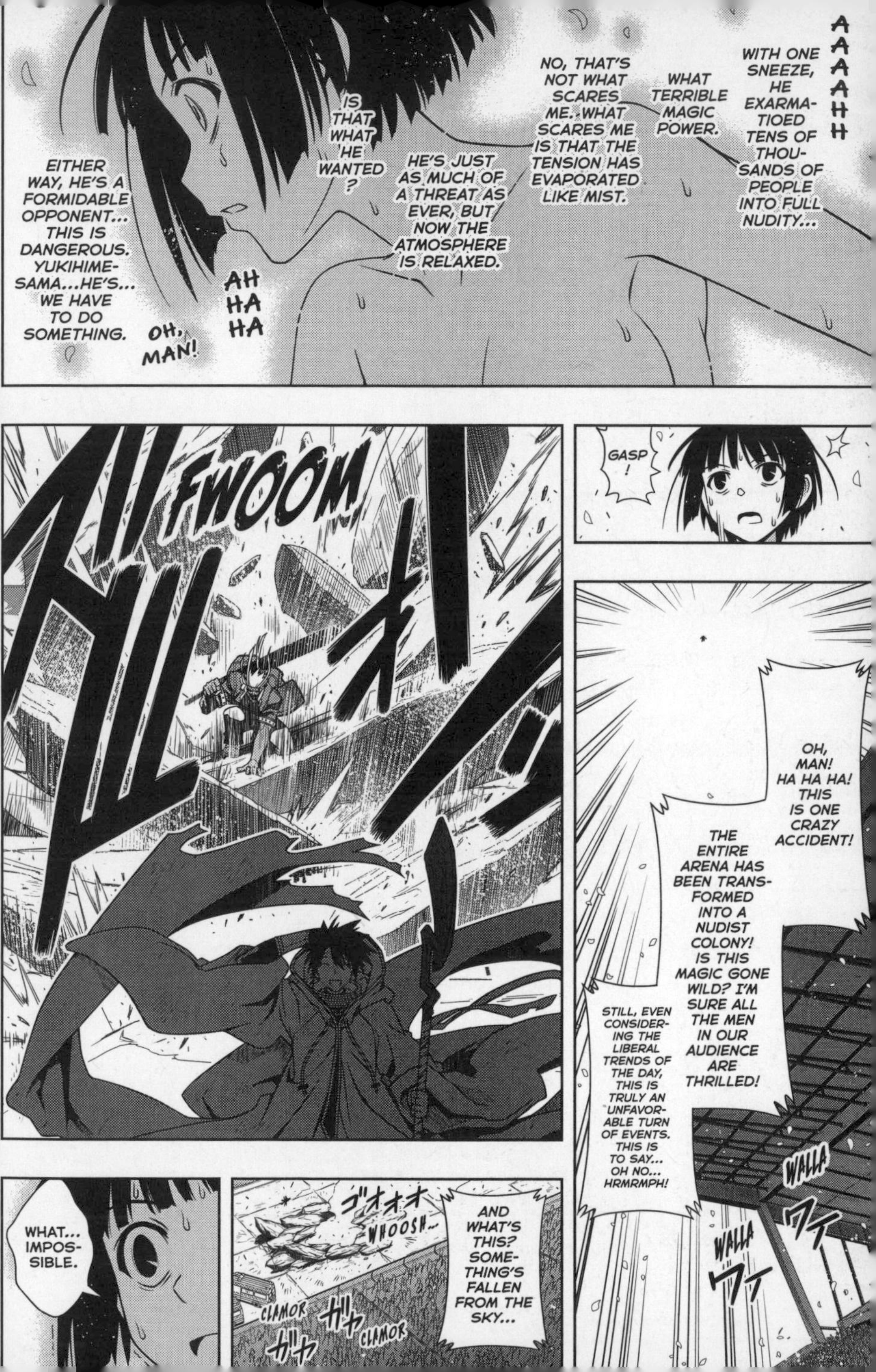
AAAAAHH
WITH ONE SNEEZE, HE EXARMATIOED TENS OF THOUSANDS OF PEOPLE INTO FULL NUDITY...
WHAT TERRIBLE MAGIC POWER.
NO, THAT'S NOT WHAT SCARES ME. WHAT SCARES ME IS THAT THE TENSION HAS EVAPORATED LIKE MIST.
IS THAT WHAT HE WANTED?
HE'S JUST AS MUCH OF A THREAT AS EVER, BUT NOW THE ATMOSPHERE IS RELAXED.
AH HA HA
EITHER WAY, HE'S A FORMIDABLE OPPONENT... THIS IS DANGEROUS. YUKIHIME-SAMA...HE'S... WE HAVE TO DO SOMETHING.
OH, MAN!
GASP!
OH, MAN! HA HA HA! THIS IS ONE CRAZY ACCIDENT!
THE ENTIRE ARENA HAS BEEN TRANSFORMED INTO A NUDIST COLONY! IS THIS MAGIC GONE WILD? I'M SURE ALL THE MEN IN OUR AUDIENCE ARE THRILLED!
STILL, EVEN CONSIDERING THE LIBERAL TRENDS OF THE DAY, THIS IS TRULY AN UNFAVORABLE TURN OF EVENTS. THIS IS TO SAY... OH NO... HRMRMPH!
WALLA
ワイ
WALLA
ワイ
FWOOM
ゴオオオ
WHOOSH
AND WHAT'S THIS? SOMETHING'S FALLEN FROM THE SKY...
CLAMOR
ガヤ
CLAMOR
ガヤ
WHAT... IMPOSSIBLE.

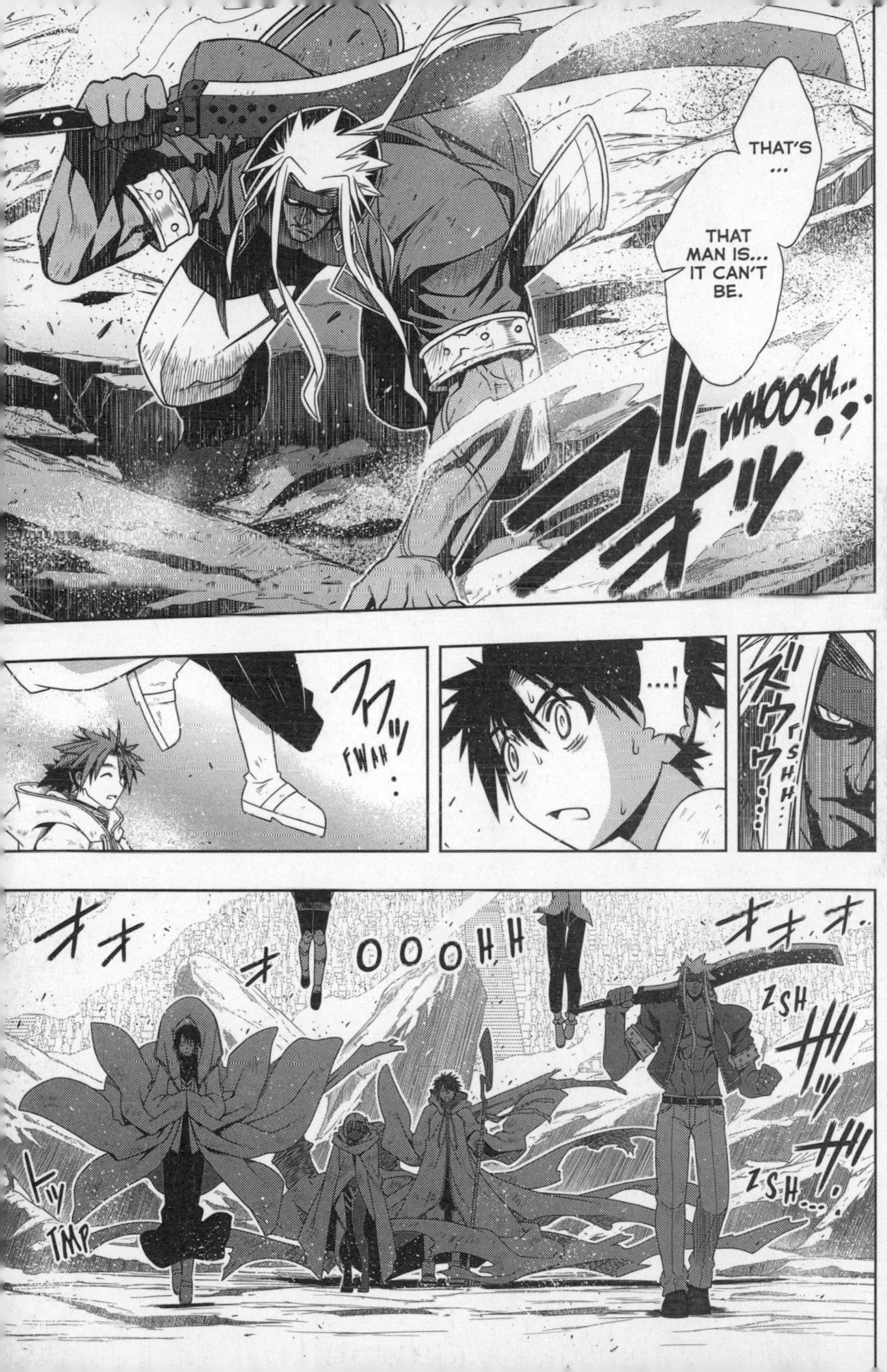
THAT'S ...
THAT MAN IS... IT CAN'T BE.
WHOOSH...
FSHH...
...!
FWAH
OOOHH
ZSH
ZSH...
TMP

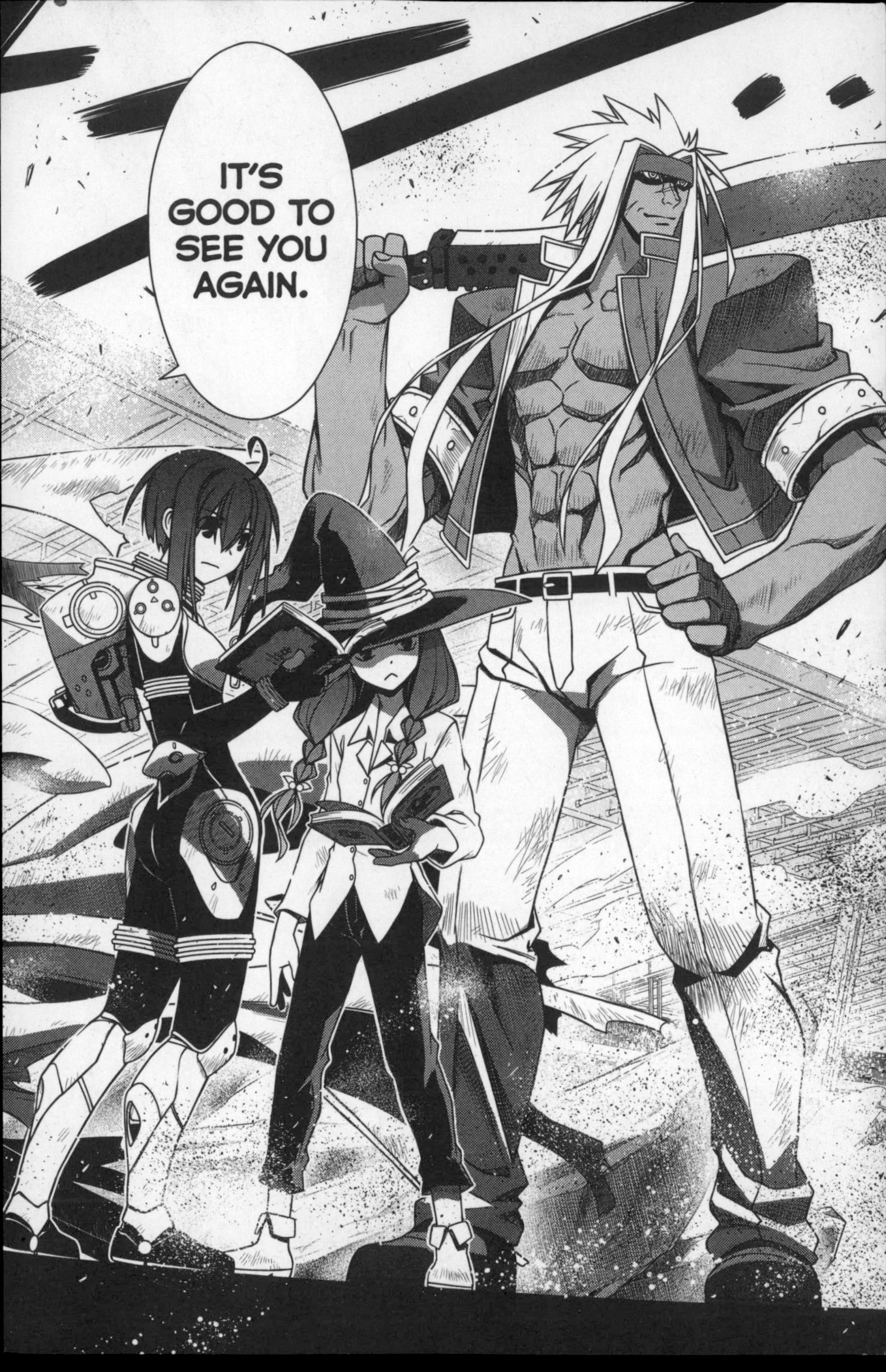
IT'S GOOD TO SEE YOU AGAIN.

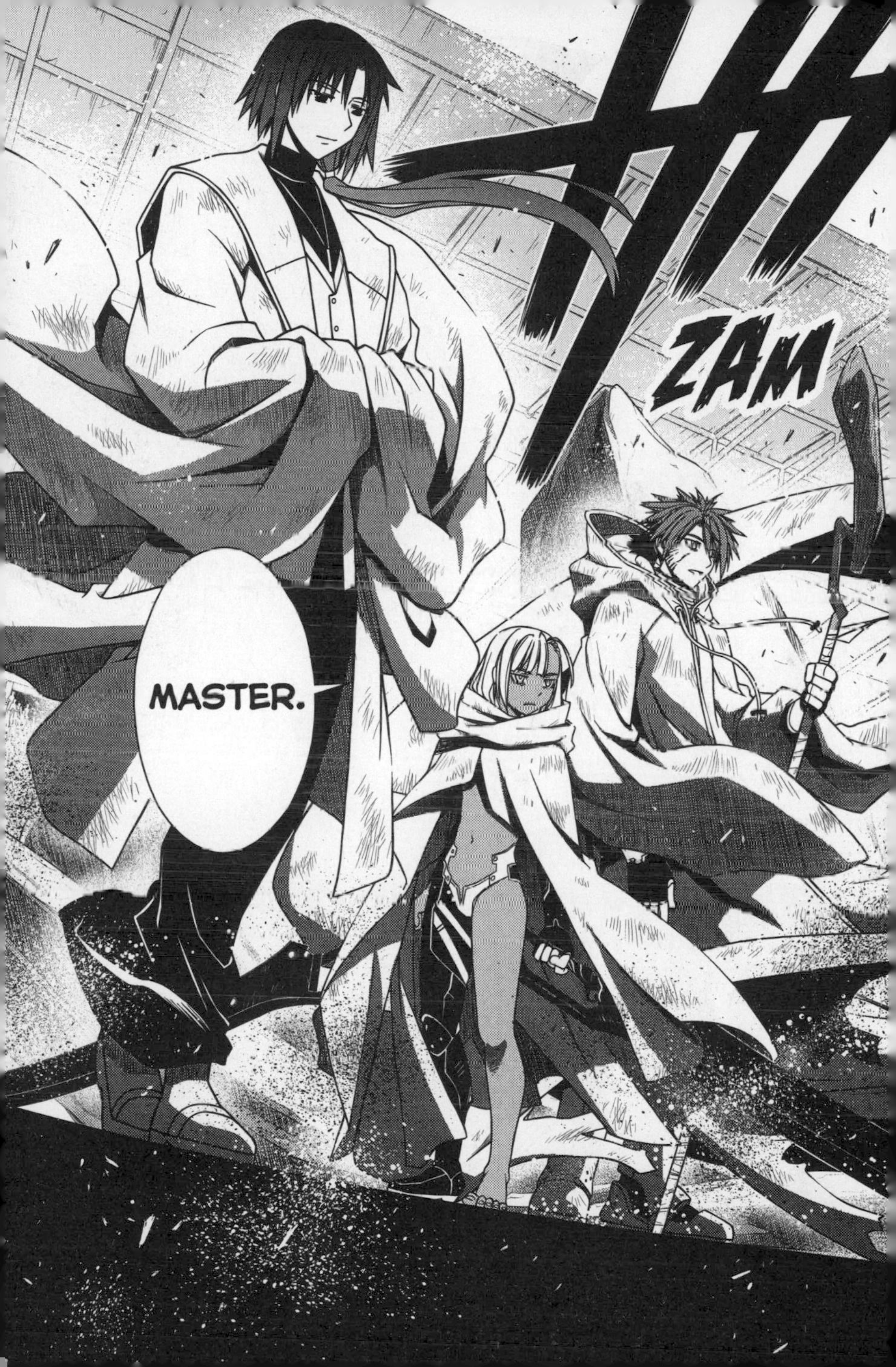
ZAM
MASTER.

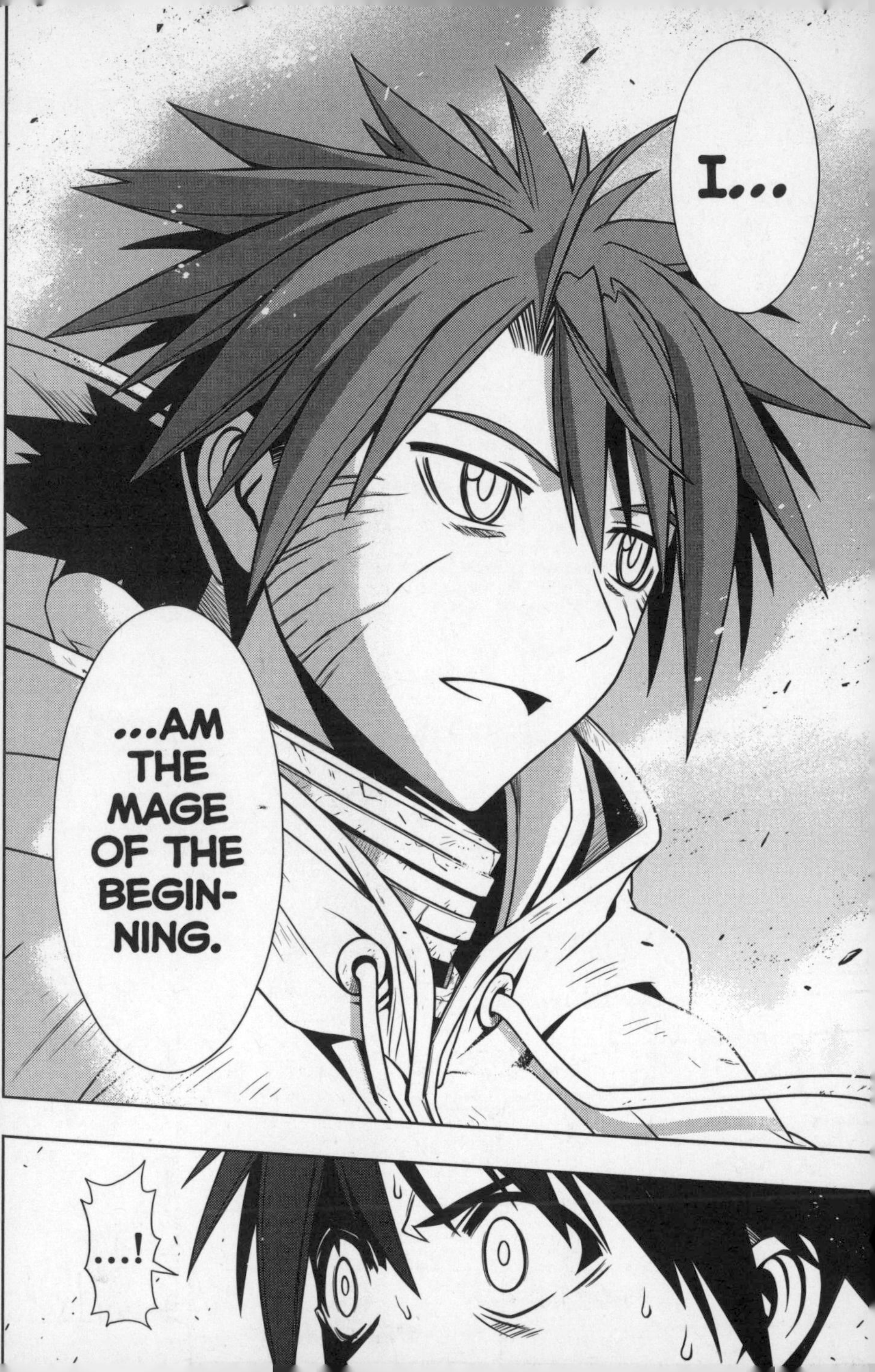
I...
...AM THE MAGE OF THE BEGIN-NING.
...!

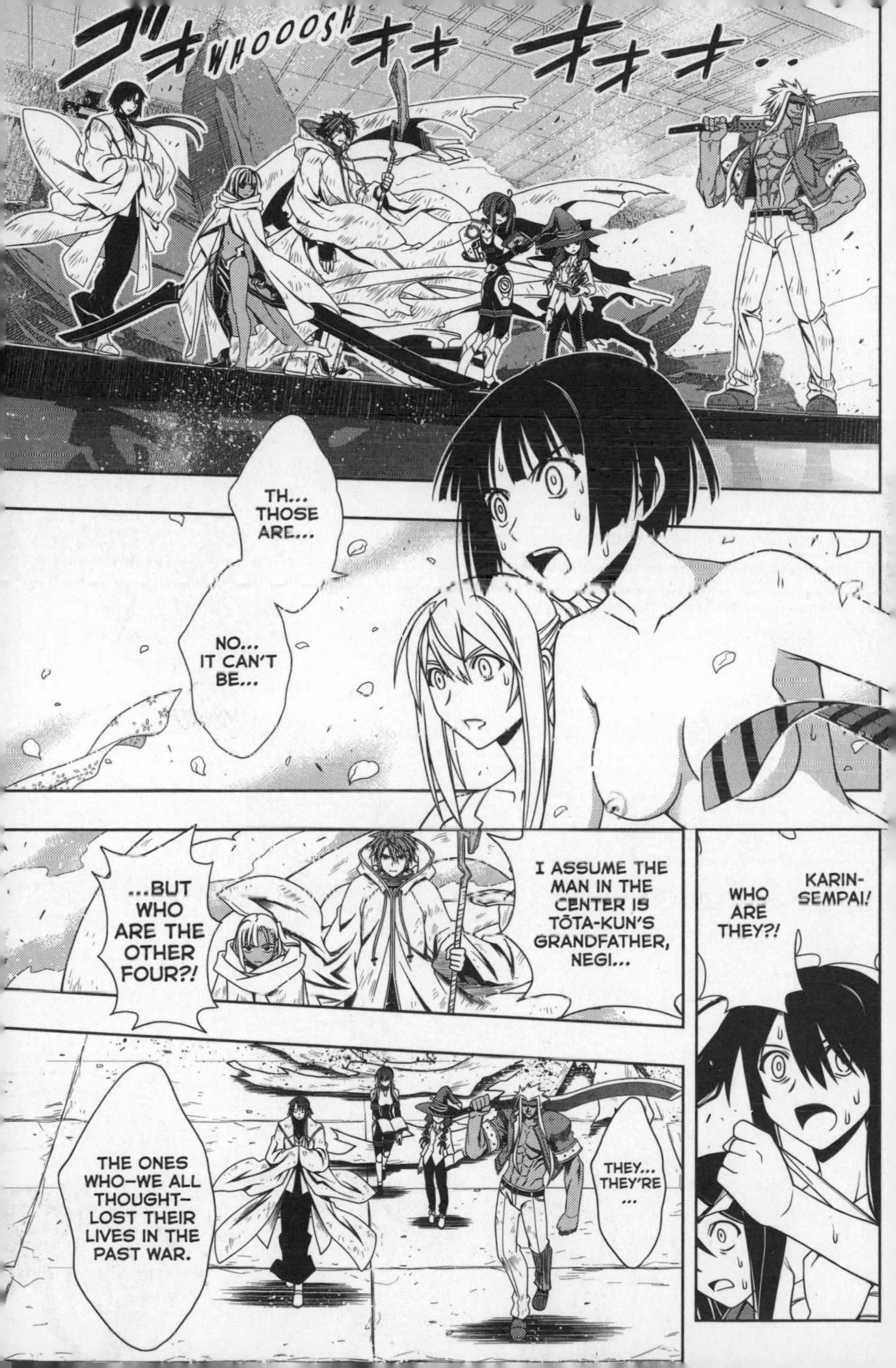
ゴオ WHOOOSH オォ オォォォ…
TH... THOSE ARE...
NO... IT CAN'T BE...
KARIN-SEMPAI!
WHO ARE THEY?!
I ASSUME THE MAN IN THE CENTER IS TŌTA-KUN'S GRANDFATHER, NEGI...
...BUT WHO ARE THE OTHER FOUR?!
THEY... THEY'RE ...
THE ONES WHO—WE ALL THOUGHT—LOST THEIR LIVES IN THE PAST WAR.

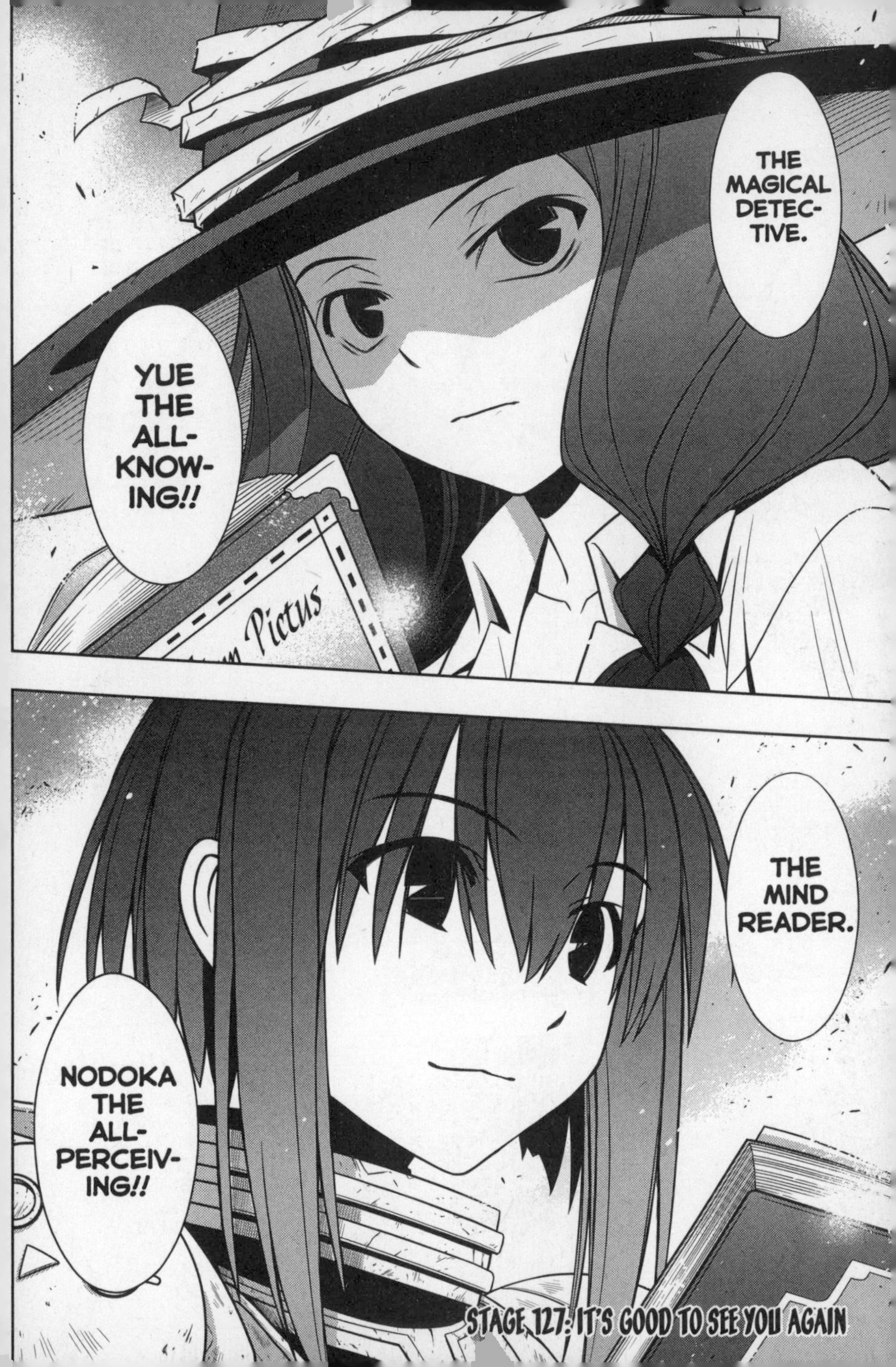
THE MAGICAL DETEC-TIVE.
YUE THE ALL-KNOW-ING!!
THE MIND READER.
NODOKA THE ALL-PERCEIV-ING!!
STAGE 127: IT'S GOOD TO SEE YOU AGAIN

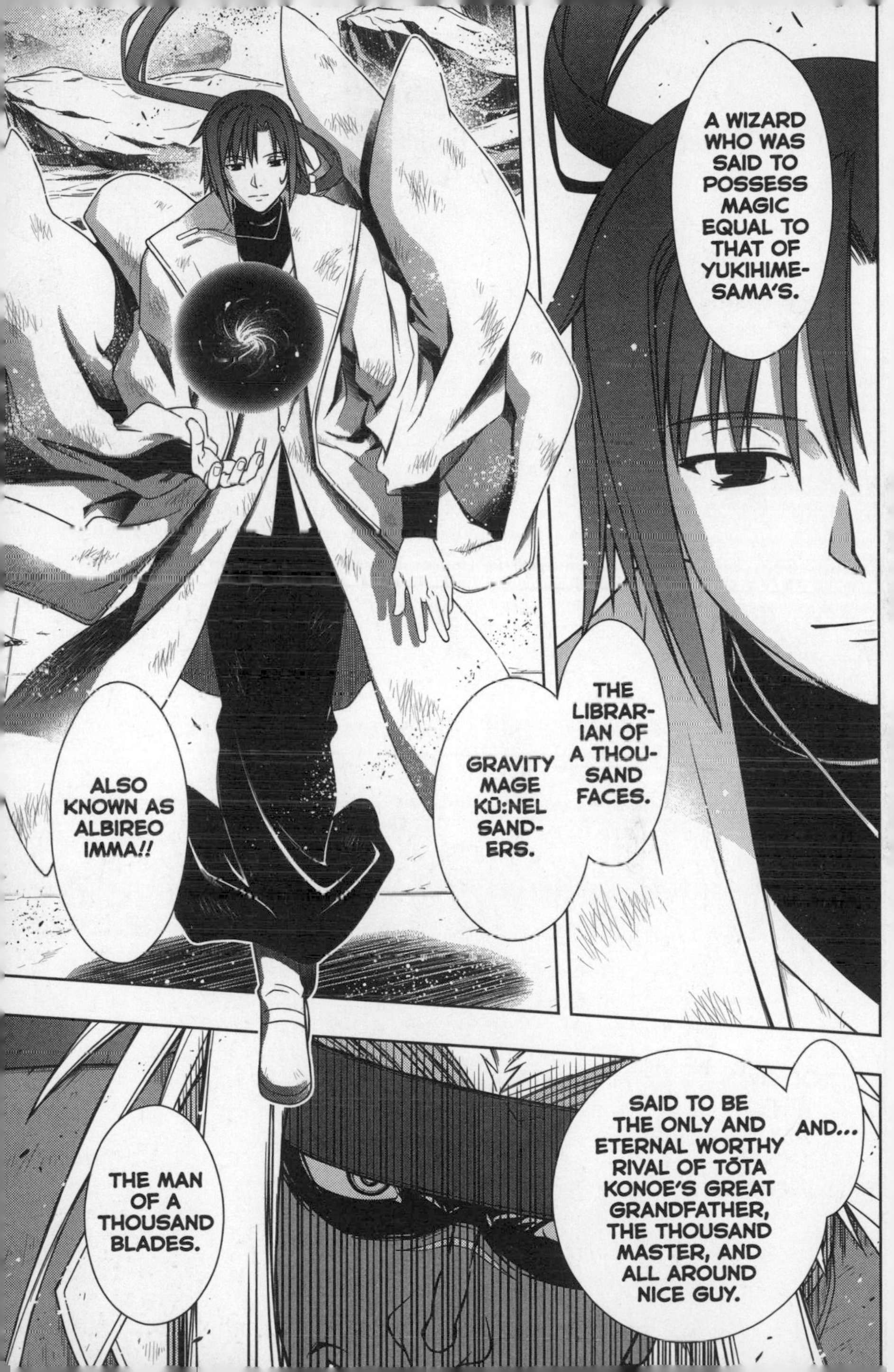
A WIZARD WHO WAS SAID TO POSSESS MAGIC EQUAL TO THAT OF YUKIHIME-SAMA'S.
THE LIBRARIAN OF A THOUSAND FACES.
GRAVITY MAGE KŪ:NEL SANDERS.
ALSO KNOWN AS ALBIREO IMMA!!
AND...
SAID TO BE THE ONLY AND ETERNAL WORTHY RIVAL OF TŌTA KONOE'S GREAT GRANDFATHER, THE THOUSAND MASTER, AND ALL AROUND NICE GUY.
THE MAN OF A THOUSAND BLADES.

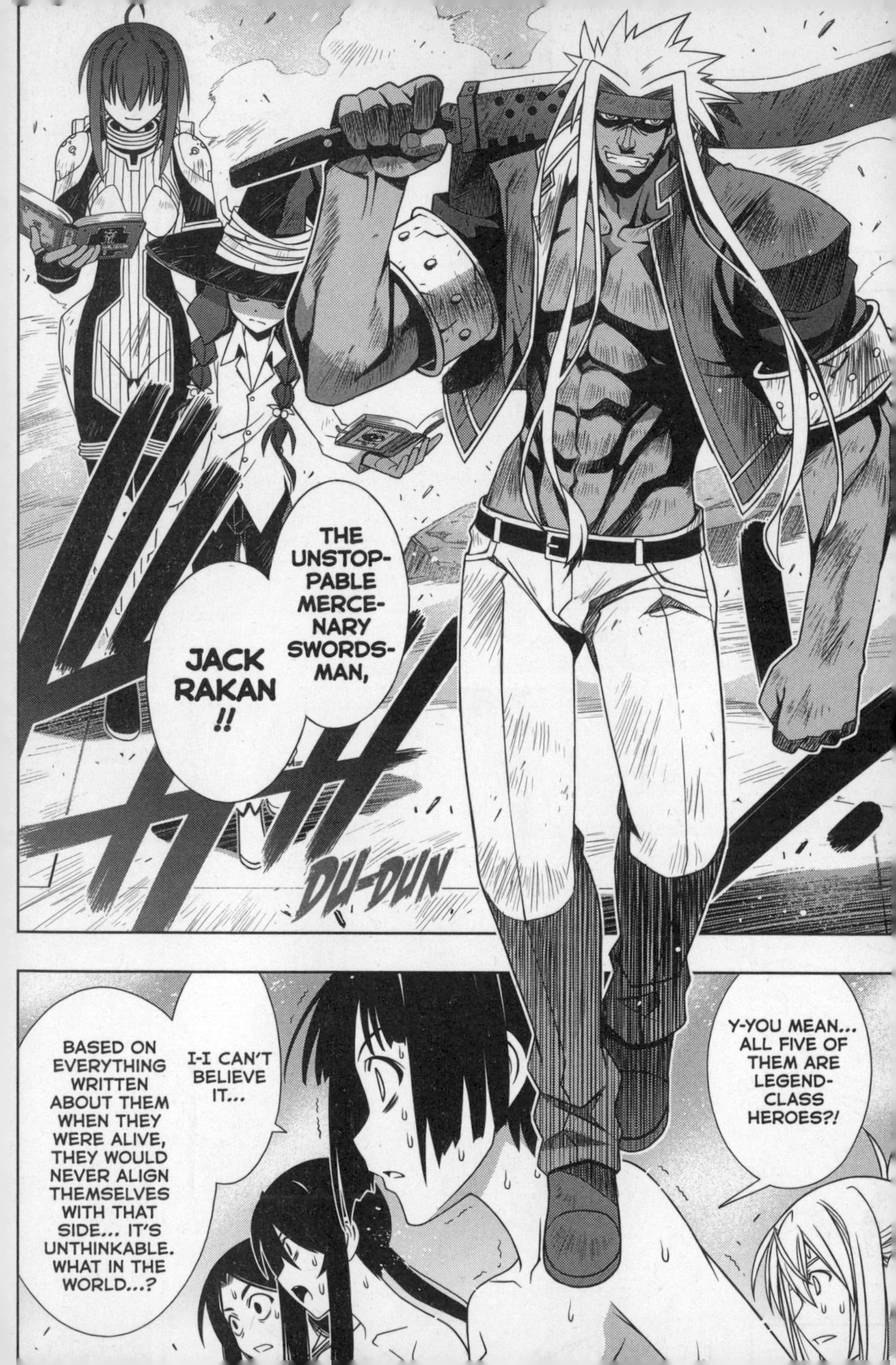
THE UNSTOPPABLE MERCENARY SWORDSMAN,
JACK RAKAN !!
DU-DUN
Y-YOU MEAN... ALL FIVE OF THEM ARE LEGEND-CLASS HEROES?!
I-I CAN'T BELIEVE IT...
BASED ON EVERYTHING WRITTEN ABOUT THEM WHEN THEY WERE ALIVE, THEY WOULD NEVER ALIGN THEMSELVES WITH THAT SIDE... IT'S UNTHINKABLE. WHAT IN THE WORLD...?

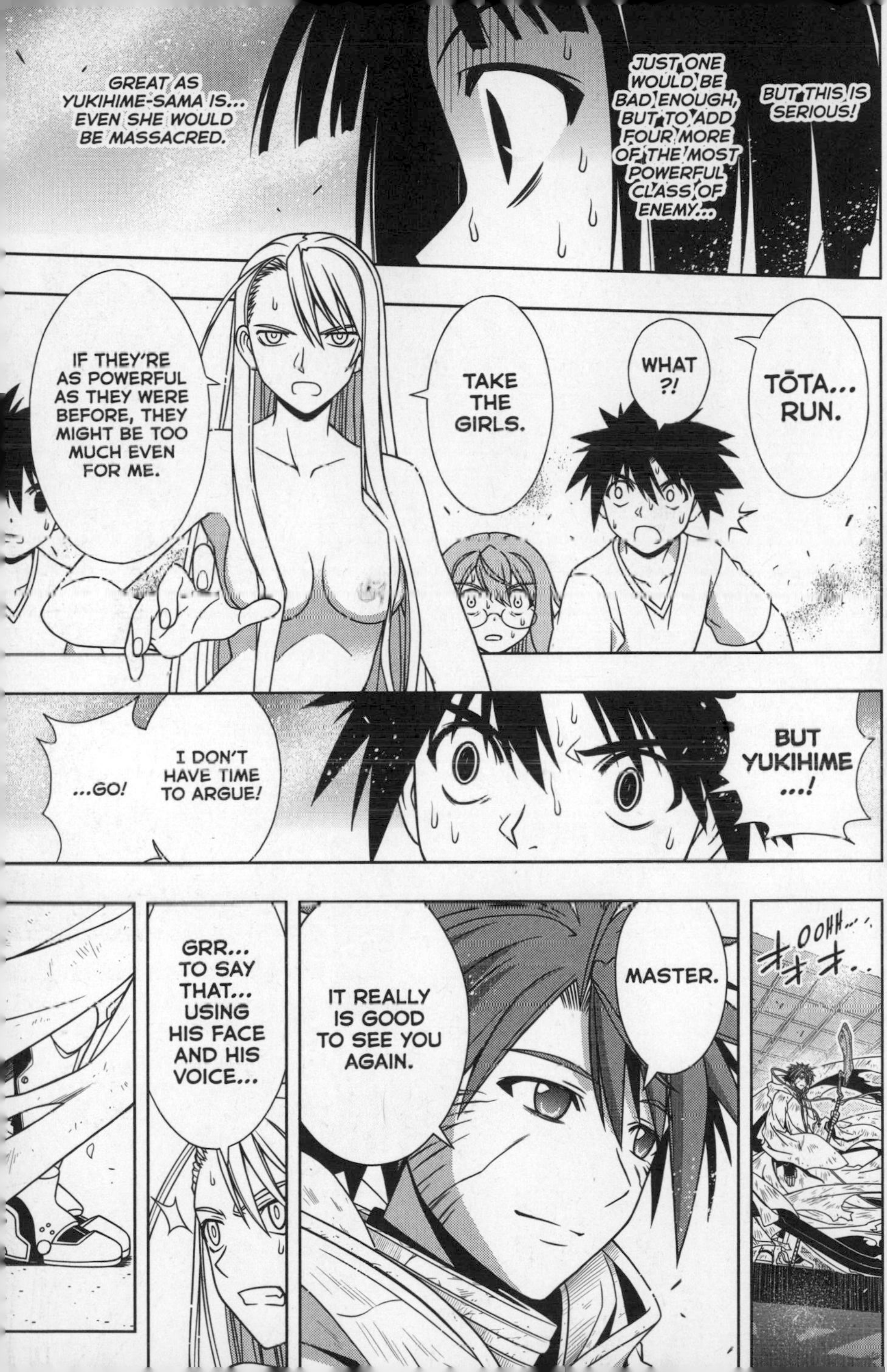
BUT THIS IS SERIOUS!
JUST ONE WOULD BE BAD ENOUGH, BUT TO ADD FOUR MORE OF THE MOST POWERFUL CLASS OF ENEMY...
GREAT AS YUKIHIME-SAMA IS... EVEN SHE WOULD BE MASSACRED.
TŌTA... RUN.
WHAT ?!
TAKE THE GIRLS.
IF THEY'RE AS POWERFUL AS THEY WERE BEFORE, THEY MIGHT BE TOO MUCH EVEN FOR ME.
BUT YUKIHIME ...!
I DON'T HAVE TIME TO ARGUE!
...GO!
OOHH...
オオオ...
MASTER.
IT REALLY IS GOOD TO SEE YOU AGAIN.
GRR... TO SAY THAT... USING HIS FACE AND HIS VOICE...

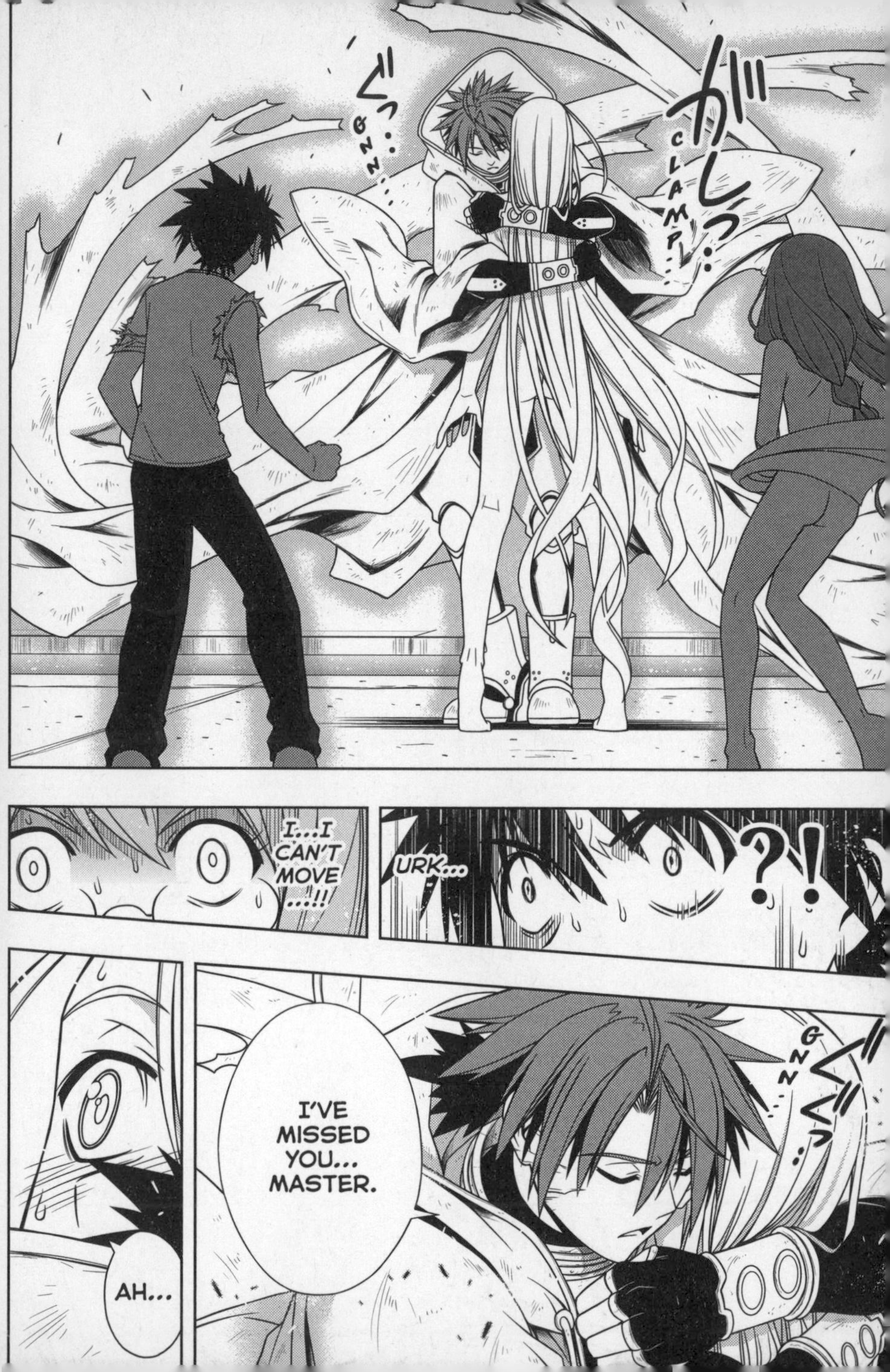
CLAMP!
GNN...
?!
URK...
I...I CAN'T MOVE ...!!!
GNN
I'VE MISSED YOU... MASTER.
AH...

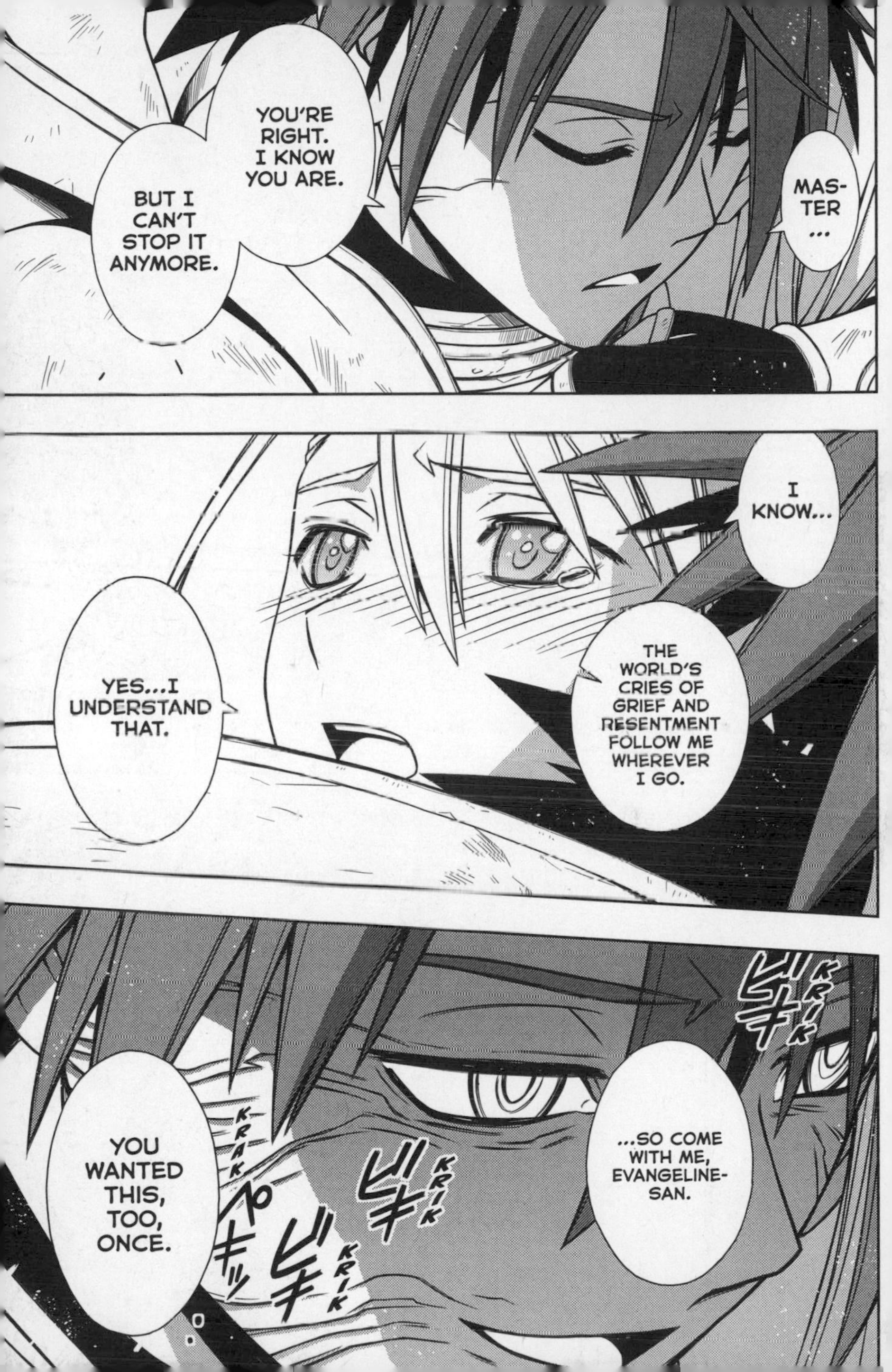
MASTER...
YOU'RE RIGHT. I KNOW YOU ARE.
BUT I CAN'T STOP IT ANYMORE.
I KNOW...
THE WORLD'S CRIES OF GRIEF AND RESENTMENT FOLLOW ME WHEREVER I GO.
YES...I UNDERSTAND THAT.
KRIK
...SO COME WITH ME, EVANGELINE-SAN.
KRIK
KRIK
KRAK
YOU WANTED THIS, TOO, ONCE.

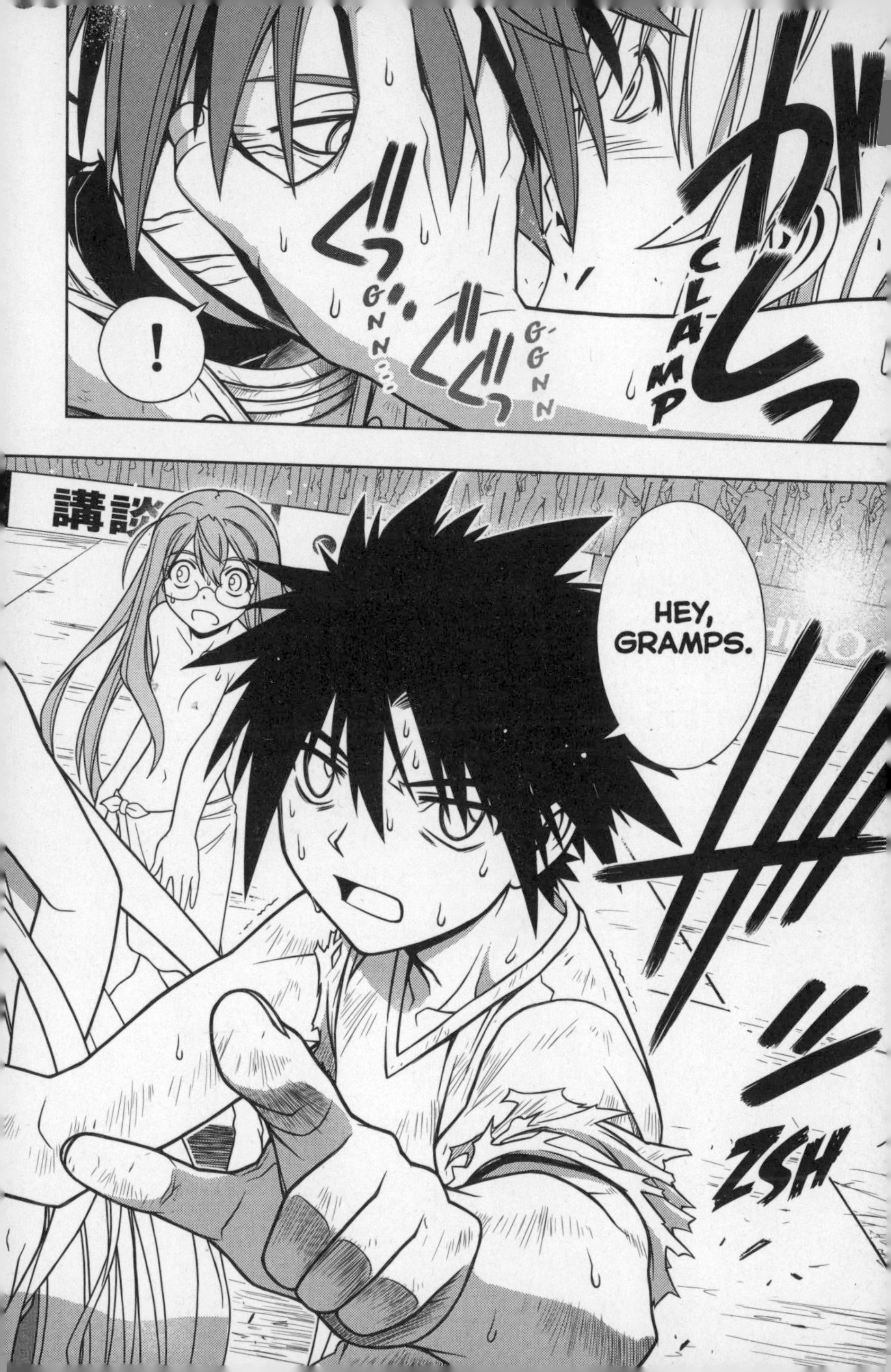

CLAMP
GGNN
GGNN...
!
HEY, GRAMPS.
ZSH
講談

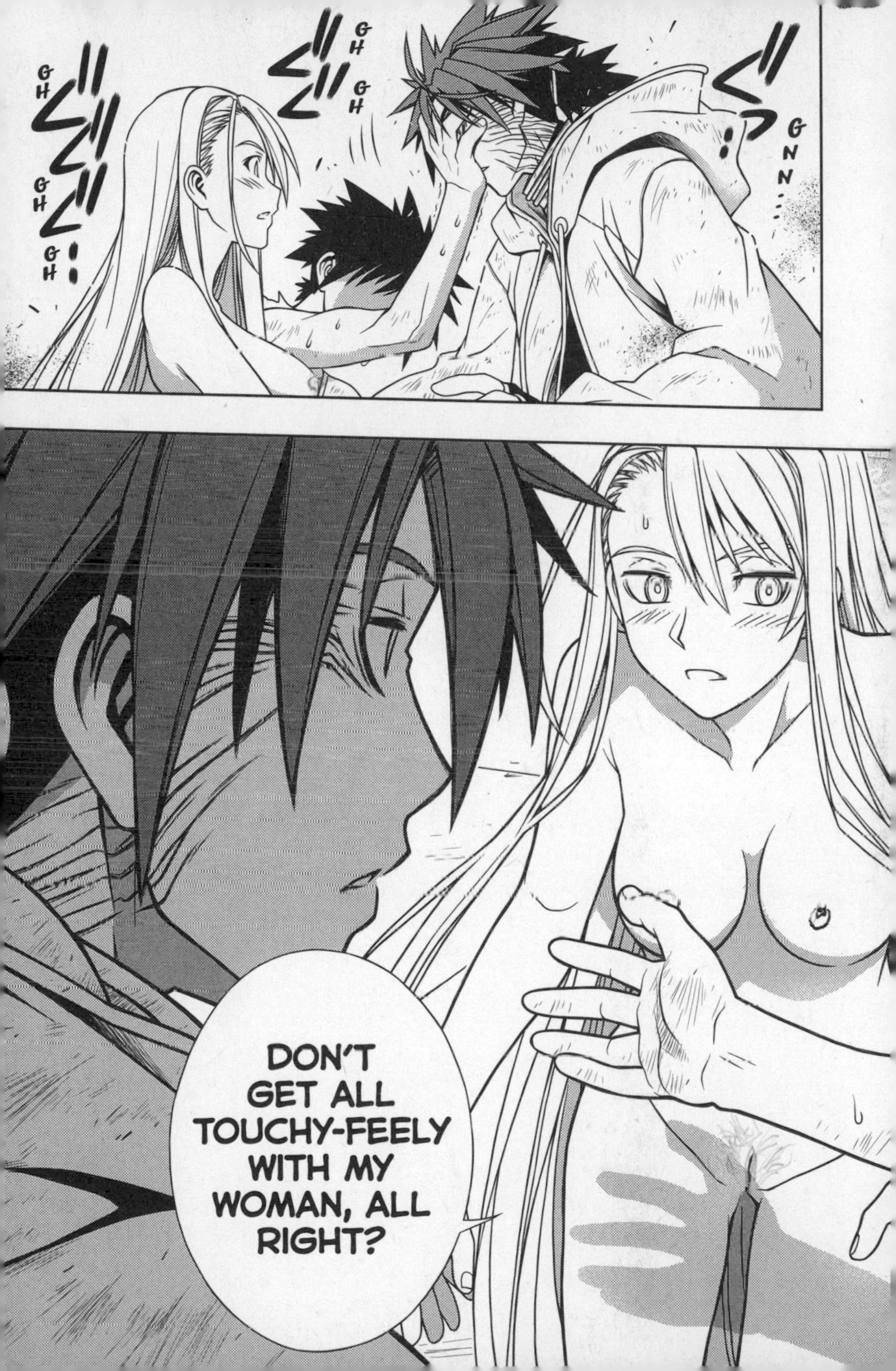
GNN...
GH GH
GH GH
GH GH GH GH
DON'T GET ALL TOUCHY-FEELY WITH MY WOMAN, ALL RIGHT?

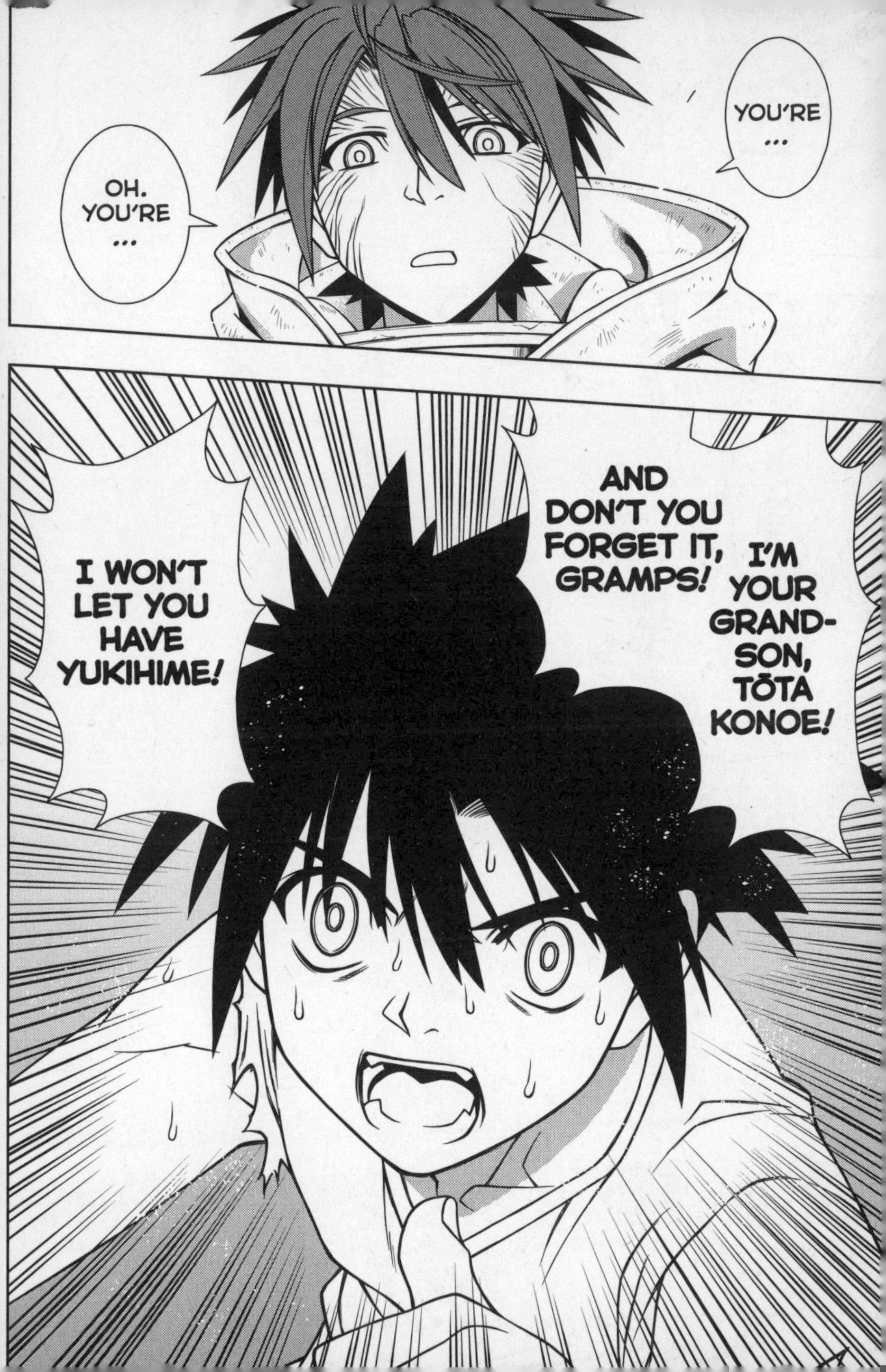
YOU'RE ...
OH. YOU'RE ...
I'M YOUR GRAND-SON, TŌTA KONOE!
AND DON'T YOU FORGET IT, GRAMPS!
I WON'T LET YOU HAVE YUKIHIME!

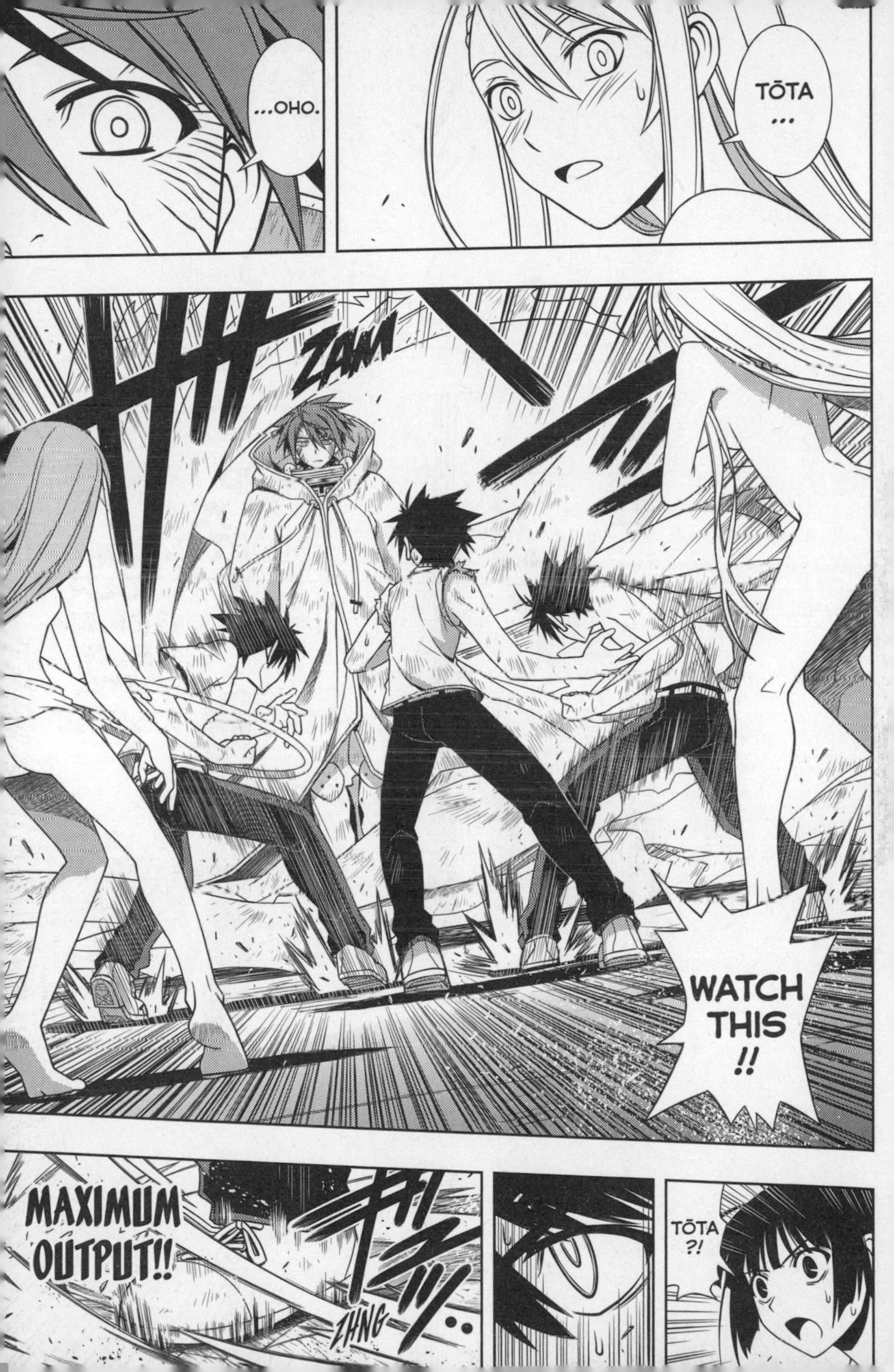
TŌTA ...
...OHO.
ZAM
WATCH THIS !!
TŌTA ?!
MAXIMUM OUTPUT!!
ZHNG

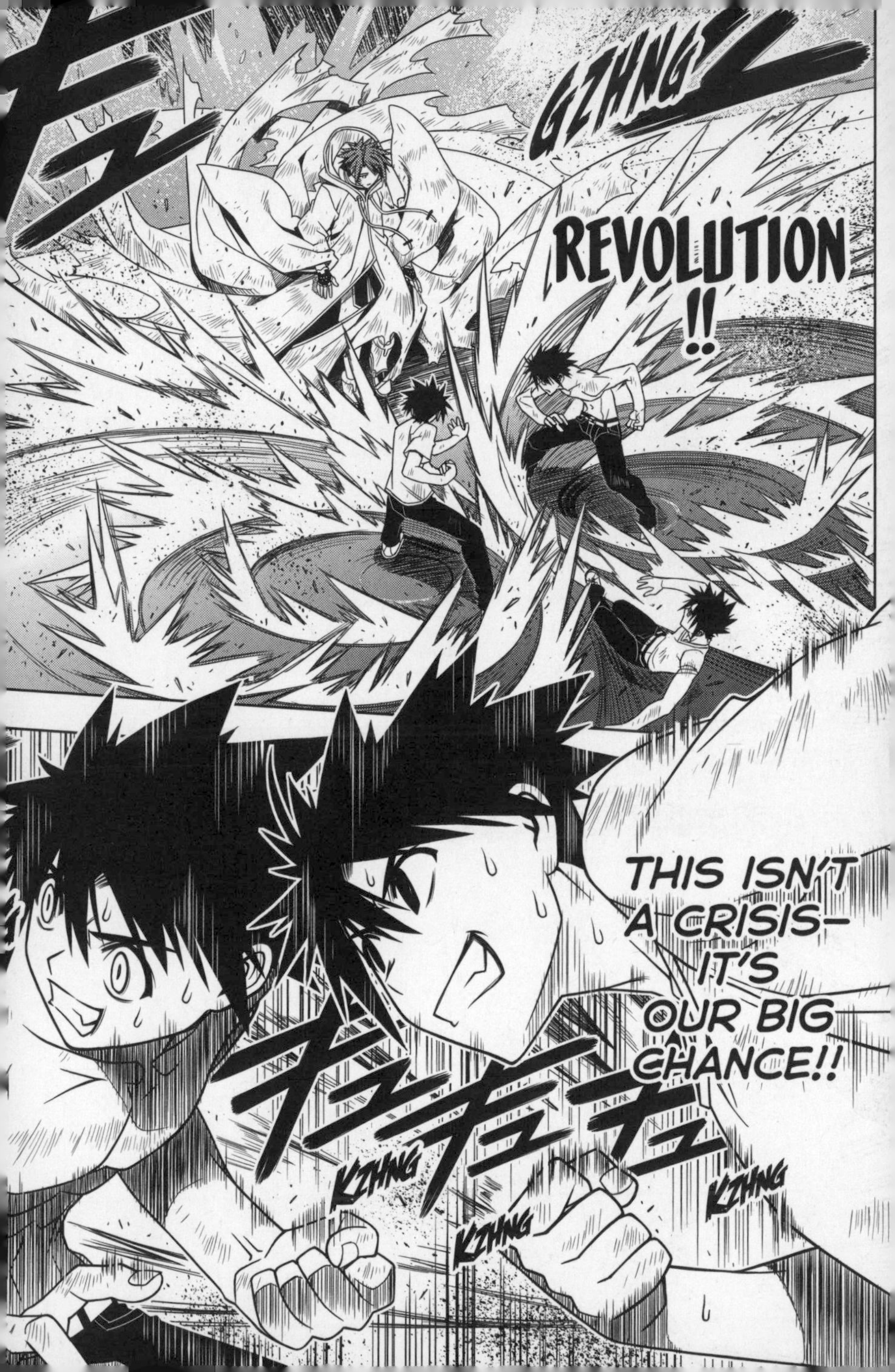
GZHNG
REVOLUTION!!
THIS ISN'T A CRISIS—IT'S OUR BIG CHANCE!!
KZHNG
KZHNG
KZHNG

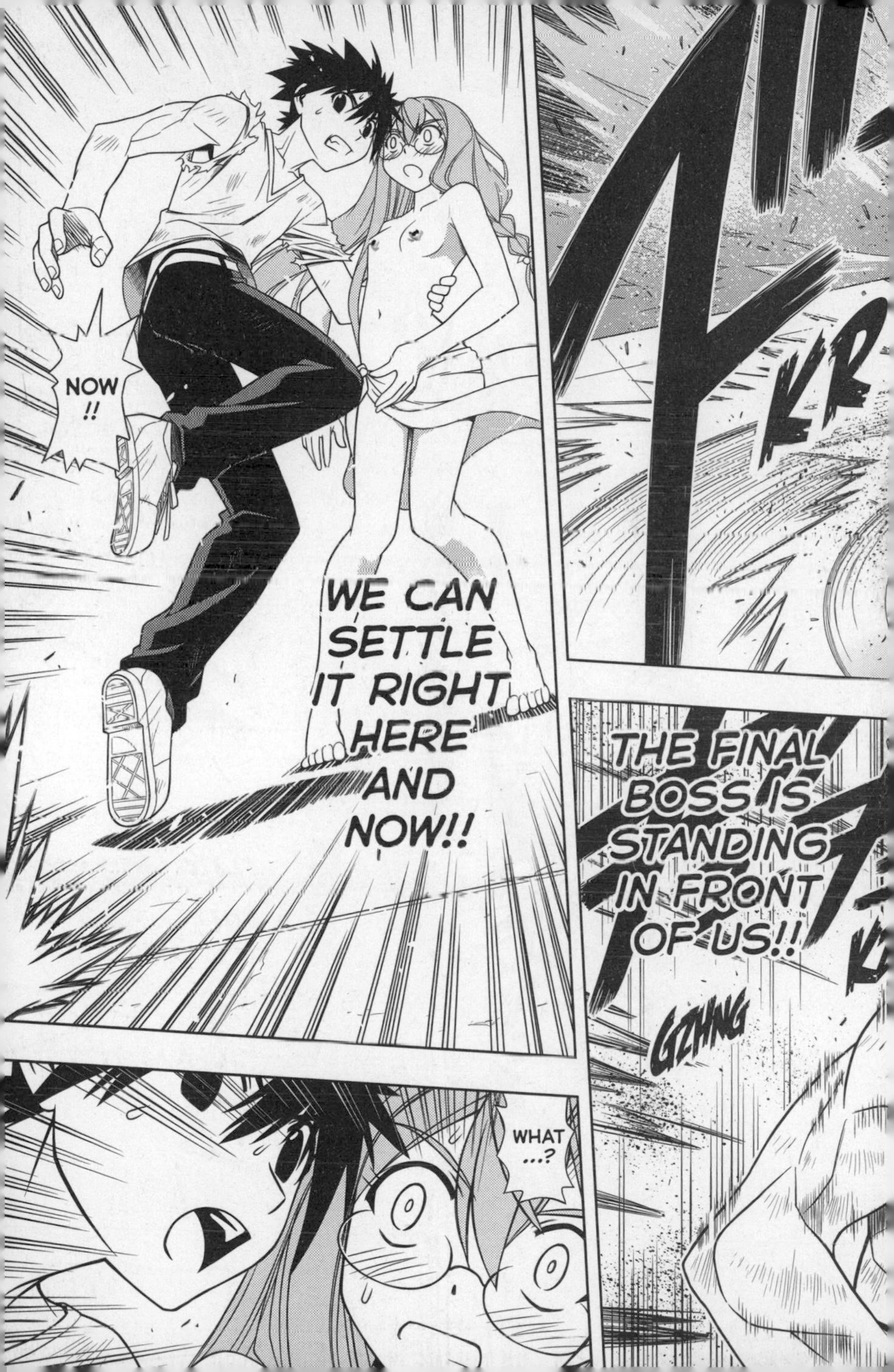
KR
NOW !!
WE CAN SETTLE IT RIGHT HERE AND NOW!!
THE FINAL BOSS IS STANDING IN FRONT OF US!!
GZHNG
WHAT ...?

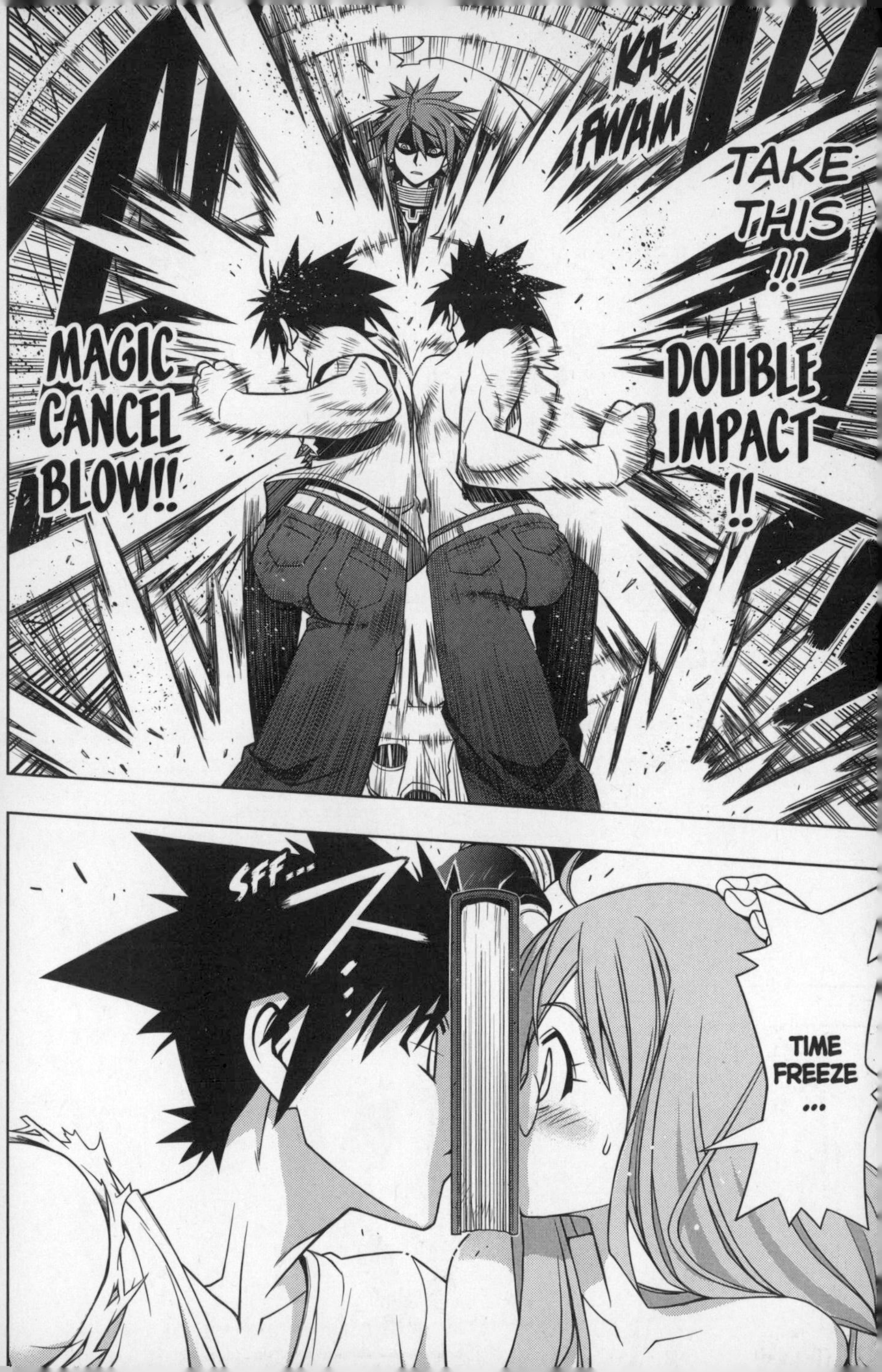
KA-FWAM
TAKE THIS!!
DOUBLE IMPACT!!
MAGIC CANCEL BLOW!!
TIME FREEZE...
SFF...

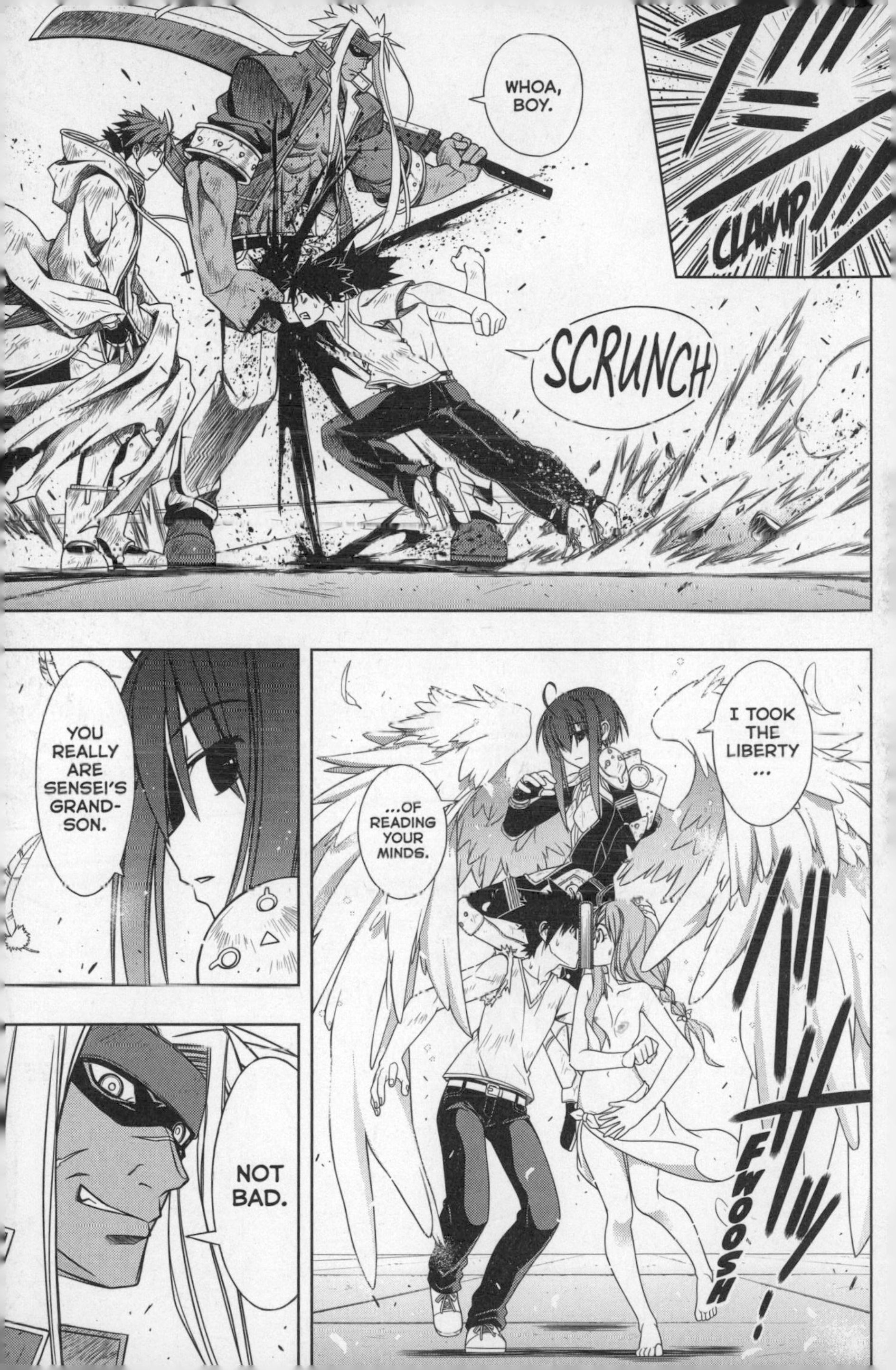
CLAMP!!
WHOA, BOY.
SCRUNCH
I TOOK THE LIBERTY...
...OF READING YOUR MINDS.
FWOOSH!
YOU REALLY ARE SENSEI'S GRAND-SON.
NOT BAD.

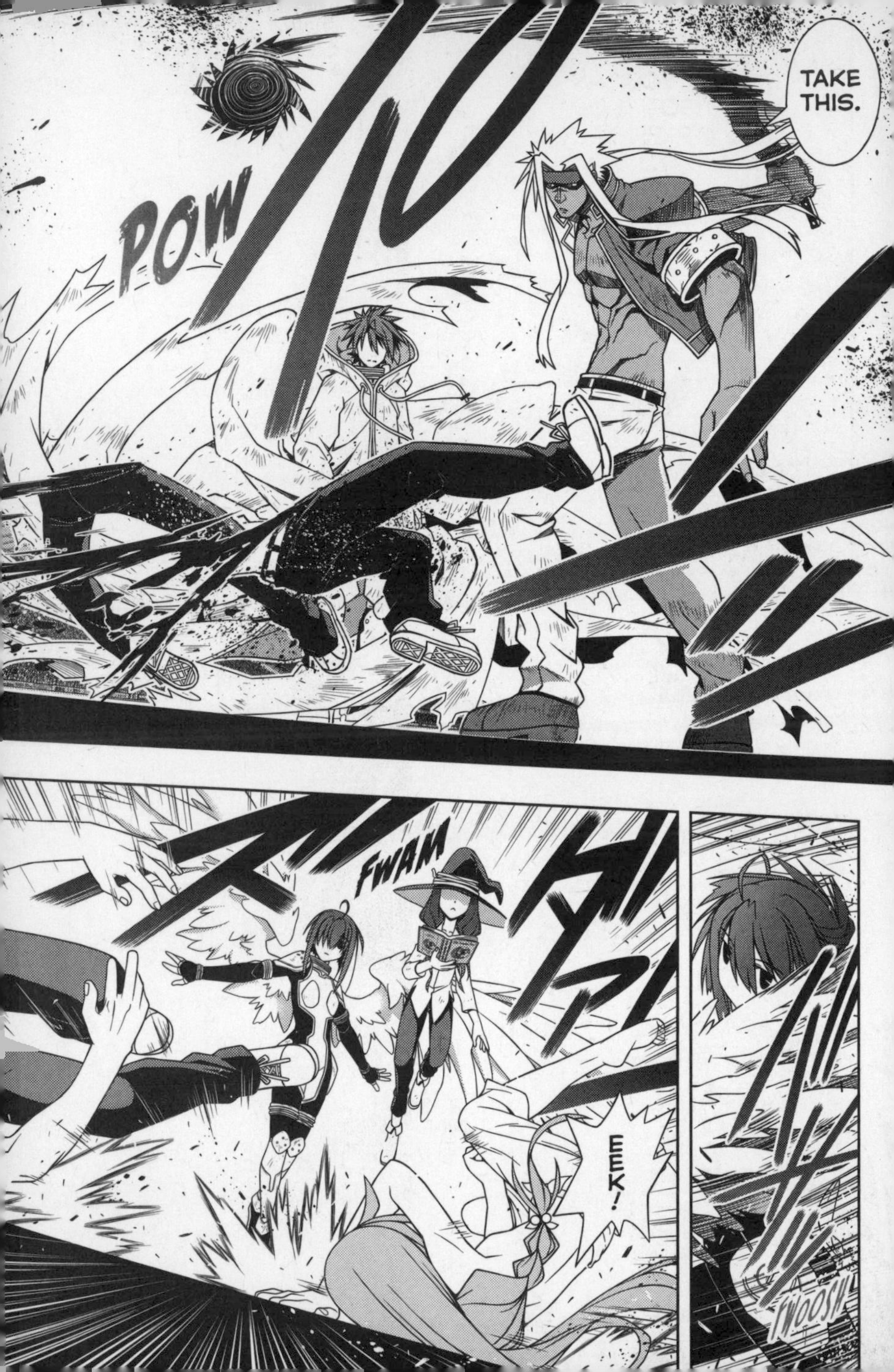
TAKE THIS.
POW
FWOOSH
FWAM
EEK!

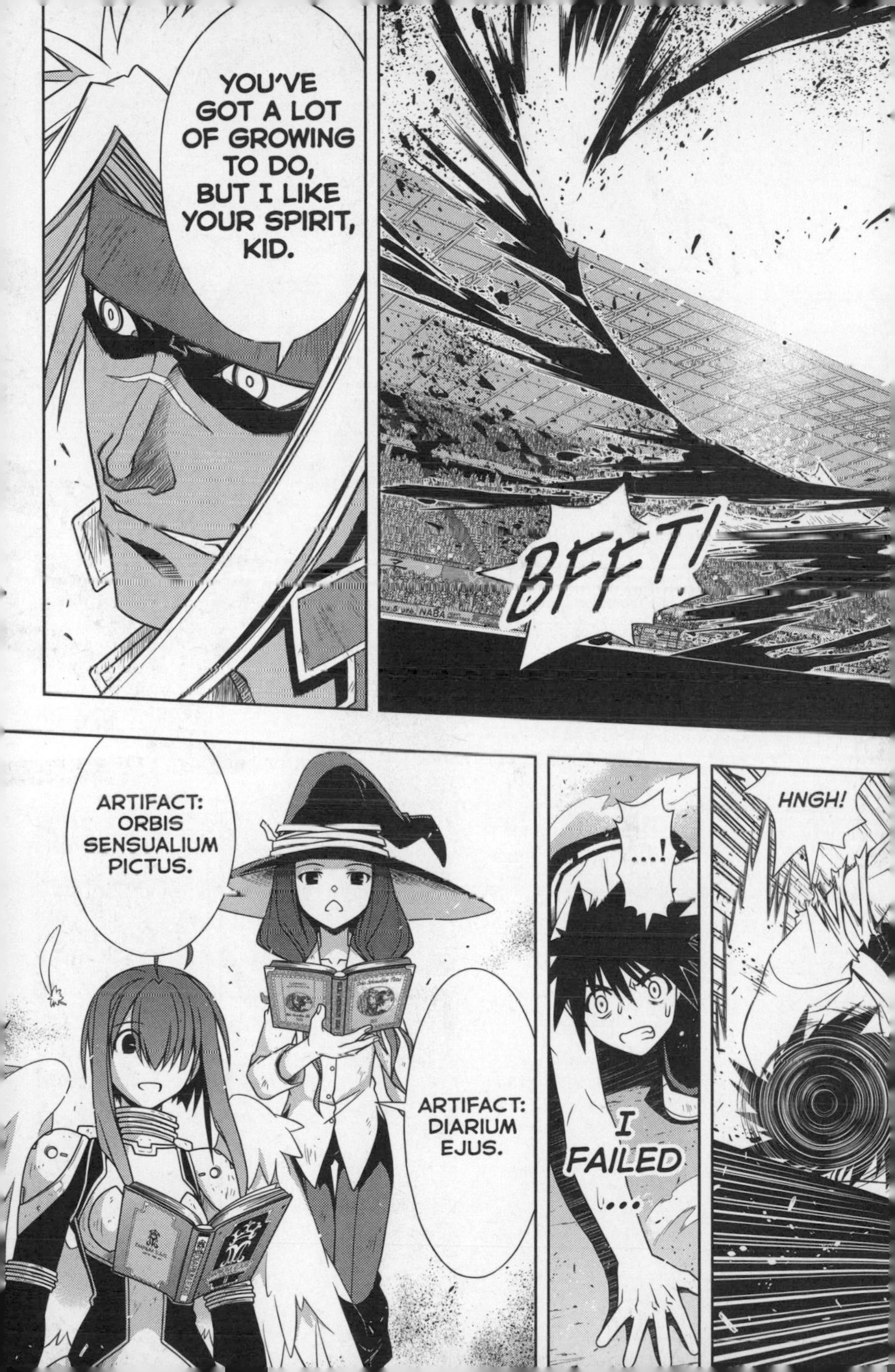
BFFT!
YOU'VE GOT A LOT OF GROWING TO DO, BUT I LIKE YOUR SPIRIT, KID.
HNGH!
...!
I FAILED ...
ARTIFACT: ORBIS SENSUALIUM PICTUS.
ARTIFACT: DIARIUM EJUS.

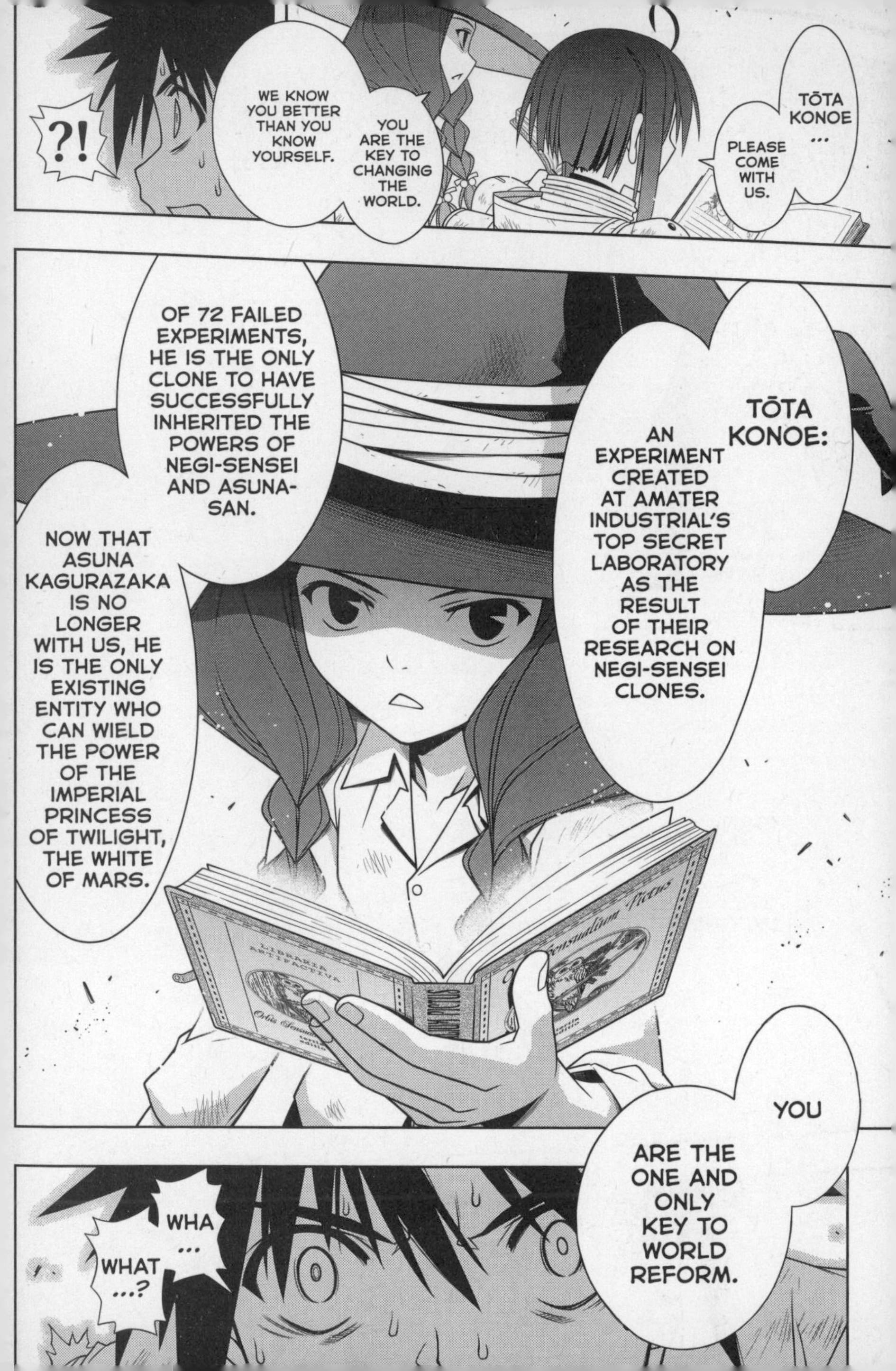
TŌTA KONOE ...
PLEASE COME WITH US.
YOU ARE THE KEY TO CHANGING THE WORLD.
WE KNOW YOU BETTER THAN YOU KNOW YOURSELF.
?!
TŌTA KONOE: AN EXPERIMENT CREATED AT AMATER INDUSTRIAL'S TOP SECRET LABORATORY AS THE RESULT OF THEIR RESEARCH ON NEGI-SENSEI CLONES.
OF 72 FAILED EXPERIMENTS, HE IS THE ONLY CLONE TO HAVE SUCCESSFULLY INHERITED THE POWERS OF NEGI-SENSEI AND ASUNA-SAN.
NOW THAT ASUNA KAGURAZAKA IS NO LONGER WITH US, HE IS THE ONLY EXISTING ENTITY WHO CAN WIELD THE POWER OF THE IMPERIAL PRINCESS OF TWILIGHT, THE WHITE OF MARS.
YOU ARE THE ONE AND ONLY KEY TO WORLD REFORM.
WHA ...
WHAT ...?

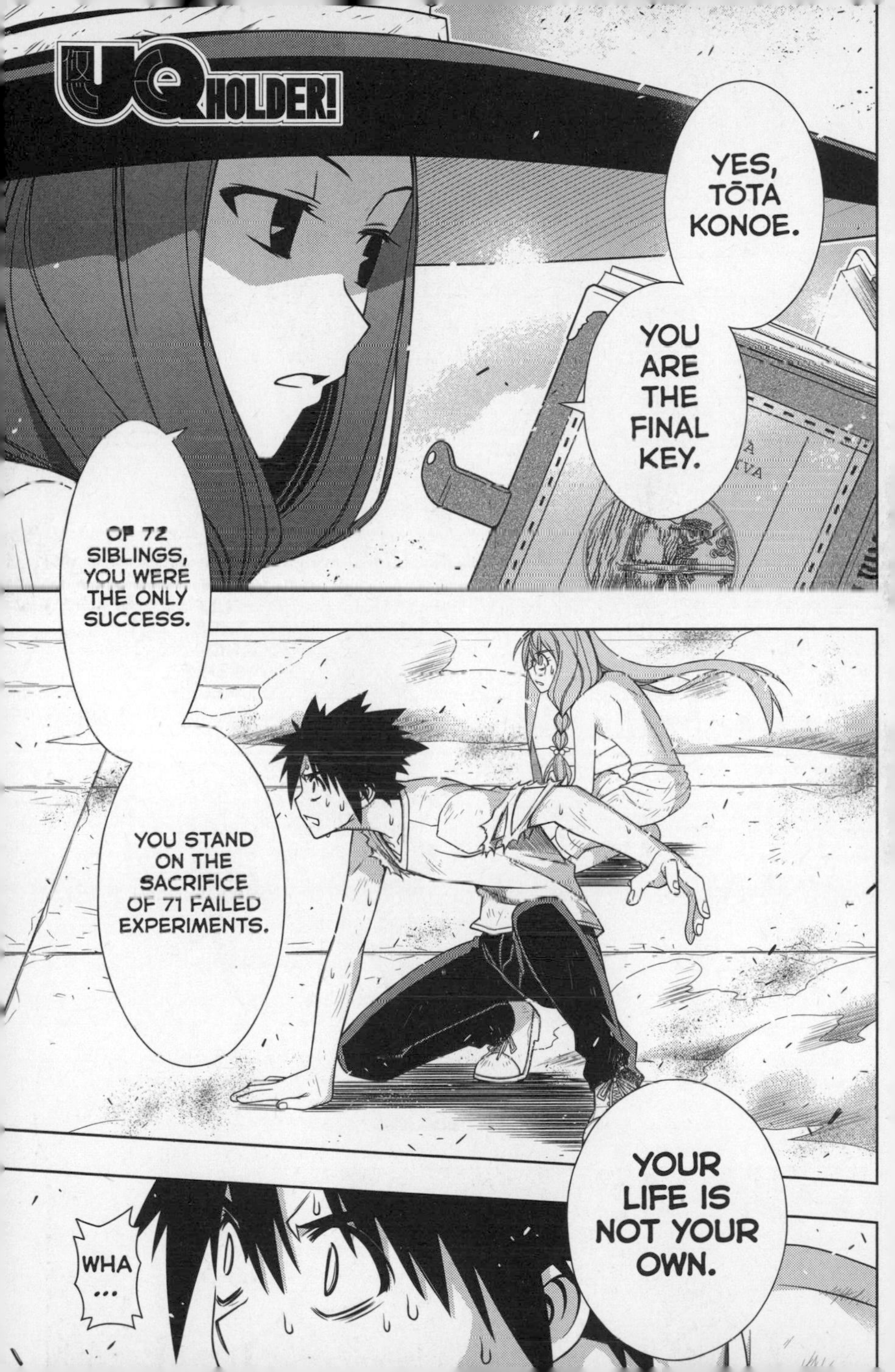
YES, TŌTA KONOE.
YOU ARE THE FINAL KEY.
OF 72 SIBLINGS, YOU WERE THE ONLY SUCCESS.
YOU STAND ON THE SACRIFICE OF 71 FAILED EXPERIMENTS.
YOUR LIFE IS NOT YOUR OWN.
WHA ...

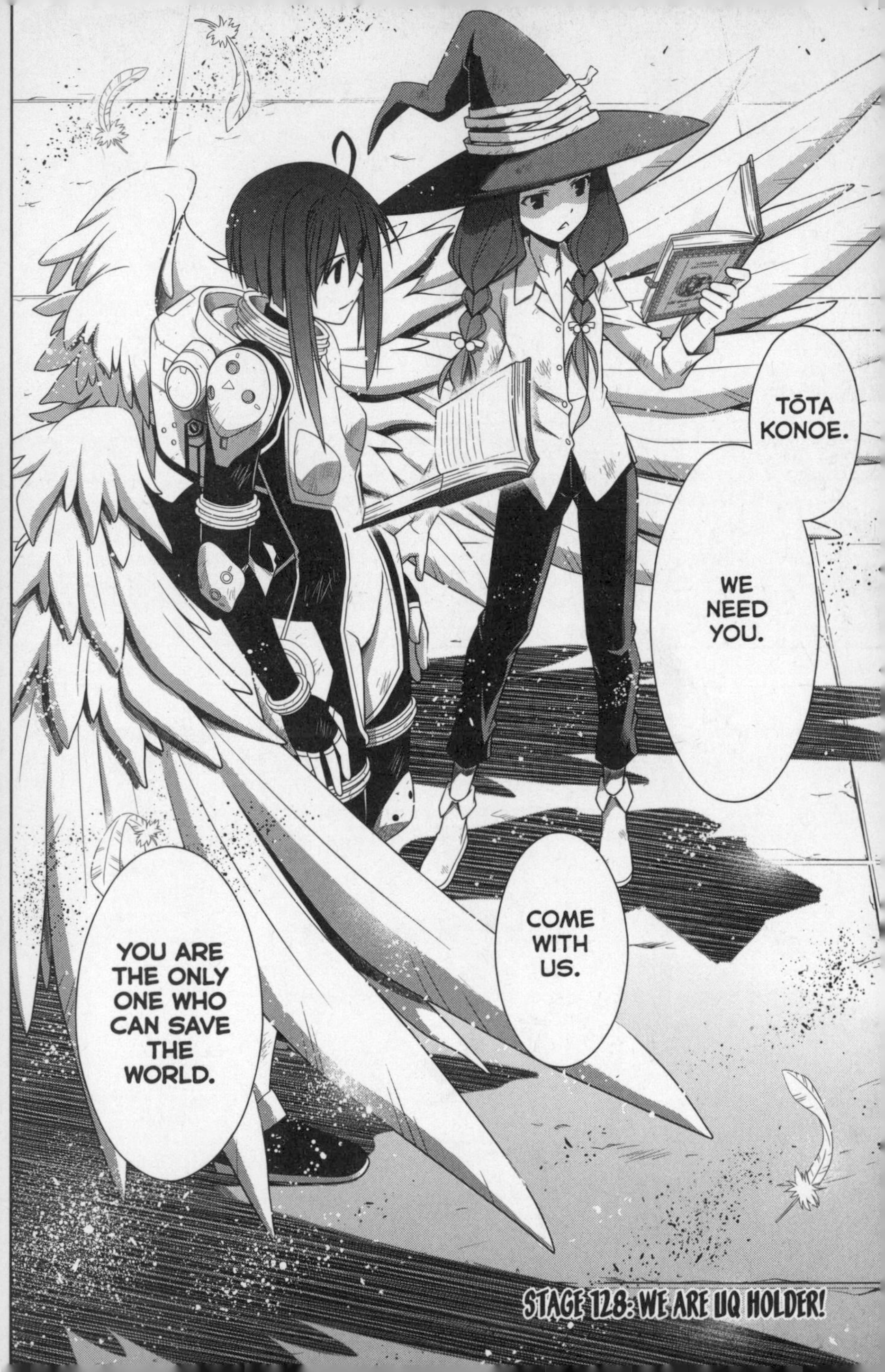
TŌTA KONOE.
WE NEED YOU.
COME WITH US.
YOU ARE THE ONLY ONE WHO CAN SAVE THE WORLD.
STAGE 128: WE ARE UQ HOLDER!

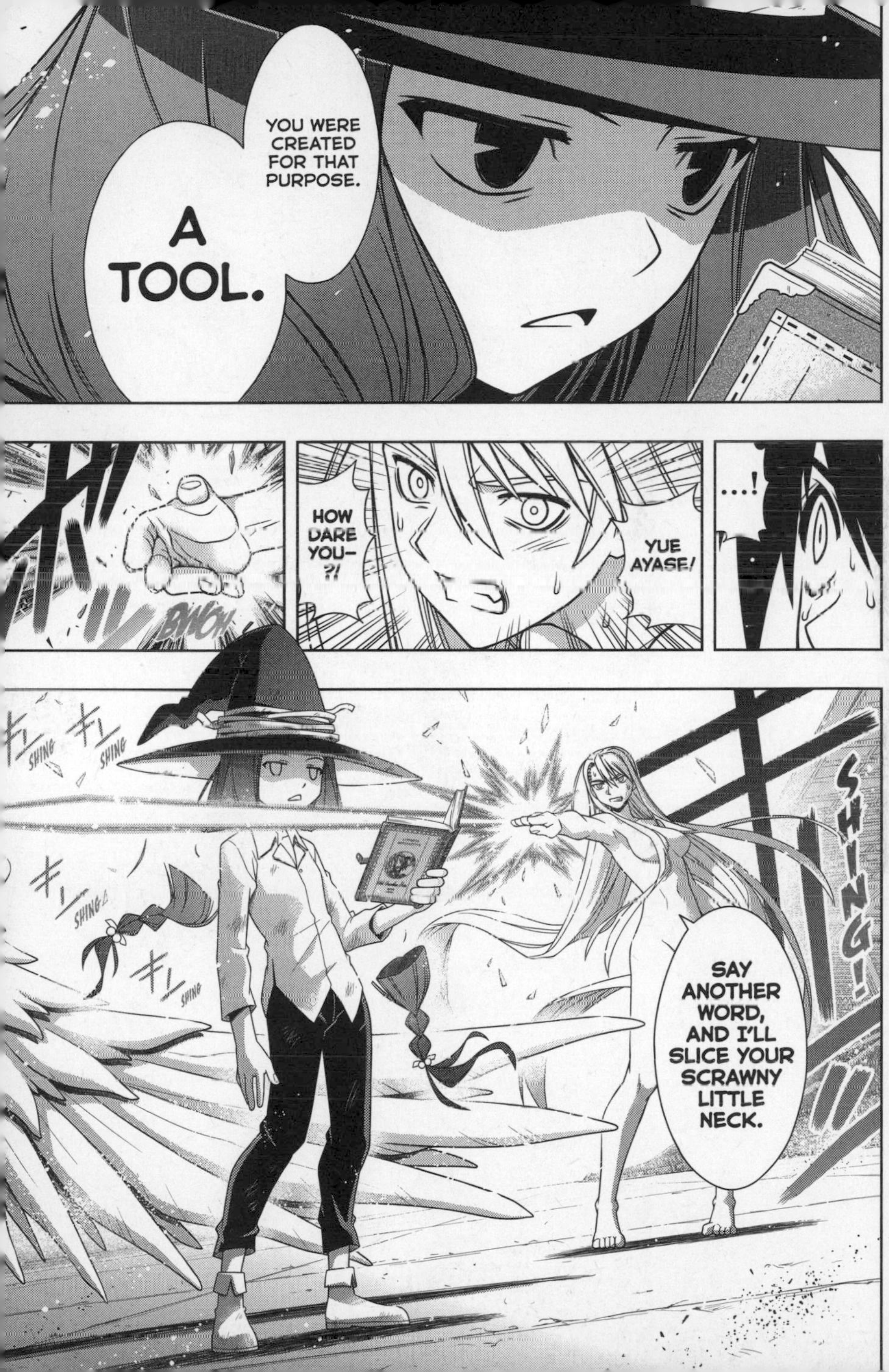
YOU WERE CREATED FOR THAT PURPOSE.
A TOOL.
...!
YUE AYASE!
HOW DARE YOU—?!
BWOH
SHING!
SAY ANOTHER WORD, AND I'LL SLICE YOUR SCRAWNY LITTLE NECK.
SHING
SHING
SHING
SHING

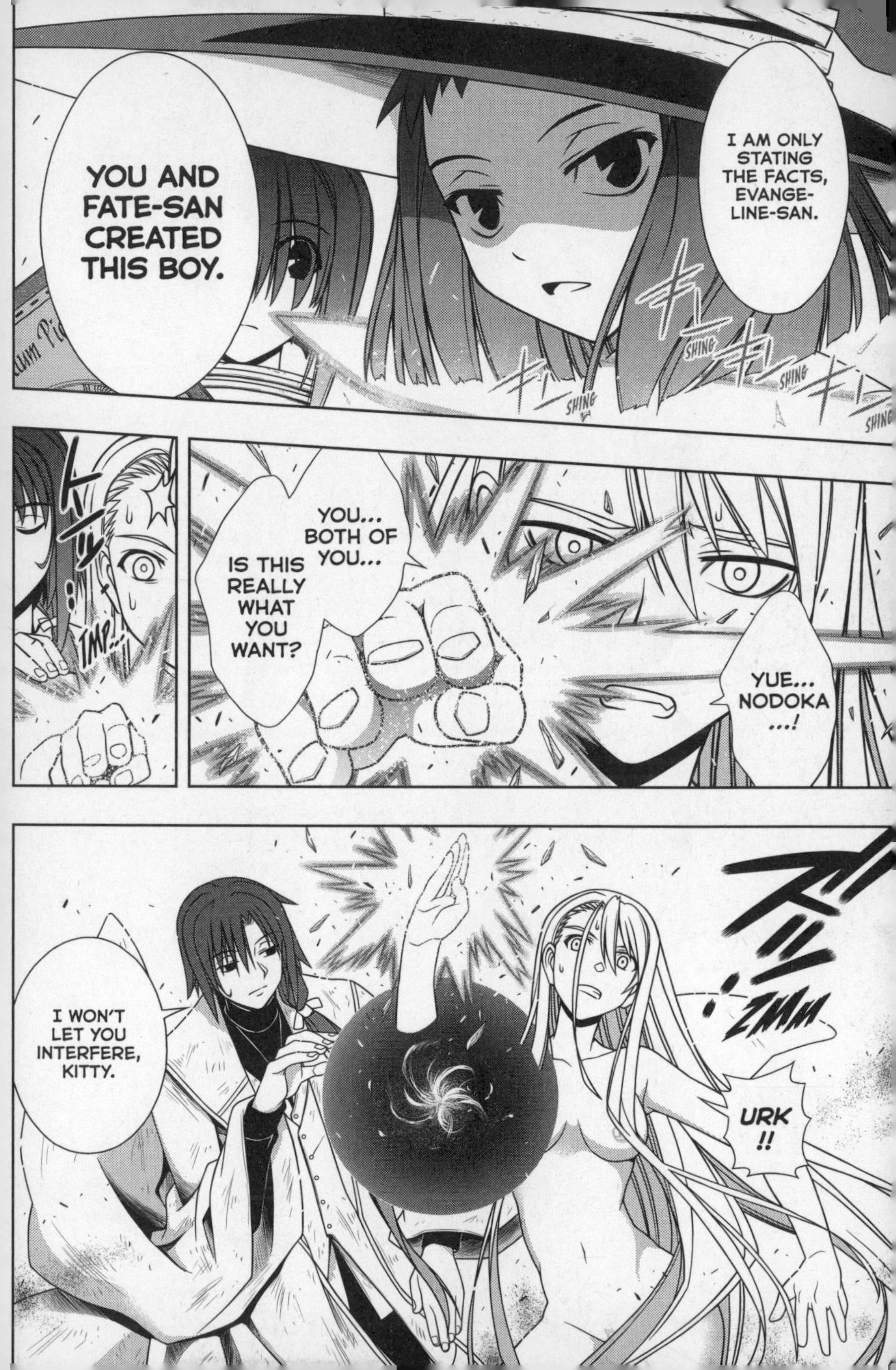
I AM ONLY STATING THE FACTS, EVANGE-LINE-SAN.
SHING
SHING
SHING
SHING
YOU AND FATE-SAN CREATED THIS BOY.
YUE... NODOKA ...!
YOU... BOTH OF YOU...
IS THIS REALLY WHAT YOU WANT?
TMP..!
ZMM
URK !!
I WON'T LET YOU INTERFERE, KITTY.

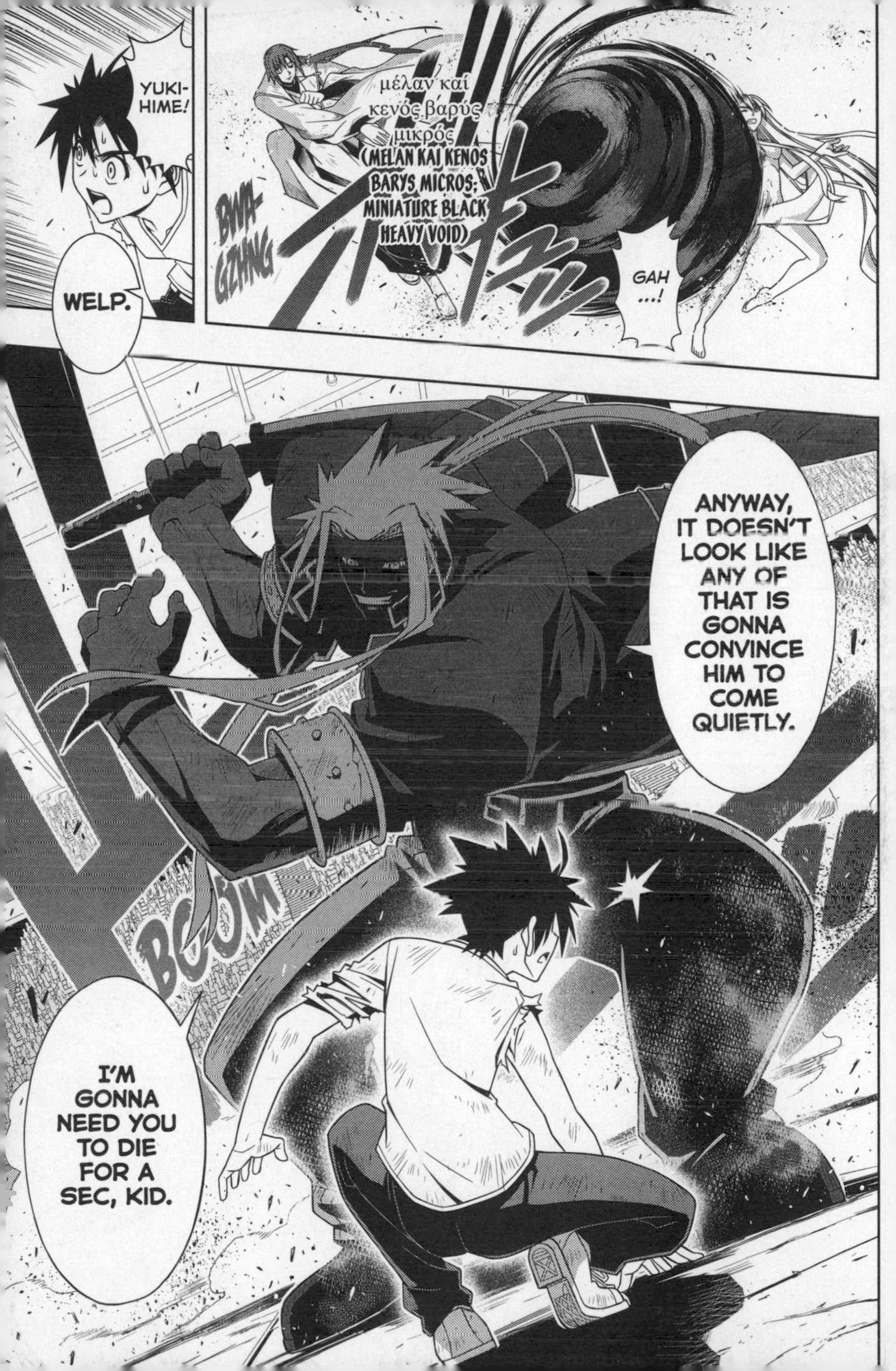

μέλαν καί κενός βαρύς μικρός (MELAN KAJ KENOS BARYS MICROS; MINIATURE BLACK HEAVY VOID)
GAH ...!
BWA-GZHNG
YUKI-HIME!
WELP.
ANYWAY, IT DOESN'T LOOK LIKE ANY OF THAT IS GONNA CONVINCE HIM TO COME QUIETLY.
BOOM
I'M GONNA NEED YOU TO DIE FOR A SEC, KID.

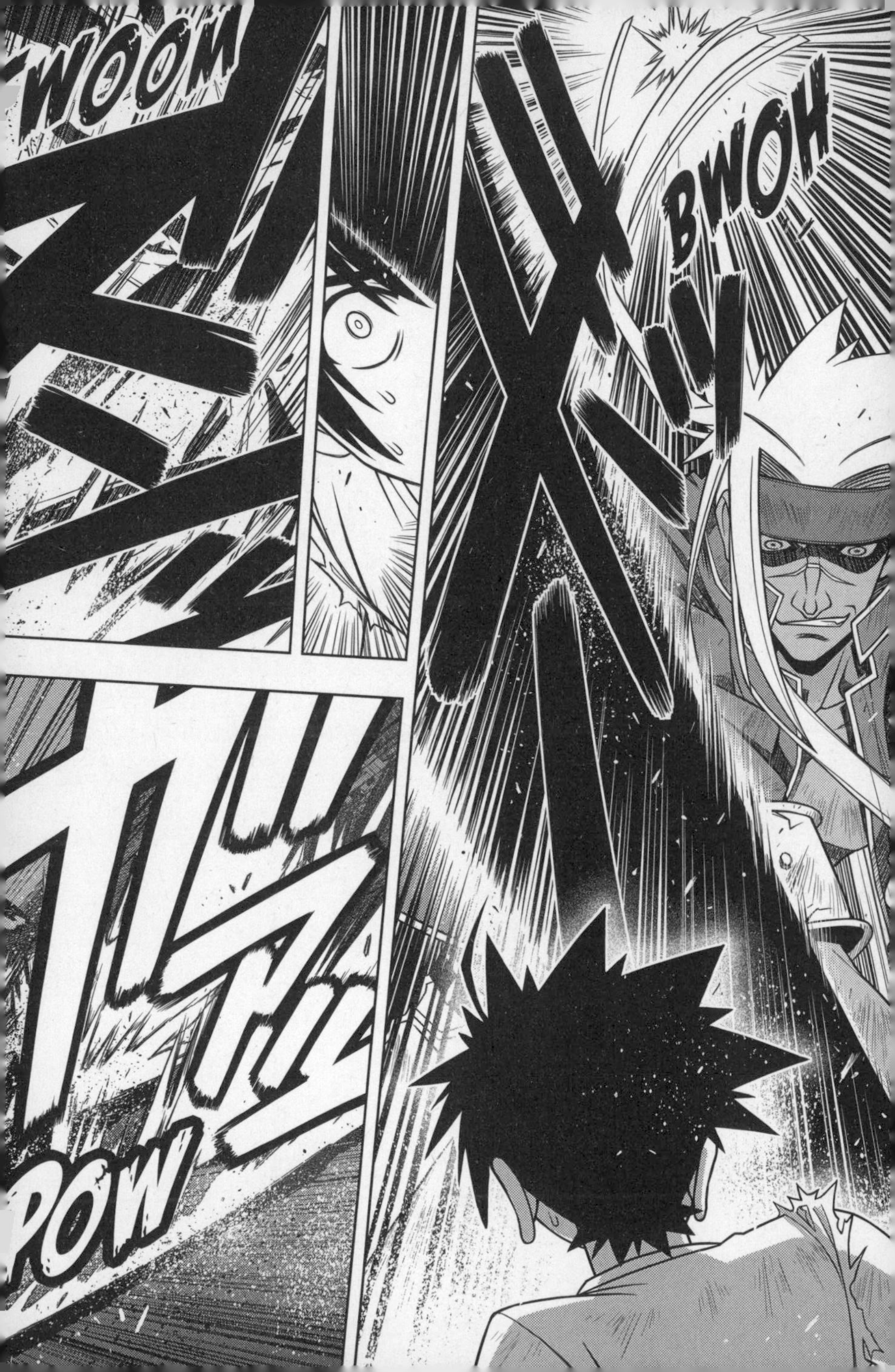
BWOH
WOOM
POW

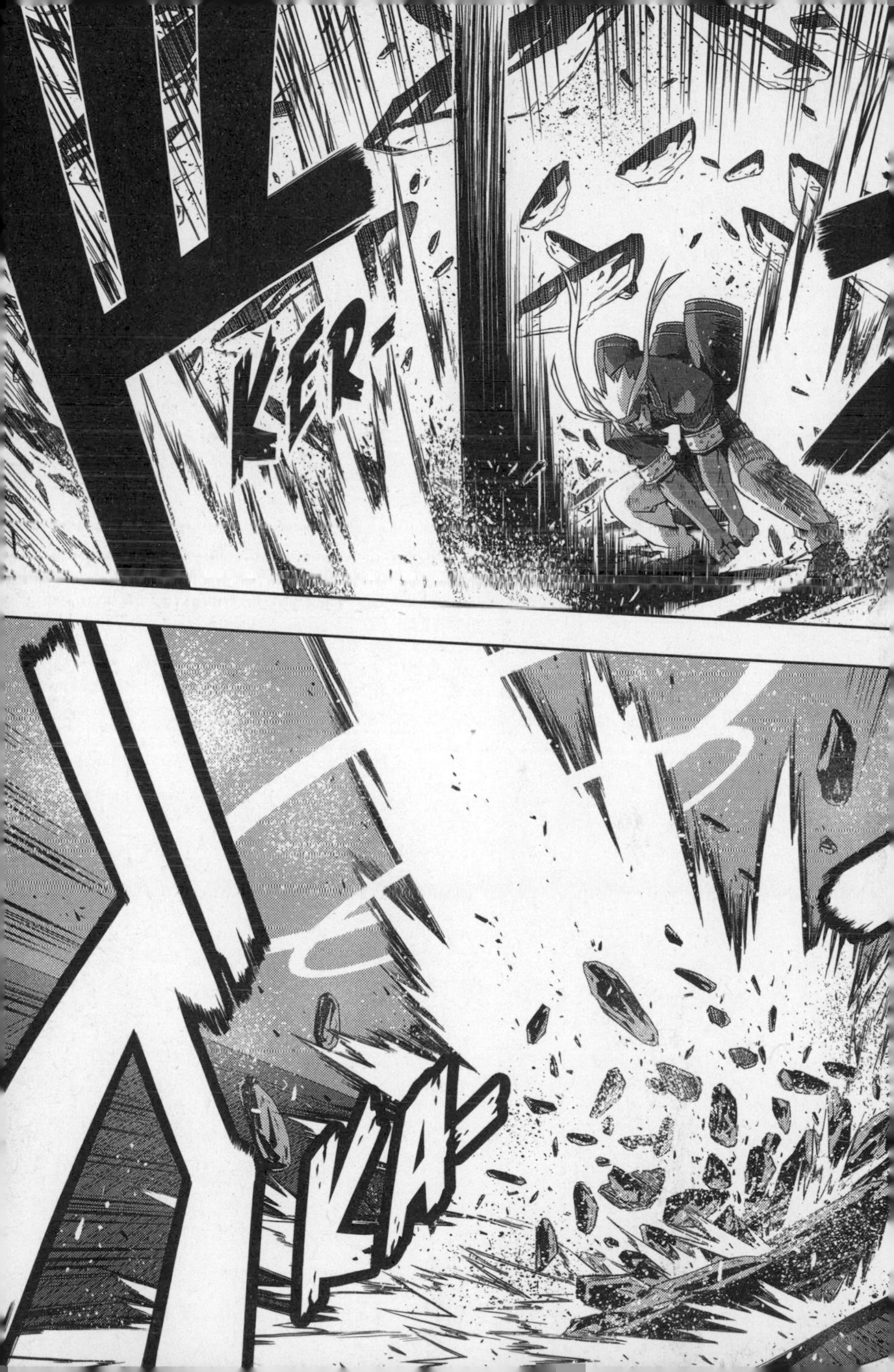
KER-
KA-

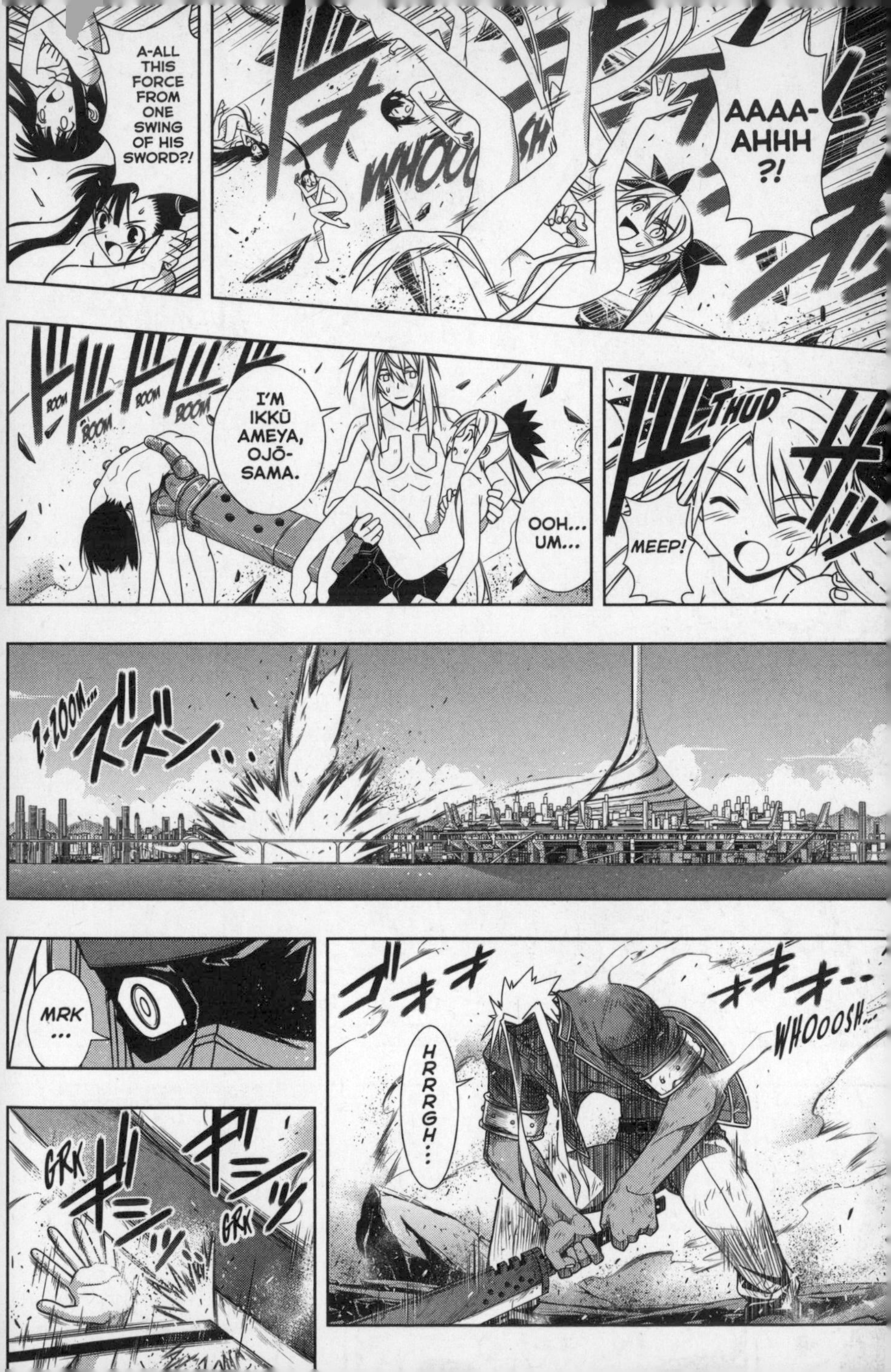
AAAA-AHHH?!
WHOOOSH
A-ALL THIS FORCE FROM ONE SWING OF HIS SWORD?!
THUD
MEEP!
BOOM BOOM BOOM BOOM
I'M IKKŪ AMEYA, OJŌ-SAMA.
OOH... UM...
Z-ZOOM...
WHOOOSH...
HRRRGH...
MRK...
GRK
GRK

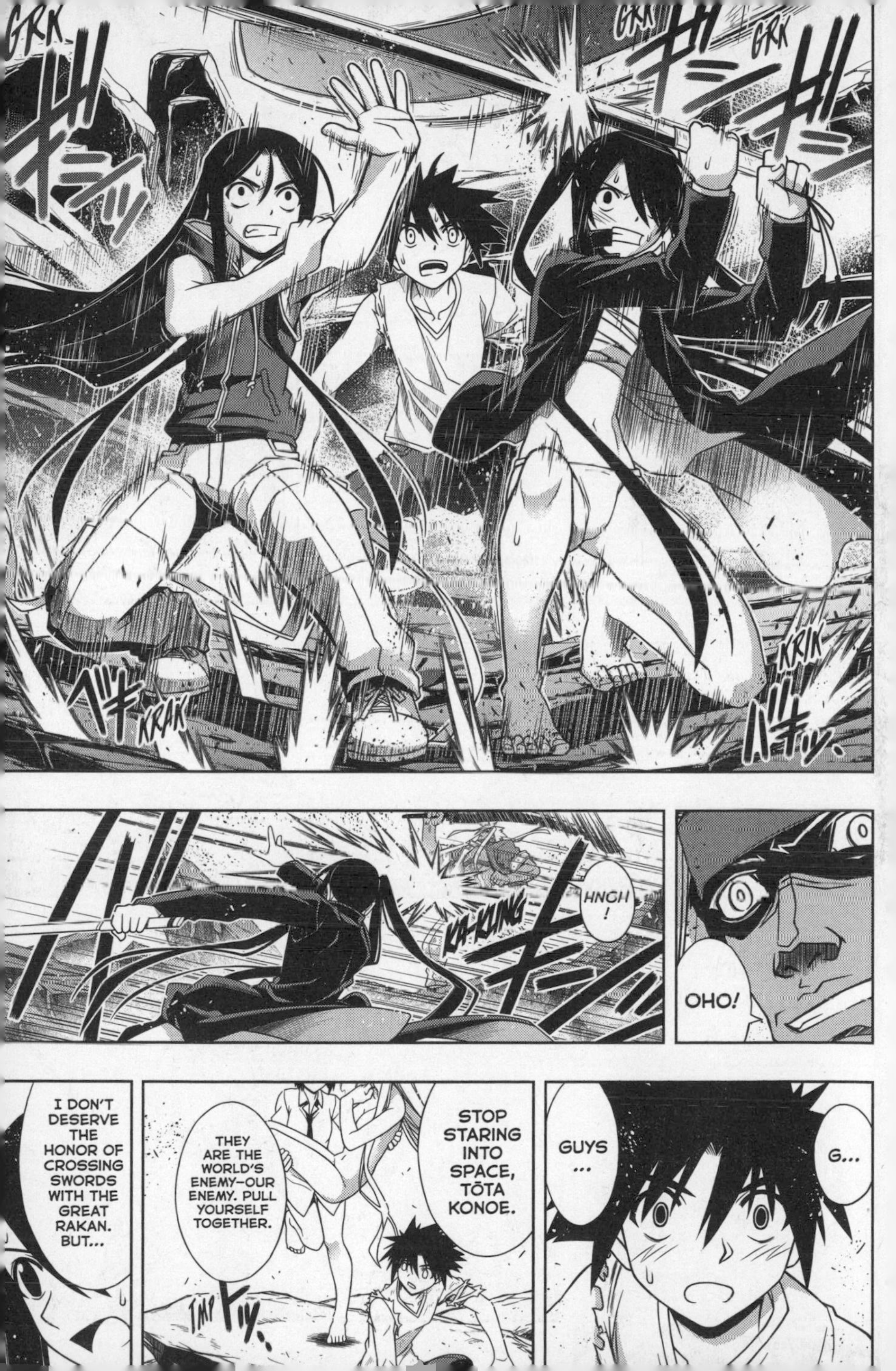
GRK
GRK
GRK
KRIK
KRAK
OHO!
HNGH
!
KA-KUNG
G...
GUYS
...
STOP STARING INTO SPACE, TŌTA KONOE.
THEY ARE THE WORLD'S ENEMY—OUR ENEMY. PULL YOURSELF TOGETHER.
TMP
I DON'T DESERVE THE HONOR OF CROSSING SWORDS WITH THE GREAT RAKAN. BUT...

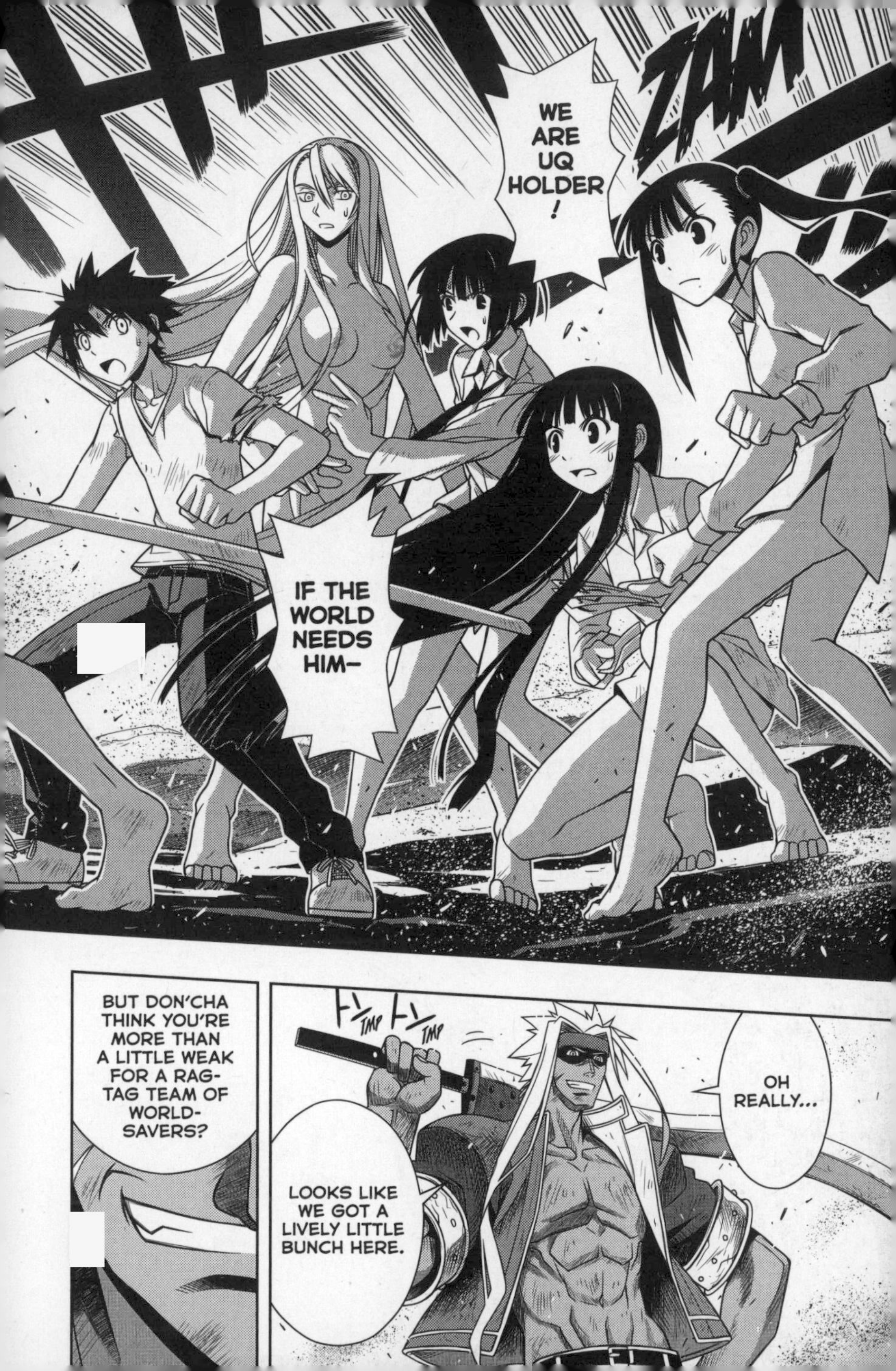
ZAM
WE ARE UQ HOLDER !
IF THE WORLD NEEDS HIM—
TMP TMP
OH REALLY...
LOOKS LIKE WE GOT A LIVELY LITTLE BUNCH HERE.
BUT DON'CHA THINK YOU'RE MORE THAN A LITTLE WEAK FOR A RAG-TAG TEAM OF WORLD-SAVERS?

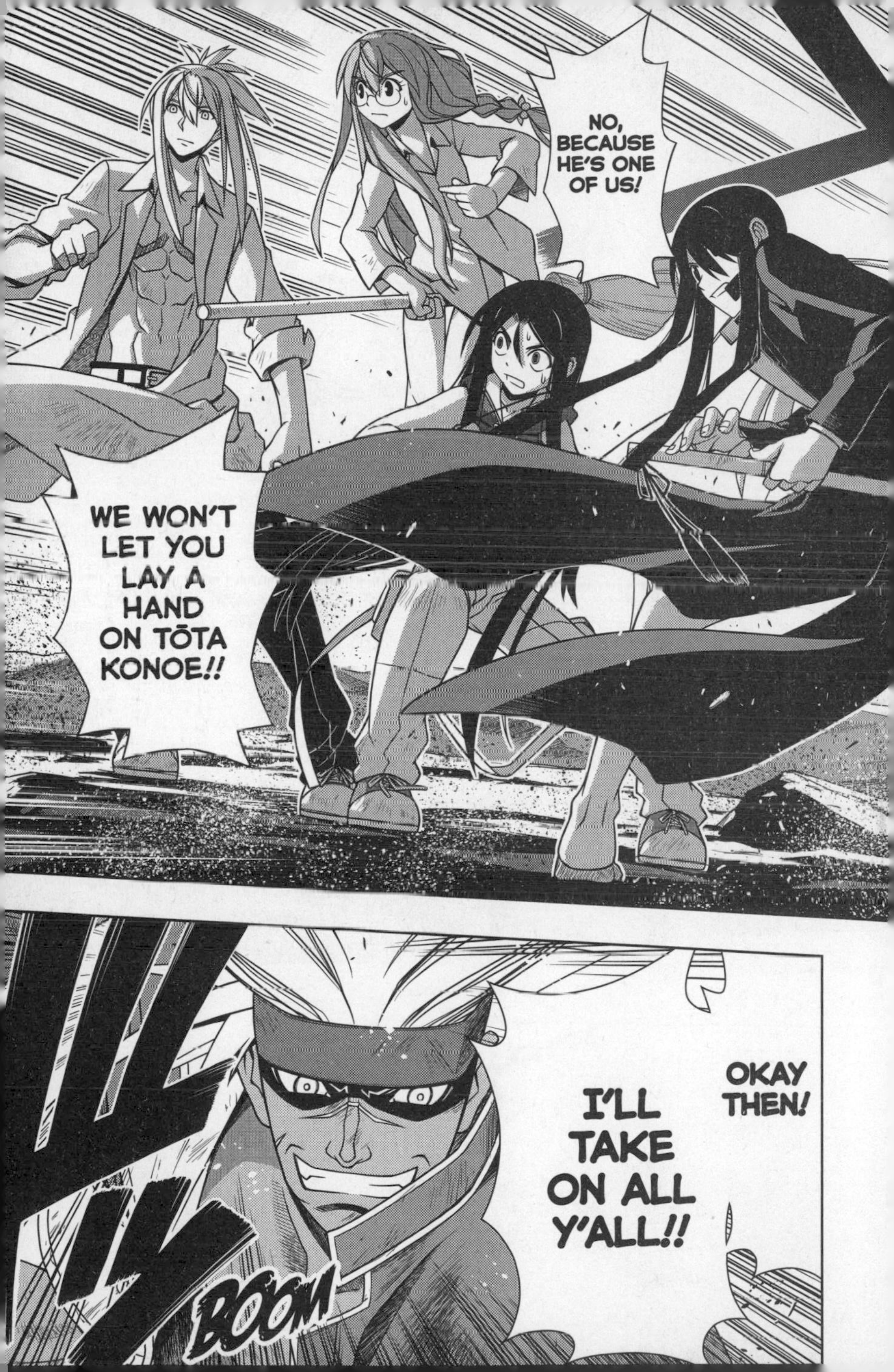
NO, BECAUSE HE'S ONE OF US!
WE WON'T LET YOU LAY A HAND ON TŌTA KONOE!!
OKAY THEN!
I'LL TAKE ON ALL Y'ALL!!
BOOM

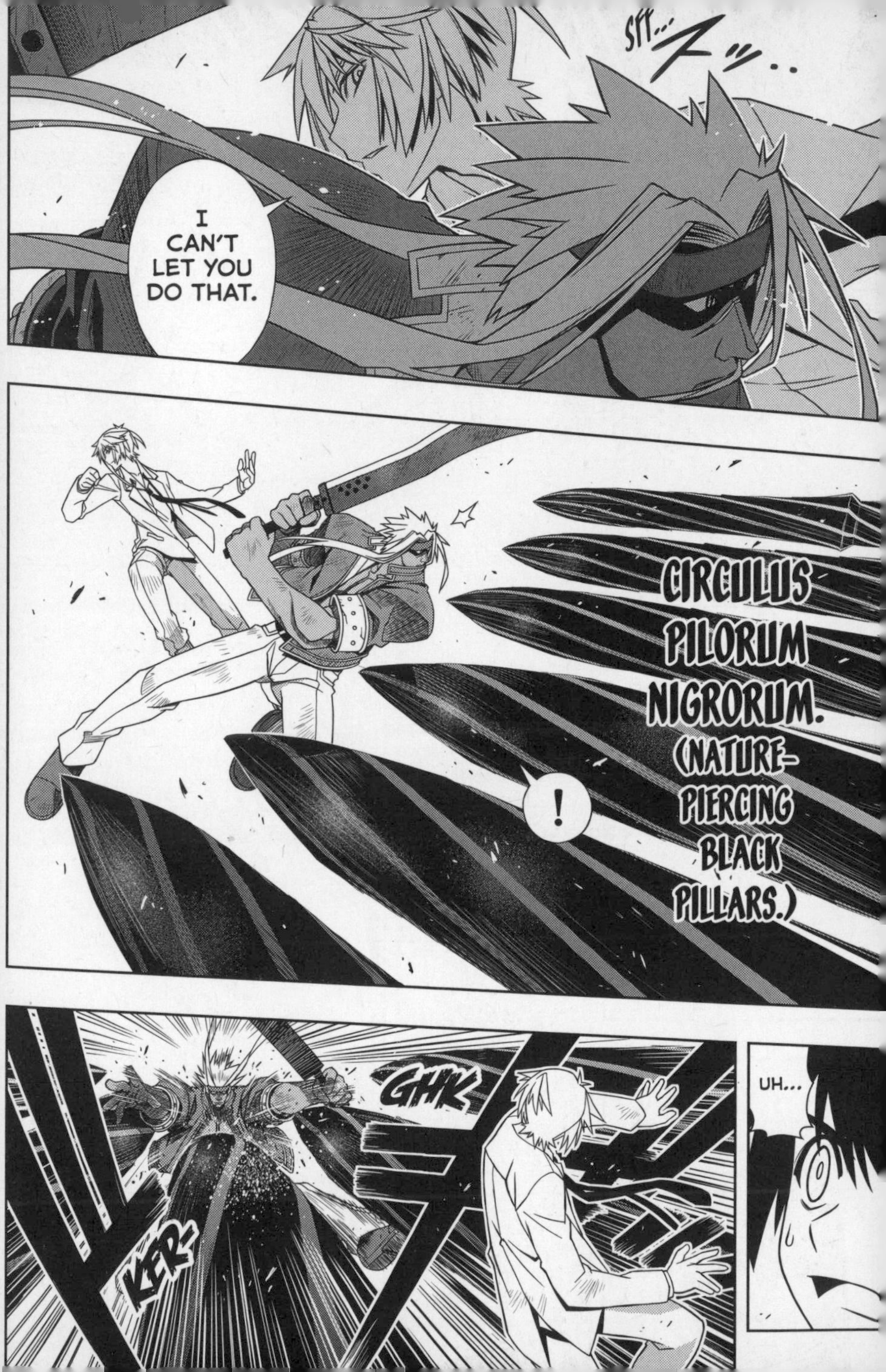
SFF...
スッ..
I CAN'T LET YOU DO THAT.
CIRCULUS PILORUM NIGRORUM. (NATURE-PIERCING BLACK PILLARS.)
!
UH...
GHK
KER-

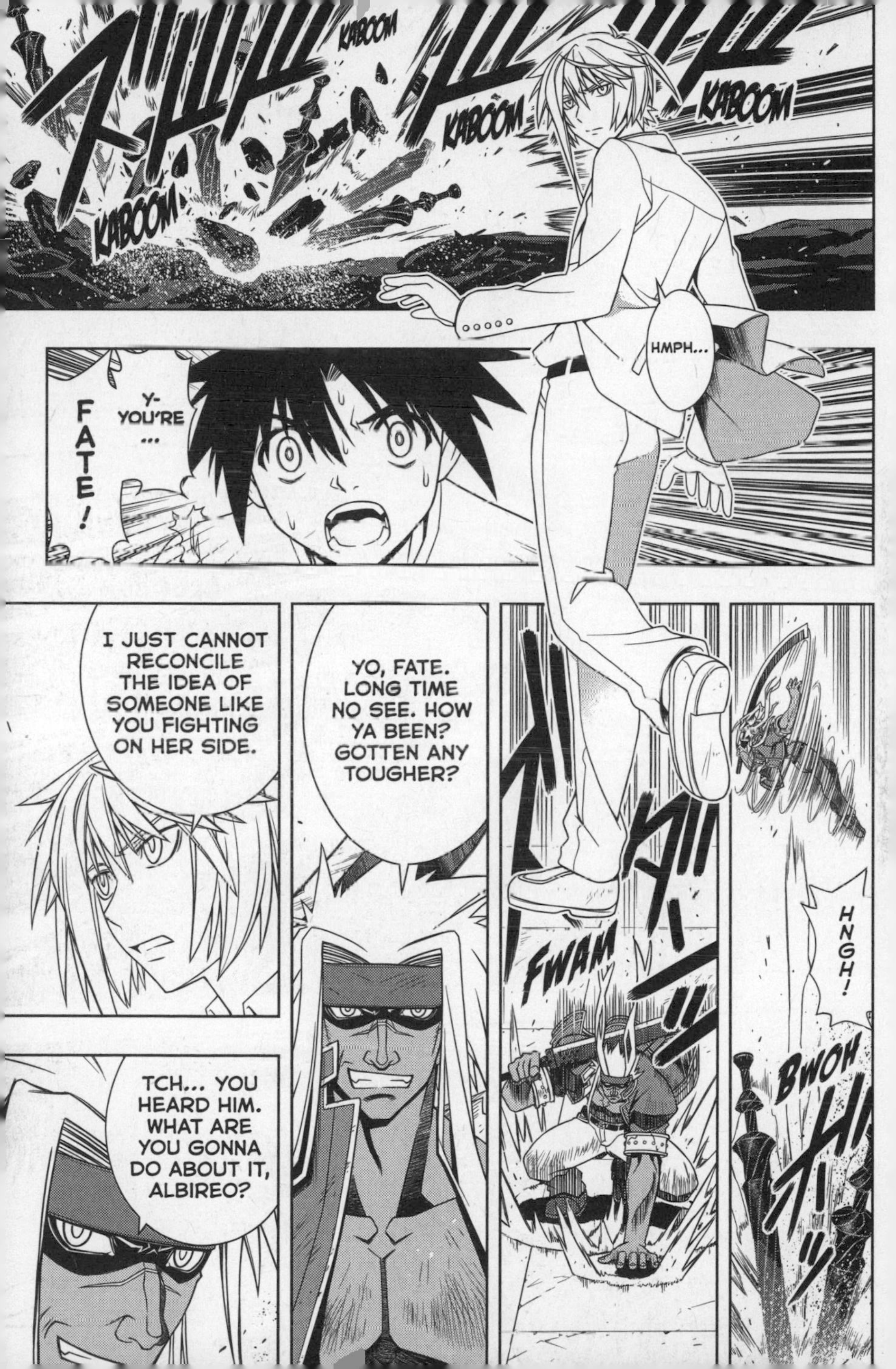
KABOOM
KABOOM
KABOOM
KABOOM
HMPH...
Y- YOU'RE ... FATE!
HNGH!
BWOH
FWAM
YO, FATE. LONG TIME NO SEE. HOW YA BEEN? GOTTEN ANY TOUGHER?
I JUST CANNOT RECONCILE THE IDEA OF SOMEONE LIKE YOU FIGHTING ON HER SIDE.
TCH... YOU HEARD HIM. WHAT ARE YOU GONNA DO ABOUT IT, ALBIREO?

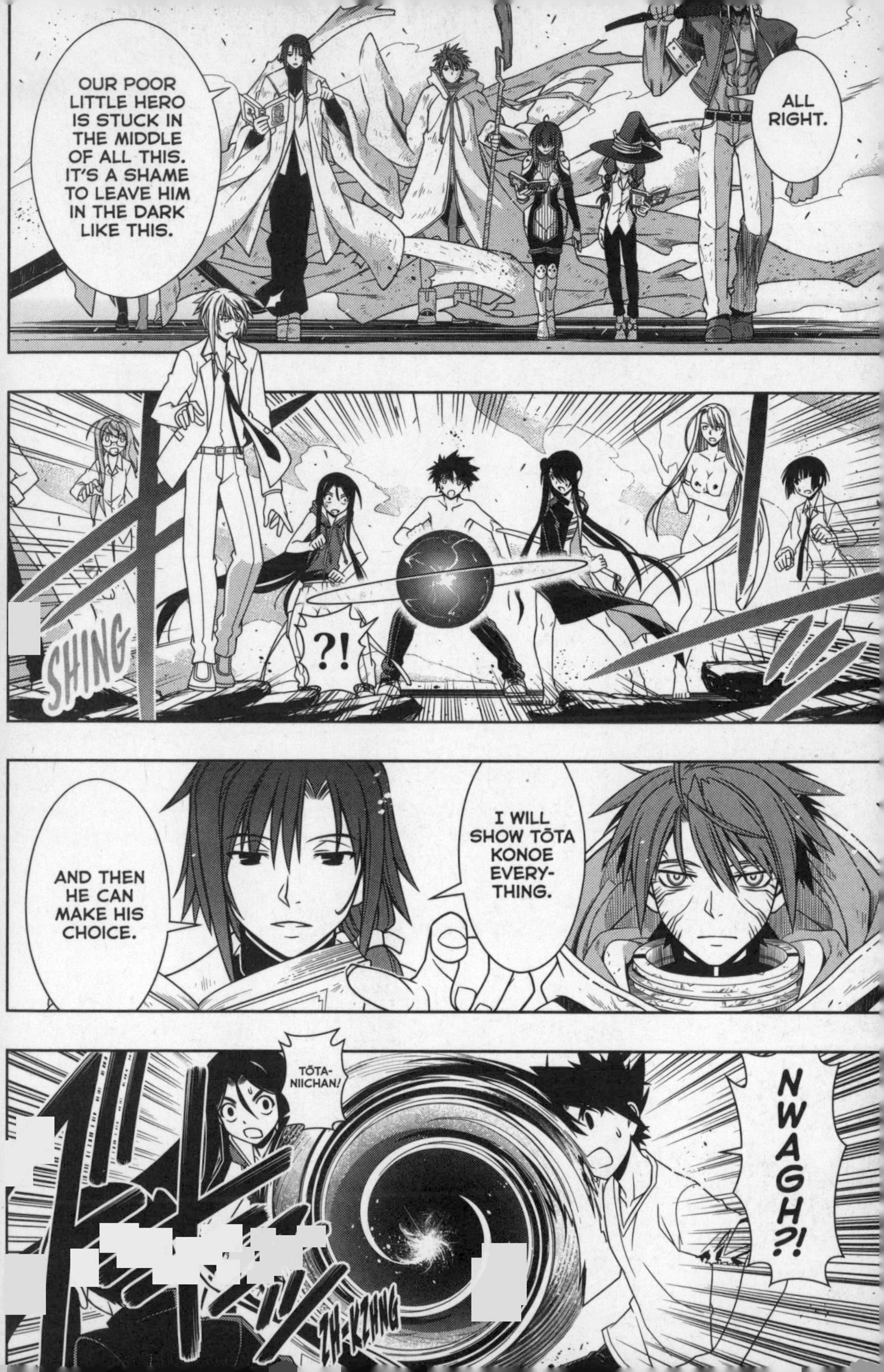
ALL RIGHT.
OUR POOR LITTLE HERO IS STUCK IN THE MIDDLE OF ALL THIS. IT'S A SHAME TO LEAVE HIM IN THE DARK LIKE THIS.
?!
SHING
I WILL SHOW TŌTA KONOE EVERY-THING.
AND THEN HE CAN MAKE HIS CHOICE.
NWAGH?!
TŌTA-NIICHAN!
ZH-KZHNG

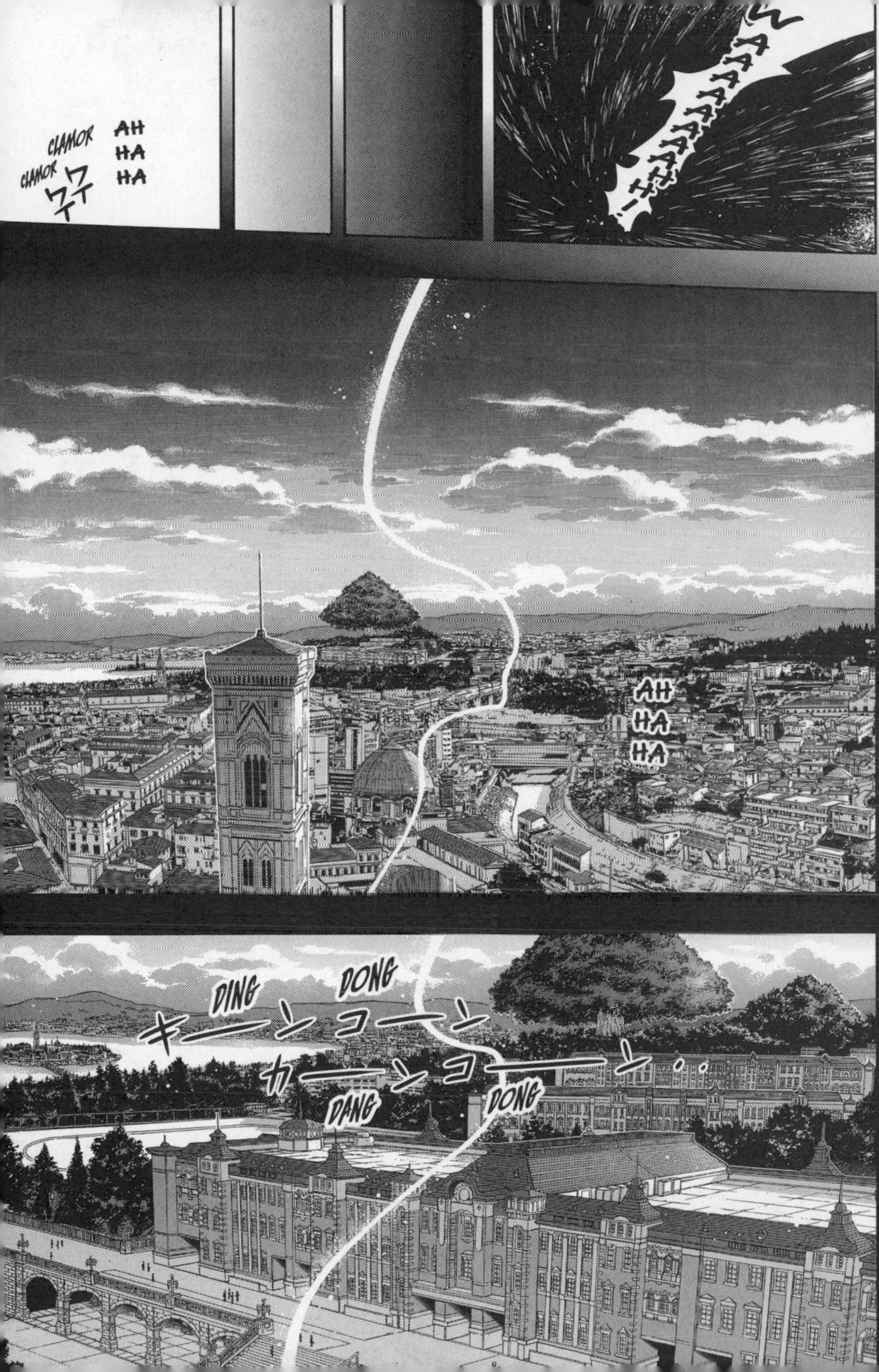
WAAAAAAAAHH!
CLAMOR
CLAMOR
ワイワイ
AH HA HA
AH HA HA
DING DONG
キーンコーン
DANG DONG
カーンコーン‥

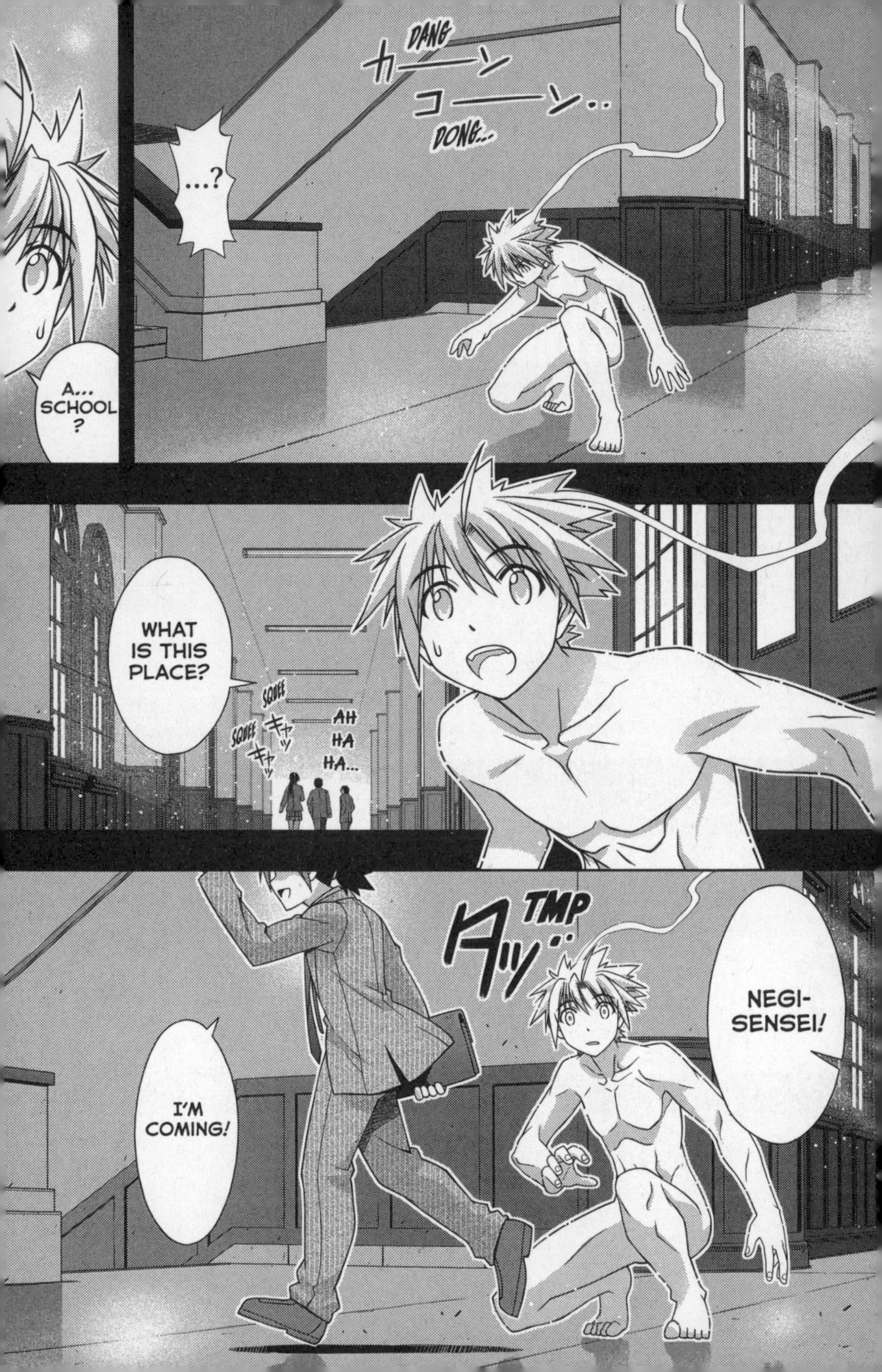
DANG
カーーン
コーーン..
DONG...
...?
A... SCHOOL?
WHAT IS THIS PLACE?
AH HA HA...
SQUEE
キャッ
SQUEE
キャッ
NEGI-SENSEI!
TMP
タッ..
I'M COMING!

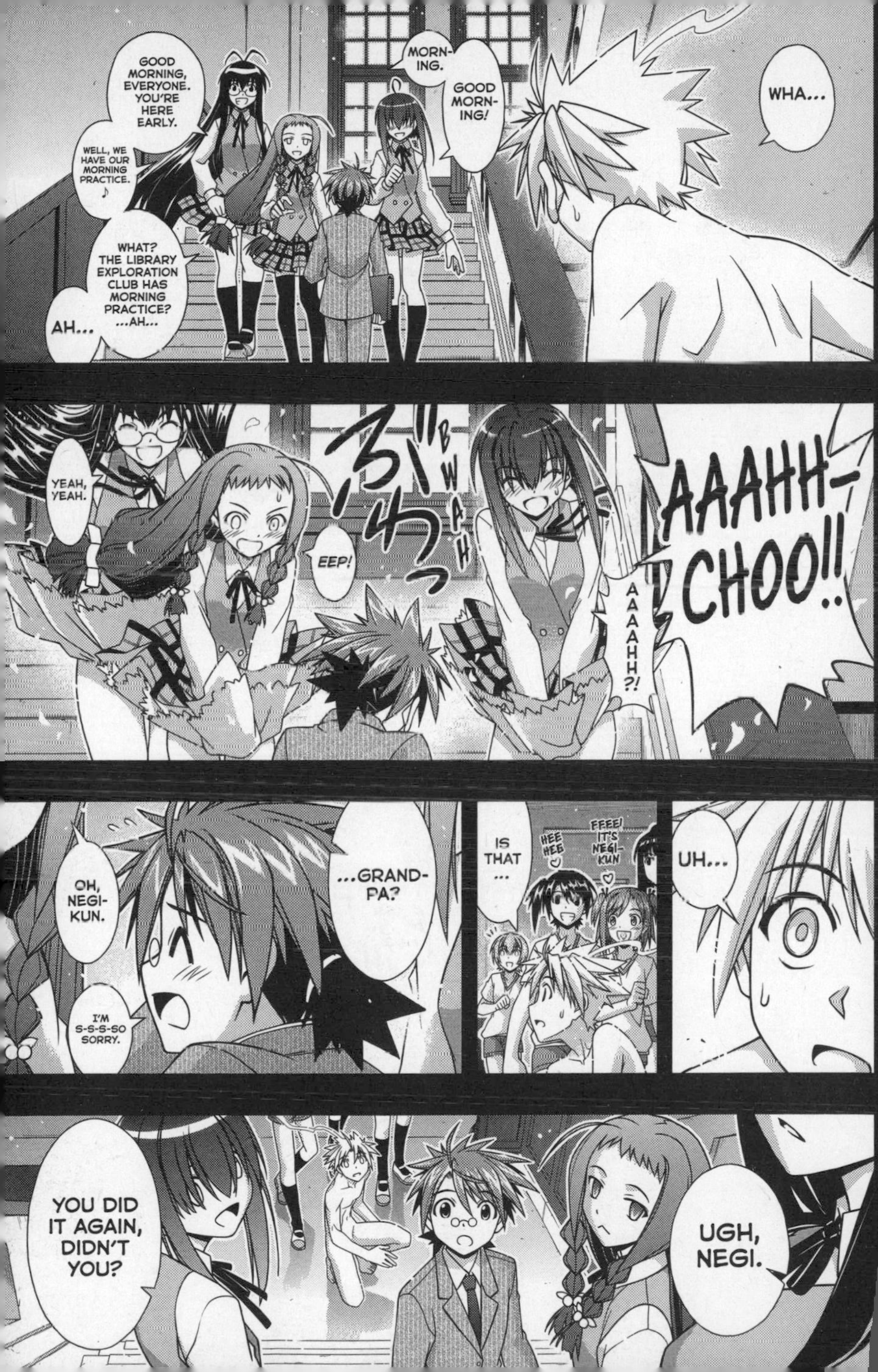
WHA...
MORN-ING.
GOOD MORN-ING!
GOOD MORNING, EVERYONE. YOU'RE HERE EARLY.
WELL, WE HAVE OUR MORNING PRACTICE. ♪
WHAT? THE LIBRARY EXPLORATION CLUB HAS MORNING PRACTICE? ...AH...
AH...
AAAHH-CHOO!!
AAAAAHH?!
BWAH
EEP!
YEAH, YEAH.
UH...
FFEEE! IT'S NEGI-KUN ♡
HEE HEE ♡
IS THAT ...
...GRAND-PA?
OH, NEGI-KUN.
I'M S-S-S-SO SORRY.
UGH, NEGI.
YOU DID IT AGAIN, DIDN'T YOU?

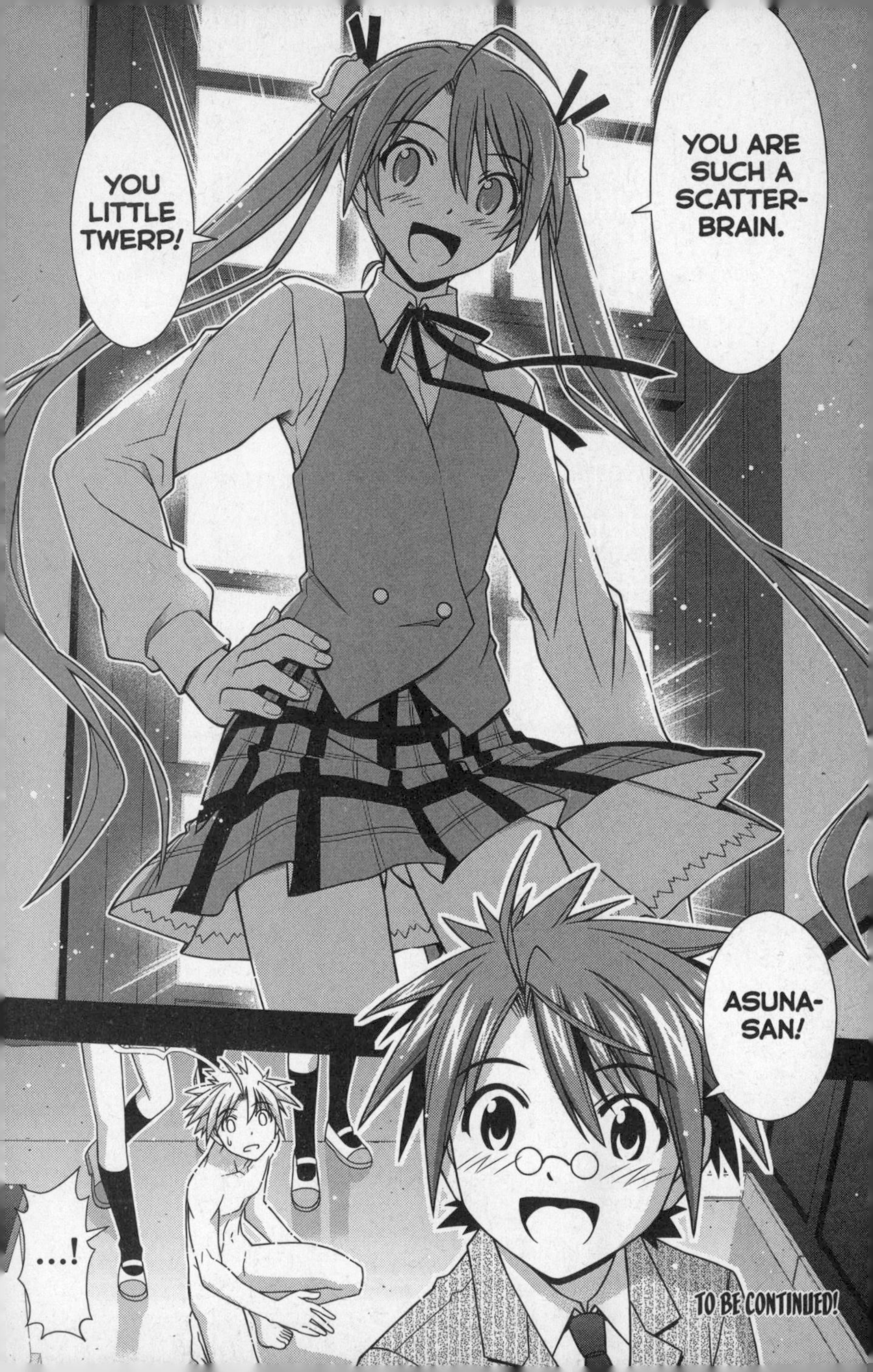
YOU ARE SUCH A SCATTER-BRAIN.
YOU LITTLE TWERP!
ASUNA-SAN!
...!
TO BE CONTINUED!

UQ HOLDER!

STAFF

Ken Akamatsu
Takashi Takemoto
Kenichi Nakamura
Keiichi Yamashita
Tohru Mitsuhashi
Susumu Kuwabara
Yuri Sasaki

Thanks to Ran Ayanaga

KC KODANSHA COMICS

A new series from the creator of *Soul Eater*, the megahit manga and anime seen on Toonami!

"Fun and lively... a great start!"
-Adventures in Poor Taste

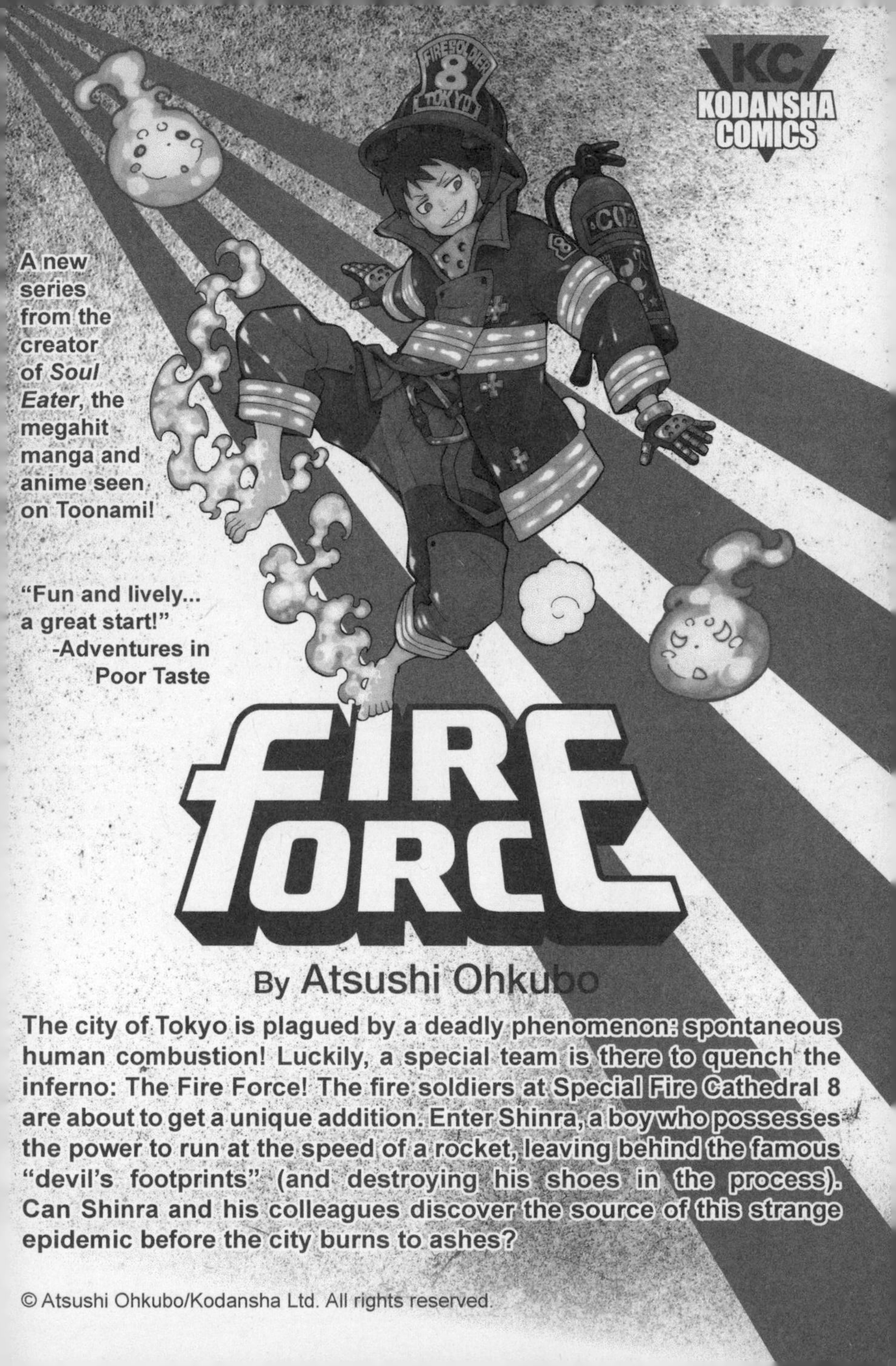

FIRE FORCE

By Atsushi Ohkubo

The city of Tokyo is plagued by a deadly phenomenon: spontaneous human combustion! Luckily, a special team is there to quench the inferno: The Fire Force! The fire soldiers at Special Fire Cathedral 8 are about to get a unique addition. Enter Shinra, a boy who possesses the power to run at the speed of a rocket, leaving behind the famous "devil's footprints" (and destroying his shoes in the process). Can Shinra and his colleagues discover the source of this strange epidemic before the city burns to ashes?

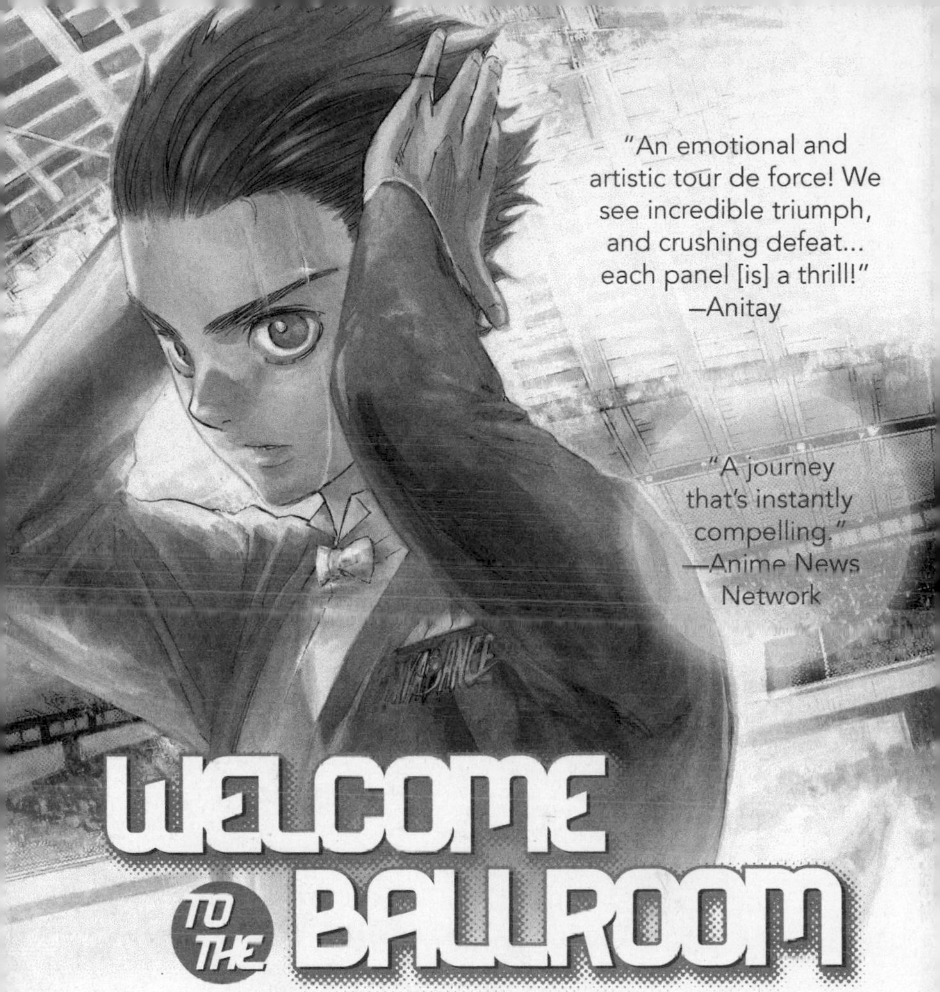

"An emotional and artistic tour de force! We see incredible triumph, and crushing defeat... each panel [is] a thrill!"
—Anitay

"A journey that's instantly compelling."
—Anime News Network

WELCOME TO THE BALLROOM

By Tomo Takeuchi

Feckless high school student Tatara Fujita wants to be good at something—anything. Unfortunately, he's about as average as a slouchy teen can be. The local bullies know this, and make it a habit to hit him up for cash, but all that changes when the debonair Kaname Sengoku sends them packing. Sengoku's not the neighborhood watch, though. He's a professional ballroom dancer. And once Tatara Fujita gets pulled into the world of ballroom, his life will never be the same.

KC KODANSHA COMICS

A KODANSHA COMICS TRADE PAPERBACK ORIGINAL

UQ HOLDER! VOLUME 12 COPYRIGHT © 2016 KEN AKAMATSU
ENGLISH TRANSLATION COPYRIGHT © 2017 KEN AKAMATSU

PUBLISHED IN THE UNITED STATES BY KODANSHA COMICS, AN IMPRINT OF KODANSHA USA PUBLISHING, LLC, NEW YORK.

PUBLICATION RIGHTS FOR THIS ENGLISH EDITION ARRANGED THROUGH KODANSHA LTD., TOKYO.

FIRST PUBLISHED IN JAPAN IN 2016 BY KODANSHA LTD., TOKYO.

ISBN 978-1-63236-578-1

PRINTED IN THE UNITED STATES OF AMERICA.

WWW.KODANSHACOMICS.COM

9 8 7 6 5 4 3 2 1

TRANSLATION: ALETHEA NIBLEY AND ATHENA NIBLEY
LETTERING: JAMES DASHIELL
EDITING: LAUREN SCANLAN
KODANSHA COMICS EDITION COVER DESIGN: PHIL BALSMAN